Limitation on Benefits Clauses in Double Taxation Conventions

EUCOTAX Series on European Taxation

VOLUME 12

Series Editors

Prof. Dr Peter H.J. Essers, Fiscal Institute Tilburg/Center for Company Law, Tilburg University

Prof. Dr Eric C.C.M. Kemmeren, Fiscal Institute Tilburg/Center for Company Law, Tilburg University

Prof. Dr Dr h.c. Michael Lang, WU (Vienna University of Economics and Business)

Introduction

EUCOTAX (European Universities Cooperating on Taxes) is a network of tax institutes currently consisting of eleven universities: WU (Vienna University of Economics and Business) in Austria, Katholieke Universiteit Leuven in Belgium, Corvinus University of Budapest, Hungary, Université Paris-I Panthéon-Sorbonne in France, Universität Osnabrück in Germany, Libera, Università Internazionale di Studi Sociali in Rome (and Università degli Studi di Bologna for the research part), in Italy, Fiscaal Instituut Tilburg at Tilburg University in the Netherlands, Universidad de Barcelona in Spain, Uppsala University in Sweden, Queen Mary and Westfield College at the University of London in the United Kingdom, and Georgetown University in Washington DC, United States of America. The network aims at initiating and coordinating both comparative education in taxation, through the organization of activities such as winter courses and guest lectures, and comparative research in the field, by means of joint research projects, international conferences and exchange of researchers between various countries.

Contents/Subjects

The EUCOTAX series covers a wide range of topics in European tax law. For example tax treaties, EC case law, tax planning, exchange of information and VAT. The series is well-known for its high-quality research and practical solutions.

Objective

The series aims to provide insights on new developments in European taxation.

Readership

Practitioners and academics dealing with European tax law.

Frequency of Publication

2-3 new volumes published each year.

The titles published in this series are listed at the end of this volume.

Limitation on Benefits Clauses in Double Taxation Conventions

Second Edition

Félix Alberto Vega Borrego

Published by:
Kluwer Law International B.V.
PO Box 316
2400 AH Alphen aan den Rijn
The Netherlands
Website: www.wolterskluwerlr.com

Sold and distributed in North, Central and South America by:
Wolters Kluwer Legal & Regulatory U.S.
7201 McKinney Circle
Frederick, MD 21704
United States of America
Email: customer.service@wolterskluwer.com

Sold and distributed in all other countries by:
Quadrant
Rockwood House
Haywards Heath
West Sussex
RH16 3DH
United Kingdom
Email: international-customerservice@wolterskluwer.com

Printed on acid-free paper.

ISBN 978-90-411-6135-2

e-Book: ISBN 978-90-411-6143-7
web-PDF: ISBN 978-90-411-9033-8

© 2017 Kluwer Law International BV, The Netherlands

All rights reserved. No part of this publication may be reproduced, stored in a retrieval system, or transmitted in any form or by any means, electronic, mechanical, photocopying, recording, or otherwise, without written permission from the publisher.

Permission to use this content must be obtained from the copyright owner. Please apply to: Permissions Department, Wolters Kluwer Legal & Regulatory U.S., 76 Ninth Avenue, 7th Floor, New York, NY 10011-5201, USA. Website: www.wolterskluwerlr.com

Printed in the United Kingdom.

MIX
FSC® C103993

To my parents, Félix and Pilar

Table of Contents

Preface   xi
List of Abbreviations   xiii

Introduction   1

CHAPTER 1
Taxation of Non-residents and International Tax Planning Through Double
Taxation Conventions   5

I   Tax Liability Criteria and Tax Treaties   5
II   Source Taxation: Limits and Conflicts with Residence Taxation   8
III   DTCs in Tax Planning: Treaty Shopping   15
    III.A   Preliminary Remarks   15
    III.B   Stages in International Tax Planning: Reduction of Global Tax   17
    III.C   Reduction of Taxation at Source Through Tax Treaties: Treaty
           Shopping Structures   21
           III.C.1   Partnership Agreements, Fiduciary Arrangements and Trusts   23
           III.C.2   The Use of Companies   27

CHAPTER 2
The Subjective Scope of Double Taxation Conventions and Limitation on
Benefits Clauses   35

I   Causes for and Consequences of the Treaty Shopping Structures   35
    I.A   Preliminary Remarks   35
    I.B   Allocation of Business Income: The Separate Accounting and
         Formulary Apportionment Systems   37
    I.C   Consequences of Treaty Shopping Structures and Reasons for the
         Adoption of Measures Against Such Structures   46

Table of Contents

II	Measures Against Treaty Shopping		55
	II.A	Application of General Anti-avoidance Rules to Treaty Shopping Structures	55
	II.B	Treaty Measures	67
		II.B.1 Subjective Scope of the OECD Model: Concepts of Person and Residence	68
		II.B.1.a Concept of Person	68
		II.B.1.b Concept of Residence	73
		II.B.2 Beneficial Ownership Concept	77
		II.B.3 Limitation on Benefits Clauses	86
	II.C	Domestic Specific Anti-treaty Shopping Measures	103

CHAPTER 3
Legal Framework and Application of Limitation on Benefits Clauses   109

I	Preliminary Remarks		109
II	Clauses That Confer the Status of Qualified Resident		113
	II.A	Individuals	113
	II.B	Governmental Entities and Other Public Agencies	115
	II.C	Tax-Exempt Organizations	118
	II.D	Pension Funds	120
	II.E	Stock Exchange Clause	123
		II.E.1 Preliminary Remarks	123
		II.E.2 Direct Access	126
		II.E.2.a Principal Class of Shares (and Disproportionate Class of Shares)	126
		II.E.2.b Substantial and Regular Trading	129
		II.E.2.c Recognized Stock Exchanges	131
		II.E.2.d Primary Place of Management and Control	133
		II.E.3 Indirect Access: Subsidiaries of Publicly Traded Companies	134
		II.E.3.a Percentage of Ownership Interest and Controlling Entities	137
		II.E.3.b The Concept of European Union, North American Free Trade Agreement and European Economic Area Member State Resident	140
		II.E.3.c Indirect Shareholding	141
		II.E.3.d Base Erosion	143
	II.F	Ownership and Base Erosion Clause	144
		II.F.1 Preliminary Remarks	144
		II.F.2 Ownership Test	147
		II.F.2.a Negative or Positive Wording of the Test	147
		II.F.2.b Percentage and Indirect Ownership	148
		II.F.2.c Qualified Residents	150

		II.F.2.d	Holding Period	153
	II.F.3	Base Erosion Test		155
		II.F.3.a	Tax Base: Concept of Gross Income	156
		II.F.3.b	Beneficiaries of the Payments: Qualified Residents	158
		II.F.3.c	Deductible Expenses	160
	II.F.4	Final Remarks		162
III	Non-qualified Residents That Are Entitled to Receive Full or Partial Treaty Benefits			163
	III.A Activity Clause			163
	III.A.1	Preliminary Remarks		163
	III.A.2	Concepts of Active Trade or Business, Indirect Activity and the Substantiality Requirement		167
		III.A.2.a	Concept of Active Trade or Business	167
		III.A.2.b	Indirect Trade or Business	170
		III.A.2.c	Volume of Activity: The Substantiality Test	171
	III.A.3	Relation Between the Income Generated and the Activity Conducted		177
		III.A.3.a	Direct Relation ('in Connection with')	177
		III.A.3.b	Incidental Relation ('Incidental to')	180
	III.A.4	Final Remarks		181
	III.A.5	Charts		181
		III.A.5.a	Activity Clause	181
		III.A.5.b	Example of the Substantiality Test ('Safe Harbour' Rule 1996 U.S. Model)	182
	III.B Headquarters Company Clause			184
	III.C Derivative Benefits Clause			187
IV	Exclusion Provisions			196
	IV.A Permanent Establishment Clause			196
	IV.B Exclusion Clause			204
	IV.B.1	OECD and U.S. Approach to Tax Treaty Measures Against Preferential Tax Regimes		204
	IV.B.2	The Special Tax Regime Clause in the 2016 U.S. Model		211
		IV.B.2.a	Preliminary Remarks	211
		IV.B.2.b	Legal Framework of the Clause	214
		IV.B.2.b.1	Introduction	214
		IV.B.2.b.2	Types of Income Covered	215
		IV.B.2.b.3	Subjective Scope: Connected Persons	216
		IV.B.2.b.4	Characteristics of the Special Tax Regime	217
		IV.B.2.b.5	Effects of the Clause	222
V	Bona Fide Clause			225
	V.A General Wording			225
	V.B Criteria for the Competent Authority Determination			230

	V.C Procedural Aspects	236
VI	The Collection of Taxes from Non-residents: The Application of Tax Treaties with LOB Clauses	238
	VI.A General Aspects	238
	VI.B Non-resident Taxation in the U.S. and the Application of LOB Clauses in the Tax Treaty Between the U.S. and the Netherlands	243
	VI.C Conclusions	248

CHAPTER 4
Limitation on Benefits Clauses and European Union Law 251

I	Preliminary Remarks	251
II	Competence of EU Member States to Conclude DTCs with Third States	254
III	Compatibility of LOB Clauses with EU Law	257
	III.A Treaties with Third States	258
	III.A.1 Individualized Analysis of LOB Clauses	258
	III.A.2 Legitimate Grounds for LOB Clauses: EU Law and Anti-avoidance Rules	273
	III.B Treaties Between EU Member States	279
IV	Consequences of the Incompatibility of the LOB Clauses with EU Law	281
	IV.A Tax Treaties with Third States: The EU Member State's Liability for Damages in the Case of a Breach of EU Law	281
	IV.B Tax Treaties Between EU Member States	289
	IV.C Possible Solutions for the Incompatibility of Tax Treaties with Third States	289
V	Final Remarks	292

Bibliography 293

Index 313

Preface

This book is an updated version of my previous book of the same title, published by Kluwer Law International in 2005. Since then, the topics of treaty shopping and the Limitation on Benefits Clauses (LOB) have undergone substantial changes due to the publication of the 2006 and 2016 U.S. Models, the tax treaties signed by the U.S. following the mentioned Models and the OECD/G20 project on Base Erosion and Profit Shifting (BEPS). Additionally, the European Union (EU) has adopted certain decisions that could affect treaty shopping strategies, and at the same time, the European Court of Justice (ECJ) has handed down several rulings that could question the compatibility of the LOB clauses with EU law.

I would like to express my gratitude to Kluwer Law International, for its interest in publishing a new edition of the book. The majority of the work carried out in order to write the updated version on this topic took place during my research stay at Georgetown University (July-December 2016). This research stay was possible thanks to an invitation from Professor Charles Gustafson and a 'Salvador de Madariaga Grant' (PRX16/00445) funded by the Spanish Ministry of Education, Culture and Sport. In this regard, I want to express my gratitude to Professor Gustafson for hosting me at Georgetown University and to my colleagues at the Autonomous University of Madrid, for taking over my duties during the period I spent in the U.S. The topic studied in this book is one of the objectives of the ongoing research project DER2015-66087-P (MINECO/FEDER) sponsored by the Ministry of Economy and Competitiveness of Spain, in which I participate along with fellow colleagues at the Autonomous University of Madrid.

Any comments that may contribute to the improvement of this book are greatly appreciated and can be sent to the following e-mail address: felix.vega@uam.es

List of Abbreviations

ALI	American Law Institute
BIT	Bulletin for International Taxation
BTR	British Tax Review
CCCTB	Common Consolidated Corporate Tax Base
CDFI	Cahiers de Droit Fiscal International
CFC	Controlled Foreign Company
CIN	Capital Import Neutrality
CT	Crónica Tributaria
DTC(s)	Double Taxation Convention(s)
ECJ	European Court of Justice
ECT	European Community Treaty
EEA	European Economic Area
ET	European Taxation
EU	European Union
FIRPTA	Foreign Investment in Real Property Tax Act of 1980
GAAR(s)	General Anti-Avoidance Rule(s)
GF	Gaceta Fiscal
HPE	Hacienda Pública Española
IBFD	International Bureau of Fiscal Documentation
IEF	Instituto de Estudios Fiscales
IFA	International Fiscal Association
IRC	Internal Revenue Code
IRS	Internal Revenue Service
IStR	Internationales Steuerrecht
ITR	International Tax Review

List of Abbreviations

LOB(s)	Limitation on Benefits Clause(s)
NAFTA	North American Free Trade Agreement
NUE	Noticias de la Unión Europea
OECD	Organization for the Economic Cooperation and Development
OECD Model	OECD Model Double Taxation Convention on Income and on Capital
OJ	Official Journal of the European Communities
PE	Permanent Establishment
PPT	Principal Purposes Test
PSF	Perspectivas del Sistema Financiero
QF	Quincena Fiscal
RDADF	Revue de Droit Administratif et de Droit Fiscal
RDFHP	Revista de Derecho Financiero y Hacienda Pública
RCT	Revista de Contabilidad y Tributación (Comentarios y Casos Prácticos)
REDF	Revista española de Derecho Financiero
RESE	Revista de Economía Social y de la Empresa
SAARs	Specific Anti-Avoidance Rules
SE	Societas Europea (European Company)
STR	Special Tax Regime
TEU	Treaty on European Union
TFEU	Treaty on the Functioning of the European Union
TIN	Tax Identification Number
TJIT	The Journal of International Taxation
TMIF	Tax Management International Forum
TMIJ	Tax Management International Journal
TNI	Tax Notes International
TPIR	Tax Planning International Review
U.K.	United Kingdom
UN	United Nations
U.S.	United States
VAT	Value Added Tax
VCLT	1969 Vienna Convention on the Law of Treaties

Introduction*

As stated in the Commentary on Article 1 of the OECD Model Tax Convention on Income and on Capital (OECD Model), the purpose of Double Taxation Conventions (DTCs) is to promote, by eliminating international double taxation, exchanges of goods and services, and the movement of capital and persons (paragraph 7).[1] In many cases, double taxation is eliminated by conferring the exclusive right to tax income on the state of residence. In other cases, the tax, which may be imposed by the source state, is limited and the state of residence has the obligation to eliminate double taxation by means of the credit or exemption method. In any case, it should be pointed out that the main effects of the conventions are noted in taxation in the source state, particularly with respect to certain types of income (dividends and royalties). Most states have adopted unilateral measures, in their capacity as the state of residence, to eliminate international double taxation. By contrast, it is not common practice for the states to unilaterally exempt non-residents from tax.

Tax treaties may be very useful in international tax planning operations, especially where the aim is to reduce taxation at source. In principle, it is sufficient to obtain income in the state that has entered into a convention with the source state where the non-resident tax liability is most reduced. For the convention to be applicable in accordance with the OECD Model, it is sufficient to be classified as a resident in the chosen state for the purposes of the convention, i.e. for the resulting worldwide income to be subject to tax in that state. The use of legal persons facilitates these operations appreciably, and often, merely incorporating a company in a given state causes the worldwide income obtained to be subject to tax therein. Accordingly, once the state in which the company wishes to earn income is chosen, it is sufficient to incorporate a legal entity in that state and attribute the income generated at source to this company for such income to be protected under the tax treaty.

---

* This book was written under the framework of the research project DER2015-66087-P (MINECO/FEDER) sponsored by the Ministry of Economy and Competitiveness of Spain, and within the framework of a Salvador de Madariaga Grant (PRX16/00445) funded by the Spanish Ministry of Education, Culture and Sport.
1. Unless otherwise specified, all references to the OECD Model refer to the 2014 OECD Model.

These operations have been given the name treaty shopping structures and are among the various international tax planning alternatives.[2] However, for such operations to be efficient, the state in which the income is obtained (intermediary state) may not significantly tax such income. Therefore, for the objectives of these operations to be achieved, when choosing which state to use, not only is it necessary to route income through the state with the best tax treaties but also to bear in mind which states' domestic laws allow for the taxation of income at very low levels. The makeup of these structures and the framework within which they are used in – international tax planning – is dealt with in the first chapter.

The use of DTCs for this type of operation (treaty shopping), particularly in the case where the operation is artificial, may cause the conventions to facilitate tax evasion and tax avoidance. As stated in the Commentary on Article 1 of the OECD Model, the DTCs should not contribute to the above (paragraph 7).[3] In the first section of Chapter 1, the consequences of using this type of structure and the rational for adopting measures to counter such operations will be analysed.

The measures against treaty shopping have been divided into two types, the first of which is the application of domestic anti-avoidance rules in order to deny the application of the tax treaty. There are doubts as to whether such rules may be applied within the scope of DTCs, especially because in such cases a domestic rule is used to override a regime already agreed to in an international treaty. This issue is discussed in the second chapter of this study. The second type of measure involves the adoption of specific provisions to counter the phenomenon of treaty shopping. The states have adopted these types of measures both in their domestic legislation and in their own treaties.

The objective of this contribution is to study the specific rules laid down in tax treaties against treaty shopping and, in particular, one type of rule, the Limitation on Benefits Clauses (LOBs). However, the makeup of the subjective scope of the conventions, i.e. the definition of the concepts of person and residence provided in the OECD Model are first analysed. Reference is also made to the concept of beneficial owner, which was introduced into the OECD Model in 1977 in order to prevent the treaties from being applied in cases of treaty shopping. Given the possible insufficiency of this concept, some tax treaties and mainly those entered into by the United States

---

2. The OECD defines treaty shopping as follows: 'treaty shopping [...] involves strategies through which a person who is not a resident of a State attempts to obtain benefits that a tax treaty concluded by that State grants to residents of that State, for example by establishing a letterbox company in that State'. OECD 2015a, p. 9.
3. The wording of paragraph 7 of the Commentary on Article 1 was slightly modified in the 2003 version of the OECD Model. Following this change, paragraph 7 makes it much clearer than the Commentaries on the 1977–2000 OECD Model that the prevention of tax avoidance and evasion is also one of the purposes of the DTCs. The BEPS project takes a step forward. In this regard, Action 6 of the BEPS project proposes to state clearly, in the title recommended by the OECD Model, that the prevention of tax evasion and avoidance is a purpose of tax treaties. It has also been proposed that the OECD Model should recommend a preamble that provides expressly that countries that enter into a tax treaty intend to eliminate double taxation without creating opportunities for tax evasion and avoidance. Given the particular concerns arising from treaty shopping arrangements, the preamble refers expressly to such arrangements as one example of tax avoidance that should not result from tax treaties. OECD 2015a, pp. 91–93.

(US) have gone one step further, precisely by introducing LOB clauses. The OECD/G20 project on Base Erosion and Profit Shifting (BEPS) has recently supported the U.S. approach by proposing the inclusion of an LOB rule in the OECD Model.[4] The concepts of person, residence, beneficial owner, and the general content of the LOBs are also addressed in Chapter 2.

According to the OECD Model, in order for the convention to apply it is only necessary to be considered a resident in one of the contracting states. The LOBs qualify the concept of residence in the OECD Model, but only for one type of taxpayer, namely a legal entity. This qualification is logical given that as opposed to individuals, legal entities enjoy a wide number of possibilities in respect of creation, establishment and transfer, which facilitate the application of the tax treaty that they intend to benefit from in each case.

Legal entities are only entitled to the benefits of the convention, if in addition to being residents in one of the contracting states, they have sufficient nexus with the state of residence or a real business purpose to obtain the income generated in the source state from this state of residence. These two criteria are specified in a series of clauses or tests, namely the stock exchange clause, the ownership and base erosion clause and the activity clause. Consequently, in order for the convention to apply, in addition to being a resident, the legal entity must fulfil the requirements of one of the aforementioned tests. However, where none of these requirements are met, the corresponding Tax Authorities may confer the benefits derived from a treaty in the event that the taxpayer proves that the purpose of its presence in the state of residence is to not take advantage of that state's network of tax treaties (bona fide provision). In Chapter 3, the legal regime of the LOB clauses provided in Article 22 of the 1996, 2006 and 2016 U.S. Models, the Commentary on Article 1 of the OECD Model, the LOB clauses proposed in Action 6 of the Organization for the Economic Cooperation and Development (OECD) BEPS project and the tax treaties between the U.S. and the European Union (EU) Member States are analysed.

As shall be observed, these clauses have been drawn up in very restrictive terms, an issue which poses two types of problems, the first of which are of a procedural nature, as, in principle, the clauses make it difficult to apply treaty benefits, especially when directly applied by the payer of the income in order to calculate the withholding tax. At the end of Chapter 3, the application of tax treaties that include LOB clauses is addressed.

The second problem relates to the compatibility of the LOB clauses provided in the tax treaties between the U.S. and EU Member States with European Union law (EU law). These provisions may restrict the freedom of establishment, movement of capital and the provision of services by both individuals and companies. Chapter 4 addresses these issues and the possible consequences of the incompatibility of LOB clauses with EU law.

Another means of carrying out the measures limiting the effect of treaty shopping is to deny taxpayers who benefit from a preferential tax regime in the state of residence

---

4. OECD 2015a, p. 20.

from applying the treaty. As noted earlier, for such structures to be worthwhile, the intermediary state must not significantly tax the income obtained under treaty shopping structures. This aim differs from that of the LOBs, as it relates to the tax regime prevailing in the state of residence and not to whether the company has sufficient attachment to this state or sound economic reasons for operating therefrom. From the standpoint of the DTCs, this aim may form part of the context of the measures undertaken by the OECD and the EU in relation to harmful tax competition. Our study is not aimed in this direction, and, accordingly, these measures are not dealt with in depth, although reference to certain aspects thereof may be required.

CHAPTER 1
Taxation of Non-residents and International Tax Planning Through Double Taxation Conventions

I TAX LIABILITY CRITERIA AND TAX TREATIES

Within the scope of the problems relating to the spatial scope of tax law, residence and territory are the two main criteria used to determine whether a taxpayer is subject to a state's power to tax.

The principle of residence is considered to be one of the criteria or forms of personal attachment. Liability by virtue of this criterion is founded on the persons' qualified attachment to a state's territory. The determination of this attachment is a matter of degree, and in each case, is based on facts, information or factors of a diverse nature which attach a taxpayer to a certain territory.[1] In spite of the fact that this type of attachment is used by the majority of states, the study of their formulation through various laws reveals that the definition of the factors and attachments which each state has chosen for the establishment of this concept varies greatly, bearing in mind that such delimitation is carried out in an autonomous and uncoordinated manner from the other states.[2]

The problems which may arise from the diverging formulation of the concept of residence will not be addressed herein. However, significance shall be given to the common result of their application or the consequence, which in principle, should be common to all the criteria or residence attachments (citizenship, domicile and residence), i.e. worldwide taxation.[3] Where liability is based on residence criteria, the taxpayer is taxed for all income obtained regardless of the location in which the income

---
1. *See* Uckmar 1956, p. 580 and Calderón 1997a, p. 27.
2. Calderón 1997a, p. 28.
3. Buhler 1968, p. 220.

has been generated. Hence, the tax levied does not depend on where the taxable event took place, but rather on the location of the person who carried out this event. From the standpoint of the spatial scope of the law, there is full tax liability since the tax is not restricted to the territory of the state with which a resident attachment has been established.[4]

The principle underlying resident tax liability is the ability to pay. The full application of this principle in respect of taxes on income requires the taxation of the worldwide income obtained by the taxpayer. Where the tax is levied on the total income obtained, only the tax imposed on the income measures the true economic capacity of the taxable persons, regardless of where the income was obtained.[5] The importance acquired by this principle of tax law in the states' tax systems is the rationale for the existence of personal taxes.

Otherwise, by virtue of the principle of territoriality, a state levies taxes on the income that has been produced or whose economic origin is within its territory. The taxpayer is subject to tax insofar as the income obtained is produced within the territory of the state which collects the tax. In this case, non-resident taxation can be considered to be a synonym of territorial taxation as, unlike resident taxation, it is founded in a direct relationship between a demonstration of wealth and a certain territory.[6] From the standpoint of the spatial scope of tax law, the non-resident tax liability is limited as long as the taxable person only pays tax on the income generated within the territory.[7]

In addition to those mentioned, there are significant differences between the tax systems in respect of their choice of tax liability criteria. Mainly, non-resident tax is levied separately on the full amount of each element of income obtained, without, as a general rule, allowing for the deduction of the possible expenses incurred to obtain such income.[8] Only in the case of resident taxation, where the entire income obtained is taxed, is it possible to personalize the tax levied, by adjusting it to the economic capacity of the taxpayer, bearing in mind his economic and personal circumstances, where appropriate.[9]

Generally, states use resident and territorial liability criteria simultaneously when establishing their tax systems. However, depending on whether the state is an importer or exporter of capital and technology, preference is given to one criterion or the other. In the former case, prevalence is given to the principle of non-resident taxation, and in the latter case, the states choose to reinforce resident criteria.[10]

---

4. Knechtle 1979, pp. 36 and 64.
5. Uckmar 1956, p. 583.
6. Baena 1994, p. 59.
7. Calderón 1997b, pp. 76–81.
8. However, this is only true in respect of the non-resident taxation of the income obtained without any mediation by a Permanent Establishment (PE). Given the high degree of attachment to the territory of a non-resident who obtains income through a PE, the tax systems have evolved and taxation is increasingly more in line with the tax regime of resident taxpayers who obtain income from economic activities. *See* Baena 1994, p. 135.
9. Calderón 1997a, pp. 72–73.
10. Primacy is given to the resident liability criterion, and, accordingly, preference is given to the state of residence over the source state in those countries which enter into DTCs following the

Chapter 1: Taxation of Non-residents and International Tax Planning

The simultaneous use of resident and non-resident taxation liability criteria can give rise to international double taxation. Consequently, for example, a resident of a state which obtains income generated in another state (source state) will observe that the state of residence, in accordance with a personal criterion, and the source state, based on the principle of territoriality, juxtapose their taxes on the same taxable event.

Bearing in mind the multiple negative connotations arising from international double taxation from tax law principle and economic standpoints, the states have adopted unilateral and bilateral methods to eliminate such double taxation.[11] Among the bilateral instruments, the DTCs entered into by the states are the most noteworthy. Most of these tax treaties have been negotiated in accordance with the successive versions of the OECD Model.

The archetypal double taxation conflict arising due to the concurrence of personal and non-resident taxation criteria is corrected in the OECD Model by means of two methods.

The first of these confers an exclusive right to tax certain income on one state. Consequently, the other state exempts this income from tax. Since the OECD Model was drafted based on the primacy of resident liability criteria, in the majority of cases the exclusive right to tax certain income is conferred on the state of residence. Exceptionally, the exclusive right to levy a tax is conferred on the source state.

In the second method, the distribution rules are not exclusive. Both the state of residence and the source state may tax the income obtained in the latter. The OECD Model foresees two classes of cumulative distribution depending on whether full or limited taxation rights are conferred on the source state. Such limitations are set forth in the convention by establishing limits on the tax which can be imposed on income in the source state. The source state may not levy a tax which exceeds the limit provided in the convention. The tax treaty establishes no limit where cumulative distribution is unlimited.

Where either the limited or unlimited distribution is cumulative, double taxation may arise as the power to tax is conferred on both states. In these cases, the state of residence is responsible for eliminating the double taxation that has arisen through one of the two methods provided for in the OECD Model (the exemption and the credit methods). The state of residence assumes the tax collection sacrifice in the event that distribution is cumulative, as, based on the international principle of the equal distribution of wealth, the source state has a pre-emptive right to impose tax on the income generated within its territory.[12]

In spite of the above, it should be noted that tax treaties based on the OECD Model substantially limit the non-resident taxation of income, and, therefore, this occurs as a

---

successive versions of the OECD Model. As a counterpoint, the states which form part of the Cartagena Agreement or the Andine Pact give absolute priority to the liability criteria of territoriality and the correlational principle of taxation in the source state. The same occurs in the case of the multilateral treaty entered into in 1994 by the Caribbean Community Member States (CARICOM). *See* Atchabahian 1975 and Bierlaagh 2000. The UN Model represents an intermediate stand between both positions.

11. *See* Knechtle 1979, pp. 3–10 and Calderón 1997a, pp. 65–89.
12. Calderón 1997a, p. 75.

result of the state of residence's exclusive right to tax conferred by the tax treaties or through the establishment of tax limits on the source state. The purpose of limiting these liability criteria is to eliminate international double taxation. However, this effect from the application of the conventions may also be useful in international tax planning.

II SOURCE TAXATION: LIMITS AND CONFLICTS WITH RESIDENCE TAXATION

Although tax treaties coordinate resident and non-resident liability criteria, the conflict between both principles has not disappeared completely.

With respect to the principle of territoriality, it may be considered a logical criterion in accordance with the establishment of the state's power to tax, understood as a declaration of sovereignty. From this standpoint, in principle, it does not appear that any state would choose to not exercise its power to tax the wealth generated within its territory, as doing so would amount to forgoing the declaration of its territorial sovereignty.[13]

In view of the significance of this principle, despite the fact that the states use resident liability criteria, they are hesitant to exempt the income obtained by non-residents within their territory from tax.

This phenomenon is observable within the scope of the DTCs. The OECD Model gives prevalence to resident taxation criteria over non-resident taxation criteria, i.e. to the state of residence over the source state. Of course, the preference given to these criteria is not as extreme as in the case of the Andean Group and the CARICOM multilateral treaties, which, from an opposite standpoint, confer the exclusive right to tax the income generated within its territory on the source state. Without reaching this extreme, the OECD does give preference to the principle of residence.

However, the conflicts between both principles are latent in the drafting of the Model. With respect to the concept of Permanent Establishment (PE), it is recognized as a criterion for the resolution of conflicts between the source state and the state of residence.[14]

Business profits are only subject to tax in the source state if they are derived through a PE situated therein. In this case, the possibility that the source state may impose taxes on business profits perfectly demonstrates that the conflict between the states that favour taxation in the state of residence and those that favour taxation in the source state is focused on the limitation or extension of the definition of this concept.[15]

A good example of the above is the concept of PE provided in the UN Model,[16] which aims to satisfy the demands of the states that are in favour of the principle of territoriality. In this regard, there are significant changes in relation to construction projects, where the term has been reduced to six months, the agency clause has been

---

13. Soler Roch 1997, p. 67 and Vogel 1997, pp. 9–10.
14. García Prats 1996, pp. 39, 48 and 85.
15. García Prats 1996, p. 46.
16. Unless otherwise specified, all references to the UN Model refer to the 2011 UN Model.

broadened, and the clauses regarding the exclusion of the consideration of PE have been limited.[17] In this connection, it is important to note the states' resistance to exempting income from tax based on the principle of territoriality, expressed in this case by the concept of PE.

Nevertheless, PE is not the only concept within the scope of the tax treaties, in relation to which, the tension between the source state and the state of residence is notable. Articles 10, 11 and 12 distribute the tax on dividends, interest and royalties. Except for in the case of royalties, the OECD Model entitles the source state to tax this income, but establishes a limit. Depending on the principle on which the tax is based, the states will attempt to negotiate a lesser or greater taxation limit in the source state.

However, the aforementioned tension is most observable in relation to the concept of royalties. According to the OECD Model, royalties are only taxable in the state of residence. However, in practice, a large majority of the DTCs concluded by the states establish a shared taxation system in which the source state's entitlement to a limited tax margin is recognized.[18]

The conflict between the source and residence principles can be most appreciated in relation to licenses to use rights or assets, authorization for the use of tangible and intangible property, the transfer of information, etc. which falls under or may fall under the definition of the concept of royalty. The autonomous concept of royalty, laid down in Article 12 of the OECD Model is characterized, *inter alia*, by the large number of reservations made by the OECD Member States. Numerous deviations in relation to this concept are also observable in the DTCs.[19]

This is due to the fact that the income derived from many transactions which could be included under the concept of royalty could also be included under the concepts of business profits (Article 7), capital gains (Article 13) or, finally, under the 'catch-all' provision laid down in Article 21 (other income). Where the aforementioned articles are applied, the consequence would always be the same: exclusive taxation in the state of residence. Therefore, in the negotiation of the conventions, the definition of the concept of royalty has a very significant role, because it directly affects taxation in the source state. The categories of income not falling within the classification of royalties give rise to the lack of taxation in the source state.

In spite of the friction between the residence and source principles observable in the tax treaties, both principles are limited by means thereof. The contracting states bring their positions face to face in the tax treaty negotiation process until a mutually agreed and balanced result is reached in relation to the licenses granted. The principle of international reciprocity presides over the conventions entered into, bearing in mind the attempt to assure that the concessions made by the states are equal.[20]

In terms of adopting regulations to avoid international double taxation, it is only logical that the states do not unilaterally adopt regulations unless there is corresponding compensation. This can be perfectly observed within the scope of

---

17. García Prats 1996, p. 57, Wijnen/Magenta 1997, pp. 574–585 and Kosters 2004, p. 9.
18. Du Toit 1999, p. 16.
19. Du Toit 1999, pp. 54–56.
20. Del Arco 1977a, p. 42.

non-resident taxation. Generally, a state will not unilaterally exempt the income obtained by non-residents from tax or limit the tax on this income unless the corresponding compensation is obtained, i.e. its residents receive the same treatment when they obtain income in third states.

In effect, the trend is to maintain and reinforce territorial taxation. A good example of this is that the criteria defined in domestic legislation are intended to determine whether income is considered to have been generated within its territory (source rules). In order to broaden non-resident tax liability, some legislation defines these liability criteria in such broad terms that in certain cases it is difficult to assert that the income has been generated within the state's territory. Since there is no international law outside of the tax treaties regime which prohibits states from taxing events which have occurred outside of their territory, there is no limit whatsoever in relation to the definition of attachments used in relation to non-resident taxation.

The opposite process is only observable in certain cases. However, in these cases it is not the main purpose of the unilateral limitation of or exemption from non-resident taxation to avoid international double taxation, although such avoidance is an immediate consequence of this measure. A clear example of the above is found in the taxation of income from movable property within Europe. Following the approval of the Council Directive 88/361/EEC of 24 June 1988, which liberalizes capital movements, the majority of EU States have established an exemption on the interest obtained by non-residents. Because of the liberalization of capital movements, taxation in the source state is a disincentive for investing in the states which require such taxation. Whether or not non-resident taxation exists has a decisive influence on capital movements. Due to the desire to avoid the 'loss of capital' and to attract investment, non-resident taxation of this type of income has been progressively disappearing.[21] This exemption is solely established for economic reasons, and is aimed at providing non-residents with investment incentives by exempting them from this tax.

It should be noted in this respect, that liberalizing capital movements without also standardizing the taxes levied on the income produced, has led to a significant degree of tax competition within the European States. In the Tax Package agreed by the ECOFIN Council of 1 December 1997 to tackle harmful tax competition, the need to adopt measures to ensure an effective minimum level of tax on savings income was established.[22] As a result of this provision, the Council Directive 2003/48/EC of 3 June 2003 on the taxation of savings income in the form of interest payments was drafted. The approval of this Directive was preceded by various proposals, among which the proposals drafted in 1998 are worth mentioning, COM (1998) 295 final, and 2001, COM (2001) 400.

---

21. Hinojosa 1997, pp. 114–122.
22. This 'Tax Package', the scope of which was agreed by the ECOFIN Council of 1 December 1997, consisted of: a Code of Conduct to eliminate harmful business tax regimes; a measure to ensure an effective minimum level of taxation of savings income; and a measure to eliminate source taxes on cross-border payments of interest and royalties between associated companies.

Chapter 1: Taxation of Non-residents and International Tax Planning

For the purposes of this study, it should be noted that the directive proposal drafted in 1998 aimed to effectively subject interest to tax in the source state, the state of residence, or in both.[23] To guarantee the above, the directive proposal allowed the states to choose between exchanging information and applying a withholding tax. If the second option was chosen, interest would be taxed at a rate of 20 percent, and the state of residence would be responsible for correcting the international double taxation arising in this case.

The 1998 proposal did not resolve the conflict between residence and source, but at least it established mechanisms enabling the income to be taxed in one of the two states. Due to the sensitivity of income from movable property to non-resident taxation, it would be logical for the states to choose the information exchange system. This is the solution provided in the 2001 proposed directive and the final directive approved in 2003. The information exchange system became the general rule and the withholding model was only upheld in a transitory manner for three states: Austria, Belgium and Luxembourg. Consequently, the interests affected by the directive are only taxable in the state of residence.

Except in isolated cases such as those pointed out, the states do not generally unilaterally exempt the income obtained by non-residents within their territory from tax. However, this stand may be contradictory to the economic principles underlying the state systems for the taxation of international income and for the methods used to eliminate international double taxation. In this regard, the states that support capital export tax neutrality tend to be differentiated from those that support capital import tax neutrality.

In accordance with the capital export neutrality (CEN) principle, a resident who obtains a portion of his income abroad must bear the same tax charge as a resident who obtains the whole of his income within the territory of the state in which he resides. To guarantee such neutrality, the state of residence eliminates double taxation by means of the credit method.[24] As sustained by experts on this subject, this method protects taxation in the state of residence on the worldwide income obtained (resident criteria) as it is the mechanism which implies the least transfer of tax sovereignty for the state applying the method.[25]

On the contrary, the states that abide by the Capital Import Neutrality (CIN) principle use the exemption method to eliminate double taxation. This method strengthens the source state's pre-emptive right to tax, bearing in mind that the state of residence exempts the income obtained outside of its territory from tax. CIN is guaranteed, as the taxpayers who carry on business activities in a state other than that in which they are residents, bear a similar if not identical global tax charge to that borne by the other taxpayers operating within that territory. As the state of residence exempts this income from tax, the taxation thereof in the source state is not altered by taxation in the state of residence.

---

23. García Prats 2000, p. 53.
24. Calderón 1997a, p. 265.
25. Vogel 1988b, p. 311 and Calderón 1997a, p. 266.

It would be beyond the object of this study to analyse these two methods in depth but the consequences arising from the use of one or the other are defined herein. The CIN principle, which implies the use of the exemption method to eliminate international double taxation, involves the implementation of a system based on the territoriality principle. On the contrary, export neutrality and the credit method protect a taxation system in the state of residence whereby the worldwide income obtained is taxed. Accordingly, international double taxation is eliminated by means of the credit method as it gives rise to the least loss of tax revenue.

On a theoretical level, a state which gives preference to taxation of worldwide income based on a resident criterion should not be overly concerned with non-resident taxation and would adopt a credit method if it were to decide to eliminate the consequences of international double taxation. Contrarily, a state which gives preference to the principle of territoriality would only tax the income obtained within its territory and would choose the exemption method. Nevertheless, neither model is uniformly applied.

An example would be the U.S. Its tax system clearly opts for resident liability criteria, i.e. taxation on worldwide income. Likewise, due to its adherence to the capital export neutrality principle, both in its domestic regulations and, within the scope of the DTCs, the credit method is the main mechanism used to eliminate international double taxation.[26]

Bearing this Model in mind, as the source state, non-resident taxation should not be greatly relevant. This is even observable in its treaty model, as when compared to the OECD Model, it significantly broadens the cases where the state of residence has the exclusive right to tax income generated within the territory of another state.[27]

However, although this is not apparently the case, it is true that the U.S. is the state most concerned with protecting taxation in the source state.[28] This may seem contradictory in view of the fact that the U.S. Model and the DTCs entered into by this state rest on resident criteria and, where possible confer the exclusive right to tax on the state of residence.[29] However, aside from cases where a tax treaty is applicable, under domestic law, the income obtained by non-residents is generally taxed at a rate of 30 percent.[30] Taxation in the source state is only considerably reduced where a treaty mediates. Taxation is not unilaterally eliminated in the source state.

---

26. Proof of this is that the U.S. Model, as opposed to the OECD Model, only provides the credit method. *See* Van Weeghel 1998, p. 111.
27. Rosenbloom 1988, p. 181.
28. Taxation based on a resident criterion (taxation of worldwide income) is also protected to the same extent. Two examples of such protection are the Controlled Foreign Corporation (CFC) rules and those which extend resident tax liability to individuals which change their residence to a low-tax territory. *See* Betten 1998.
29. The U.S. is one of the few states which uses citizenship as a resident taxation liability criterion. Consequently, regardless of their residence, the worldwide income obtained by citizens of the U.S. is subject to tax in the U.S. Although citizenship is the main residence criteria, the principle of residence is also used. Obviously, the latter criterion is only applicable to those who are not citizens of the U.S.
30. McDaniel/Ault 1998, pp. 63–66.

Chapter 1: Taxation of Non-residents and International Tax Planning

Furthermore, even within the scope of the treaties, the U.S. has developed significant measures to protect non-resident taxation. The provisions being studied herein, namely LOB clauses, were first introduced and further developed by the U.S. within the scope of the DTCs.[31] The purpose of these clauses is to guarantee that the benefits laid down in the convention are only conferred on those who are considered to have a legitimate claim thereto. As shall be observed, these provisions only authorize the conferral of an exemption or limited taxation at source following verification that the person residing in another contracting state has not established his enterprise therein for the sole purpose of claiming treaty benefits. The LOB clauses restrict the use of the DTCs, and accordingly the application of the regulations provided therein which eliminate or reduce taxation in the source state.

The stand taken is justified based on the fact that in relation to the negotiation of its treaties, the U.S., like any other state, aims to enter into the convention that most adapts to its taxation premises. As discussed earlier, in the case of the U.S., taxation is in accordance with resident criteria and involves the levying of tax on the worldwide income obtained. Like the other states, the U.S. provides for a strong non-resident taxation system under its domestic law and introduces rules in its treaties to limit the taxpayers who may claim the benefits thereof, for the purpose of improving its initial position in the negotiation of treaties.[32] The existence of a high level of non-resident taxation is used as an instrument to improve its negotiating position.

Accordingly, for example, if a state wishes to negotiate the exemption of interest from tax at source with the other contracting state, or what amounts to the same, the exclusive right to taxation in the state of residence, the other state is more likely to accept such an agreement if interest is taxed under domestic legislation. Otherwise, the other state will have no incentive to accept this clause as it would not be materially obtaining any benefit when acting as the state of residence given that the source state's domestic legislation unilaterally provides that this income shall not be taxed.[33]

As shall be observed, territorial taxation can be founded on causes other than on the choice of territory criteria as the tax system's main liability rule. States which give preference to resident criteria do not exempt income from non-resident taxation if parallel treatment is not obtained in exchange for such exemption in the source state. It should be noted that taxation at source also gives rise to a cost for the state of residence, which may be higher or lower, based on the method used to eliminate double taxation (exemption/credit).[34] Accordingly, the extension of non-resident taxation is normally reduced through the DTCs, since reciprocal treatment in the other state is usually achieved by means thereof.

---

31. In a report released in 2007, the U.S. Deparment of the Treasury stated the following: 'In addition, the United States has been a longstanding world leader in the development of limitation on benefits rules to prevent the inappropriate use of a bilateral tax treaty by residents of third countries, known as "treaty shopping"'. U.S. Department of the Treasury 2007, p. 73.
32. Uckmar 1983, p. 39, García Prats 1996, p. 401 and Van Weeghel 1998, p. 116.
33. Another example is the Netherlands. Even though the tax authorities considered that the dividends paid by a subsidiary to its parent company should not be subject to non-resident taxation, in 1965 tax on such income was created specifically to improve its negotiating position in respect of DTCs. Van Weeghel 1998, p. 108.
34. Kaplan 1993, p. 175.

LOB clauses aim to prevent residents from third party states, other than the state with which the DTC has been concluded, from indirectly applying this treaty. If the treaty is indirectly applied, the source state has no justification for exempting the income generated within its territory from tax or limiting the tax levied on such income, in view of the fact that there is no reciprocity when it acts as the state of residence, i.e. its residents do not benefit from the same reductions in the source state.[35]

Finally, it should be pointed out that within the scope of the application of EU law, the states' resistance to exempting income from non-resident taxation is also notable in the event that parallel benefits are not obtained when the state acts from the contrary standpoint, i.e. as the state of residence.

The Council Directive 2011/96/EU of 30 November 2011 on the common system of taxation applicable in the case of parent companies and subsidiaries of different Member States, 'harmonizes' the taxation of the dividends paid by an EU subsidiary to its parent company where the company is a resident of an EU Member State. The regime was established based on the idea that dividends should not be subject to either legal or economic double taxation. Therefore, the source state in which the subsidiary paying the dividends resides may not tax such dividends. Likewise, since the profits out of which dividends are paid are subject to corporate income tax in the source state, the parent company's state must eliminate the double economic taxation, by either exempting the dividends from tax (exemption method) or granting a tax credit for the amount of corporate income tax paid by the subsidiary on the profits out of which the dividends are paid (credit method).

Pursuant to the directive, states may not levy non-resident tax on the dividends paid by subsidiaries to its EU parent company. However, EU Member States have not generally significantly improved the directive regime, and require lesser ownership interest in the capital of the subsidiary or have broadened the types of companies which may apply the regime. In other words, except where strictly necessary to comply with the directive mandate, they have not limited non-resident taxation.[36]

All the above is meant to demonstrate the conflict between source and residence, in addition to the states' resistance to exempt income from tax at source. The conflict between residence and source is notable in terms of all concepts included under the DTCs. The concepts of PE and royalty, and the use of the exemption or credit methods are good examples of the above. As a general rule, the states do not exempt the income obtained by non-residents within their territory from tax, despite the fact that both from a domestic standpoint as well as from the standpoint of the treaties entered into, clear preference is given to the taxation on worldwide income in the state of residence. When there is compensation for such an exemption, as normally occurs in the DTCs, taxation is significantly limited in the source state in order to avoid international double taxation.[37]

In view of the importance of territorial taxation, either due to the fact that the taxation model is in line with this principle or, for other reasons, some states have

---

35. Schaffner 1997, p. 165.
36. Vanistendael 2001, pp. 154–155.
37. Menck 1993, p. 253.

introduced rules in the DTCs to prevent their application in cases where such application is not considered to be justified. As shall be observed, one of the causes of this problem relates to the weakness of the requirements for being under the personal scope of tax treaties, which is exactly what the LOB aim to resolve.

III DTCs in Tax Planning: Treaty Shopping

III.A Preliminary Remarks

It is evident that economic operations have expanded well beyond the limits of territoriality. The internationalization of economic life has materialized in the phenomenon commonly known as globalization.[38] In view of the demands of this phenomenon, in order to compete in a globalized market, it is necessary to be present in more than one state. Consequently, it is no longer surprising that a company has located the various chains of its productive cycle in various states.[39] In this sense, as pointed out in the OECD/G20 BEPS Action Plan, 'globalisation has resulted in a shift from country-specific operating models to global models based on matrix management organisations and integrated supply chains that centralize several functions at a regional or global level'.[40] This process multiplies international cash flows and, likewise, the possibility that international double taxation may arise, bearing in mind the simultaneous use of resident and non-resident liability criteria, as discussed at the beginning of this study.

To prevent the phenomenon of double taxation from giving rise to an obstacle or from reducing one's competitive stand, at least minimal international tax planning is necessary.[41] Nevertheless, the tax structure designed for the group should be subordinate to and congruent with its business structure, so that it is justified by the economic and organizational benefits achieved, regardless of the structure's effect on the tax borne by the group.

The group structure must be in line with its operations. The tax aspect should only become relevant once the appropriate business structure required to compete in a globalized market has been determined. Artificial structures, whose purpose is exclusively of a tax nature will be attacked by tax authorities and will not be efficient in the medium term. As shall be observed, with respect to the purpose of our study, artificial structures are not entitled to access the regime of the DTCs as a result of the LOB clauses. Consequently, the international tax planning structure adopted must avoid being artificial, given that this is the source of its weakness.[42]

Tax treaties contribute to the aforementioned international tax planning in an essential manner. One of the purposes of all tax planning is to avoid uncertainty, or in other words, to achieve maximum legal security. When operating on an international

---
38. Ramallo 2001, p. 12.
39. Jeffery 1999, p. 18.
40. OECD 2013, p. 7.
41. Manokhin 2013, p. 339.
42. Spitz 1991, p. 117.

scale, the level of uncertainty rises, because, in addition to the usual volatility of tax regulations, there is also a need to bear in mind the changes which may arise in all the states in which an enterprise operates.[43] In this regard, in addition to forming common legal systems for the coordination of tax powers in order to avoid international double taxation, tax treaties provide a more stable legal framework than the states' domestic legislation, since the modification of these conventions is subject to a more complex and specific procedure than the modification of domestic law.

Of interest here, with respect to the double taxation treaties' role in international tax planning, is the fact that such treaties provide a means by which to eliminate or reduce taxation in the source state. As discussed earlier, the purpose of adopting these means in the tax treaty is to avoid international double taxation, either by conferring the exclusive right to tax on the state of residence or by limiting taxation in the source state and establishing a method by which to eliminate international double taxation in the state of residence.

In view of the characteristics of non-resident taxation or taxation in the source state, in certain cases, the reduction thereof may be essential to guarantee the viability of some operations. The taxation of non-residents is characterized by the levying of tax on the gross income obtained in the territory, without any deduction of expenses. This configuration of the tax is justified given the taxpayer's clear difficulty in determining the sum of expenses applicable to the income obtained in the territory and the tax authorities' difficulty in verifying this amount. The non-deductibility of expenses is meant to be compensated with moderated tax rates. However, these tax rates are normally higher than the maximum tax rates authorized by the DTCs where they allow for limited taxation in the source state.

Where the source state is authorized to impose a limited tax, the application of the percentages laid down under domestic legislation, which are proportionally higher than those laid down in the DTCs, may give rise to the levy of taxes on operations in which no profit is actually obtained and even on operations that may actually give rise to a loss. An operation's economic profit margin may be absorbed, or even exceeded by the non-resident tax levied, since it is applied on the gross sum of the operation. Accordingly, the viability of an operation may only be feasible where the tax imposed in the source state is reduced or eliminated, an objective which may be achieved if a DTC is applied.[44]

The need to reduce the tax in the source state may also be justified due to the insufficiency of the methods provided in domestic legislation for the elimination of double taxation. In accordance with the ordinary credit method, the deduction of the taxes paid in the source state may not exceed the tax charge which would have been payable if the income had been obtained in the state of residence. Due to this method's

---

43. Briones 1993, pp. 33–34.
44. Saunders 1995, p. 21 comments on the case of a company residing in the U.K. which tendered a successful bid for a series of projects in Malaysia. However, because of the non-resident tax imposed, the economic profit relating to the operation completely disappeared. Therefore, this project was carried out through a subsidiary created ad hoc in Germany, since in view of the DTC entered into with Malaysia the tax imposed was much lower causing the operation to be profitable.

limitations in relation to eliminating the effects of double taxation, the lesser the tax in the source state, the greater the taxpayer's possibilities of fully applying the deduction of taxes paid abroad and avoiding the limit established by the ordinary credit method. The DTCs reduce taxation in the source state, and, accordingly, where the ordinary credit method is applicable, contribute to the full application of the deduction of taxes paid abroad.

However, these are not the only cases where an entity may try to improve the means by which it obtains income in another state in order to reduce the tax imposed at source. Furthermore, even the reduction achieved in the source state by simply obtaining income through a state with which it has concluded a DTC, or whose taxation is more favourable than that which would be applied in principle, may not be sufficient to achieve the objective of all international tax planning. This objective is to minimize the global tax imposed on the exercise of business activity or the holding of assets, where there are international implications, through the choice of the most efficient means among all the possible alternatives.[45]

Accordingly, although this study is focused on the tax structures used to reduce taxation at source by means of the DTCs, it is necessary to refer to the framework within which they are applied, given that the reduction of taxation at source is normally only one of the phases that must be covered in all international tax planning.

III.B Stages in International Tax Planning: Reduction of Global Tax

Three levels of tax can be differentiated in all international investments.[46]

The first of these is the tax levied in the location where the investment is made ('destination tax'). When planning for tax purposes, this variable must only be taken into account where the investment is made through a 'vehicle' which is liable for tax on the income obtained by means of the operations carried out in that state.[47] The basic techniques for reducing 'destination tax' include, *inter alia*, the claiming of the tax benefits provided in a state's legislation,[48] the generation of deductible expenses and the choice of the most appropriate investment vehicle. The attribution of deductible expenses to the investment vehicle will decrease its tax base. This technique also serves to transfer profits to another state. The income, which is turned into an expense, flows towards a third state.[49] As for the investment vehicle, the use of a transparent entity whose partners reside in another state will cause the 'destination tax' to be reduced.

---

45. Arespacochaga 1998, p. 437.
46. Briones 1993, pp. 34–35.
47. This will normally be when the operation is carried out through a subsidiary or PE. As is common knowledge, although the PE is not considered to be a resident for tax purposes, the taxation thereof is similar to that of resident entities.
48. Easson 2004.
49. This technique is also called extraction of profits. As shall be observed, in order for the transaction to be efficient, the income which gives rise to the deductible expense must either not be subject to non-resident tax, or must only be taxed minimally in the 'destination state'. Ogley 1993, pp. 4–5.

When operating through a subsidiary, or when transferring profits from an entity's PE to its head office, reducing the tax base by crediting deductible expenses also allows profits to be transferred to another state in a more simplified manner than distributing profits through dividend payments. The distributed portion of the profit is not a deductible expense and is generally subject to tax at source, even in the event that a double taxation agreement is applied. Although the majority of states do not tax the profits remitted by a PE to its head office, there are some states, including Spain, that do tax these profits. In the event that this tax – the so-called branch tax – is imposed, the operation has the same disadvantages as the payment of dividends.

The second phase of international tax planning is aimed precisely at reducing the taxation of income transferred to another state. As indicated at the beginning of this study, when acting as the source state, the majority of states levy a tax on the income obtained within their territory by non-residents. This shall be the object of our study. DTCs are the main instrument used to achieve the elimination or reduction of taxation at source, or 'route tax'.[50]

Although these shall be discussed in more depth later, two forms for using tax treaties in this second phase of international tax planning should be differentiated. Although the two mechanisms differ, they can be used simultaneously for the same transaction.

First, there are practices or operations known as treaty shopping.[51] Taxation is reduced at the source through the application of a tax treaty. These types of strategies seek the application of the tax treaty authorizing the source state to apply the least tax possible. In principle, the chosen treaty is not applicable. However, a series of operations are carried out in order for the taxpayer to be included within its scope of application. Normally, this is accomplished through the incorporation of a company in a state that has entered into the ideal treaty with the state where the income is obtained:

> Example: A person residing in Spain has a 10% holding in the capital of a company, which for tax purposes, resides in the U.S. If there were no DTC between the U.S. and Spain, the dividends paid by the American company to the Spanish resident would be subject to non-resident tax in the U.S. at a rate of 30%. Since there is a DTC, the dividends are only taxed at a rate of 15%. However, this person could improve the tax treatment of these dividends in the U.S. if they were obtained through The Netherlands. Where the dividends are obtained in the Netherlands the DTC which that state has entered into with the U.S. would be applied and the dividends would only be taxed at a rate of 5%. To obtain dividends in this state, in principle it would be sufficient to incorporate a company in The Netherlands and for this purpose, to contribute the holdings in the American company. Following this operation, the dividends would be obtained from the company residing in the Netherlands.

---

50. Briones 1993, p. 35.
51. The term is from the U.S. It comes from the expression forum shopping, the use of which is widespread in U.S. civil procedure and consists of searching for a court from which the most favourable sentence is hoped to be obtained when trying a case. The same occurs in the case of treaty shopping, an operation which is arranged in order to obtain income from the state which has concluded the most beneficial treaty with the source state. Becker/Wurm 1988, pp. 1–2 and Brignoli 2013, pp. 15–16.

Chapter 1: Taxation of Non-residents and International Tax Planning

Our study focuses on this aspect of the use of DTCs in international tax planning. Later the development of this type of structure and the conditions in which they should be developed will be addressed.

The main objective of the second type of operation, known as rule shopping, is not to achieve the application of a convention, but rather to assure that the income obtained is classified under the category of income that reduces taxation at source the most, once a tax treaty is considered to be applicable.[52] The problem essentially relates to the categorization of income.

This aspect was indirectly referred to in the above paragraph when analysing some of the problems raised by the definition of a royalty in tax treaties. The problem relating to the categorization of certain operations in which the right to use intangible assets or movable property as either royalties, business or professional profits or 'other income' in accordance with the OECD Model may lead to the lack of taxation in the source state. If the operation is presented in appropriate terms, a categorization authorizing the levying of tax in the source state may be avoided or what amounts to the same, a categorization which confers the exclusive right to tax income on the state of residence may be achieved.

Finally, the third phase of the tax planning strategy consists in minimizing the tax imposed in the investor's state of residence ('residence tax'). The reduction obtained in the 'destination' and 'route tax' paid may be lost in the event that it is not possible to reduce the tax imposed in the investor's state of residence, since the tax savings obtained abroad will give rise to a higher tax base in this state. To reduce this third type of tax, several strategies may be used.

From this viewpoint, the optimization of the investment can be channelled through domestic or tax treaty rules which establish the tax exemption on the income obtained outside of the state territory. In this regard, in many cases the DTCs use the exemption method to eliminate double taxation. In accordance with such DTCs, the state of residence exempts foreign income from tax, which gives rise to a lack of taxation in the investor's state of residence. There are also similar provisions in both state and EU law. In addition to the possible measures for avoiding international double taxation, both domestically and by means of the DTCs, the possible tax benefits which may be adopted by the states to foster foreign investments should also be borne in mind. The application of these benefits, where provided, may lead to a significant 'minimizing effect' in respect of the tax payable in the investor's state of residence.

Another type of alternative for reducing taxation at this level consists of changing the state in which the income is obtained. On the one hand, the investor may change his residence to a low-tax territory. However, such changes are problematic from a tax standpoint, both in the case of individuals and legal entities.

With respect to individuals, domestic legislation tends to establish rules, the effects of which extend tax liability. According to these rules, the taxpayer continues to be considered a resident and will be required to pay tax on the worldwide income obtained during a period commencing when the taxpayer changes residence.[53]

---

52. Vogel 1997, p. 119 and Van Weeghel 1998, p. 3.
53. Betten 1998.

With respect to the transfer of the tax residence of legal entities, such a change leads to serious difficulties both from a tax and business standpoint, particularly where a DTC is not applicable. It should be considered, for example, that it would be extremely difficult for a company incorporated in accordance with Spanish law, to be able to change its tax residence, since the mere fact that it was incorporated in accordance with Spanish law, means that the company would be considered a resident of Spain for corporate income tax purposes. In the case that there is no mediating tax treaty, the company must be dissolved and a new company must be incorporated in the location where it is to be considered a resident for tax purposes. From a tax standpoint, the taxes on the unrealized gains arising when an entity transfers its tax residence to a third state – the so-called exit tax – will also be of significance.

The second option involves accumulating the income obtained in an entity residing in a low-tax state. As opposed to the previous case, the initial investor does not change his residence, but rather 'shifts' the income to an entity created ad hoc in a low-tax territory (shifting the income from the taxpayer to the Base Company). This option requires the incorporation of an entity in a low-tax area. The function of this company would be to receive the income which would otherwise be directly obtained from the company originally holding it.

In international language, this type of company is known as a base company,[54] and is used to reduce 'residence tax'. From a legal standpoint, the income shifted to the base company cannot be credited to the original owner thereof, and, accordingly, tax liability in the state in which the original company is resident is avoided. However, from an economic standpoint, this income could be credited to the original owner, bearing in mind that it controls the capital of the base company.

The 'residence tax' is reduced as long as the base company does not remit the accumulated income to its original owner's state of residence through, for example, the distribution of income. A deferral of the 'residence tax' is fundamentally obtained using base companies.[55] However, it is also possible to avoid taxation where something other than a mere deferral is achieved when remitting the income (secondary sheltering).[56]

Despite the fact that the base company concept tends to be used to describe the previous case, it is not always solely tax related. In many cases, a base company is not formed exclusively to reduce residence tax, but rather, for example, to centralize certain group operations.[57] Such a company may exist for valid economic reasons.

The use of base companies implies an erosion of the taxation principle which applies to the worldwide income obtained in the state of residence. Worldwide taxation is clearly minimized by avoiding this rule of liability through the use of a base

---

54. This is the term used by the OECD in its report 'Double Taxation Conventions and the use of Base Companies'. *See* OECD 1997.
55. Rapakko 1989, pp. 16 and 171.
56. In its report on base companies ('Double Tax Conventions and the Use of Base Companies', paragraph 12, in OECD 1997), the OECD mentions the following: (a) distribution as income of a type which is tax-exempt; (b) reinvestment abroad of income sheltered in the base company; (c) ploughing back as a loan to the shareholder company; (d) alienation of the company holding in the base company, with the shareholder thereby realising a gain which is tax exempt or taxable at reduced rates.
57. Rapakko 1989, pp. 1–3 and 87–89.

Chapter 1: Taxation of Non-residents and International Tax Planning

company. Therefore, rules have been laid down under the states' legislation to directly attribute the income obtained to its economic owner, regardless of whether or not the base company has already remitted these profits Controlled Foreign Company (CFC rules).

Through the application of CFC rules, under certain circumstances, the income obtained by non-resident entities (base companies) will be taxed in the state of residence of the individual or legal entities which control them.[58] These rules aim to provide coherence to tax systems based on the residence principle. For such a system to be coherent, it must be impossible to omit the tax liability on worldwide income by diverting the income into non-resident entities.[59]

As pointed out by the OECD, these measures protect the taxation on worldwide income in the state of residence (taxation from the top).[60] However, it is important to note that these rules will only be applied when the sole activity of the base company is to obtain passive income. Generally, if it carries out a business activity, CFC rules will not be applicable. Tax authorities will only challenge artificial structures, arranged exclusively for tax purposes.

In conclusion, international tax planning should aid to optimize 'destination, route and residence tax'. The tax structure adopted should be congruent with the business structure, because otherwise it could be affected by both unilateral and bilateral measures to avoid planning which is exclusively for tax purposes and which is clearly of an elusive nature.

III.C Reduction of Taxation at Source Through Tax Treaties: Treaty Shopping Structures

Treaty shopping structures are included in the second phase of international tax planning, i.e. when the income is 'on route' to the state of residence. The objective of these structures is to eliminate or reduce non-resident taxation in the state in which income has been generated (source state) through the use of a tax treaty.

The situation is typically as follows: A company residing in state R (residence) obtains income in state S (source). The latter heavily taxes the income obtained within its territory by non-residents, except in the event that a DTC is applicable. As a result of the application of the DTC, this income is not taxed by state S (because the convention confers the exclusive right to tax on the state of residence), or the tax it would bear is significantly lower because the convention establishes a limit on the tax which can be imposed by the source state. There is no applicable tax treaty between the states R and S. Another possibility is that despite the fact that there is an applicable tax

---

58. Sanz Gadea 1996, p. 14.
59. Sanz Gadea 1996, p. 14.
60. 'Double Tax Conventions and the Use of Base Companies', paragraphs 18 and 19. These measures to protect taxation in the state of residence (taxation from the top) counteract those which protect taxation at source (taxation from below). The LOB clauses set forth in tax treaties are included in this second group, since they are aimed at denying the application of the DTC in respect of treaty shopping structures which are solely meant to minimize taxation at source.

treaty; state S has entered into other treaties which reduce taxation at source to a greater extent than the treaty entered into with state R.

The entity residing in state R will develop a treaty shopping structure to benefit from the advantageous conditions offered by the DTCs entered into by third states with the source state. Generally, it will do so through the incorporation of a company in the state that has entered into the desired convention with the source state. The intermediary or conduit company must be considered a resident for the purposes of the application of the convention. If this were not the case, it is very likely that the operation would not achieve the required result.

As with all tax planning, the objective consists of reducing global tax. Therefore, in order for the development of this type of structure to make economic sense, not only is it necessary to reduce taxation in the source state, it is also necessary to make sure that there is no tax liability or that tax liability is minimal in the state of residence of the intermediary or conduit company.

Normally, the objective is not for the income obtained to remain at the intermediary or conduit company, but rather for this income to be distributed to the original owner's state of residence or, for the income to be accumulated in a company residing in a low-tax territory (base company). In the second phase, in order to guarantee the structure's efficiency and viability, it is also essential that the income transferred abroad is not subject to non-resident taxation in the intermediary company's state of residence.

If the two conditions detailed above are not met, i.e. a lack of or reduced effective tax on the income obtained by the intermediary company (resident tax) and its subsequent transfer (non-resident tax), the benefit gained by the treaty shopping structure, i.e. reduced taxation in the source state under a DTC, would be lost.

As can be observed, this structure is not solely the result of using the most beneficial tax treaty. It also requires the skilful combination of such a treaty with the domestic legislation of the intermediary state chosen to carry out the transaction.[61] Accordingly, tax treaties are not the sole variable which should be borne in mind, although the principle effect desired, i.e. the reduction of taxation in the source state, is achieved by means thereof.[62] It should also be considered that not only tax aspects are relevant. Among other aspects, the facilities provided by the states' civil and commercial legislation for the creation of entities' considered legal persons for the purposes of applying the treaties are also of basic significance.

As in all decisions relating to tax planning, a cost-benefit analysis of the structure used is fundamental. Logically, income should only be channelled through these types of structures if the final tax charge resulting from the chosen tax planning is substantially lower than that which would originally have been borne. Furthermore,

---

61. UN 1988, paragraph 22 and De Broe 2008, p. 15.
62. As stated in paragraph 22 of the UN report (1988), the same effect could be achieved through a domestic law, but tax treaties offer a higher level of legal security, given that they eliminate the uncertainty caused by the volatility of domestic laws. Within the European Union, the aforementioned legal safety can be guaranteed through the approval of the corresponding Regulation or Directive, taking into account that the amendment thereof requires unanimity by the Member States (Article 115 TFEU).

the business structure of the intermediary company must have a certain degree of economic substance and coherence to avoid the attack of these structures by the tax authorities and fundamentally, through the LOBs introduced in tax treaties.

The details of the basic structures used follows. It should be borne in mind that due to the characteristics of this study, these issues can only be analysed from an abstract standpoint. In each case, given that the structure's design is closely related to the DTCs and the legislation in force in each state, the tax planner must consider these factors when defining its structure. However, for illustrative purposes, the jurisdictions which can best meet the basic requirements already mentioned will be indicated.

Two types of techniques will be differentiated, i.e. those which do not involve the use of a company created for this purpose and those whose structure is designed based on the establishment of a company in a state which has concluded the desired treaty with the source state.

III.C.1 *Partnership Agreements, Fiduciary Arrangements and Trusts*

Treaty shopping structures are normally arranged through the incorporation of a company in the state that has entered into the desired convention.

The purpose of treaty shopping is to access the regime of a tax treaty that is not originally applicable.[63] In order for this to be possible, it is necessary to locate a person who is considered as a resident for the purposes of the conventions within this state.

The income will then be obtained through this company, which will accordingly control the assets that generate income in the source state, such as shares in the capital of a company which pays dividends. Otherwise, operations will be performed by this company (granting loans or licenses for the use of intangible property), notwithstanding the subsequent distribution of the income to a base company or to the company that originally controlled the assets or performed the above operations.

From a strictly legal standpoint, in these cases, the intermediary or conduit company is the owner of the assets which produce the income generated in the source state, and can freely dispose of it. The income is obtained on this company's behalf and on its own account. However, in certain cases, access to the regime of a convention does not require the company to obtain the income on its own behalf and on its own account.

In some cases, the same objective, i.e. obtaining income through a state that has concluded the convention that provides the greatest taxation reduction with the source state, can be achieved through contracts involving the management of outside affairs (mandatorys, agents, nominees, representatives, etc.). For example, the tax treatment of reinsurance companies performed with non-residents has given rise to these types of operations. Non-resident reinsurance agencies which are unable to benefit from a

---

63. OECD 2015a, p. 9.

convention entered into with Spain have frequently used brokers (agents) located in states with which Spain has concluded a tax treaty for the purpose of channelling the ceded premiums.[64]

Normally, in order to facilitate the application of the tax treaty in the source state, the representative actions of the person residing in the state which has concluded the chosen tax treaty will be of an intermediary nature, since the fact that he is acting for a third party is not to be revealed.[65] Consequently, the intermediary will act in his own name (*agere nomine proprio*), although, logically, the measures he takes would always be on behalf of a third party because he acts on his account. The effects of the managed affair fall within the principal's sphere.[66]

By applying the tax treaty, the desired effect will be achieved, since the manager will make the income obtained, e.g. from the collection of a dividend, available to the principal residing in a state which has not concluded a treaty with the source state.

However, in such cases the source state may deny the application of the convention, because, although the person who receives the income is a resident of the other contracting state, rather than being the owner of the assets giving rise to the income, he is solely an intermediary in the obtainment thereof. Even so, in many cases verification of the above can be extremely difficult due to the lack of information. Therefore, the tax treaty will still be applied since the person who receives the income is apparently a resident of the other contracting state.

In order to prevent the lack of legal ownership of the income leading to the application of the convention being denied, the use of legal figures such as fiduciary arrangements and a trust may resolve this matter. In the case of fiduciary arrangements and the trust, the fiduciary or the trustee formally own the assets and rights which have been transferred to them.

With respect to Spanish law, according to legal opinion and case law, the double effect theory arises in the case of fiduciary arrangements. The original owner transfers the property title of an asset or of a credit, in a definitive or unlimited manner. Such a transfer can be made for guarantee or administration purposes, and in this case, it is made for the latter. The fiduciary shall then be the owner, and shall hold all related powers in respect of the original owner and all others (*erga omnes*). The fiduciary is only personally obligated to the original owner, to use the acquired ownership in a manner which does not contradict the purpose for which he was consigned.[67] Even if the fiduciary agreement was broken and the asset transferred to a third party, such transfer would be fully valid, and the stand of the acquirer incontestable. The legal position of the original owner is very weak with respect to the asset transferred to the fiduciary for his management.

---

64. Vega 2003, pp. 55–56.
65. Díez-Picazo 1979, p. 249.
66. For example, under Spanish law, the acquisition or disposal of an asset on its own behalf by the agent for the principal, does not give rise to two transfers, from the principal to the agent and from the agent to the third party, or vice versa, but rather to the direct acquisition of the asset from a third party (purchase order) by the principal or the direct acquisition of the asset from the principal by a third party (disposal order). *See* Díez-Picazo 1979, pp. 270–275.
67. De Castro 1972, p. 6.

However, from the standpoint of civil, commercial and tax law, the use of a fiduciary arrangement may have some disadvantages. First, the original owner's stand is very weak, as he would be unable to recover the property in the case that the fiduciary agreement was broken, and would only have the right to claim compensation. Accordingly, the original owner's insecurity in respect of his legal stand is sufficient to discard the use of an arrangement.

Second, a unanimous decision with respect to the circumstances under which a fiduciary arrangement leads to the effective transfer of ownership has not been made in either legal opinion or case law.[68] Accordingly, the source state may not recognize the application of the convention since the fiduciary is not considered the legal owner of the income.[69]

Third, from a tax standpoint, once the disadvantages of the operation have been overcome, it is essential that the income obtained by the fiduciary not be subject to resident or non-resident tax in the fiduciary's state of residence, both when the income is obtained and when it is made available to the settlor.

With respect to trusts, the institution of English common law originally proceeding from the *fiducia cum amico* of Roman law, may also give rise to a series of disadvantages which should be considered when using them in a treaty shopping structure.

The trust is separate property governed by a notarial document or deed created by the settlor, which is transferred to a series of individuals (trustees), in order for the assets to be managed and disposed of in accordance with the instructions provided in the notarial deed in the interests of one or more individuals (the beneficiaries).[70] The trust is unique in that it gives rise to a division of property unknown in the civil law legal systems because, in these systems, property is of an indivisible nature.[71] Legal ownership resides in the trustee, who is granted the right to manage the property and dispose of it in the manner established by the settlor but always in benefit of other individuals. Consequently, his ownership is limited, in that he cannot sway from the instructions of the settlor contained in the notarial deed. Additionally, he must manage and dispose of these assets in the interest of those who have material or economic ownership thereof (beneficial ownership), i.e. the beneficiaries.

However, it should be borne in mind that the instructions contained in the notarial deed could be completely varied in nature, covering matters that range from

---

68. De Castro 1972, pp. 15–20. According to this author, a fiduciary arrangement does not give rise to a full and final transfer to the fiduciary under either German or Italian law.
69. One of the cases discussed by the OECD in its report 'Double taxation conventions and the use of conduit companies', (paragraph 13) to deny the application of the treaty to conduit companies consists of those cases in which the assets and rights giving rise to the dividends, interest and royalties have not effectively transferred to the company so that it acts as a mere nominee when receiving payments of such income. *See* OECD 1986.
70. Arespacochaga 2000, p. 33.
71. Trost 2001, p. 597.

granting the trustees with the utmost discretion in the management and disposition of the transferred property, to the establishment of very detailed rules with respect to the use and disposition of the assets.[72]

As can be observed, trusts resolve some of the fiduciary arrangements problems in that there is no doubt as to the effective transfer of the property. Furthermore, in this connection, the law provides sufficient guarantees to respond to unlawful acts by the trustee (incompliance with the settlor's instructions).

From this standpoint, this legal figure can be of use for treaty shopping structures. The tax residence of the trust must simply be located in the chosen state. Furthermore, as in all structures of this type, the income obtained through the trust must not be subject to resident tax and when the income is subsequently transferred to the beneficiaries, the non-resident taxation thereof must be avoided.

This alternative can also give rise to some disadvantages. Trusts are not usually recognized in states with civil law legal systems. The fact that they are not recognized hinders the application of the DTCs, as the first requirement for the application of such conventions is to be a person (Article 1 OECD Model). Even where the existence of a trust is recognized for the purposes of the application of the conventions, a question arises as to the determination of its tax residence. There is no unanimous answer in this respect, which makes it even more difficult to use them in treaty shopping structures.[73] Being a tax resident in the desired state opens up the possibility of using all the tax treaties signed by that country. Consequently, a certain degree of certainty is required in this respect, as on the contrary, the pillars (due to problems with the determination of the state of residence) of such a structure could collapse.

Significant problems may also arise with respect to the classification of the income received by the beneficiaries of the trust. For example, under Spanish law, there are doubts as to the classification of income paid through a trust to an individual beneficiary under Individual Income Tax. Technically, such income could not be classified as income from movable property, since the amounts received by the beneficiaries are not derived from an equity holding, or from compensation for the transfer of capital or any other right to a third person. As pointed out by a certain author, it may even be considered income subject to inheritance and gift tax.[74] If this was the case, the taxation of this income could be particularly harsh, bearing in mind the high tax rates imposed on gifts between unrelated individuals.

In view of the difficulties that arise in relation to the trust tax regime, especially in legal systems which do not recognize such an institution, the intervention of a trust

---

72. It should be noted that the trust beneficiaries are not always entitled to receive the income obtained through the trust immediately. For example, among the basic trust models, the discretional trust is included, in which case the trustees are broadly empowered to manage the assets and are only limited by the instructions contained in the foundational document. Within these premises, the trustees may decide when, how and to whom the income and earnings from the trust are to be distributed, or even when ownership of the assets is to be transferred. By contrast, such discretion does not exist in the case of participation trusts, where the beneficiaries have the right to share in a certain portion of the income from the trust. With respect to the types of trusts, see Arespacochaga 2000, pp. 35–38.
73. IFA 1988, Avery Jones 1989 and Arespacochaga 2000, pp. 83–85.
74. Trost 2001, p. 609.

in these states would be arranged through a legal entity. Accordingly, the treaty shopping structure would not be channelled through the direct intervention of a trust, but rather through the use of a company. Such an arrangement is discussed in the following section.

III.C.2 The Use of Companies

In this type of operation, the income originated in the source state is obtained through a company residing in a state which has concluded a tax treaty with the source state. As shall be observed, it is not necessary for the intermediary company to have been created solely for performing this operation. Additionally, it is not essential for the intermediate company's capital to be controlled by the company which uses it to obtain income therefrom.

From a legal standpoint, in this case as opposed to the above cases, there is no doubt as to the intermediary company's ownership of the income generated in the source state, and accordingly, the holdings in the capital of the company which pays dividends in the source state will have been transferred to the intermediary company.

For such an operation to make sense, it is not sufficient for the applicable convention to eliminate or reduce non-resident taxation in the source state. The income received by the intermediary company, which is the company created or used for the purpose of accessing the tax treaty that reduces taxation in the source state, must not be effectively subject to tax, or the tax to which it is subjected must be minimal. The concurrence of this second aspect is essential when these types of structures are used, because otherwise, the advantage obtained through the application of the convention concluded with the source state would be compensated with the tax arising in the state in which the conduit company resides. Finally, when the income accumulated at the intermediary company is distributed, and regardless of the method used, it must not be subject to non-resident taxation in that company's state of residence.

Two types of strategies or structures are differentiated based on how the resident tax on the income obtained by the intermediary company is eliminated or reduced.[75]

(a) Direct Strategy (Direct Conduit)

The income obtained by the intermediary company is not taxed, either because the company itself is not subject to corporate income tax, or where the company is subject to this tax, in view of the fact that the income is exempt.

When referring to this strategy, some authors point out that the lack of taxation is due to the fact that the company enjoys a preferential tax regime. However, in our opinion, this is not necessarily the case. For example, under Spanish legislation, like that of many other states, the dividends obtained as a result of holding an ownership interest of more than 5 percent in a non-resident company in Spain are exempt from corporate income tax as long as there are a series of concurring circumstances.

---

75. In this regard, Grundy 1984, p. 71 states that both strategies give rise to interaction between domestic law and the DTCs. The type of strategy used will be based on how the interaction arises.

However, this exemption may not be classified as a 'preferential tax regime'. The purpose of this measure is to prevent the dividends received suffering international legal and economic double taxation.

Finally, as in the case of all treaty shopping structures, the income received by the intermediary company must not be subject to non-resident tax when shifted to a third state. The lack of tax at source, in this second phase, may arise as a result of the application of domestic law or of a tax treaty.

(b) Indirect Strategy (Stepping Stone Conduits)

The main difference lies in the fact that the income obtained by the intermediary company is not exempt from tax in the state in which it resides. To prevent the income from effectively being taxed in the intermediary state, the income generated is compensated with expenses billed by companies residing in a third state. As a result of these expenses, the intermediate company's tax base is eroded (base erosion) effectively causing the income obtained in the source state to not be taxed in the intermediary company's state of residence.

The income/expenses do not have to be fully compensated. It is normally necessary to leave a certain tax margin, to assure that the intermediate company's tax authorities accept this operation.

It should be noted that in the stepping stone structure, the income obtained in the source state flows towards a third state other than that of the intermediate company via expenses. These expenses are normally billed by a base company located in a low-tax state. In order for the structure to make sense, the income obtained by the company which bills the expenses to an intermediary company may not be subject to non-resident taxation.

Consequently, this structure eliminates resident tax in the intermediary state through the compensation thereof with expenses billed by companies residing in third states. To allow for such compensation, the expense must be deductible from the intermediary company's tax base.

Regardless of whether a direct or indirect strategy is adopted, it should be borne in mind that the intermediary company must be established in states with an extensive network of DTCs. The network of tax treaties will not only provide for the elimination or reduction of taxation in the source state. It will also assure that non-resident tax is not imposed on the income when distributed towards another state by the intermediary company, because in stepping stone conduits the income is distributed through the expenses billed by a company residing in a third state.

Nevertheless, other factors should be taken into account when making a decision regarding the state in which to incorporate the intermediary company, including, first, the level of formalities, accounting and audit requirements and, in general, the administrative controls required for the incorporation and operation of companies. The number of demands required by the 'legal vehicle' will be fundamental when choosing one state or another. Aspects such as the existence of restrictive exchange control laws or the fact that a state's currency is strong are also fundamental. From a tax standpoint, and particularly when operating through stepping stone conduits laws relating to the deductibility of expenses in the intermediary company's state of residence should not

Chapter 1: Taxation of Non-residents and International Tax Planning

be restrictive. In this respect, laws against thin capitalization or transfer pricing should be avoided. As a consequence of the application of these laws, the expenses billed by the company residing in a third state may not be deductible from the intermediary company's tax base.

Following is a brief analysis of the some of the typical operations for which intermediary companies are used. This analysis will show how treaty shopping structures are arranged in specific cases.

(a) Intermediation in the License to Use Intangible Assets

This type of company is basically used to channel all the income classified as royalties within the scope of the application of tax treaties. Royalties means payments received for licensing the use of an intangible asset to a third person (intellectual property rights, know how, etc.).

The structure is basically formed as follows: company T residing in state T (state of origin) has developed a patent, and wishes to assign the right to use this patent to companies residing in third states. If the license to use the patents is directly assigned to company S, a resident in state S (source), the latter will impose non-resident tax on the payments made by S to T. To avoid the tax at source, T could structure the investment in the two following manners:

First, it could be structured through the assignment of the patent to a company formed in a low-tax state (base company). Subsequently, the base company would grant a license to use the patent to a company formed and residing in another state (intermediary company) for 98 units of account. The intermediary company would then grant a sublicense to use the patent to company S for 100 units of account. The intermediary company must be located in a state which has entered into a treaty with state S and which confers the exclusive right to tax the royalties on the state of residence. Likewise, either in accordance with a convention, or through the application of domestic law, the intermediary company's state must not impose non-resident tax on the royalties paid to the state of residence of the base company.

As can be observed, the above is a stepping stone structure. The royalties paid by company S to the intermediary company are not taxed in S due to the application of the tax treaty. The intermediary company is liable for tax in its state of residence on only two units of account, following the compensation of the income obtained in S (100) with the billed expense, which in this case is the payment of a royalty to the base company (98). The 98 units of account paid to the base company are not subject to non-resident tax in the intermediary company's state. As the base company resides in a low-tax state, it will not be taxed, or will only be minimally taxed on the 98 units of account received. This income will only be taxed when they are distributed to company T in the form of dividends, notwithstanding the fact that another technique, which reduces or eliminates taxation, may be arranged for the distribution of the dividends (secondary sheltering).

The second alternative merely consists of dispensing with the interposing of a base company. The intermediary company obtains the usage license from company T, and then assigns it to company S. In this case, the reduction of the global tax charge may be less in the event that company T's state imposes a high resident tax on this income.

Regardless of whether a base company is also used, it is of prime importance that the intermediary company is established in a state that has entered into a DTC, which confers the exclusive right to tax royalties in the state of residence, with the source state. Resident taxation is eliminated through the billing of a royalty by an entity residing in a third state. The royalty payment is not subject to non-resident tax in the intermediary state.

Many expert opinions in this field refer to the Netherlands as being among the states that make the use of this operation the most accessible. In this state, there are a series of ideal elements for this purpose. First, there is an extensive network of tax treaties which confer the exclusive right to tax royalties on the state of residence or at least, only allow for minimal tax in the source state. Furthermore, under domestic legislation the royalties generated in Dutch territory and paid to non-residents are not taxed. Additionally, the deductibility of the royalties from the tax base of the intermediary company has been assured through a system of advance tax rulings.

These types of transactions are normally carried out between associated companies. To avoid applying domestic laws relating to transfer pricing, the Dutch tax system provided a tax ruling system to determine the tax margin to be left by the intermediary company and, accordingly, respect this type of operation.

The possibility of obtaining tax rulings significantly contributes to increasing the legal security of the operation, which is understood to be the possibility of calculating the tax consequences of a given operation in advance, and as legal security in the planning of economic decisions.[76]

Obtaining one of these royalty rulings was relatively simple.[77] The ruling determines the tax margin that should remain in the Netherlands for this operation to be accepted, i.e. the Dutch tax authorities allowed the royalties paid by the intermediary company to be fully deducted as an expense.[78] As explained in the above example, the ruling basically consists of calculating the amount of the royalty to be received by the intermediary company from the entity to which it sublicenses the intangible property. That amount was determined as a result of increasing, by a certain percentage, the sum of money paid by the intermediary company to the entity which previously assigned the intangible property to it.

---

76. Zornoza 1984, p. 223.
77. *See* Betten 1992 and 1993.
78. The tax margin was generally 7 percent. Nevertheless, it should be noted that the regime of these rulings in the Netherlands was modified, among other reasons, as a result of the 1998 EC Code of Conduct. In this regard, the objective was to make the tax ruling system more transparent, in addition to adapting it to the international transfer pricing regulations. This system for calculating the tax margin to remain at the intermediary company had been criticized since it was not considered to be in line with the methods proposed by the OECD. *See* Hamen 2001, pp. 19–20, Pijl/Hählen 2001, pp. 614–629 and De Broe 2008, p. 16.

If the operation is performed under these terms, the deductibility of the amount paid by the intermediary company is not questioned from the standpoint of the rules on transfer pricing. The existence of this type of ruling facilitates and assures the success of this operation.

(b) Financial Intermediation

Directly granting loans may involve high tax costs that an intermediary company can reduce. Accordingly, the intermediation of a company between a business group's borrowers and either group or independent lenders can contribute to reducing the additional costs that arise in the event of a cross-border operation.

The operation is structured in similar terms to stepping stone conduits, although in this case, the income with which the companies are operating is interest.[79] As shown in the above example, the intermediary company receives a loan from another company, and subsequently lends these funds to the company to which the loan will be granted. The interest rates on the loan are fixed in a manner by which a tax margin is left in the intermediary state.

As in the case of any other operation, the interest received and the interest paid by the intermediary companymust not be subject to non-resident tax. Taxation is eliminated in the intermediary state through the compensation of the interest paid and received. In order to guarantee such compensation, it is essential that there are no hindrances with respect to the deductibility of interest under the legislation of the intermediary state, or at least that such hindrances are not applicable in the specific case in question.

Among the tax laws that must be taken into account in this connection, those relating to transfer pricing, thin capitalization and other rules limiting interest deductions are of particular relevance. These laws may be applicable given that the operations are between associated entities. The possibility of obtaining a tax ruling from the intermediary state indicating the tax margin which should remain at the intermediary company will be of particular aid in eliminating doubt as to the laws' applicability. Furthermore, the interest which the loans bear must respect the arm's length principle, as the DTCs do not protect interest that does not abide by this principle.[80]

---

79. A loan is to be granted to a Group Subsidiary (GS) residing in State S (source). Two companies are incorporated (or already exist). The first is the Intermediary Company which will be established in a state that has concluded a treaty with State S which confers the exclusive right to tax the interest on the state of residence. The second is the base company, which is incorporated in a low-tax state. Either as a result of a convention or its own domestic legislation, the intermediate company's state does impose non-resident tax on the interest. The base company loans one million units of account to the intermediary company at an interest rate of 6 percent. Subsequently, the intermediary company loans the same amount to the subsidiary (GS) but at an interest rate of 6.125 percent. When the GS pays the intermediary company the interest on the loan (61.250 units of account), this interest is not taxed in the state of source. The intermediary company earns income of 61.250 units, which is compensated with the expense relating to the payment of interest to base company (60,000 units of account). Non-resident tax is not levied on the interest paid by intermediary company to base company. The SI's tax base is 1.250 units of account (61.250 minus 60.000).
80. Article 11.6 OECD Model.

The numerous tax laws that 'monitor' operations between associated companies may complicate the viability of this operation. However, this disadvantage may be avoided in the event that the intermediary company is not related to the companies which lend and receive the loaned capital, i.e. where a back-to-back loan is used.[81] The intermediary is usually an unrelated financial institution. The company that wants to grant the loan makes a deposit in the financial institution and receives interest relief in compensation for this deposit. Subsequently, the financial institution grants a loan to the company that the funds were originally to be loaned to, with a charge to the deposited funds. The profit earned by the financial institution consists of the difference between the interest received on the loan and the interest paid on the deposit, in addition to possible commissions charged for these services.

In many cases, back-to-back loans allow the domestic laws on associated operations to be avoided and also achieve the intended aims of treaty shopping. However, the cost of the operation may be higher than the cost incurred in cases where the operation is directly between associated companies.

(c) Intermediary Holding Companies

Such companies are used to optimize the taxation of the dividends and capital gains resulting from the holding of shares in the capital of companies which are residents of other states. This optimization involves eliminating or reducing taxation in the source state and eliminating or reducing taxation in the company's state, which is the holder of the shares. Likewise, where the profit is subsequently distributed towards a third state the objective is to avoid non-resident taxation. With respect to these types of companies, a direct strategy or direct conduit is typically used.

With regards to the reduction of resident tax, a large number of states have introduced regimes which favour the establishment of holding companies.[82] Those regimes contain an exemption from tax on the dividends paid or the capital gains arising from the transfer of shares. From this standpoint, many states may be suitable for the establishment of these types of companies (participation exemption). However, the aim of treaty shopping structures is to reduce taxation at source, meaning that these companies will tend to be established in states where treaties reduce non-resident taxation the most.

With respect to dividends compared to interest or royalties, there are significantly fewer tax treaties that eliminate taxation at the source, or in other words, that confer the exclusive right to tax on the state of residence. The above is only observed in a generalized manner in the treaties concluded by some states such as Luxembourg, the

---

81. IBFD 1996, p. 26.
82. These regimens are only applied to the shares in the capital of the companies of a business or control nature (direct invesment) and not to those merely formed as a portfolio investment. The expression 'business holding' refers to a holding which is of a business rather than of a portfolio nature. While there is no ontological division between them, practice evidences that commencing from a certain degree of ownership interest, the economic position of the shareholder varies essentially due to the variation in the costs assumed. One of the criteria for determining the different between a business and portfolio holding is the percentage of ownership interest. Article 10(2) of the OECD Model fixes a percentage of 25 percent.

Netherlands and Switzerland.[83] Nevertheless, although not set forth within the scope of the treaties, where Directive 2011/96/EU is applicable, the distributions of profits between parent companies and community subsidiaries are not taxed in the source state. Capital gains are not taxed at source because tax treaties confer the exclusive right to tax on the state of residence (Article 13 OECD Model).

The third matter that should be considered when choosing the state in which to incorporate the holding company is whether the profits distributed by the holding company are subject to non-resident tax. Where a treaty or domestic law does not exempt the distribution of dividends from tax, the distribution can be channelled through another means which is not subject to taxation at source (the liquidation of the company, transfer of the shares, etc.)

(d) Coordination, Financing and Distribution Centres

These entities are used to centralize certain business group services and activities (financing, research and development, audit, collection management, etc.).

This is not actually a treaty shopping structure, as its aim is to reduce 'destination tax', i.e. the profits generated by the various group entities through the billing of a series of expenses by the coordination centre. Therefore, it would not be included within the second phase of international tax planning, i.e. reduction of the route tax, but rather in the first phase, according to the outline detailed in the previous section (III.B).

Obviously, the income obtained by the coordination, financing or distribution centre in the state where the group entities are billed may be subject to non-resident tax. Therefore, the centres are established in states with tax treaties that confer the exclusive right to tax this income on the state of residence, or at least which only allow the source state a minimal tax margin. In this respect, there is a certain degree of treaty shopping, as the existence of DTCs that reduce taxation at source is a decisive factor when choosing which territory to establish the company in. However, the income obtained by these entities must also be exempt from or only subject to low corporate income tax in the state of residence. States which favour establishing these types of entities within their territory tend to establish low tax rates or tax base definitions which give rise to reduced taxation.

The definitive aim of these entities is to localize the group's profits in jurisdictions where there is an extensive network of DTCs that give rise to low taxation, in order to avoid or reduce the tax at source levied on the income billed to the rest of the group entities by the coordinating centre.[84] As a result of the centralization of services, it is typical for these entities to carry on a certain degree of business activities, which, as shall be observed, hinders the application of LOB clauses, or rather, prevents the application of these rules, as there is a concurring valid economic reason for establishing the company within the territory.

---

83. Van Raad 1988, p. 245.
84. In this respect, in addition to treaty shopping, a form of country shopping may be evidenced by the states which establish these regimens. *See* Hinnekens 1996, pp. 98.

The main problem relating to these 'centres' arises in states where income is decreased due to the reduction of resident companies' tax bases as a result of the billing by these entities. This income is not subject to non-resident tax either, since the DTCs are applicable. Finally, it is difficult to apply CFC rules since these entities do carry on business activities to a certain extent.

The problem lies in the reduced non-resident tax offered by the states which establish these regimes,[85] favours centralization and accordingly, the relocation of the services to these jurisdictions. Little can be done to prevent the loss of taxation at source by means of the DTCs, except where resident tax is not imposed on the worldwide income obtained under the tax regime of the coordination centre.

(e) Use of a PE

The following structure is a case of a direct strategy. In this structure, taxation in the intermediary company's state of residence is eliminated in the following manner. The income obtained by the intermediary company in the source state is attributed to a PE which belongs to the same company and is located in a low-tax territory. A taxation reduction in the source state is achieved because, the applicable tax treaty is that entered into with the state of residence of the company that owns the PE. In order for the tax to be eliminated in the intermediary state, the income obtained in the source state must not be taxed by the intermediary company's state. Consequently, the income must be exempted from tax by the treaty due to the fact that it is attributed to a PE located in a third state. Likewise, the state where the PE is located is required to be a low-tax territory.

As can be evidenced, the success of this structure essentially depends on assuring that the income attributed to the PE is exempt from tax in the intermediary state. This exemption may be provided either in the intermediary state's legislation or in a DTC concluded by an intermediary state with the state where the PE is located.[86] In any case, the obtainment should not be excessively strict bearing in mind that the PE must be in a low-tax territory or a preferential tax regime must be applicable.

---

85. As mentioned, this is a problem which to the most extent lies in the fact that a preferential tax regime is enjoyed in the state of residence of the coordination, financing or distribution centre. As shall be observed, this is not the objective of the LOB clauses, i.e. to deny the application of the tax treaty as a result of the tax regime enjoyed in the intermediary company's state of residence. This does not mean that the decision not to apply the treaty can be made due to the fact that a preferential regime is enjoyed. In this regard, in these cases the application of the treaty is denied by including an exclusion clause in the treaty (*see* section IV.B, Chapter 3).
86. This structure has normally been arranged by placing the PE in the Dutch Antilles or in Switzerland and then locating the company to which it belongs in the Netherlands. *See* Van Weeghel 1998, pp. 125–126. Therefore, for example, a company residing in the Netherlands, which obtains dividends in the U.S., will allocate the shares arising from these dividends to a PE located in the Dutch Antilles. These dividends are not taxed in the U.S. due to the tax treaty concluded with the Netherlands. The dividends are not taxed in the Netherlands, as they are exempt as they are allocated to a PE. They are not significantly taxed in the territory where the PE is located either, taking into account the Dutch Antilles' low taxation.

CHAPTER 2
The Subjective Scope of Double Taxation Conventions and Limitation on Benefits Clauses

I CAUSES FOR AND CONSEQUENCES OF THE TREATY SHOPPING STRUCTURES

I.A Preliminary Remarks

The way in which tax treaties are used in international tax planning, and particularly, as an instrument for reducing taxation at source, was addressed in the first chapter. The reduction of the global tax burden by means of tax planning is the result of the appropriate combination of DTCs and the states' legislation. Treaty shopping structures allow for the reduction of the global tax charge, by combining the reduced tax at source provided for under a tax treaty and a favourable tax regime in the conduit or intermediary's state of residence.

Regarding the application of tax treaties, this type of structure is possible because in principle, access to the tax treaties is relatively simple. Although this issue will be analysed in detail below (*see* section II.B.1 of this chapter), it should be noted that for a tax treaty to be applicable, it is only necessary for a taxpayer to be liable to tax in a state on worldwide income. In principle, a state's resident taxpayers have the right to apply a tax treaty in accordance with Articles 1 and 4 of the OECD Model.

Tax liability on worldwide income is expressed in abstract terms, i.e. a taxpayer must be subject to resident tax regardless of whether he is effectively taxed.[1] Accordingly, for example, with direct or indirect strategies, the company is subject to tax on worldwide income. However, in the case of either an exemption provided for under domestic law (direct conduit), or the compensation of foreign source income

---

1. ALI 1992, p. 128.

with expenses (stepping stone conduit), tax liability may not exist in the company's state of residence which obtains income. It is only necessary for resident tax liability to formally exist in abstract terms for a taxpayer to be considered a resident in a state for DTC purposes, and accordingly, to be included within the subjective scope of a tax treaty.

It is relatively easy to achieve this, especially for legal entities. In many jurisdictions, the mere incorporation of a company in accordance with a state's laws gives rise to tax liability on worldwide income.[2] The states' corporate laws also facilitate access to tax treaties, bearing in mind that the majority do not significantly hinder the incorporation of companies by non-resident taxpayers. From a material standpoint, the development of business activity is generally not required for legal personality to be recognized. Therefore, in principle, a company which is merely incorporated in accordance with a state's laws has the right to apply all DTCs entered into by that state.[3]

In view of the relative ease in obtaining the right to apply double taxation treaties, the existence of planning structures like those described is understandable. However, when deciding in which state income should be obtained, it is important to bear in mind that not only the tax treaty entered into with the source state should be valued, but also the possibilities offered by domestic legislation for the elimination of resident tax.

On first consideration, it should be noted that the reason for introducing LOB clauses in a tax treaty is precisely to affect the subjective scope of the DTCs.[4] Pursuant to these clauses, it is not sufficient to be merely liable to resident tax in a state to be included within the subjective scope of a treaty for the purpose of requesting its application, particularly in respect of the laws which limit taxation in the source state. These clauses mainly 'qualify' the requirements that a company must meet to be able to request the application of the DTCs entered into in the state in which it resides.[5]

However, prior to analysing the basis for and wording of these clauses in detail, it is essential to address the method used by the OECD Model and also included in the tax treaties' drawn up in accordance with this model, to distribute taxable income among several tax jurisdictions. In our opinion, this method, is not only the reason behind the existence of this type of clause, but also, that the rest of the rules included in both treaties and each state's legislation for preventing international tax avoidance (transfer pricing, CFC rules, thin capitalization, etc.).

These rules have been recently reviewed by the OECD in the context of the OECD/G20 project on Base Erosion and Profit Shifting (BEPS). This initiative started with the OECD report 'Addressing Bases Erosion and Profit Shifting' released on 12

---

2. Rohatgi 2002, pp. 146–152.
3. The place of incorporation is not the only criterion used by the states to subject a company to taxation on worldwide income. The place of effective management and tax residence are also criteria used by most tax systems. However, special attention should be paid to the place of incorporation, since it is the criterion which most evidences the easy access to the subjective scope of the DTCs.
4. Almudí/Serrano 2001, pp. 82–83.
5. Vogel/Shannon/Doernberg/Van Raad 1989, Article 16, p. 4.

February 2013. Following the release of this report, the OECD and G20 countries adopted a fifteen-point Action Plan to address BEPS in September 2013. The Action Plan identified fifteen actions along three key pillars: introducing coherence in the domestic rules that affect cross-border activities, reinforcing substance requirements in the existing international standards, and improving transparency as well as certainty. The Action Plan ruled out the possibility to introduce fundamental changes to the international tax architecture and the current source and/or residence dichotomy.[6] After two years of work, in October 2015 the fifteen actions were completed and the OECD released the final documents of each action. Some of these actions are closely related with the object of this book (treaty shopping and LOB clauses), especially Action 6 (titled: Preventing the Granting of Treaty Benefits in Inappropriate Circumstances) as it identifies treaty abuse, and in particular treaty shopping, as one of the most important sources of BEPS concerns.

I.B Allocation of Business Income: The Separate Accounting and Formulary Apportionment Systems

The current OECD Model is a result of the work performed by the League of Nations following World War I. In 1933, the Fiscal Committee of the League of Nations carried out a study on the income allocation systems used by states for enterprises which operate on an international level (Carrol Report).[7] The two systems mainly considered were the separate accounting and the formulary apportionment methods.

These systems use different techniques for allocating the income obtained by a company which carries on its operations in more than one state.

Previously, it is important to bear in mind that the definition of an enterprise adopted within the League of Nations and subsequently within the OECD is limited. Legal personality plays a significant role where income is allocated. Commencing with the first studies carried out by the League of Nations, bodies corporate with their own legal personality were considered to be separate entities, and, accordingly, to be autonomous income allocation centres, regardless of whether they were included under the same operating and control unit from a business standpoint.[8] Therefore, for example, the fact that a company or various companies are controlled by another entity does not convert the group into a single income allocation centre. On the contrary, tax systems treat each company as a separate and autonomous income allocation centre.

This same phenomenon is observed in domestic tax systems. Income tax is levied based on the legal person's, rather than the enterprise's ability to pay. Evidence shows that in practice, these two concepts are not always the same. However, it cannot be disregarded that the existence of polycorporate enterprises is considered under tax law, where traditional regulations which are based on legal personality and on identity in

---

6. Panayi 2016, p. 629.
7. Picciotto 1992, pp. 27–31.
8. Picciotto 1992, p. 23.

formal terms rather than in business practice are incapable of meeting tax objectives. The most significant example of this is that tax systems tend to establish a specific tax regime for groups of companies.

As shall be observed, this restricted definition of enterprise facilitates the use of treaty shopping structures. The income obtained in the source state can easily be 'redirected' to a state that has the desired treaty. The income is simply allocated to the intermediary company established for this purpose since this intermediary company's tax base is not required to be consolidated with the tax base of other entities. It should be noted that the intermediary company is normally controlled by the original owner of the income. If a broader definition of enterprise were applied for tax purposes, the income earned by all parts of the enterprise would be consolidated and taxed as single unit.

Due to the limited definition of enterprise on which the OECD Model is based, these methods only apply to the taxation of the PE. As is common knowledge, income of a business nature is only taxed in the state of residence, unless the person who obtains the income has a PE in the source state. Each of the two methods establishes a different criterion for determining which portion of the global income obtained by the person is allocated to the PE.

The objective of the separate accounting system is for each PE to be taxed as if it were an independent business, distinct and separate from the home office or other PEs with which it legally and economically forms a unit.[9] The tax base is determined based on the accounting records relating to the PE's operations, regardless of the profit or loss which may be recorded by the business as a whole, which is considered to be completely and absolutely separate. Due to the fictitious consideration of the company as a separate enterprise, transactions between the PE and other company units are recorded for accounting purposes as if they were carried out between separate entities.

In this regard, the PE is taxed as a separate entity because it is an autonomous income allocation centre, and independently because its transactions should be carried out in terms similar to those in which they would be performed by an independent entity, even if transactions are performed between the PE and its home office or other parts of the company.[10]

To guarantee that the PE operates as an independent company, i.e. that it respects the arm's length principle, both the tax treaties and domestic legislation allow for adjustments in the value of the PE's transactions where such transactions are performed with companies with which the PE is associated, and, where it is estimated that these transactions do not adapt to the requirements of the arm's length principle.

The ability to make such adjustments is necessary to assure the proper assignment of income to the territory of each of the parties to the transaction, and accordingly, the arm's length principle is used as a parameter to do so. If such a possibility were to not exist, the PE's profit or loss could easily be altered in cases

---

9. Forns 1960, p. 155.
10. García Prats 1996, p. 265.

Chapter 2: Scope of Double Taxation Conventions and Limitation

where it performs transactions with the head office, other parts of the company or even legal entities which are independent, but, associated with the legal entity under which the PE is included.

Consequently, the separate accounting system requires a significant effort by the tax authorities to verify that the transactions are actually performed as an independent entity. However, this problem not only relates to the taxation of the PE, but, also to all transactions between taxpayers which are formally considered to be separate entities but are related or associated.

Therefore, although in principle, separate accounting may appear to be a simple system by which to allocate income, it requires that a significant effort be made to verify the value of the transactions in order to assure that the 'assumed' independence reflected on a formal level is also reflected on a material level. As evidenced by the enormous number of expert studies both on a national and an international level, the application of this system is quite complicated.[11]

Actually, determining the value of effectively performed transactions in an independent manner is particularly difficult. Not even the methods proposed by the OECD have completely resolved this problem. Likewise, it should be remembered that it is physically impossible for the tax authorities to individually verify all transactions between associated parties in order to determine whether they meet the requirements of the arm's length principle.[12]

The use of the separate accounting method as a criterion for the determination and allocation of income to the PE and to entities with their own legal personality is not as simple as it may first appear; especially when considering that which is required for its correct application. However, this has come to be the preferred method both in tax treaties and domestic law.[13]

The formulary apportionment system is based on a definition of an enterprise as a unit which may not be divided. The income that may be allocated to this unit is a synthetic sum, which takes the various parts into account.[14] In principle, this definition of an enterprise would transcend beyond legal personality and would take into account all entities under the same operation and control unit in which there is a common interest. Based on this definition of enterprise, entities with their own legal personality would not be considered separate and independent where they are included under the same operation and control unit.[15]

However, as has been observed, this is not the definition of enterprise which has prevailed. Entities with legal personality are considered to be separate entities, meaning that they operate as separate and autonomous income allocation centres despite the fact that on a business level they are included under a higher business unit.

---

11. Viñuales 1977, p. 192, Avi-Yonah/Benshalom 2010, pp. 6–7 and OECD 2015b, pp. 9–10.
12. Sadiq 2001, p. 281.
13. Picciotto 1992, p. 31.
14. Del Arco 1977b, p. 173.
15. Blázquez 1999, pp. 152–153.

Accordingly, this method is used exclusively for the attribution and distribution of income between the head office and the different PEs included under the same legal entity.

Although the problem relating to the limited definition of enterprise is disregarded for the time being, it should be noted that the formulary apportionment method considers the total income obtained by the enterprise unit and subsequently divides it among the various parts of the enterprise using several distribution variables or methods.[16]

Total income is distributed among the various parts of the enterprise using a formula. The distribution formula used should distribute income based on the contribution by each part of the enterprise to the overall generation of income. Therefore, the formula's perfection will depend on the exactitude with which it calculates each contribution, made by each part of the enterprise to the total generation of profit.[17]

As pointed out by García Prats, where the enterprise is considered a unit, the international tax dimension must be understood in a different manner. The enterprise's total income is distributed among the states in which the income was generated in accordance with the requirements of the 100 percent test. According to this test, the enterprise may not be taxed for more income than that which was actually obtained. Each state may only tax the portion of income which has been assigned to it. Consequently, international double taxation does not arise as two taxes, one being the result of the residence principle and the other being the result of the territoriality principle, are not juxtaposed.

Compared to the separate accounting system, this system is more advantageous because verification on whether transactions between associated companies comply with the arm's length principle is not required, as long as income is calculated jointly.

This method resolves most of the problems that arise in relation to the separate accounting systems and the treatment of entities with their own legal personality as separate entities, even though they fall under the same operation and control unit. As income is calculated jointly, the use of transfer pricing to fictitiously relocate income is avoided. Likewise, the tax authorities are not required to control whether associated companies respect the arm's length principle in their transactions because this parameter is not used to value the transactions.

---

16. García Prats 1996, p. 266. Accordingly, for example, a group of companies with subsidiaries in various states may obtain income as a whole. However, if the accounting records of each subsidiary are analysed separately, it is possible that some may show profit while others show a loss. According to this method, the subsidiary's state of residence will levy the tax corresponding to the portion of the group's profit which is attributable to this part of the company. On the contrary, if the enterprise unit records a loss, the state of residence of each of the parts thereof would not be able to levy any tax, in spite of the fact that the group as a whole has recorded a profit.
17. The criteria commonly used can be grouped into three main categories, namely those which are based on the receipts of the enterprise, its expenses or its capital structure. The first category covers allocation methods based on turnover or on commission, the second on wages and the third on the proportion of the total working capital of the enterprise allocated to each branch or part. See Commentaries on Article 7 of the OECD Model (paragraphs 52–55 of the annex).

Based on our study, the formulary apportionment system limits the effectiveness of treaty shopping structures. As a result of this method, a state only has the right to tax the income effectively earned by the enterprise within its territory, i.e. only the income which the part of the enterprise located within its territory has contributed to generating. Consequently, based on this method, the mere fact that income is allocated to an entity with legal personality does not mean that the state in which it resides or is located has the right to tax this income.

Based on this method, it would be difficult to fully allocate the income obtained to the conduit company using stepping stone strategies. It should be noted that the aforementioned company acts as an intermediary in the transfer of the asset that generates income. From the standpoint of this method, this entity is not considered to be the company that generated the income simply because it operates as an intermediary. The entity that has generated a profit, i.e. which has effectively contributed to the production of the asset generating income, is that to which the income should be allocated. Accordingly, the income should not be considered to have been obtained in the state of the entity that records such income in its accounting records, but rather in the state of the entity which actually produced the asset giving rise to the aforementioned income.

From this perspective, it should also be remembered that the formulary apportionment method eliminates international double taxation differently to the system applied in tax treaties drawn up in line with the OECD Model.

In principle, each state may only tax the income attributed to its territory. The worldwide income obtained by the part of the enterprise located within its territory may not be taxed as in the case of the OECD Model. As non-resident and resident tax may not be juxtaposed, no international double taxation arises. However, this method does not exclude the residence principle, bearing in mind that in a preliminary phase, it only determines the income obtained in each state. This does not prevent the state of residence from establishing a tax on the worldwide income obtained, notwithstanding the adoption of appropriate measures to eliminate the international double taxation arising from the juxtaposing of tax at source and resident tax. Nevertheless, the fact that an enterprise's state of residence is difficult to determine cannot be disregarded, particularly if a broad definition of enterprise is used, i.e. all parts of the company are included, even if they are considered to be separate entities from a legal standpoint.

Despite the above, in our opinion, if a broad definition of enterprise is used, the state of residence should be the state in which the part of the enterprise managing the unit as a whole is located.[18] Based on the above, the applicable DTC will be that entered into by the various states to which the income obtained is allocated (source state) and the state of residence from which the enterprise as a whole is managed.

From this standpoint, treaty shopping structures in which there is no underlying business activity would be unable to achieve their objectives, since the tax treaty entered into by the source state and the state of residence of the company formally receiving the income would not be applicable. Only the tax treaty entered into with the

---

18. Lodin/Gammie 1999, p. 291.

state in which the part of the company managing the enterprise unit as whole is located would be applicable. As can easily be deduced, it would be relatively simple to incorporate a merely instrumental company in a state for the purpose of obtaining income and consequently, being able to apply the DTC entered into with the source state. However, it would not be as simple as transferring the company's head office to a state that has entered into the desired tax treaty with the source state, in order to be entitled to apply the DTC.

Formulary apportionment, as defined above, was neither the general method finally adopted in double taxation treaties nor in the state's legislation. In the OECD Model, the formulary apportionment method was only provided for as a subsidiary method to the separate accounting method until the 2008 version of the model. It was only applied to calculate the profit assigned to the PE. This method was ruled out in the 2010 version of the Model, due to the modification of Article 7 of the OECD Model and the 2008 OECD report on 'Attribution of Income to Permanent Establishments'.[19]

The reasons which led to the formulary apportionment method being rejected relate to the initial difficulties involved in its application, particularly in view of the fact that this method requires a degree of uniformity in the state's tax systems which is difficult to achieve.

First, there is a question as to whether the definition of the concept of enterprise relates to a company's legal personality, or is it extendable to a group defined by the existence of a common interest or control unit. It seems that in order to be correctly applied, legal personality should not be a determinant factor in deciding which parts are included in an enterprise. In contrast, starting with the League of Nation's first reports, taxpayers with their own legal personality were always considered to be separate entities, i.e. autonomous and separate income allocation centres.[20]

Second, to fully achieve this objective, all the states in which the enterprise operates must determine the overall profit obtained in a uniform manner. The use of this method would not make sense unless the states did not previously agree on the apportionment of the enterprise's profit in the jurisdictions that generated it.

Third, even if an agreement were to be reached in respect of the profit to be apportioned, a formula for establishing such apportionment would still be lacking.[21] Determining this formula would be as difficult as determining the normal market value of transactions between associated companies, taking into account that not just any parameter is valid. The apportionment formula should be in line with the nature of the business carried on by the various parts of the enterprise, and also respect a reasonable assignment of the income based on the importance of the contribution of this part to the general profits of the enterprise unit. It is impossible to consider all factors coinciding in the production of the enterprise's total profits. The fact that productive factors vary from one company to another must be recognized, meaning that problems arise in relation to the allocation of the income among the different parts.[22]

---

19. OECD 2008.
20. Picciotto 1992, pp. 23 and 27.
21. Lodin/Gammie 1999, pp. 29 and 293.
22. García Prats 1996, p. 268.

Chapter 2: Scope of Double Taxation Conventions and Limitation

In spite of the objective difficulties involved in the use of this method, it is unlikely that the implicated states would come to an agreement in this regard. This does not mean that this method is not objectively capable of improving the resolution of the problems which arise in relation to the taxation of international income. In fact, this method continues to be used in some cases for the distribution of the income obtained by an entity which operates in various territories. However, in such cases, the implicated territories have a common authority which can impose a uniform method for the determination and allocation of income.[23]

Consequently, although the formulary apportionment method may appear to be preferable, in practice, in order to achieve the objectives thereof, a consensus of the states involved was required in order to put a system for the determination of income into practice based on the same criteria, and such a consensus was never reached. Therefore, the problems which were supposed to be resolved through the creation of this method led to greater problems where the system was not accepted by all of the various states.

The latter does not mean that the use of this method has been completely discarded on an international level. In fact, recently there has been support for its implementation on a European level.[24] In this regard, the most significant proposal of the EU is the Common Consolidated Corporate Tax Base (CCCTB). This project was launched in 2011 and re-launched in 2016 by the European Commission. The CCCTB is a harmonized system to calculate companies' taxable profits in the EU. It offers one set of rules for companies to determine their tax base, rather than multiple national ones. It will enable businesses to file a single tax return for all their EU activities. Once a company's consolidated tax base has been established, each Member State in which the company has activities will have the right to tax part of this base. The proportion of the company's base that a Member State can tax will be decided based on three equally weighted factors: the assets of the company in that Member State; the workload the company has in that Member State; and the sales that the company has made in that Member State. The CCCTB intends to combat tax avoidance, as consolidation will remove the need for complex transfer pricing, which is one of the main vehicles for profit shifting within international groups.

Despite this EU CCCTB project, so far, the truth is that the separate accounting method has prevailed over the formulary apportionment method in the context of international tax law. This is evidenced in the OECD/G20 BEPS project, insofar as it maintains the separate accounting method, while attempting to clarify and to strengthen the arm's length principle.[25]

In this regard, the initial position and the assumptions on which the separate accounting and the formulary methods are founded are very different. While the formulary apportionment system corresponds to a global conception of the

---

23. *See* Picciotto 1992, pp. 230–249 and Martín Jiménez 1999b, pp. 55–59.
24. *See* Lodin/Gammie 2001, the Communication from the Commission of 23 October 2001, COM (2001) 582 final, titled 'Towards an Internal Market without tax obstacles. A strategy for providing companies with a consolidated corporate tax base for their EU-wide activities' and McLure 2004.
25. OECD 2015b, p. 9.

international taxation phenomenon and of the problems resulting from the direct taxation of a company with an international dimension, the separate accounting system is mainly based on a bilateral and isolated concept of the resolution of problems which arise in this area.[26]

The separate accounting model's definition of a separate and independent enterprise is based on an eminently formalistic concept of the international dimension of the entities which operate on an international level. The mere fact that taxpayers operating on an international level have their own legal personality converts them into separate and independent entities. This allows for the relocation of income, through its formal attribution to a taxpayer incorporated ad hoc in a chosen state, or through transfer pricing in the case that the transactions are carried out between associated taxpayers.

Additionally, in many cases, the significance of the formal aspects reduces the tax treaties to a mere bilateral matter. When negotiating these treaties, the states only distribute taxation on the flows of income produced between both states. The assessment and determination of these income flows is limited to those produced between both states, and in particular, between the residents of each of these states. The analysis is performed from the limited viewpoint of what occurs between both states. A more in-depth analysis would exhaust the possibilities offered by the separate accounting method, because the legally separate entities residing in third states are autonomous and independent allocation centres, which may not be treated or taken into consideration.

From this standpoint, the tax regime finally established under the DTC will clearly be subordinate to each party's economic situation at the time the DTC is drawn up. This system fails to harmonize any aspect of the determination of income subject to taxation and only distributes the income produced in each state from a position which places great importance on legal personality.

Notwithstanding the above, the objective of this study is not to resolve the problems relating to the separate accounting method or to propose the adoption of the formulary apportionment method. This study only aims to highlight the assumptions on which the DTCs negotiated in line with the OECD Model are based, in order to be able to situate the LOB clauses in the framework in which they appear.

In view of the formal concept of separate entity underlying this method, an autonomous and independent income allocation centre can be formed by simply incorporating a company with its own legal personality. As a result of the above, the mere incorporation of a company in another state is sufficient for the income formally attributed to this company to be subject to taxation in that state. Accordingly, on the one hand, it is possible to incorporate companies, with the purpose of accumulating income in low tax jurisdictions (base companies), and on the other, the income obtained may be attributed to a company residing in a certain state, with the sole purpose of enabling this company to apply the tax treaty entered into with the source state.

---

26. This also explains the reason that the OECD Model does not resolve triangular cases. *See* Van Raad 1993, p. 298 and Easson 2000, p. 620.

In principle, these avoidance schemes may not be neutralized with the separate accounting method. Since this method requires the arm's length principle to be respected, the allocation of the resulting income to a different taxpayer is prevented. The parameters considered are limited to the transactions between separate and independent entities located in the contracting states. The fact that these entities may be included under a higher unit of operation and control becomes irrelevant for the purposes of this treaty, although it may have some effect materially. As the states and the DTCs are considered in completely isolated terms, when negotiating the treaty, each treaty is a different instrument drawn up in accordance with the particular viewpoints of the contracting states. Considering the treaties are negotiated based on a limited viewpoint, or in other words, a viewpoint restricted to the events which have occurred in the states entering into the tax treaty, without acknowledging those events which have formally taken place in third states, but do have a direct effect on the economy of these states, each treaty is invariably unique.

The consequences arising from the differences between tax treaties along with the differences in the various state's legislation may be very costly for international companies (double or triple taxation), but may also enable companies which skilfully combine these differences to significantly reduce or even eliminate taxation in any of the states in which they operate. In this respect, the differences lead to an opportunity for tax planning.

For this reason, not only the states but also certain economic sectors reject the formulary apportionment method. As has been observed, the adoption of a uniform stand to resolve the problem of international double taxation also implied the elimination of tax planning opportunities resulting from the differences in tax regimes.

The different anti-avoidance or anti-abuse rules which have been introduced in DTCs and domestic law in recent years specifically aim to resolve the shortages of the separate accounting method, particularly in relation to the excessively formalistic concept on which the definition of a separate and independent enterprise is based.

The formal manner in which the concepts of separate entity and independent entity are understood within the scope of the DTCs give rise to the appearance of avoidance conduct within this scope. The measures which have been adopted are not aimed at changing the system, but rather at correcting the aspects where a problem has been detected. The OECD/G20 BEPS project is the best example of this trend.[27]

Following are some examples which illustrate the above. First, to guarantee that the transactions performed between associated taxpayers are in accordance with the arm's length principle, extensive transfer pricing laws have been developed. Second, the problems created by the incorporation of companies in low-tax territories in order to accumulate income of a passive nature have been dealt with through the adoption of CFC rules in domestic legislation. This regime is specifically aimed at overcoming the legal personality barrier by allocating the income accumulated at the base company to the participating shareholders. Lastly, as observed above, the separate accounting

---

27. Panayi 2016, p. 629.

method allows for the state where the income is obtained to be easily modified, allowing for the development of treaty shopping structures.

Measures to restrict or reinforce the subjective scope of these treaties have been adopted within a conventional scope in order to avoid the application of the tax treaty regime to these structures. As shall be observed, this is the main effect of the introduction of the LOB clauses in the tax treaties. Contrary to the case of CFC rules, legal personality is not an unknown factor. LOBs only deny taxpayers who do not comply with its requirements from applying the treaty. However, the corporate veil of legal personality is lifted to a certain extent, as one of the criteria used by these clauses to deny the application of the tax treaty is where the shareholders reside.

I.C Consequences of Treaty Shopping Structures and Reasons for the Adoption of Measures Against Such Structures

As discussed in the previous section, one of the consequences of the separate accounting method sanctioned by the OECD Model is that entities with their own legal personality are considered to be separate entities and, accordingly, to be autonomous income allocation centres. A separate entity may obtain income in different states. Under the OECD Model tax scheme, such income is only considered to have originated from the state in which the separate entity is resident, i.e. where this taxpayer is liable to tax on worldwide income.

The essential feature of treaty shopping is a change in the state from where income is obtained. This change results from the modification of the taxpayer to which the income obtained is allocated. The purpose of this change is to claim the application of a tax treaty which eliminates or significantly reduces the actual tax levied in the state where the income is obtained (source state). To do so effectively, the taxpayer to which the income is allocated must be a resident in accordance with the OECD Model in the state which has entered into a treaty with the source state, the effect of which is to eliminate or significantly reduce taxation at source.

The treaty concept of a separate and independent entity facilitates the change in the state from where the income was obtained. As long as the income or the assets which generate such income are effectively transferred, the transferee will be understood to be the taxpayer which the income should be attributed to. Likewise, to change the state from where the income is obtained for the purposes of the tax treaty, the new entity where the income is allocated is only required to reside in the state that has entered into the desired convention with the source state. In principle, the taxpayer only needs to be liable to tax in that state on worldwide income. The framework of this operation is *a priori* relatively simple.

On first consideration, the immediate harm resulting from this type of structure is suffered by the source state. Pursuant to the treaty, the source state may not levy a tax on the income generated in its territory which is higher than that established in the treaty. If the treaty were not applicable, the existing tax in the source state would have been applicable without any type of limitation. The state in which the income is generated experiences economic damage, bearing in mind that the tax revenue earned is lower than that established by domestic law. Consequently, the immediate effects of treaty shopping are evidenced on non-resident taxation.

Despite the fact that most of the DTCs' provisions are based on the OECD Model, by essence these tax treaties are of a bilateral nature. A tax treaty concluded by two states is the result of a negotiation in which each one has requested recognition of its interests and in particular, of the interests it has in the other state. Obviously, the interests that converge in each negotiation process are different, the results of this process also materialize differently in each treaty. Therefore, the tax treaties concluded by a state are inevitably different when entered into with distinct states.[28]

By simply examining the royalties' tax regimes at source in the network of DTCs entered into by Spain; it can be observed that the tax ceiling fluctuates between margins of zero (DTC Spain-Bulgaria) to 20 percent (DTC Spain-India). Each contracting state's economic interests in the other state lead to the negotiation of a higher or lower tax ceiling at source. The existing volume of capital flows between the states unavoidably affects the outcome of the negotiation expressed in the tax treaty.[29]

In this regard, as Kingson correctly points out,[30] in relation to tax treaties, 'more is less'. A state's negotiating position is inversely proportional to its investment volume in the other state, particularly when the treaty is aimed at significantly reducing taxation at source. The reciprocity principle governing the DTCs should not only be examined from a formal viewpoint, i.e. the fact that a treaty establishes the same tax ceiling at source for both states does not mean that the material consequences are the same for each state that is a party to the convention. From a material point of view, the reciprocity principle assumes that the amount of income flows produced between the states which are party to the treaty are the same. If these flows are identical, the financial sacrifice required by the state, because it does not tax this income, will be compensated by the other state's waiver.

Consequently, for example, if two states have agreed that the royalties will only be taxed in the state of residence, there will only be reciprocity in material terms if the volume of the royalties from each state is comparable.[31] As Kingson points out, the volume of the investment flows is particularly important in determining whether there is reciprocity in the agreed regime. In order to avoid this problem, some tax treaties establish different regimes for each source state to assure that the mutually agreed concessions made by the states when concluding a tax treaty are comparable.

Treaty shopping structures can undermine the assumptions based upon which states have agreed to a certain tax regime. The economic elements on which the negotiation of the different regimens rests, depends on the base of income flows

---

28. Rosenbloom/Langbein 1981, p. 402, Jian 2015, p. 140 and Kerekes 2016, p. 154.
29. Rosenbloom 1983, pp. 734-735.
30. Kingson 1981, p. 1169.
31. Each financial year, state S pays royalties amounting to 1,000 units to state R. Each year state R pays 100 units of resident royalties to state S. Under the domestic law of both states, tax is levied at a rate of 30 percent. However, this tax is eliminated in accordance with the tax treaty. Although both states apply the same treatment, the concessions mutually made are not comparable. Whereas state S sacrifices the collection of 300 units of account, state R only fails to collect 30 units of account. The tax loss is ten times greater for state S than for state R by virtue of the tax treaty.

between the party states. Treaty shopping may artificially alter the above.[32] The main consequence of such structures is a substantial change in the assumptions based upon which each particular tax treaty was drawn up.

The sacrifice of non-resident tax revenues agreed in the tax treaty may be substantially altered by these types of structures. In the above example, as royalties are not taxed at source as a result of the tax treaty concluded between state R and S, it is possible that investors residing in third states which obtain royalties in state R may try to obtain royalties from state S, in order to enjoy the exemption at source. If this type of structure is used on a general basis, the volume of royalties originating in state R but obtained from state S may rise significantly. As a result of the change in the assumption which led to the agreed upon exemption at source, state R will likely to try to modify the DTC in view of the fact that the sacrifice of tax revenues has increased significantly.[33]

The assumption based upon which a state has negotiated a tax treaty may be significantly altered when treaty shopping structures are used on a general basis. Under the same circumstances, it is very likely that the state would have negotiated the terms of the convention in a different manner since the underlying economic assumptions have changed. Given the bilateral nature of tax treaties, it is reasonable to believe that a state is only willing to maintain the agreed conditions as long as the circumstances which led to the conclusion of the convention have not substantially changed (*rebus sic stantibus*).[34]

Therefore, the investment flow is clearly relevant when determining the tax regime agreed upon in the convention. Treaty shopping structures may undermine this assumption because they lead to a change in the state from where the income is obtained. The immediate consequence of this type of structure is a loss of non-resident tax revenue of a higher amount than that initially projected based on the economic situation which prevailed at the time the convention was entered into.

However, the problems caused by these structures should not be assessed exclusively from the standpoint of the source state. The fact that the same state which enters into a tax treaty negotiates as both the source state and the state of residence cannot be ignored.[35]

From this perspective, when a state's interests are proportionally higher, it will try to strengthen the residence principle in the tax treaty by reducing the limits on taxation at source as much as possible. The reduction of taxation at source gives rise to important consequences for the state of residence. The tax revenue cost of the measures provided for in the state of residence to eliminate international double taxation will be substantially reduced given that the convention eliminates and reduces

---

32. UN 1998, paragraph 28.
33. Based on the same data as in the above example, if due to the general use of this type of structure in state S, the volume of royalties which residents of this state obtain in state R is increased to 2,000 units of account, the concession made by state R with respect to tax revenue will rise from 30 units of account to 600 units of account.
34. It is precisely the *rebus sic stantibus* clause which enables states to conclude a treaty in accordance with the 1969 Vienna Convention on the Law of Treaties. *See* Vamvoukos 1985.
35. Vogel/Shannon/Doernberg/Van Raad 1989, Article 16, p. 4.

Chapter 2: Scope of Double Taxation Conventions and Limitation

taxation at source. Thus, as a result of the tax treaty, the non-resident tax revenue losses suffered by a state are compensated by the higher resident tax revenue collected.

Treaty shopping structures can also negatively affect resident tax liability. Generally, the states unilaterally adopt measures to eliminate legal international double taxation and where applicable, economic double taxation. The cost of these measures is significant for the states, and as it has been observed, is reduced by tax treaties.

By using these structures, a taxpayer may gain access to a tax treaty which in principle, is not applicable. The state in which the income is obtained suffers from a loss of non-resident tax revenue. However, where there is no tax treaty or where the tax treaty is less favourable, the residents of that state do not receive reciprocal treatment in the taxpayer's state of origin that develops the structure. This situation indirectly leads to a loss of tax revenue in that state, bearing in mind that the residents will make use of the measures provided under domestic law to eliminate the international double taxation produced.[36] The loss of non-resident tax revenue suffered by the state is not compensated by higher resident tax revenue.

Consequently, it should be noted that the treaty shopping structures not only have an influence on non-resident tax liability but also on resident tax liability. These structures directly affect non-resident taxation and indirectly affect resident taxation.

Materially, this situation significantly undermines the principle of reciprocity, as the states suffer from a loss of non-resident tax revenue which is not compensated by higher resident tax revenue, because, the extent to which measures to avoid international double taxation should be applied is not limited by decreased taxation in the source state. If a tax treaty had been entered into with the original state of residence, the state would have borne a lesser tax expense since the tax credit (credit method) required would be as equally reduced as the taxation at source.[37]

Nevertheless, the consequences of the generalized use of this type of structure is not limited to those already discussed above.

A state's negotiating position may be weakened.[38] As discussed in Chapter 1 of this study (section II), one of the reasons for the states maintenance of a strong non-resident tax liability is that it is an instrument used to improve the state's negotiating position. A state whose intention is to reduce the tax levied on its residents in another state is in a better position to achieve this objective in the negotiation of a

---

36. Based on the example used in the previous notes, the residents of state T that access the treaty entered into by state R and state S will be subject to less tax in state R as a result of the treaty concluded by these two states. However, the tax to which the residents in state R are subject will not be reduced in state T when they receive income produced in the latter states. The higher tax at source levied in state T with respect to the treaty between state R and S, will lead to a lesser tax revenue in state R as a result of the application of the methods to eliminate double taxation.
37. It is important to note that if a state adopts the exemption method in a general manner under its domestic law, no tax revenue is lost regardless of whether or not a DTC is applied, because the state unilaterally waives this tax. However, the residents of this state still suffer from higher taxation at source, which is not the case for the residents of the latter state which develops treaty shopping structures, since taxation is limited through the use of these structures to access the DTCs which that state has entered into.
38. Amico 1989, p. 226.

treaty, if its domestic legislation provides for the taxation of income obtained by non-residents in terms similar to those of the other state. On the contrary, the other state would not have any incentive to agree to reduce taxation because its residents directly obtain this treatment in the other state under this state's domestic laws.

Treaty shopping allows residents in third states to indirectly claim the benefits of the tax treaty provisions not applicable to them. As pointed out by the OECD, this may imply that these 'third parties' state of residence has a minimum incentive or interest in initiating the negotiation of a tax treaty, given that its residents are able to apply tax treaties concluded by other states.[39]

This situation may significantly weaken the state's negotiating position, as the state of residence of the taxpayer who uses these structures, may indirectly obtain a reduction at source. It may be more difficult for the state in which such structures are used to negotiate a tax treaty where preference is given to the residence principle through the reduction of cases where the state may levy non-resident tax, if it does not materially offer any benefits other than those that the state's may already obtain.

Another consequence of this type of structure is that it fosters international tax evasion. The purpose of the DTCs is not only to eliminate international double taxation, but also to avoid international tax evasion. Exchange of information clauses are included in the DTCs for this purpose.

Obviously, for a state to levy tax on the worldwide income obtained, it is unavoidably required to provide an information exchange system which extends beyond its borders. The lack of incentives to conclude DTCs may also affect this issue, in view of the fact that where a tax treaty is not concluded, the necessary instruments to facilitate the exchange of tax information are not adopted either.

In line with the above, it should also be noted that treaty shopping contributes to the performance of artificial transactions without any economic substance.[40]

As observed in the previous chapter, the state in which income is obtained is normally modified by means of the incorporation of a company in a state that has entered into the tax treaty whose use is desired with the source state. On many occasions, intermediary company does not perform any business activity in the state of residence. Although it is considered to be a resident for tax purposes, its presence in that state is merely formal, given that it lacks material elements linking its business activity to the state's economy.

---

39. OECD 1986, paragraph 7 and Van Weeghel 1998, pp. 122-123. In this regard, the case of the U.S. and Canada is significant. Prior to the 1992 modification of the DTC entered into by the U.S. and the Netherlands, the Canadian government refused to negotiate a new DTC with the U.S. to reduce taxation at source. The investments of Canadian multinational enterprises in the U.S. were channelled through the Netherlands, since the DTC entered into with the latter state and the U.S. gave the state of residence the exclusive right to tax interest and royalties. Since the Netherlands was a suitable state for the development of this type of structure, Canadian residents were not taxed on the income obtained in the U.S. However, the residents in the U.S. bore a high tax charge in Canada. Only after the modification of the tax treaty between the U.S. and the Netherlands, which consisted precisely in the introduction of an extensive number of limitations on benefits clauses, did Canada negotiate a new tax treaty with the U.S. to reduce taxation at source. Boidman 1989, pp. 370-371 and Morrison/Bennett 1993a, p. 322.
40. UN 1988, paragraph 28.

Chapter 2: Scope of Double Taxation Conventions and Limitation

As a result of these structures, the existing income flows between the states are artificially modified. There is no underlying economic substance relating to the income which flows between the source state and the intermediary company's state of residence, given that the true source of the income flow is located in a third state.

Lastly, it should be remembered that these structures contribute to the full elimination of the taxation of international profits. The purpose of the DTCs is to eliminate double taxation but they should also prevent the opposite phenomenon from occurring, i.e. the lack of taxation (double non-taxation).[41] In this regard, when intermediary companies are combined with base companies, both non-resident and resident tax liability on the income obtained in any state may be avoided. From the point of view of the principles of international tax law, *a priori* the above is unacceptable, not only due to the tax authorities' loss of tax revenue, but also because such a case is contrary to the tax justice principle.

With respect to the problems that arise in relation to international double taxation, it was previously pointed out that the ability to pay principle does not imply that foreign source income may not be taxed under domestic law.[42] The limitation which appears to follow the application of this principle lies in the fact that the state of residence should take into account the tax borne in the source state, so as to levy tax on the taxpayer in accordance with his true ability to pay.

International double taxation could also be a breach of the equality principle. The mere fact that a taxpayer obtains income in states other than his state of residence may cause his tax burden to be higher than that of another taxpayer with the same ability to pay, and obtains all of his income from domestic sources.[43]

In the above respects, DTCs contribute to the effective fulfilment of the ability to pay and equality principles by eliminating international double taxation. Therefore, it is also reasonable to conclude that the DTCs should not contribute to causing the opposite to occur, i.e. the avoidance of any type of taxation merely due to the fact that the income is of an international nature. The lack of taxation of international income is as unfair as the double taxation thereof. Accordingly, mainly from the standpoint of the equality principle, measures against treaty shopping should be adopted to prevent only taxpayers who obtain domestic source income from contributing to the payment of public expenditure.

International organizations like the OECD, states and experts in this field base the need to adopt measures limiting the use of these types of structures on the aforementioned reasons. As can be verified, the reasons discussed (breach of the reciprocity principle, tax revenue losses, disincentives for DTCs, fostering of international tax evasion, breach of the tax justice principles) are closely linked and some are the consequence of others.

The reason which appears to have the most weight is the breach of the reciprocity principle, where a state waives or reduces non-resident tax but does not receive the corresponding compensation in the taxpayer's state of origin. Treaty shopping may

---

41. Rosenbloom 1983, p. 766.
42. Calderón 1997a, p. 67.
43. Calderón 1997a, pp. 68–69.

artificially change the assumptions on which the tax treaty entered into is based, thereby upsetting the balance reached as a result of the negotiation.

However, it should be noted that the treaty shopping problem does not arise in the case of all tax treaties. It may be asserted that there are tax treaties which suffer more from these types of operations. One of the treaties most affected by these structures is the 1965 DTC between the U.S. and the Netherlands. The change thereto in 1992 led to the existence of the convention with the most complex and exhaustive LOB clauses.

In this regard, one cannot lose sight of the fact that treaty shopping is not only the result of a tax treaty with a favourable non-resident tax regime, but also of the intermediary state's domestic legislation. Consequently, perhaps the reproaches from which these structures may suffer should not be aimed at the residents of third states that indirectly access these tax treaties, but rather at the states that establish tax regimes favouring the use of these structures.

As discussed in Chapter 1, the three elements required for a state's domestic law to serve the purpose of treaty shopping structures are the existence of exemptions on foreign source income, regimes that are flexible in terms of the deductibility of expenses billed by non-residents and, a lack of non-resident taxation, either under domestic law or by means of DTCs. In view of the above, one of the measures proposed by the OECD to prevent this phenomenon is not to enter into DTCs with those states whose domestic legislation is fit for this purpose (abstinence approach).[44] This approach has been further reinforced in the OECD/G20 BEPS project, whereby Action 6 provides for a series of tax policy considerations that, in general, countries should consider before deciding to enter into a tax treaty with another country.[45]

However, this approach should not be adopted in a general manner, as the consequences of the lack of a tax treaty may seriously harm the existing trade relationship between two states. It is common knowledge that tax treaties are instruments which significantly favour the international movement of capital, goods and services, taking into account that they eliminate the significant obstacle represented by international double taxation. For this reason, the abstinence method should only be used in the cases of states whose only asset is the tax treaty, i.e. those states with which there are no significant trade relations, the exclusive purpose of which is to channel income between states.[46]

Two types of measures against the phenomenon of treaty shopping have been developed. First, tax authorities may invoke General Anti-Avoidance Rules (GAARs) found in domestic law to deny tax treaty benefits. The application of these rules gives rise to numerous problems, not only in relation to the content thereof, but also to the doubts that exist regarding whether they can be applied within the scope of international treaties. In this regard, it must be highlighted that Action 6 of the BEPS

---

44. OECD 1986, paragraphs 17–18.
45. OECD 2015a, pp. 94–98.
46. This is the exact position adopted by the U.S. beginning in 1981 with respect to the DTCs entered into with former colonies of European states (Virgin Islands, Dutch Antilles, etc.). The U.S. withdrew from these treaties since these states had become hosts for treaty shopping structures. *See* Grady 1983, p. 636.

project proposes to introduce, in the OECD Model and tax treaties, a GAAR, the so-called Principal Purposes Test of 'PPT' rule, in order to address treaty shopping and other forms of treaty abuse.[47] These aspects will be analysed in the following section.

The second type of measure against treaty shopping, relates to provisions that are specifically against treaty shopping. These provisions can be adopted unilaterally by one of the contracting states or may be directly provided for in the tax treaty. This study focuses on the latter and specifically on the one type of rule, LOB clauses introduced in tax treaties. Nevertheless, some references will be made to the problems arising in relation to unilateral rules in this respect (section II.C of this chapter).

It should be noted that, regardless of whether they are included in a tax treaty or in the domestic legislation of a contracting state, specific anti-treaty shopping provisions are characterized by their limitation or reduction of the subjective scope of the DTCs. Consequently, the approach adopted focuses on the regime where access to convention benefits is given and not on the tax system of the state which acts as the intermediary in each case. However, except for the abstinence method, no reproach to the intermediary state's legislation was found in the OECD report on this subject published in 1986.[48]

In this regard, reference must be made to the measures adopted by the OECD and the EU to eliminate harmful tax competition.

In 1998, the OECD published the report, Harmful Tax Competition: An Emerging Global Issue.[49] This report laid the foundations for the OECD's work in the area of harmful tax practices and created the Forum on Harmful Tax Practices to carry out this work. It was published in response to a request by governments to develop measures to counter harmful tax practices with respect to geographically mobile activities. The 1998 OECD report laid down a series of factors to determine whether a preferential regime is potentially harmful.

The purpose of these measures is to assure that taxation does not distort investment decisions. The report on this subject matter provides a series of criteria to establish when a tax regime gives rise to harmful tax competition. Generally, for the regime to be qualified as such, it must lead to the relocation of business activities or operations to its territory, either by virtue of a zero (or very reduced) tax regime or due to the state's opacity, which will allow for cases of tax evasion. The measures which allow for reduced taxation may take many different forms (exemptions, artificial definitions of the tax base, non-application of the OECD rules relating to transfer pricing, etc.)

The OECD's work on preferential and harmful tax regimes has continued since the 1998 Report. The BEPS project is the latest stage of this work, Action 5 deals expressly with this topic.[50] However, the final document of this Action does not provide any proposals to modify the OECD Model in order to include a general clause with the objective of excluding treaty benefits for taxpayers who benefit from

---

47. OECD 2015a, pp. 18–19.
48. OECD 1986.
49. OECD 1998.
50. OECD 2015c.

preferential tax regimes. Neither were such proposals provided for in Action 6 of the BEPS project, apart from a reference, included at the very end of the final document, to the Special Tax Regime (STR) clause provided in the 2015 U.S. Draft.[51] Nonetheless, it should be mentioned that one of the objectives of Action 6 is to clarify 'that tax treaties are not intended to be used to generate double non-taxation'. This clarification is provided through a reformulation of the title and preamble to the OECD Model.[52] This objective appears in other actions of the BEPS project creating a strong double non-taxation language.[53]

Moreover, on 1 December 1997, the ECOFIN Council of the EU adopted the Code of Conduct on business taxation to counter 'harmful tax competition'. The Code contains a series of criteria to determine when a specific measure should receive such a qualification. These criteria are similar to those adopted by the OECD.[54] Both the OECD and the EU aim to progressively eliminate domestic tax measures which are capable of giving rise to harmful tax competition. The EU's Finance Ministers established the Code of Conduct Group (Business Taxation) at a Council meeting on 9 March 1998 to assess the tax measures that may fall within the scope of the Code of Conduct for business taxation.

Among other EU work related to harmful tax practices, the Action Plan adopted by the Commission on 17 June 2015 for fair and efficient corporate taxation in the EU should be mentioned. The Action Plan deals with issues related to harmful tax practices and to the work of the Code of Conduct Group. In this regard, the Anti-Tax Avoidance Package adopted on 28 January 2016 is part of the Commission's agenda for fairer, simpler and more effective corporate taxation in the EU. The Package contains concrete measures to prevent aggressive tax planning, boost tax transparency and create a level playing field for all businesses in the EU. Finally, as part of the commitment in the EU Code of Conduct on business taxation, the Commission committed itself to publishing guidelines on the application of the State Aid rules to measures relating to direct business taxation. The guidelines were adopted by the Commission on 11 November 1998. The latest Commission report on their action taken in the field of tax aid was adopted by the Commission on 9 February 2004.

A more detailed discussion of this subject matter is beyond the scope of this study.[55] However, it is worth noting that states whose domestic regulations enable treaty shopping structures to eliminate or reduce taxation in an intermediary state and to transfer income into a third state without subjecting it to any non-resident tax may be qualified as harmful preferential tax regimes. In fact, this type of structure is used frequently in certain states not only due to their network of DTCs but also as a result of their domestic legislation. Consequently, it is understandable that a state which aims to

---

51. OECD 2015a, pp. 96–98. *See* section IV.B.2 of Chapter 3.
52. OECD 2015a, pp. 96–98 and pp. 91–93.
53. Brauner 2014, p. 28.
54. Osterweil 1999, p. 199.
55. *See* Nouwen 2017.

foster these types of operations within its territory relies on an extensive network of tax treaties and provides for alternatives which allow for the reduction of tax on income shifted to its territory under its laws.

The analysis of treaty shopping from the position that a state of residence's tax regime differs to that used by the rules unilaterally adopted by states and included within its DTCs. As shall be observed, particularly in the case of LOB clauses, the level of taxation levied in the state of residence is not the criterion used by these rules for granting access to treaty benefits, but rather whether there is sufficient nexus with this state or a real business purpose to obtain the income generated in the source state from this state of residence.

However, the measures promoted by the OECD and the EU in respect of harmful tax competition should not be rejected, since they may eliminate one of the elements which allow for treaty shopping structures. Nevertheless, it should be borne in mind that these are not measures undertaken when the two states conclude a DTC but rather external measures, the acceptance of which depends largely on the affected states willingness to adapt to them. Likewise, the continued use of such measures should not be disdained based merely on the criticism received,[56] particularly in view of the fact that the measures may be understood to be an unjustified attack against the state's tax sovereignty.[57] Despite the aforementioned disadvantages, it should be noted that these measures appear to be successful in practice.[58]

II MEASURES AGAINST TREATY SHOPPING

II.A Application of General Anti-avoidance Rules to Treaty Shopping Structures

The terms used on an international level to qualify treaty shopping structures indicate that they may be unlawful. These structures have been qualified as an 'abuse of tax treaties', 'improper use of tax treaties', 'treaty fraud', etc.[59]

Without making any prejudgments about whether or not treaty shopping is lawful, the qualification of this conduct as a case of tax evasion or fraud should be ruled out. The concept of tax evasion assumes that a taxable event has taken place. The taxpayer's conduct consists precisely in concealing the existence or the exact amount of a tax liability from the tax authorities by means of fraudulent manoeuvres.[60] In principle, treaty shopping conduct does not involve concealment. The non-resident taxpayer does not conceal the income obtained from the source state's tax authorities, but rather changes the state from where the income is obtained in order to reduce the

---

56. Ellis 1999, pp. 78–80 y Zagaris 2001, pp. 2298–2306.
57. Martín Jiménez 2001, p. 86.
58. OECD 2004.
59. Van Weeghel 1996, p. 10 and 1998, p. 119.
60. According to Uckmar 1983, pp. 20–21, 'avoidance of payment without avoidance of the tax liability certainly falls within the definition of evasion in all legal systems'.

tax burden it bears in that state. The reduction is a result of the application of the tax treaty concluded between the source state and the 'new state' from where the income is obtained.

This type of conduct may fall within the framework of tax avoidance.[61] However, it is necessary to define the scope of this concept to prevent all cases of such conduct from being prematurely labelled as unlawful.

In this regard, although their opinion is not unanimous, experts in this field tend to differentiate between lawful and unlawful avoidance. The latter is identified through the application of assumptions made in the general rules used by the states to correct the conduct of taxpayers, whose only objective is to reduce their tax burden by means of certain manoeuvres.[62] Accordingly, the concept of abuse of law (*fraus legis*) should not be confused with the concept of tax avoidance, notwithstanding the fact that in all abuse of law cases there is avoidance. As pointed out by Palao, the concept of avoidance may be considered to be broader than abuse of law (*fraus legis*), which is limited exclusively to the avoidance or reduction of the scale of the taxable event.[63]

Although it is not our intention to fully undertake the complex study regarding abuse of tax law (*fraus legis*), this concept refers to the following phenomenon. The use of legal means to achieve the economic result projected by the taxable event gives rise to a tax debt. However, on occasions, this same result 'may be indirectly reached by other legal means, which naturally and primarily tend towards the achievement of various objectives, and which are either not taxed, or are taxed to a lesser extent than the usual means.'[64] This figure presupposes that there are dual legal rules, one being the avoided rule which gave rise to tax liability in a specific case, and the other being the coverage rule which may or may not tax the event in question to a lesser extent or, which declares the event to be exempt or not subject to tax.

Abuse of tax law (*fraus legis*) does not presuppose nor is it necessarily carried out by means of non-tax abuse, although it does not exclude it. 'The legal form adopted as an abusive contrivance may be perfectly lawful and valid for non-tax purposes.'[65] Additionally, the rule does not limit a private person's ability to choose the legal acts and transactions offered by private law which best adapt to their needs, within the limits established by a legal order. As Palao points out, tax laws do not directly prohibit any activity per se due to its substantive significance, but rather as a result of its relationship with the tax event itself. Consequently, the figure of abuse of law (*fraus

---

61. Uckmar 1983, p. 183 and Brignoli 2013, p. 22.
62. The majority of legal orders provide instruments to prevent legal rules from being avoided through manipulation by the taxpayers who take part in legal traffic (business purpose test under American law, *fraus legis* under Dutch law, 'abuse of legal forms' under German law, etc.). The formulas used have either been directly established under the law or have been developed by case law. In any case, as Palao affirms 2001, p. 131, the formulas used give rise to the same result and, accordingly, are interchangeable. See Ward 1985, pp. 68–123 and Vanistendael 1997b, pp. 131–155.
63. Palao 1977, p. 776.
64. Palao 1966, p. 678.
65. Palao 1966, pp. 678–679.

legis) only corrects tax matters, respecting the lawfulness of the objective pursued and therefore, leaving the private situation created intact.[66]

The difference between abuse of tax law (*fraus legis*) and a mere case of tax avoidance is the unlawfulness of the means employed to avoid the consequences of the tax rule. The method used is a legal transaction carried out in a manner contrary to its natural purpose, making it void of cause and definitively, using it in an artificial manner. Consequently, the transaction is not deemed unlawful because its purpose is avoidance, but rather due to the objective artificiality of the legal form used. However, in practice, the purpose of avoiding tax must be proven externally and it is precisely the artificial nature of the transaction used, i.e. the lack of any other plausible justification for the means chosen (business purpose referred to in Common law) which causes this purpose to be evidenced.[67]

In conclusion, avoidance should be understood as a concept that is broader than abuse of law (*fraus legis*). Avoidance only becomes an abuse of law when the method used to avoid tax is unlawful. As pointed out earlier, the unlawfulness is a result of the 'abuse of legal forms'. Only unlawful avoidance that is considered an abuse of law would be identified. The cases of avoidance that are not considered abuses of law are lawful, and consequently, should be respected by law. In this regard, lawful tax avoidance, which is identified with the concept of tax planning by Vogel, could be differentiated from unlawful tax avoidance which is tied to the abuse of law concept or *fraus legis*.[68]

However, the fact that the term tax avoidance has also been identified exclusively with cases considered to be lawful cannot be disregarded. Therefore, perhaps a more restrictive definition of tax avoidance could be applied, where it would only include those cases considered an abuse of law.

If this were the case, tax avoidance would only arise when the consequences of the taxable event were avoided or reduced due to the artificiality of the legal transaction used or the lack of any other plausible justification for the means chosen. In any case, this is a question of terminology. The truly relevant issue is to determine when the abuse of law or *fraus legis* exists.[69] In this regard, the main problem lies in proving how the transaction is artificial and explaining the reasons that the qualification intended by the taxpayer is not acceptable.

Bearing in mind the above, the treaty shopping phenomenon could be considered as a case of tax avoidance in the restrictive sense discussed earlier, and accordingly, could be corrected by anti-abuse rules. The purpose of this type of structure is to avoid taxation in the source state, by shifting the income obtained to a third state with which the source state has concluded a treaty that significantly reduces non-resident taxation. The coverage rule is the tax treaty entered into with the state where the income is shifted.

---

66. Palao 1966, p. 684.
67. Palao 1996, pp. 7–8. The artificiality of the legal transaction used and the lack of valid business purposes are criteria which are also applied in other legal orders.
68. Vogel 1997, p. 118.
69. OECD 1987, p. 16.

This conduct would be qualified as tax avoidance where it was evidenced that the income was artificially obtained through the state where the tax treaty was concluded without any justification whatsoever except for the mere elimination of taxation at source.

In principle, it could be claimed that these operations should not be objected to in any manner as they meet the necessary requirements for the tax treaty that used to be applicable.[70] However, it must be remembered that the purpose of these types of rules are precisely to avoid the use of formal or restrictive interpretation criteria which cause the wording of the rule to prevail over its final aim in order to favour unlawful avoidance. For this reason, these rules give rise to a more flexible interpretation where the most weight is placed on the teleological element, and from the standpoint of acts or transactions to which the law is applied, on its business significance and practical purpose.

The abuse of law mechanism presupposes compliance with the coverage rule requirements. There is verification as to whether it is used in artificial manner, i.e. for a purpose other than that for which it is intended. This verification corresponds to the tax authorities, but their actions may be subsequently reviewed by the courts.

The main objective of tax treaties is to eliminate double taxation. However, one should not lose sight of the fact that this aim is instrumental, bearing in mind that the DTCs final purpose is to promote the movement of capital, persons and services between contracting states by removing obstacles from these movements, among which include international double taxation.[71]

In principle, from this stance treaty shopping should not be reproached in any manner, since it contributes precisely to this aim by eliminating the possibility of double taxation. If the legitimacy of treaty shopping were to be accepted, the international movement of goods, capital, persons and service would be promoted, in that not only is double taxation eliminated when the tax treaty is accessed directly, but also when it is accessed indirectly. However, confining this matter exclusively to this standpoint would be excessively limited and would not fully consider the assumptions on which tax treaties are based.

Nevertheless, tax treaties should not protect all types of operations, but rather those backed by a sufficient economic basis in the contracting state of where the taxpayer is resident. On the contrary, tax treaties would contribute to distorting the flow of capital movements. As observed in the previous section, the generalized use of these structures may artificially modify the existing economic flows between states that are party to a convention. The state suffering from the consequences of such a structure may see a significant increase in the economic flows from the other contracting state. This could undermine the assumptions on which the treaty was based and could even give rise to unbearable economic harm. It is reasonable to conclude that tax treaties are not meant to favour these types of economic flows. Only taxpayers which have a due nexus with the state of residence may be protected under the convention.

---

70. Oliver 1989, p. 330.
71. Lüthi 1989, p. 336.

Furthermore, tax treaties should not contribute to the avoidance of all types of taxation on international income. As observed in Chapter 1 of this study, the combination of base and intermediary companies may be used for such a purpose, and consequently it is necessary to adopt measures to avoid these combinations in order to guarantee the integrity and efficiency of tax systems.[72]

Therefore, conduct contrary to the purposes assigned to the tax treaties may arise even though the coverage rule terms are complied with (those of the tax treaty). In this regard, the decisive criterion applied to determine whether the convention is used in an artificial manner is the inexistence of a sufficient business nexus, or in other words, a real business purpose which justifies residence in that state.[73]

In this regard, according to the Commentaries on the 1992–2003 OECD Model, 'anti-abuse measures' should only be used to maintain the equity and neutrality of the states' tax systems:

> It would be contrary to the general principles underlying the [OECD Model] and to the spirit of tax treaties in general if counteracting measures were to be extended to activities such as production, normal rendering of services or trading companies engaged in real industrial or commercial activity, when they are clearly related to the economic environment of the country where they are resident in a situation in which these activities are carried on in such a way that no tax avoidance could be suspected.[74]

As discussed above, it can be deduced from this paragraph taken from the Commentaries of the 1992–2003 OECD Model, that there is only abuse when residence in a state does not also involve integration in its economic environment. When this degree of integration does exist, the conduct should be lawful, and therefore should not suffer from any reproach from the standpoint of rules against tax avoidance. Moreover, should a rule be applied in these cases, it would be contrary to the purposes of the tax treaties, as it would unjustly hinder them.

'Abuse of legal forms' arises due to the fact that a company establishes residence in a state for the sole purpose of accessing the tax treaty's regime. To a certain extent, this could be considered as an abusive use of legal personality, since the company's incorporation is only justifiable for tax purposes and there is no accompanying element which implies the development of a business activity. The attachment to the state of residence of the legal person used is merely formal. There is no business element that provides for an attachment of the territory to the taxpayer who obtains the income or to the operation which generates income in the source state.

In summary, the criteria used to determine if an operation is artificial, and accordingly, unlawful from a tax avoidance position, is whether or not there are elements which evidence that the transaction or the taxpayer is sufficiently integrated in the state of residence.

---

72. Vanistendael 1999, p. 165.
73. Hübner 1988, p. 210.
74. Paragraph 26 to the Commentaries on Article 1 of the 1992–2000 OECD Model. The Commentaries on Article 1 of the 2003–2014 OECD Model do not include the contents of the aforementioned paragraph. However, the idea underlying the same can be deduced from the whole of the Commentaries relating to Article 1 of the 2003–2014 OECD Model.

It should be recognized that although this parameter may appear to be abstractly valid, in specific cases, the exactness required to determine whether there is a sufficient degree of integration is lacking.

However, it should be borne in mind that this is a drawback of the GAARs. As Palao correctly states, 'the delimitation of cases of abuse of tax law is inevitably based on concepts with a considerable degree of uncertainty and, consequently, gives rise to certain legal insecurity. This is the price to be paid for preventing the legal rule from being circumvented.'[75] In contrast, the rules lack the limitations of the Specific Anti-Avoidance Rules (SAARs), whose factual basis can easily be avoided. Furthermore, given the limitation of their scope of application these rules are unable to resolve cases outside of this scope.[76]

Furthermore, the OECD Model does not provide sufficient useful means to determine when there is a sufficient level of integration. However, as shall be observed in the following section, the definition of resident provided in Article 4 of the OECD Model requires a factual attachment between the taxpayer and the territory of the party state for the convention to be applicable. Mere formal attachments are not sufficient to be considered a resident.

In accordance with the above and notwithstanding the problems arising from the abstract formulation of the GAARs, it appears that in principle under a domestic GAAR, the application of a tax treaty could be denied in cases where treaty shopping structures are used. In this regard, the Commentaries on Article 1 of the OECD Model, at least since 2003, support this proposition, even though it has to be highlighted that some scholars, tax authorities and courts question this.[77] In this regard, the Commentaries provide for a 'guiding principle' that a transaction should be considered abusive where the main purpose of the transaction is to obtain treaty benefits and, in the circumstances, providing treaty benefits would be contrary to the object and purpose of the relevant provision of the treaty. Action 6 of the BEPS project also gives support to this proposition.

However, as in the case of the legal rules or principles used by other states, the application of domestic GAARs to counter such situations on an international level may give rise to some additional problems. A good example of this is that addressing treaty shopping by means of GAARs 'has proved to be difficult and unsuccessful attempt by [tax authorities]'.[78]

First, from a factual standpoint, as the operations take place in more than one state, the tax authorities may have serious difficulties in identifying the operations that may constitute an abusive use of a tax treaty. However, this is not a problem

---

75. Palao 2001, p. 8. This author adds that although the general anti-avoidance rules give rise to certain legal insecurity, its existence is justified because it aims to avoid unfair results, which are only apparently supported by the coverage of legal rules, whose substantial purpose was not to provide such coverage. However, the sacrifice of legal security must be reasonable. The general anti-avoidance rule should only be applied when the abuse of law is evident. In the end the scope and effectiveness of such clauses is in the hands of the courts, whose prudence is relied upon for its application.
76. Cooper 1997, p. 40.
77. De Broe/Luts 2015, p. 124, Irawan 2016, p. 38 and Báez 2017.
78. Báez 2017 and Rädler 1999, p. 297.

specifically relating to anti-avoidance rules. Nevertheless, it cannot be disregarded that because the case takes place on an international level, it is more difficult to apply these rules than in cases where the operations are fully developed within the territory of the same state.[79]

Second, it must be taken into account that the application of the tax treaty is denied based solely on a domestic rule in force in the source state. In application of this rule, the source state's tax authorities deny the taxpayer, who resides in another contracting state, from applying a tax treaty as it is deemed to have been used in an abusive manner.

As in the case of a domestic rule, GAARs should be applied with the utmost caution at an international level. This caution should be even greater when a tax treaty is applicable. For the convention objectives to be achieved, the states are required to apply it in a uniform manner.

In the case that they are used, despite the similar formulation of these types of rules or principles in the various states, not all aspects thereof are necessarily the same, or at least, they may be interpreted in a different manner.[80] As this is the case, the results arrived at by each state may differ because there is no international consensus regarding the dividing line between what is and what is not considered to be acceptable in this regard. As previously mentioned, although the parameter to bear in mind is whether the operation or taxpayer is sufficiently integrated in the state of residence, in view of the generality of its formulation, it is possible that different results are produced depending on which state applies the convention.[81] Consequently, it may be asserted that the unilateral application of these provisions gives rise to a problem relating to the possible asymmetry of the results that may arise between the states involved.

From this stance, although in principle, it is desirable for states to be able to implement their domestic anti-avoidance rules, materially the application thereof gives rise to serious problems, particularly because the uniformity required in the application of the tax treaty by the contracting states may be contravened.[82]

Although related to the above, the third problem that arises is of a formal nature. The application of these domestic measures does not tend to be provided for in the tax treaties which follow the OECD Model. In principle, if the tax treaty does not expressly authorize these measures, the states should not deny its application to a taxpayer who complies with the requirements for its application, despite the fact that his 'conduct' is reproachable from the standpoint of domestic rules relating to anti-avoidance. In this regard, as pointed out by the OECD in 1986, it could be concluded that if the tax treaty does not provide such authorization, the tax treaty regime should be applied based on the *pacta sunt servanda* principle, although a taxpayer might be deemed to be using it in an abusive manner.[83] However, as shall be observed below, the OECD's position regarding the relationship of domestic anti-avoidance clauses and tax treaties has

---

79. Laule: IFA 1995, p. 37. The international mechanisms for assistance and the exchange of tax information contribute to the resolution of this problem prior to the application of the rule.
80. Torrione: IFA 1995, pp. 30–31 and Wasserneyer: IFA 2001, p. 19.
81. Van Weeghel 1996.
82. Gustaffson: IFA 1995, p. 36.
83. OECD 1986, paragraph 23.

evolved over time, culminating in the Commentaries on Article 1 of the 2003–2014 OECD Model. Action 6 of the BEPS project confirms this approach and, at the same time, proposes the incorporation of a GAAR into the OECD Model, i.e. the so-called PPT rule.

DTCss are international treaties. In accordance with Articles 26 and 27 of the 1969 Vienna Convention on the Law of Treaties (VCLT), once they enter into force, the treaties obligate the parties entering into them and should be complied with by these parties in good faith. The *pacta sunt servanda* principle prevents a party from using domestic law as justification for the breach of a tax treaty.

A *priori*, the application of domestic anti-avoidance rules without authorization could be a breach of the tax treaty. In fact, although the application of these rules is authorized based on 'the wording of the treaty', domestic law prevents them from being applied.[84] From this standpoint, these rules would not be accommodated within the scope of the tax treaties.

Experts in this field have attempted to include GAARs within the scope of tax treaties. Ward points out that under the *pacta sunt servanda* principle provided for in Article 26 of the VCLT, compliance of the treaties is required in accordance with the principle of good faith. This principle would prohibit the opposite, i.e. the abuse of law, from occurring.[85] Accordingly, prohibition of the abuse of law would be a principle of international law, which must be taken into account in the interpretation and application of treaties.[86] In this respect, a state which is party to a treaty would not be acting in a manner contrary to the principle of good faith where it denied the treaty's application to a specific taxpayer whose actions have been deemed to fall within the parameters of anti-avoidance rules.[87]

For tax purposes, this principle is accepted by the majority of states as their legal orders contain similar domestic anti-avoidance rules or judicial doctrines. Bearing in mind these two circumstances, the application of the rules provided in the state's legislation might be acceptable, although the treaty does not expressly stipulate that this is the case. This also seems to be the stand taken by the Commentaries on the

---

84. Even so, the lack of authorization in a convention has prevented the courts and authorities of various states from applying these rules when a DTC is involved. See the decisions mentioned by Vogel 1997, pp. 120–121. Nevertheless, it also true that the courts in some states have been reluctant to apply this type of rule within the scope of the DTCs. The arguments put forward are of a very wide nature. *Inter alia*, it is worth noting that from a formal point of view it was considered that the general anti-avoidance clause set forth in legal orders could not be applied to residents requesting the application of a DTC. Examples of the above are the German and Canadian legal orders. In this regard, *see* Füger/Rieger 1998, Rädler 1999, p. 297 and Goyette 1999, p. 23.
85. Ward 1995, p. 178.
86. Ward 1995, pp. 178–179 mentions some decisions handed down by the International Court of Justice which use this principle. As pointed out by Martín Jiménez 2002, p. 547, public international law recognizes the prohibition on the abuses of treaties, which basically means that the execution and interpretation of a treaty must be carried out in good faith. This allows one to search for the limits on the rights derived by states and individuals from a treaty beyond its literal wording.
87. In our opinion, this principle should be understood in this manner, since the VCLTs principle of good faith is aimed at states which are party to the convention and not at the taxpayers which may benefit therefrom. *See* Martín Jiménez 2002, pp. 545–546.

OECD Model since 2003, which after varying in its opinion, expressly provides for the possibility of applying these rules or principles although they are not expressly authorized in the treaty.[88]

However, even though this is the case, these rules give rise to the same problems discussed earlier, i.e. the formulation thereof is not the same in all states and there is no uniform international rule in this regard. Therefore, irregularities might arise in the application of the treaty, which in certain cases could hinder the achievement of their aim, i.e. to eliminate international double taxation.

For this reason, some authors have proposed that they are only applicable when the rules provided under the legislation of the contracting states are the same.[89] On the contrary, it is Vogel's understanding that where a treaty is applied, an effort must be made to interpret the existing 'domestic anti-avoidance rules' in the contracting states, in order to bridge the differences in their meaning and prevent this conduct from being protected. In this respect, this author proposes that the substance over form principle, which in his understanding is a principle of international law, is used as a parameter for making these rules more similar.[90] Even so, Vogel points out that their application should be exceptional and that without a doubt, it would be best for the parameters on which their application is based, to be determined by the contracting states.[91]

Thus, it could be concluded that although the cases of unlawful tax avoidance or abuse of law should not be protected under the DTCs on an international level, there is reluctance to apply the states' domestic rules in this regard. The reason for the above lies in the different wording and scope of these domestic rules, which could give rise to irregularities in the application of the treaty. Consequently, when not expressly authorized by the treaty, legal doctrine advises its application only in exceptional cases.

In the latter case where authorization is provided under the treaty, the application of these rules is formally safeguarded. However, in material terms, the same problems as those previously discussed arise, especially when the contracting states domestic rules or judicial doctrines clearly differ in this regard.

Given that this is the case, the conclusion reached by some experts is that in view of the difficulty involved in redirecting this conduct to the taxable event when such rules are applied (anti-avoidance, abuse of law, substance over form test, etc.), this should be done when the rules are drawn up, i.e. by introducing specific measures to combat this conduct in the treaty itself. As Uckmar pointed out, 'including detailed provisions in double-taxation conventions seems to be the most appropriate means of dealing with the problem'.[92]

In our opinion, although it is true that the specific rules strongly facilitate the denial of the regime provided under the treaty, the 'conventional lawmaker' alone cannot be relied upon to counter tax avoidance. As in the case of domestic legal orders,

---

88. *See* Martín Jiménez 2002, pp. 547–549 and Irawan 2016.
89. Lucas 2000, footnote 378.
90. Vogel 1997, pp. 122–125.
91. Vogel 1997, p. 125.
92. Uckmar 1983, p. 48.

there must be a general reactive instrument to combat the ongoing new tax avoidance schemes that arise. In this regard, the general reactive instrument may be that provided in each legal order or in a GAAR introduced in the tax treaty itself.[93]

Where a general anti-avoidance clause is not set forth in a treaty, the application of domestic rules must be allowed. These rules should be applied with utmost caution in order to prevent consequences contrary to the purposes of the DTCs from arising. In this respect, where such rules are applied, it would be appropriate for the source state to allow for the participation of the state of residence in some form, by means of the cooperation mechanisms established by the treaty. If the context in which the domestic rule is applied is considered and the aforementioned precautions are taken, it is likely that a uniform result will be achieved.[94]

It is also plausible to include SAARs in the treaty. As shall be observed, the LOB clauses are included under this type of rule.

As it has already been mentioned, the last stage of the OECD work to prevent the granting of treaty benefits to treaty shopping schemes and in other inappropriate circumstances is Action 6 of the BEPS project. Action 6 provides for a three-pronged approach to address treaty shopping.[95]

First, it proposes to introduce in the title and preamble of the OECD Model a clear statement that tax treaties do not intend to create opportunities for non-taxation or reduced taxation through tax evasion and avoidance, making an express reference to treaty shopping arrangements.

Second, Action 6 proposes to include in the body of the OECD Model a specific anti-avoidance rule based on the LOB (LOB provision) provided for in the U.S. Model and U.S. tax treaties.[96]

Third, in order to avoid other forms of treaty abuse, including treaty shopping situations that would not be covered by the LOB provision, the final report recommends including, in the OECD Model, a GAAR based on the principal purposes of transactions or arrangements, i.e. the so-called PPT rule. According to the PPT rule, the treaty benefits:

> shall not be granted in respect of an item of income or capital if it is reasonable to conclude, having regard to all relevant facts and circumstances, that obtaining that benefit was one of the principal purposes of any arrangement or transaction that resulted directly or indirectly in that benefit, unless it is established that granting that benefit in these circumstances would be in accordance with the object and purpose of the relevant provisions of this Convention.

Additionally, it should be mentioned that the Multilateral Convention to Implement Tax Treaty Related Measures to Prevent BEPS published by the OECD on 24

---

93. Essers: IFA 2001, p. 60.
94. Torrione: IFA 1995, p. 43 and West: IFA 2001, pp. 54–55.
95. Palao 2015, p. 603 and Irawan 2016, p. 43.
96. Action 6 of the BEPS project provides for a 'detailed LOB provision'. This is the one based on the U.S. Model. At the same time, the final report envisages a 'simplified LOB provision'. OECD 2015a, pp. 21–22.

November 2016 (hereinafter, 2016 BEPS Multilateral Instrument) also contains the PPT rule proposed in Action 6 of the BEPS project.[97]

The PPT rule proposed by the BEPS project merits some comment. As it has been pointed out by some scholars, the PPT rule has lowered the anti-abuse standard previously defined in the guiding principle included in the Commentaries on Article 1 of the 2003 Model.[98] According to the Commentaries' guiding principle, a transaction should be considered abusive only where the main purpose of the transaction is to obtain treaty benefits. Hence, treaty benefits should not be rejected when a transaction or arrangement is inspired by one (or various) principal purpose(s) that are in no way related to obtaining treaty benefits, even though obtaining a treaty benefit was also a principal purpose.[99] On the contrary, under the application of the PPT rule, treaty benefits could be denied to taxpayers merely 'because one of their (principal) motives was the obtaining of those benefits'.[100] This aspect of the PPT rule has been highly criticized, as, among other reasons, the OECD does not provide any guidance on how one should distinguish between principal purposes and ancillary purposes on the one hand, and between various principal purposes on the other hand.[101] In this regard, some scholars have proposed that the PPT rule should only be applied if a transaction or arrangement was solely or at least predominantly inspired by treaty benefits.[102] At the same time, the elimination of the subjective approach of the PPT rule has also been proposed, by building the 'anti-abuse standard of the PPT upon the concepts of artificiality or business purpose test' as these concepts will help to avoid the inconveniences of a strict subjective approach.[103] In fact, these concepts are used in some of the Commentaries on the PPT rule set forth in the final document of Action 6 and, at the same time, are more in line, as it will be analysed in Chapter 4, with the European Court of Justice (ECJ) Standards on abuse of tax law.

Moreover, the final document of Action 6 contains some considerations on the relationship between special and GAARs. These considerations refer to the relationship between the LOB provision and the PPT rule, as the BEPS project recommends a joint incorporation of both rules in tax treaties. According to the final document of Action 6:

> the fact that a person is entitled to benefits under [the LOB clauses] does not mean that these benefits cannot be denied under [the PPT rule]. [The LOB clauses, contained in] paragraphs 1 to 6 are rules that focus primarily on the legal nature, ownership in, and general activities of, residents of a contracting state. [These]

---

97. The Multilateral Convention is the outcome of Action 15 of the OECD/G20 BEPS project. Action 15 provided for an analysis of the possible development of a multilateral instrument to implement tax treaty related BEPS measures 'to enable jurisdictions that wish to do so to implement measures developed in the course of the work on BEPS and amend bilateral tax treaties'. *See* OECD 2016.
98. De Broe/Luts 2015, p. 131 and Báez 2017.
99. De Broe/Luts 2015, p. 131.
100. De Broe/Luts 2015, p. 132.
101. De Broe/Luts 2015, p. 132.
102. De Broe/Luts 2015, p. 132.
103. Báez 2017.

rules do not imply that a transaction or arrangement entered into by such a resident cannot constitute an improper use of a treaty provision.[104]

The position of Action 6 should be criticized, as compliance with any of the tests that conform to the LOB rule guarantees that the taxpayer either has a sufficient nexus to the state of residence or a real purpose to obtain the income generated in the source state from the state of residence.[105] This situation could discard the fact that the principal purpose (or one of the principal purposes) of the arrangement or transaction was to obtain treaty benefits regarding an item of income. It is our understanding that this approach is crystal clear under some of the LOB tests, such as the activity clause and the bona fide clause. Under the activity clause, treaty benefits only apply if the taxpayer is engaged in the active conduct of a trade or business in the state of residence and the income derived from the source state is derived in connection with, or is incidental to, that trade or business. The same conclusion should be drawn when the taxpayer gets access to treaty benefits under the bona fide clause, as treaty benefits are only applied with respect to an item of income if the taxpayer provides sufficiently clear and consistent evidence that the establishment, acquisition or maintenance in the state of residence did not have as one of its principal purposes the obtaining of treaty benefits.

However, this conclusion is not so clear under other LOB tests, as the stock-exchange clause and the ownership and base erosion clause give access to all treaty benefits without looking into the specific situation of how each item of income is derived from the source state. From this point of view, it is possible that a taxpayer who complies with any of the mentioned LOB clauses may act as a conduit in certain transactions or arrangements in order to provide treaty benefits to residents in third states. If this were case, the denial of treaty benefits may be justified on those transactions or arrangements under the application of a GAAR, but not in other cases. In this regard, we agree with those scholars who hold the view that the PPT rule should only be applied when the principal purpose of the arrangement or the transaction was to obtain the treaty benefit, but not when this purpose concurs with other principal purposes that are in no way related to obtaining treaty benefits.[106] In fact, as suggested by Báez, it will be more advisable to build the anti-abuse standard of the PPT rule upon concepts of artificiality or the business purpose test in order to avoid the inconvenience of a strict subjective approach, which is the one that seems to follow both the guiding principle of the Commentaries on Article 1 of the OECD Model and the PPT rule proposed in Action 6 of the BEPS project.[107]

---

104. OECD 2016a, pp. 55–56.
105. *See* section II.B.2 of this chapter.
106. De Broe/Luts 2015, p. 131.
107. Báez 2017. This author also considers that general anti-avoidance rules (including the PPT rule) should be inapplicable to taxpayers who comply with the LOB clauses, this kind of rule describes what is abusive according to the legislator but, at the same time, clarifies *a contrario* what arrangements might not be considered abusive. 'Applying the GAAR (the PPT) in this context would be hardly reconcilable with the principle of legal certainty and a bona fide application of tax law provisions. Being more precise, one could think that the GAAR is applicable but just to conclude that, when the taxpayer is within the legal limits of the SAAR,

If the above conclusions are correct, the PPT rule will only be potentially applicable to certain transactions performed by taxpayers who comply with certain LOB rules, i.e. the stock-exchange clause and the ownership and base erosion clause. From this point of view, as it will be analysed in section II.B.3 of this chapter, the relationship between LOB clauses and the beneficial owner concept will be similar, as the meaning of the latter concept given by the Commentaries of the OECD Model has substantial similarities to the GAARs.

Finally, it should be pointed out that the position taken by some states, which consists of directly including specific rules in their domestic legislation, by which the application of the treaties is prevented, should be included under the same scope. These rules are briefly referred to below in section II.C, given that the object of our study is the specific measures included in the treaties. The main problem relating to these measures is that they may be contrary to tax treaties, since they unilaterally limit their personal scope.

II.B Treaty Measures

First, the concepts already provided for in the treaties should be analysed to determine their specific scope and how they may be useful against these structures, without requiring the most extreme solution involving the amendment of a treaty in order to include these specific measures, which is what occurs in the case of the LOB clauses.[108]

In this regard, the concept of residence and person laid down in the OECD Model, which are the two parameters used to delimit the subjective scope thereof, will be analysed. Attention will also be paid to the concept of beneficial owner provided in Articles 10, 11 and 12 of the OECD Model. It is essential to delimit the definition of the beneficial ownership concept, as the need to include LOB clauses in the treaty largely depends on the scope given to this concept. Finally, the general wording of the limitations on benefits clauses will be examined.

---

the arrangement can never be considered abusive'. Additionally, according to Baéz, this interpretation could be sustained under the wording of the PPT rule proposed in Action 6 of the BEPS project. In this regard, those other provisions mentioned in the wording of the heading of the PPT rule –'Notwithstanding the other provisions of this Convention...'- could be identified not with the LOB clauses 'but rather with the distributive rules whose application the tax payer aims to provoke by means of abusive arrangements. According to this interpretation, the benefits intended by the taxpayer would be denied notwithstanding the provisions of the Convention that would be applicable at first glance if the PPT did not exist. This would be consistent with the wording of certain treaties that nowadays already incorporate a GAAR (more or less similar to the PPT). These conventional GAARs –often not accompanied by LOB provisions- are always headed with the expression "Notwithstanding the other provisions of this Convention..." demonstrating thereby that these words do not refer to the LOB, but rather to other provisions of the treaty'. This author concludes the PPT rule should be just applicable to arrangements leading to rule shopping whereas treaty shopping strategies should be considered to be covered comprehensively by the LOB clauses.

108. OECD 1986, paragraph 14.

II.B.1 Subjective Scope of the OECD Model: Concepts of Person and Residence

The subjective scope of the DTCs is understood to be the group of persons who the treaty may affect. In accordance with Article 1 of the OECD Model, the convention shall apply to persons who are residents of one or both of the contracting states.

As previously discussed, treaty shopping structures materially broaden the subjective scope of the DTCs, as they enable residents in third states to indirectly access the regime of the treaties. These structures mainly aim to reduce the source state taxation by applying the restrictions which the treaty imposes on it when levying tax on the income obtained within its territory by residents of the other contracting state. As graphically demonstrated by the U.S. Internal Revenue Service (IRS), the treaty is converted into a 'treaty with the world' and not only with the state with which it was originally concluded.[109]

The problem lies precisely in the definition of the subjective scope of the treaty, which as was pointed out earlier, is due to the concurrence of two requirements which consist in being a person and a resident in at least one of the contracting states.[110]

II.B.1.a Concept of Person

The concept of person is defined in rather broad terms in Article 3 of the OECD Model. The term 'person' includes an individual, a company and any other body of persons. As can be observed, this concept is not restricted to individuals and bodies with legal personality. Moreover, the OECD Model's definition of the concept of a company not only refers to legal persons but also to any entity that is treated as a body corporate for tax purposes.

Due to the broad definition of the concept, compliance with this requirement rarely constitutes a problem for treaty application purposes. The main issues do not arise in relation to this requirement, but rather to the concept of residence.[111]

A good example of this is the treatment of partnerships in international taxation. These types of entities are not considered to have legal personality under all legal orders. However, as stated by the OECD in its report on the problems relating to the application of the OECD Model to these types of entities,[112] this does not prevent them from being included within the Model's concept of person. Partnerships will also be considered as 'persons' either because they fall within the definition of 'company', in

---

109. ALI 1992, p. 152.
110. It is noted by Vogel/Shannon/Doernberg/Van Raad 1989, Article 16, p. 4, that the development of LOBs is precisely due to the weakness of the concept of residence provided in the OECD and U.S. Models. The above is only partly true. As previously observed the treaty-shopping structures also depend, to a large extent, on the intermediary state regime. A state with very strict rules in relation to transfer pricing or thin capitalization would not be an appropriate location for conducting the operation, especially in the case of a stepping stone conduit.
111. Van Weeghel 1998, p. 39.
112. OECD, *The Application of the OECD Model Tax Convention to Partnerships*, OECD, Paris, 1999.

the sense that they are treated as a body corporate for tax purposes, or where this is not the case, because they constitute other bodies of persons.[113]

The clarity with which this matter is resolved is not comparable to the solution provided for determining whether a partnership is considered a resident under the terms of the OECD Model.

It should be pointed out that while in some countries the income tax obtained is borne by the partnership itself, which is considered to be an independent body of the partners, in other states the tax is applied to the partners based on their share of the partnership's income. In the latter case, the partnership does not have the right to apply the treaty, as it is not subject to tax on worldwide income. The treaty is applied to this type of entity where the partnerships are liable to tax on worldwide income. This will not occur in the case where a transparency regime is applied. However, experts have questioned whether the partners would have the right to apply the treaty in these cases.

The problems relating to the taxation of partnerships will not be addressed in this study. However, it is important to note that the determination of whether or not the treaty will be applied mainly depends on whether the taxpayer that requests its application is considered to be a resident in any of the contracting states. Therefore, knowledge of the taxation regime established in the state from which the partnership requests the application of the treaty is unavoidable. As can be evidenced, the problems arising in relation to the application of tax treaties to partnerships stem from Article 4 of the OECD Model (concept of residence) rather than Article 1 of this Model (concept of person).

In this respect, the scope of the definition of the concept of person leaves little space for denying the application of the treaty in the case that a treaty shopping structure arises, even where a partnership is used. Nevertheless, the problems arising from the application of tax treaties to partnerships relates to the fact that corporations are normally used in treaty shopping structures.

Entities on which legal personality is conferred are subject to corporate income tax, because the states' tax law normally relates a taxpayer's liability to the type of legal organization.[114] As shall be observed, liability to corporate income tax in a state is a basis for being considered a resident for the purposes of the application of DTCs. Therefore, prior to studying the concept of residence provided in the OECD Model, the systems used under international corporate law for the recognition of legal personality shall be briefly analysed. Since liability to corporate income tax depends on the recognition of legal personality, the tax planner should bear these aspects in mind, given that the determination as to whether the treaty is applicable depends on whether the entity is subject to tax on worldwide income in the state from where the income is intended to be obtained.[115]

---

113. *See* Commentary on Article 3 of the OECD Model (paragraph 2).
114. Albiñana 1986, pp. 185–186.
115. Ebenroth/Daiber 1990, p. 176.

With respect to the determination of the law governing companies (*lex societatis*), there are fundamentally two theories: the incorporation theory and the theory of the 'real seat'.[116]

Based on the incorporation theory, the *lex societatis* is the state law in accordance with which the company has been incorporated.[117] This is strictly a legal criterion for connection in view of the fact that it does not take material aspects of the company into account such as the location of the company's head office or the main operating centre (real seat). This theory only requires the company's statuary seat to be located in the state of incorporation.

This theory facilitates the free international movement of companies for two reasons. First, the state adopting this theory facilitates the recognition of foreign companies, as these companies will be recognized where they have been properly incorporated in accordance with the law chosen by the partners.[118] Second, the transfer of the company's real seat to a third state does not give rise to the termination or dissolution of the company. Consequently, the geographic continuity of the company's legal personality in international traffic is assured.[119]

However, several objections to this theory have been raised. The theory makes it possible for a company to be incorporated in accordance with a state's legal order without requiring any other relationship of an objective nature between the state and the company. This can give rise to a separation between the company's 'centre of gravity' and the legal order governing it, which, as shall be observed, is unacceptable in line with the real seat theory. It has also been pointed out that this theory fosters competition between the legal systems, leading to a 'race to the bottom', in the sense that the states will make their corporate law more flexible in order to attract the incorporation of companies within their territory.[120]

In contrast, according to the real seat theory, a company should only remain subject to the law of the state where it actually maintains a particular and specific relationship of a factual nature, limited to the state in which its real seat is located.[121]

---

116. Garcimartín 1999, p. 647.
117. Vischer 1994, p. 14.
118. Fock 2000, p. 43.
119. Rivier 1987, p. 50.
120. One of the examples of the drawbacks of this theory of incorporation which tends to be used is the corporate legislation of the state of Delaware (U.S.), which fostered the massive incorporation of companies in this state due to the flexibility of its legislation. See Blanco-Morales 1997, pp. 53–56.
121. There is no univocal solution in the legal orders which adhere to this theory (especially the European systems) with respect to the element which determines a company's real seat. The elements commonly used refer to two aspects: central management (decision-making body) or company operations (execution of these decisions). In the first case, the real seat is identified with central management: the place where corporate decisions are ordinarily made (the place where the company is managed and directed). In the second case, the real seat is identified as the place where the company has its main business activity centre (main operating centre). The first alternative (place of central management) is that which is defended by most experts in this field, although the solution is not formulated in this manner in all legal orders. In any case, it should be noted that is a predominantly factual concept. See Garcimartín 1999, p. 650 and Blanco-Morales 1997, pp. 72–77.

The consequences of the use of this theory are more clearly evidenced by first examining *ex post* and then *ex ante*.[122] From an *ex post* perspective, this theory implies that where a company has not been incorporated in accordance with the law of the state in which its real seat is located, it will not be deemed to be validly incorporated, and consequently will not be recognized as such. From a *ex ante* perspective, this theory requires the shareholders to incorporate a company in accordance with the law of the state in which its real seat is located, otherwise, it will be not be recognized.

Under this theory, foreign companies will only be recognized if the companies have been validly incorporated in accordance with the law of the state where their real seat is located. Where the state in which the company was incorporated and the state in which the real seat is located are not the same, the company will not be deemed to be validly incorporated under this theory. However, under the incorporation theory, it would be validly incorporated. Where this theory is applied, the transfer of the real seat to a third state is not viable in view of the fact that it gives rise to the aforementioned separation. The transfer of the head offices to a foreign location would decisively lead to the company's dissolution and liquidation.

The advantages of this theory are rightly the reverse of the disadvantages of the incorporation theory. In the first place, the *lex societatis* will be determined by the law of the state where the company's operations are established (real seat). Second, the real seat theory avoids the 'race to the bottom' phenomenon which occurs under corporate law.

Even so, as experts in this field have noted, this theory does not always achieve the above, and also gives rise to certain drawbacks, those worth mentioning include the lack of a definition for the concept of real seat, which is based on two criteria, the location of the company's head offices and the location of the company's main operations. Thus, once one of these two possible criteria has been chosen, determining the state in which it is located can give rise to problems.[123]

The main objection to the real seat theory is that it would considerably hinder the free movement and establishment of companies, as the company would not be recognized where there was a separation between the place where the company was incorporated and its real seat. Furthermore, any change in the real seat, even where it was unintentional, would lead to the dissolution and liquidation of the company.[124]

For the purposes of this study, the effect of these company theories on the concepts of person and residence set forth in the OECD Model must be taken into account.

---

122. Garcimartín 1999, p. 650.
123. In this respect, a question arises in regard to the main operations of a company with various centres with the same line of business. Also, the criterion of central management may be easily manipulated, since a company may be understood to have its real seat in the U.K. if it holds its Board of Directors' meetings there, even though its operations take place in a third state.
124. Imagine a company incorporated in accordance with French law with two operating centres, one in France and another in Spain. When the Spanish centre gains more relevance than the French centre, the strict application of this real seat theory would obligate France to stop recognizing the legal personality of this company.

In principle, from the following point of view, they would not have a considerable effect. Imagine that a company which has adopted the incorporation theory is incorporated in state A, and that the company's real seat is located in state C, which has also adopted the incorporation theory. However, the company obtains income in state B, which has adopted the real seat model. State B would not recognize the company incorporated in state A because the state in which it was incorporated is not the same as the state in which its real seat is located. Nevertheless, this company would still be considered a person according to Article 3 of the OECD Model, as long as it is liable to tax on worldwide income in state A, which is very likely, since the incorporation of a company in accordance with the laws of a state is a criterion that determines its liability to tax on worldwide income.

However, this theory can give rise to drawbacks in the following case. Taking treaty shopping structures into account, when the corporate theory adhered to by a state is the real seat theory; it will be more difficult to achieve the application of the treaties entered into by this state solely by means of the incorporation of a company.

In principle, only legal entities are subject to corporate income tax, and accordingly, recognition of legal personality is a primary requirement for being included within the scope of this tax.[125] According to the real seat theory, legal personality is only recognized where the company is incorporated in accordance with the state's rules and where the company's real seat is located within its territory. Consequently, the mere incorporation of a company as part of the treaty shopping structure would not be sufficient, as the state would also require that the company's real seat be located within its territory. If the company were not a legal entity, it would not be liable to corporate income tax, a requirement which is essential for being considered a resident for the purposes of the application of tax treaties.

In the previous case, the problem could not be resolved by transferring the company's real seat from a third state to the state referred to above, as this state would not recognize the company's legal personality because the location of its real seat is not the same as the state where it was incorporated. Accordingly, the company that is being transferred would be required to be dissolved and incorporated in accordance with the laws of that state.

Consequently, the states that apply the real seat theory are less suitable for channelling treaty shopping structures as it is more difficult to be considered a resident for the purposes of DTCs. This is precisely because, in order to be liable to tax on the overall income obtained, it is first necessary for the company's legal personality to be recognized, a requirement usually met under the real seat theory because the company's real seat is located in the same state in which it was incorporated in accordance with this state's laws. Therefore, the states usually used for these structures apply the incorporation theory (the Netherlands, the U.K.), and the fact that no material connection with the state of incorporation is required greatly facilitates the development of the structure.

---

125. Ebenroth/Daiber 1990, 176 and Frommel 1989, pp. 267–274.

Finally, it is important to note that the real seat theory has been under scrutiny within the EU, precisely due to its adverse effect on the freedom of movement and establishment of companies (Articles 49-54 TFEU, ex 43-48 EC Treaty). In this respect, following the decision handed down by the ECJ on 9 March 1999, *Centros*, C-212/97, experts are practically unanimous in their view that where the state of incorporation is not the same as the state in which its real seat is located, a state cannot refuse to recognize this company when it has been incorporated in accordance with the law of a Member State, solely based on the argument that its legal order adheres to the real seat theory.[126] However, in accordance with Article 54 of the TFEU, this obligation only exists when the real seat, which is understood to be the head office or the main operating centre, is located within EU territory.[127]

II.B.1.b   Concept of Residence

To be considered a resident it is necessary to be liable to tax on worldwide income in a state. Any other criterion under a state's legislation which does not give rise to this degree of liability (full tax liability) is an insufficient basis on which to consider a taxpayer as a resident in accordance with Article 4 of the OECD Model, even though such consideration is nominally given under a state's legislation.[128] In this respect, Article 4 of the OECD Model states that the expression 'resident of a Contracting State [...] does not include any person who is liable to tax in that state in respect only of income from sources in that state'.

In principle, this criterion is sufficient for the objective of the tax treaties. As observed in the first part of this study, tax treaties are aimed at resolving the archetypical double taxation conflict which entails the juxtaposition of non-resident and resident tax liability. Pursuant to the convention, the source state limits the tax established under legislation in order to eliminate or reduce double taxation. Correspondingly, the state of residence eliminates double taxation by means of the exemption or credit method where the treaty authorizes the source state to establish a tax on the income obtained within its territory in a limited or unlimited manner.

The structure of this system assumes that the taxpayer that obtains income at source is liable to resident tax in the other state. Likewise, the state of residence applies the measures provided in the treaty to eliminate double taxation because the source state has levied tax on the income obtained.

Nevertheless, the requirement of liability to tax on the worldwide income obtained is only abstractly established, without requiring income to be effectively taxed.[129] In some tax treaties, subject to tax clauses are established in order to assure

---

126. There are other subsequent EJC cases relating to international corporate law in which the doctrine of the Centros decision was confirmed. These include the decisions handed down in cases C-208/00 (*Überseering*) and C-167/01 (*Inspire Art*).
127. *See* Garcimartín 2001, pp. 82-83 and Frommel 1988, p. 412.
128. *See* Shannon 1988, p. 206, Vogel 1997, p. 229 and Marino 1999, pp. 197-198.
129. ALI 1992, p. 128 and Vogel 1997, pp. 229 and 364. In this manner, although a company transforms all the income received into expenses, in a stepping stone structure, without giving rise to taxation, it would not lose the condition of resident.

that the source state only applies the treaty limitation when the income is effectively taxed in the state of residence, or that the state of residence only applies the exemption method where the income is effectively taxed at source.[130] However, such clauses are not common in tax treaties.[131] Furthermore, the OECD Model does not include a liability and non-exemption clause similar to that provided in Article 2(1)(c) of the Directive 90/435/EEC, on the common system of taxation applicable in the case of parent companies and subsidiaries of different Member States, to prevent taxpayers, which are formally liable to tax but exempt from taxation, from benefiting from the DTC.[132]

Therefore, one of the assumptions on which the concept of residence is based (taxation on worldwide income), does not only require the income obtained at source to be effectively taxed in the state of residence; because the definition of the concept of residence is not only based on this parameter, but also on the fact that the persons liable on worldwide income have a fixed and stable nexus with the state of residence.

This presumption follows from the criteria on which liability to tax in a state on the worldwide income obtained is based. Article 4 of the OECD Model states that, the term resident of a contracting state 'means any person who, under the laws of that state, is liable to tax therein by reasons of his domicile, residence, place of management or any other criterion of a similar nature'. The criteria expressly stated in the Model at least appear to imply that there is a factual nexus to the state of residence's territory.[133]

Accordingly, Article 4 of the OECD Model does not expressly mention any other liability criteria, such as the citizenship of individuals, or correspondingly, in the case of entities, of a company's place of incorporation.[134] Therefore, on first consideration, not just any criteria which, pursuant to domestic legislation, gives rise to liability to taxation on worldwide income is sufficient to deem a taxpayer as resident for the purposes of the application of the treaty. A person will only be considered a resident for the purposes of the treaty if the domestic criterion for liability to tax on the worldwide income obtained is one of those provided for in the OECD Model.[135]

---

130. Vogel 1997, pp. 364–365.
131. Lang 2000, p. 38.
132. However, it should be borne in mind that the Commentaries on Article 4 of the OECD Model (paragraph 8) state that taxpayers will not be considered as residents in the case of 'foreign-held companies exempted from tax on their foreign income by privileges tailored to attract conduit companies. This, however, has inherent difficulties and limitations'. In essence, their intention is to include a liability and non-exemption clause. However, the vague terms in which the Commentaries are worded, demonstrates the doubts that the OECD has regarding the ability to make this non-exemption requirement unless it is expressly provided. Vogel 2001, pp. 91–92, cites several resolutions by the American Internal Revenue Service which confirm that being formally liable to tax in a state on worldwide income is sufficient to satisfy the requirement of residence (*see also* the decision of the Supreme Court of India dated 7 October 2003, which is commented by Thacker 2004, p. 72). Lastly, it is important to bear in mind that paragraphs 8.2 and 8.3 of the Commentaries on Article 4, which were included in the 2000 version of the Commentaries on the OECD Model, state that an entity exempt from taxation in its State of Residence may be considered to be a resident for the purposes of a DTC.
133. Shannon 1988, p. 206.
134. Shannon 1988, p. 207 and Vogel 1997, p. 233.
135. Ismer/Riemer 2015, p. 259.

Although these are criteria (citizenship and place of incorporation) used to determine the liability to taxation on the worldwide income obtained, they would not be valid criteria for determining whether a taxpayer would be considered a resident in the conventions that follow the OECD Model.[136] Additionally, as pointed out by experts in this field, these criteria would not be included under the final paragraph of the first section of Article 4 of the OECD Model, 'or any other criterion of a similar nature'.[137] A systematic interpretation of Article 4 requires that any other criteria take into account factual elements which attach the taxpayer to the territory. Citizenship and place of incorporation cannot be considered similar criteria, as they relate to a nexus which is of a purely legal nature.

Nevertheless, the opinion in this respect is not unanimous.[138] The question depends on how the concept is to be developed. If the concept is developed exclusively based on the liability to tax on worldwide income, any attachment criteria under the state's legislation which establishes such a degree of extension of liability to tax is valid as a basis for being deemed a resident for the purposes of the application of the convention. However, if the nature of the criteria on which liability is determined is also taken into account, a systematic interpretation of Article 4 of the OECD Model would require that these criteria be expressed taking factual elements into account.

The concept of residence which appears to stem from the OECD Model is a hindrance to the development of treaty shopping structures. The tax planner is required to provide a legal vehicle which has the necessary factual elements to assure that liability to tax on the worldwide income obtained arises as a result of the criteria accepted in accordance with Article 4 of the OECD Model. In this respect, although the mere incorporation of a company in accordance with the laws of the state gives rise to liability to tax on worldwide income, it is not sufficient for the purpose of being included within the scope of the application of the treaty.

From this viewpoint, the treaty concept of residence (Article 4 of the OECD Model) is an efficient instrument for use in countering some treaty shopping structures, and accordingly, there is no need to resort to mechanisms such as the application of domestic anti-avoidance rules. Note that in this case not even the requirements for the application of the DTC are applicable.[139]

However, the concept of residence is not sufficient to resolve all problems arising from the development of these structures. The fact that the entity used is liable to tax

---

136. Therefore, for example, a company incorporated in accordance with Spanish law would be liable to resident corporate income tax. However, if the criterion of incorporation is the only basis on which liability to resident tax is determined, and not any other, such as domicile or place of effective management, this company would not be considered a resident for the purposes of DTCs entered into by Spain which are worded in accordance with Article 4 of the OECD Model.
137. Shannon 1988, pp. 206–207, Vogel 1997, p. 233 and Marino 1999, p. 199.
138. Rivier 1987, p. 135 and Van Raad 1988, p. 243.
139. This concept excludes the so-called letter-box companies from applying the convention. These are companies which only exist on a legal level and which lack a material nexus to the state of incorporation. See Huiskamp/Bracewell-Milnes/Wisselink 1979, p. 52.

in the intermediary state in accordance with the liability criterion accepted under Article 4 of the OECD Model does not exclude the possibility that these structures may arise. The company may have either its registered office or its place of effective management in this state but, still lack a sufficient degree of integration within the territory, which as pointed out earlier, is one of the parameters used to judge whether the structure is lawful from the standpoint of GAARs.[140]

Additionally, the fact that the place of incorporation criterion is not admitted under the OECD Model does not mean that it is not actually applied. For this reason, there is a singular phenomenon with respect to the liability criteria used by the states.

States generally do not use citizenship as a criterion to determine if individuals are liable to tax on the worldwide income they have obtained. However, in the case of entities, place of incorporation is a criterion used in most domestic legislation.[141] The fact that this criterion is generally accepted in the states' legislation is relevant, as it could be used to support its inclusion within the 'similar criteria' (criterion of a similar nature) stipulated in Article 4 of the OECD Model. In this regard, it should be borne in mind that the place of incorporation criterion is expressly provided in a large number of tax treaties. As a result, any doubts as to the admissibility of this criterion are fully removed, although only in the tax treaties in which the criterion is provided.

Regarding the above, it is well known that the U.S. tax treaties were particularly concerned with the issue of treaty shopping and have included the most LOB clauses, therefore, it is worth pointing out that the U.S. tax treaties still maintain that the incorporation criterion is sufficient to be considered a resident. The 1996, 2006 and 2016 U.S. Models and earlier versions expressly provide for the criterion of incorporation.[142] This is due to the fact that U.S. legislation only uses this criterion for taxing entities on worldwide income.[143] Given that these tax treaties may be understood to have included an additional criterion not admissible under Article 4 of the OECD Model, the weight of the conventional concept of resident is placed on the fact that the criterion applied under the state's domestic law establishes liability to tax on the worldwide income obtained, regardless of the nature of the aforementioned criterion.

There is no doubt that this concept of residence greatly facilitates the development of treaty shopping structures since residence is only established in consideration of formal elements which, in principle, do not guarantee the company's presence in the state of residence. In this regard, it is important to consider how paradoxical the position of the U.S. is. On the one hand, it is the driving force behind the inclusion of the place of incorporation criterion in tax treaties, but on the other hand, it is also the main driving force behind the inclusion of LOB. The purpose of these

---

140. Vogel 1997, pp. 263–264.
141. Rohatgy 2002, p. 146.
142. Doernberg/Van Raad 1997, pp. 28–29. It also expressly includes the concept of citizenship of individuals. The 1980 UN Model does not include the criterion of citizenship of individuals. With respect to entities, the 1980 version of the UN Model does not include the place of incorporation criterion. However, the 2001 version does include this criterion.
143. Rivier 1987, p. 125. With respect to individuals, the citizenship criterion is used but not exclusively.

clauses is precisely to reinforce the criterion of residence in order to correct the consequences arising from an attachment factor which is excessively formal.

In summary, from the point of view of the treaty concept of residence, there are two clearly distinguishable groups of treaties. First, there are treaties that follow Article 4 of the OECD Model. In these treaties, the concept of residence takes into account not only the liability to tax in a state on worldwide income, but also the nature of the liability criterion. The criterion of incorporation has no place in this concept, since the nexus to the state of residence is merely legal and not of a factual nature. In these tax treaties, the correct application of the conventional concept of residence is an instrument which is significant, though not sufficient to deny the application of the treaty in certain cases of treaty shopping.

Second, there are tax treaties which include the place of incorporation criterion. The conventional concept of residence is defined exclusively by reference to liability to tax on worldwide income. This definition does not even allow for the denial of treaty benefits to the crudest treaty shopping structures and even fosters their development. Entities, as opposed to individuals, are provided with extensive possibilities for creation, establishment and transfer, which allow them to incorporate in, or move to the state with the most advantageous treaty.[144] This is also the reason that LOBs are essentially applied to entities, due to their mobility, such entities may more easily obtain residence in a state for the sole purpose of applying a DTC.

In this respect, one option for resolving the problems caused by this conduct would be to modify the concept of resident, defining it in terms similar to the OECD Model. However, this is not the alternative which has been used in the DTCs entered into by the U.S.[145] The solution that has been adopted is to include specific rules, i.e. LOB clauses, to guarantee that the treaty benefits are only applied to taxpayers with a sufficient nexus to the territory of the state of residence, or at least, a real business purpose for obtaining the income generated at source from this state.

In any case, the taxpayer must be liable to tax on worldwide income, as on the contrary, it could not be considered a resident for the purposes of applying the treaty, regardless of whether or not the place of incorporation criterion were admissible.

II.B.2 Beneficial Ownership Concept

In this section, the concept of beneficial ownership provided in Articles 10, 11 and 12 of the OECD Model will be analysed. It would be beyond the object of this study to

---

144. Rosenbloom 1983, pp. 810–811 and Grundy 1984, p. 27.
145. This alternative could be worded in another manner so as to be accepted in the U.S. The DTCs would accept the criterion of incorporation only to determine the residence of entities in the U.S. To be considered a resident in another contracting state, the companies would be required to be liable to tax on the worldwide income obtained in accordance with a criterion included in Article 4 of the OECD Model. Consequently, the incorporation criterion would only be used to determine residence in the U.S., but not in any other state with which it has entered into a treaty.

analyse this concept in depth. However, it is important to examine the most significant matters which have arisen in relation thereto for the purpose of studying the LOB clauses.[146]

The concept of beneficial ownership is included in Articles, 10, 11 and 12 of the 1977 version of the OECD Model. This concept is also included in the U.S. and the UN Models.[147]

Apparently, this concept gives rise to a new requirement which must be satisfied in order for the source state to apply the limits established in the OECD Model on the taxation of dividends, interest and royalties. The source state will only be obligated to apply the limits stipulated in a treaty if the beneficial owner of the dividends, interests or royalties is a person who resides in the other contracting state. Logically, in the case where the taxpayer who resides in another state is not considered to be a beneficial owner, the treaty limits will not be applicable.[148]

This concept was included in tax treaties in order to prevent a treaty from being applied in cases of treaty shopping.[149] However, it does not cover all treaty shopping conduct, but rather conduct which relates to dividends, interest and royalties. As is evident, the consequences arising from the inclusion of the beneficial ownership clause are more limited than those which arise from the inclusion of LOB. Whereas the LOB clauses exclude taxpayers who do not comply therewith from the personal scope of a tax treaty, the beneficial ownership clause only excludes taxpayers from applying a treaty in specific cases, and always in relation to three types of income, i.e. dividends, interest and royalties. This means that the taxpayer could be protected under the treaty where he obtains another type of income, or where he obtains other dividends, interest or royalties, if he is considered the beneficial owner thereof.

Most controversial in relation to this concept is precisely the determination of the term's meaning.[150] In this regard, the OECD Model is not very helpful as it does not provide any definition, giving rise to a highly relevant question from the viewpoint of the interpretation of DTCs. Article 3(2) of the OECD Model states that:

> as regards the application of the Convention at any time by a Contracting State, any term not defined therein shall, unless the context otherwise requires, have the meaning that it has at that time under the law of that State for the purposes of the taxes to which the Convention applies.

In principle, from this rule it follows that the meaning of terms not expressly defined in a treaty should be determined in accordance with domestic legislation.

---

146. For a more in depth analysis *see* Van Weeghel 1998, pp. 64–91, Du Toit 1999, Oliver/Libin/Van Weeghel/Du Toit 2000, Martín Jiménez 2010, Zuk 2013, Hernández 2015 and Armelin 2016.
147. Rohatgi 2002, p. 367.
148. The wording of the 1977 OECD Model was rather confusing, since in the case that the person receiving the income and the beneficial owner were not the same, it seemed to require that both taxpayers reside in the other contracting state. The successive modifications to the OECD Model, and its Commentaries (1995, 1997 and 2003) clarified that only the beneficial owner of the income is required to reside in the other contracting state. See Vega 2003, pp. 130–133.
149. *See*, among others, Loukota 1989, p. 352 and Vogel 1997, p. 147.
150. Lukoff 1977, p. 566 and Vargas 2004, pp. 18–20.

However, this reliance on domestic law depends on the weight given to the other part of the rule ('unless the context otherwise requires').

Most experts in this field consider that the context of the treaties require this concept to be interpreted autonomously, in order to guarantee that the DTCs are applied in a uniform manner by the contracting states.[151] Therefore, with respect to determining the concept's meaning, preference should be given to an autonomous interpretation of the concept rather than to the interpretation which would prevail under each state's domestic law. However, as shall be observed below, it should be borne in mind that reference to domestic law is not always appropriate because the majority of legal orders do not provide a similar concept.[152]

Accordingly, if the concept of beneficial ownership should be interpreted autonomously, the concept's meaning must then be determined. Without a doubt, this is a complicated matter because the OECD Model does not define this concept.

As pointed out by experts in this field, the concept of beneficial ownership under the OECD Model is taken from legal orders of English common law.[153] In principle, civil law regulations do not provide a similar concept, since contrary to the English common law, there cannot be different levels of ownership in relation to a single asset, i.e. legally, no distinction may be made between a legal owner and a beneficial owner.[154] Nevertheless, even though such a distinction cannot be formally made, it should be taken into account that under civil law, it is possible for persons other than the owner of an asset to enjoy the rights resulting therefrom, either as a result of a personal right or a right *in rem* (e.g. an usufruct). It should also be noted that concepts and regimes that are similar to the English common law concept of beneficial ownership could be found in tax laws under the states' civil law systems.[155] One of the most significant examples is the concept of 'economic ownership' (*wirtschaftliches Eigentum*) as provided for in Article 39(1) of *Abgabenordnung* under the German legal system.[156] This rule establishes for tax purposes, that the ownership of an asset or right is generally allocated to the person to whom it corresponds under civil law. This rule assumes that the ownership of an asset and its economic disposal correspond to the same taxpayer. Consequently, this rule is separated from the provisions of civil law for the purposes of allocating income, where both elements (ownership and economic disposal of an asset) do not correspond to the same person.[157]

---

151. Edwardes-Ker 1994, p. 2 (Chapter 7), Vogel 1997, p. 562, Du Toit 1999, p. 173 and Lüthi: IFA 2000, p. 20. Of the opposite opinion are Eynatten/De Haen/Hostyn 2003, p. 538.
152. However, this assertion should be clarified, at least within the scope of the states that form part of the EU, in view of the approval of the Directives 2003/48/EC of 3 June 2003 on taxation of savings income in the form of interest payments and 2003/49/EC of 3 June 2003 on a common system of taxation applicable to interest and royalty payments made between associated companies of different Member States (Article 1.4). Both directives use the concept of beneficial ownership.
153. Baker 1994, p. 229.
154. Vega 2003, p. 144.
155. Eynatten/De Haen/Hostyn 2003, pp. 530–532.
156. Vogel 1994, p. 88, seems to identify the concept of beneficial ownership with that of *wirtschaftliches Eigentum*.
157. *See* Combarros 1984, p. 487 and Vega 2003, p. 145.

Based on the above, it can be asserted that although the concept of beneficial ownership comes from English common law, the contents thereof are not completely absent from civil law systems, since the tax laws under these systems include similar concepts and regimes, particularly within the scope of the allocation of income. As shall be observed below, this circumstance may be useful in determining the meaning of the concept of beneficial ownership.

As mentioned earlier, the body of the OECD Model does not include a definition of the beneficial ownership concept. However, in the Commentaries on the aforementioned Model, some references in relation to its meaning can be found.[158] It should be noted that the 2003 and 2014 OECD Models have included significant modifications in this respect.

The Commentaries on the 1977–2000 OECD Model only state that taxation limits in the source state will not be applicable when an intermediary, such as an agent or nominee, is interposed between the beneficiary and the payer, unless the beneficial owner is a resident of the other contracting state. As can be observed, the Commentaries consider that taxpayers who act on the account of a third party are not considered to be beneficiary owners. This is only logical as in these cases, although the aforementioned taxpayers are those who materially receive the income, the fact that they are acting on behalf of another party means that they are not obtaining the income on their own behalf and are obligated to put the income at the disposal of a third party, i.e. the person on whose behalf they are acting. In this respect, it is considered irrelevant whether the taxpayer who acts on behalf of a third party does so in his own name or in the name of a third party.[159] In both cases, this person cannot be considered the beneficial owner, since he is not receiving the income on his own behalf.[160]

Nevertheless, it should be noted that from a practical position, when the intermediary acts in his own name, it may be complicated for the tax authorities of the source state to verify whether or not the taxpayer who receives the income is the beneficial owner thereof, as they do not know whether he is acting on his own behalf or on behalf of a third party.[161]

Therefore, if the meaning of the concept of beneficial ownership is that which seems to be derived from the wording of the Commentaries in the 1977–2000 OECD Model (which excludes taxpayers who act on behalf of a third party), it can be asserted that this provision is clearly insufficient to counter all treaty shopping conduct, because in those structures where an entity is used (direct conduit and stepping stone conduit), at least formally, the interposed taxpayer acts on his own behalf. Moreover, in reality,

---

158. In the 1986 OECD report 'Double taxation conventions and the use of conduit companies' (paragraph 14) some references can also be found. The 2003 modifications in the OECD Model have included the conclusions of the 1986 report to a greater extent than earlier versions.
159. Verdoner 2003, p. 152.
160. Eynatten/De Haen/Hostyn 2003 p. 540, consider that an intermediary can only be denied from being considered a beneficial owner when he acts in the name of a third party, but not in cases where he acts in his own name.
161. Martín Jiménez 2004b, p. 678.

if the concept of beneficial ownership is interpreted in the manner discussed above, in the majority of cases no additional requirement actually arises for the application of Articles 10, 11 and 12 of the OECD Model.

In our opinion, when the person receiving the income acts on behalf of a third party, there is no obligation to apply the treaty, since the taxpayer who requests its application will not satisfy the requirements provided for this purpose in Articles 1, 3 and 4 of OECD Model (to be considered a person and to reside in one of the contracting states). Logically, the intermediary must be liable to tax on this income in the state of residence in order to be able to apply the treaty. In most cases, the state of residence would not levy tax on the income of this intermediary, because, for tax purposes its income allocation regulations will logically allocate this income to the taxpayer on whose behalf the intermediary is acting. Moreover, it is likely that under the source state's own regulations regarding the allocation of income, the taxpayer who must be liable to tax on this income is not an intermediary, but rather the person on whose behalf he is acting. Therefore, even when the corresponding treaty does not include this concept, it seems reasonable for the state to deny the application of the treaty to an agent because the state of residence did not levy tax on this income, as it will be allocated to its principle.

Regarding the interpretation of the beneficial ownership concept, the position seemingly taken by the U.S. tax authorities in its Technical Explanation to the 1996 and 2006 U.S. Models; is that the beneficial owner is the person residing in a contracting state to whom this state allocates the income for tax purposes.[162]

If the concept of beneficial ownership were to be interpreted in these terms, it is clear that no new requirement for the application of Articles 10, 11 and 12 of the OECD Model would be established. It would simply serve as a 'reminder' that the satisfaction of the general requirements that enable a taxpayer to apply the DTCs would have to be verified in each case. If this were the case, it appears to be clear that the corresponding provisions of the DTC would not be applied when the treaty shopping conduct were developed in one of the manners discussed in section III.C.1 of Chapter 1, i.e. using agents, fiduciaries and certain types of trusts. There would be no obligation to apply the treaty because the person receiving the income is not liable to tax thereon in the state of residence. Under this state's regulations on income allocation, it would be allocated to a different taxpayer, i.e. the principal, the trustee, etc.[163]

The modifications contained in the 2003 Commentaries on the OECD Model seemed to be aimed in this direction, although as shall be seen below, they also intend to extend the scope of this concept to other cases. Specifically, the Commentaries state that where an item of income is received by a resident of a contracting state acting in the capacity of agent or nominee it would be inconsistent with the object and purpose of the Convention for the source state to grant relief or exemption merely on account of the status of the immediate recipient of the income as a resident of the other contracting

---

162. Doernberg/Van Raad 1997, pp. 85 and 305.
163. Obviously if the principal also resides in the intermediary state, the tax treaty will have to be applied, although the general requirement must be satisfied, i.e. the beneficial owner must reside in the other contracting state.

state. The immediate recipient of the income in this situation qualifies as a resident but no potential double taxation arises as a consequence of that status since the recipient is not treated as the owner of the income for tax purposes in the state of residence.[164]

In summary, if the concept of beneficial ownership were interpreted in the above manner, the effectiveness of the concept within this scope would be shown to be very limited. This would also mean that the concept is clearly insufficient in preventing the application of treaty benefits to all types of treaty shopping conduct.

Experts in this field have pointed out that this interpretation of the concept would be excessively formal.[165] In essence, the objective resulting from the wording of this concept would not be achieved, in the respect that not only must the formal owner of the income be taken into account, but also the person who actually disposes of this income from an economic standpoint. In other words, an analysis of both the form and substance of the operation is required to determine whether the person who requests the treaty benefits is the beneficial owner of the income. To a certain extent, the aim of this approach is none other than creating an economic interpretation of this concept. If not properly understood, this approach may give rise to serious obstacles for the tax authorities of many states as their legal orders do not allow for an economic interpretation of the rules.[166] In principle, in these legal orders, the interpretation should be strictly legal. However, it should be taken into account that in certain cases there are principles and rules under these legal orders which allow for an interpretation which extends beyond a strictly legal and private interpretation.[167] These are precisely the GAARs and principles.

In our opinion, based on the fact that the meaning of beneficial ownership is broader than that discussed above, in cases where the beneficial ownership clause is to be applied, the circumstances that will be valued are very similar to those which would be taken into account when general anti-avoidance clauses are applied. In this respect, for example, in a stepping stone conduit, it would be necessary to judge whether the structure has been developed solely to achieve the application of a treaty. In order to determine whether there were economic grounds, other than those indicated earlier, behind these operations, it would be necessary to analyse the conditions under which each specific operation was performed. To the extent that the operation was proven to be artificial, it would be determined that the intermediary taxpayer is not the beneficial owner. In order to value the above, it would be necessary to bear in mind, among other

---

164. OECD 2003, pp. 26–29. In our opinion, for the determination of whether or not a taxpayer is the beneficial owner of income, it is indifferent whether the person is taxed on income in the state of residence. It is not relevant as to whether the income is actually taxed, but rather if the taxpayer is liable to tax on this income. Therefore, a certain person could be considered to be the beneficial owner of an item of income if the state of residence taxes this income, regardless of whether or not the taxpayer actually bears the effective tax. In this respect, although the income is subject to taxation, it is possible that it may not actually be taxed, because a regime which gives rise to this effect may be applicable, e.g. an exemption. In line with the above, it must be remembered that there is no general provision on tax liability in the OECD Model. *See* Commentaries on Article 1 of the 2003 OECD Model (paragraph 15).
165. IBFD 1981 and IFA 2000.
166. Eynatten/De Haen/Hostyn 2003 pp. 528–530.
167. Palao 1997, p. 242.

facts, the date on which the agreements between the different parties were entered into, the financial amount of each of the agreements, etc.

In our opinion, in view of the 1986 report in this regard, and particularly, based on the modification to the Commentaries on the 2003 OECD Model, this is the stand taken by the OECD.

The purpose of the modification of the Commentaries in 2003, is to show that the scope of the beneficial ownership concept is broader than that which could be deduced from a simple reading of the references contained in the Commentaries until that date. Its aim, is to broaden the concept of beneficial ownership to cover other cases in which, despite the fact that the owner of the income is a certain person, it is another person who materially acquires this income. Specifically, the 1986 report states that although the Commentaries 'mention the case a nominee or agent [the provisions] would, however, also apply to other cases where a person enters into contracts or takes over obligations under which he has a similar function to those of a nominee or an agent. Thus, a conduit company cannot normally be regarded as the beneficial owner if, through the formal owner of certain assets, it has very narrow powers which render it a mere fiduciary or an administrator acting on behalf of the interested parties (most likely the shareholders of the conduit company)'. Although a slight change may have been made, this is the paragraph that was included in the Commentaries on Articles 10, 11 and 12 of the 2003 OECD Model.

The above clearly demonstrates that the 2003 modifications aim to highlight that the concept of beneficial owner has a broader scope than that which was evidenced in the Commentaries on the 1977–2000 OECD Model. However, the application of this concept to other cases requires a case-by-case analysis of the circumstances to verify the conditions under which each taxpayer receives the income.

In our opinion, if this interpretation of the concept were to be accepted, the practical result would be very similar to that arising from the states' application of GAARs. In this respect, whether or not the conduct has a real business purpose would be considered. Accordingly, for example, when the structure is presented as a direct conduit, whether or not the intermediary company actually acquires the income obtained in the source state would be determined, or on the contrary, is a mere intermediary, as the control exercised by the company's shareholder requires that the person who received the income put it at the shareholder's disposal, through the distribution of profits or by other means of transferring the income accumulated by the shareholders.[168] It would also be necessary to consider whether or not the intermediary company was incorporated exclusively as a means for obtaining the dividends generated in another state. This would be determined on the basis of *inter alia*, the following factors: the fact that the company does not carry on any other business activity in addition to the mere holding of shares, that it has no other assets, that it has no employees, etc.

As in the case of the application of GAARs, this matter can only be resolved by examining the circumstances of each specific case. The same occurs with stepping

---

168. *See* Vogel 1997, p. 563 and Vega 2003, pp. 157–159.

stone conduits. Obviously, as previously discussed, the extent to which a narrow connection is evidenced between the operation and the interposed taxpayer, whereby, for example, he obtains a patent license solely to sublicense it to a third party, this taxpayer would not be considered as the beneficial owner. In essence, it would be concluded that the two contracts lack their own substance and that this is an operation where the intermediary company's only purpose is to gain access to the treaty benefits entered into with the source state by the state where the interposed taxpayer resides.[169]

If this second interpretation of the beneficial ownership concept were also accepted as possible, it would be necessary to bear in mind, that from a material standpoint, it does not add anything to the OECD Model. The treaties could achieve the same objectives using measures that already exist. Note that this interpretation uses parameters similar to those used by the states to apply GAARs. Accordingly, the results achieved would be similar to those where general anti-avoidance clauses or principles were applied.

As previously observed, it is possible to achieve this result without the inclusion of beneficial ownership clauses as clarified by the Commentaries on Article 1 of the 2003 OECD Model, GAARs may be applied within the scope of tax treaties.

Without a doubt, the conclusion reached following the analysis of the beneficial ownership concept is clearly discouraging, because, based on the meaning of the beneficial ownership concept, the OECD Model remains unchanged by including it in its text. Furthermore, this formulation of the beneficial ownership concept does not relieve the tax authorities of the difficulties involved in applying anti-avoidance rules, because the parameters used for this purpose would be similar.[170]

It is only possible to point out one advantage which might be provided by this concept from a procedural standpoint, a good example of which is the Spanish legal order.

In the case where the Spanish tax authorities wish to apply the domestic GAAR under the legislation in force, a special procedure which is not free from complexities is required.[171] In our opinion, when the aim is to apply the beneficial owner concept in the terms discussed above, the tax authorities could use the same parameters as when the GAARs are applied to deny a taxpayer from being considered as a beneficial owner, but without the need to formally apply the rule in this specific case, bearing in mind that the objective is to verify whether or not the person who receives the income is

---

169. In the case that the courts of the different states were faced with this question, these were the elements valued when applying the concept of beneficial ownership. *See* Vega 2003, pp. 160–162.
170. In fact, the 1986 OECD report highlights the above, stating 'in practice, however, it will usually be difficult for the source country to show that the conduit company is not the beneficial owner. The fact that its main function is to hold assets or rights is not itself sufficient to categorize it as a mere intermediary, although this may indicate that further examination is necessary. This examination will in any case be highly burdensome for the source country and not even the conduit company's country of residence may have the necessary information regarding the shareholders of the conduit company, the company's relationships with the shareholders or other interested parties or the decision-making process of the conduit company'. OECD 2003, pp. 30–31.
171. Palao 2004, pp. 116–117.

considered to be the beneficial owner. If this is the case, it would not be necessary to follow the special procedure required under Spanish law and it would be sufficient to follow the general procedural rules established for this purpose.

Notwithstanding the above, it is important to remember that defining the beneficial ownership concept is a very complex matter. The most appropriate solution for resolving this problem would be for the OECD Model to establish an exact definition of what this term means.

In this regard, the modifications introduced in the Commentaries on the 2014 OECD Model have not solved the problems highlighted in this section. The Commentaries have developed some aspects of the concept by including some new paragraphs in the Commentaries on Article 10 –some similar paragraphs have also been added to the Commentaries on Articles 11 and 12.[172]

First, paragraph 12.1 states that the term 'beneficial owner' was added to address potential difficulties arising from the use of the words 'paid to [...] a resident' in Article 10(1) of the OECD Model. Therefore, it was intended to be interpreted in this context and not to refer to any technical meaning that it could have had under a specific country's domestic law. Hence, according to the Commentaries, the term 'beneficial owner' is not used in a narrow technical sense (such as the meaning that it has under the trust law of many common law countries). This term should be understood in its context, particularly in relation to the words 'paid [...] to a resident', and in light of the object and purposes of the OECD Model, including avoiding double taxation and the prevention of fiscal evasion and avoidance.

Second, the Commentaries try to clarify when an entity should not be considered the beneficial owner when it is acting as a conduit. According to paragraph 12.4 of the Commentaries on Article 10 of the 2014 OECD Model, the direct recipient of a dividend will not be the beneficial owner when that recipient's right to use and enjoy the dividend is constrained by a contractual or legal obligation to pass the payment received on to another person. In this respect:

> such an obligation will normally derive from relevant legal documents but may also be found to exist on the basis of facts and circumstances showing that, in substance, the recipient clearly does not have the right to use and enjoy the dividend unconstrained by a contractual or legal obligation to pass on the payment received to another person.

Third, the Commentaries describe the relationship between the beneficial ownership concept and other anti-avoidance provisions:[173]

> The fact that the recipient of a dividend is considered to be the beneficial owner of that dividend does not mean, however, that the limitation of tax provided for by paragraph 2 must automatically be granted. This limitation of tax should not be granted in cases of abuse of this provision [...] [There] are many ways of addressing a conduit company and, more generally, treaty shopping situations. These include specific anti-abuse provisions in treaties, general anti-abuse rules and substance-over-form or economic substance approaches. Whilst the concept

---

172. Zuk 2013, pp. 320–321.
173. Commentaries on Article 10 of the 2014 OECD Model (paragraph 12.5).

of 'beneficial owner' deals with some forms of tax avoidance (i.e. those involving the interposition of a recipient who is obliged to pass on the dividend to someone else), it does not deal with other cases of treaty shopping and must not, therefore, be considered as restricting in any way the application of other approaches to addressing such cases.

As can be seen, the latest development of the beneficial ownership concept in the Commentaries has not really clarified its exact meaning. In this regard, the trend is to categorize this term as a specific anti-abuse which uses similar standards as GAARs, but that is only applicable in the context of dividends, interest and royalties.[174]

Finally, with respect to the relationship between the concept of beneficial ownership and the LOBs, it is only important to note that the concept of beneficial ownership, interpreted in a broad sense, gives rise to the same drawbacks that the LOB clauses aim to resolve in respect of the GAARs, i.e. the problems relating to the application of these rules. However, it should be pointed out that the concept of beneficial ownership and the LOB clauses are not necessarily incompatible, although as shall be observed, it is unlikely that a taxpayer who complies with the LOB clauses will not be considered as a beneficial owner, since compliance with one of these clauses guarantees that the aforementioned taxpayer has, either a sufficient nexus to the state of residence or a real purpose to obtain the income generated in the source state from the state of residence.

However, it is true that this may not always be the case, especially when the taxpayer gains access to the treaty benefits by means of either the stock exchange or the ownership and base erosion clauses. In these cases, compliance with these clauses enables the taxpayer to obtain all the treaty benefits, without considering, as with the activity clause, under which conditions each item of income generated in the source state is received. Since this is the case, the beneficial ownership clause complements LOB clauses, and it is possible to conclude, in a specific transaction, that the person who qualifies under the stock exchange or ownership and base erosion LOB clauses is not the beneficial owner.

II.B.3 Limitation on Benefits Clauses

In this section, the general wording of the LOB clauses which have been included in tax treaties will be detailed. The legal regime of each of these clauses will be analysed in Chapter 3. This analysis will be based on the U.S. Models (1996, 2006 and 2016), the OECD Model, the LOB rules proposed in Action 6 of the BEPS project and the tax treaties concluded between the U.S. and EU Member States.

First, it should be pointed out that the current body of the OECD Model (2014) does not establish specific and definitive methods for preventing the abuse or improper use of the treaty in a strict sense (treaty shopping). However, a series of clauses (the look-through approach, exclusion, subject-to-tax approach, channel approach and a series of moderate clauses) were included in the Commentaries on Article 1 of the 1992

---

174. Armelin 2016, p. 516.

OECD Model to prevent the abusive use of the treaties, and in particular, treaty shopping structures.[175] These are the clauses proposed by the 1986 OECD report on conduit companies.

The 2003 OECD Model maintained these clauses in the Commentaries on Article 1 (paragraphs 13-19).[176] Paragraph 20 of the Commentaries on Article 1 of the 2003 OECD Model also added a group of clauses which are similar to the previous ones but represent a different approach for dealing with the problem of treaty shopping. This group of clauses aims at reinforcing the personal scope of tax treaties by materially increasing the requirements that must be met in order to be able to claim treaty benefits. As shall be observed, where the clauses of paragraph 20 are included in a treaty, being a person and being considered a resident in one of the contracting states shall not be sufficient to gain access to a DTC.

Bearing in mind the above, it can be asserted that the Commentaries on Article 1 of the 2003-2014 OECD Model provide two different approaches in this regard.

The first approach is contained in the clauses included in paragraphs 13-19 of the Commentaries on Article 1 of the 2003 OECD Model (isolated approach). The treaties where any of these clauses are introduced, do not modify the subjective scope of the DTCs as formulated in versions prior to the 2003 OECD Model and in the body of text of the latest versions. With these treaties, it is sufficient to be considered a person and a resident in order to be able to request the application of a treaty, notwithstanding the inclusion of any of the indicated clauses in the treaty. The application of these rules can cause the affected taxpayer, i.e. the person who makes assumptions of fact in relation to these rules, to be deprived of the treaty benefits.

The new approach, introduced in 2003 by the clauses proposed in paragraph 20 of the Commentaries on Article 1 of the OECD Model, materially reshapes the subjective scope of the treaties in which they are included (comprehensive approach). These treaty benefits will only apply to persons, who in addition to being residents, comply with one of the clauses established. This comprehensive approach provided for in the Commentaries on Article 1 of the OECD Model is similar to the U.S. approach, which consists of introducing a complete set of LOB clauses into the tax treaties. However, until 2015, due to the BEPS project, there was an appreciable difference between both Models. The LOB clauses were only mentioned in the Commentaries on Article 1 of the OECD Model and, therefore, these provisions were not a so-called must-have-as-is provision in the same way as LOB clauses and other provisions of the U.S. Model are, such as, the U.S. branch tax rules and the Foreign Investment in Real Property Tax Act of 1980 (FIRPTA).[177]

It will be mentioned later on, the OECD approach has changed in 2015 due to the BEPS project. The final report on Action 6 of the BEPS project proposes to include, in the body of the OECD Model, an LOB rule similar to the one provided for in the U.S.

---

175. Vid. paragraphs 13-21 of the Commentaries on Article 1 of the 1992-2000 OECD Model.
176. However, as indicated in the following section, the exclusion clause (former paragraphs 15 and 16 of the 1992-2000 OECD Model) is moved to paragraph 21 and the subsequent paragraphs of the Commentaries on Article 1 of the 2003 OECD Model. This change in location is caused by the different nature of the exclusion cause. *See* section IV.B.1 of Chapter 3.
177. Harrington 2015.

Model. Additionally, it should be emphasized that the 2016 BEPS Multilateral Instrument contains a simplified version of the LOB rule proposed in Action 6 of the BEPS project. This provision deviates in some respects from the (detailed) LOB rule provided for in Action 6 of the BEPS project and the U.S. Models. In Chapter 3, some references will be made towards the simplified version of the LOB rule provided for in the 2016 BEPS Multilateral Instrument.

Moreover, Article 22 of the 1996, 2006 and 2016 U.S. Models contains a complete set of LOB clauses. Each version of the U.S. Model (1977, 1981, 1996, 2006 and 2016) includes clauses that have been progressively more developed.[178]

The clauses contained in the 1996, 2006 and 2016 U.S. Models are substantially the same as the proposals in the Commentaries on the OECD Model and in particular, those introduced in the Commentaries on Article 1 of the 2003 OECD Model (paragraph 20). The clauses of the U.S. Models are those which have actually been used in practice. Commencing with the 1989 DTC between the U.S. and Germany, all DTCs entered into by the U.S. include a uniform group of these provisions.[179]

As can be observed, in principle, the positions taken by both the OECD and the U.S. in this regard are similar, especially commencing in 2003, and following the inclusion of a complete group of LOB clauses similar to those provided in Article 22 of the U.S. Models in paragraph 20 of the Commentaries on Article 1 of the 2003-2014 OECD Model. Prior to 2003, the Commentaries only proposed the adoption of isolated LOB clauses. The 2003 version of the Commentaries does not eliminate this first alternative. However, in conjunction with the above, it provides for the possibility of introducing a part of the LOB clauses similar to those included in the U.S. Model. Despite the fact that the OECD's stance seems to be the same as that of the U.S., we believe that there is a very significant difference, at least until the final documents of the BEPS project, which were released in October 2015. As opposed to the U.S. Model, these clauses are not included in the body of the OECD Model but rather in the Commentaries. Without doubt, this reflects a difference in attitudes with respect to the inclusion of these clauses when negotiating treaties. Specifically, the Commentaries on Article 1 of the 2003-2014 OECD Model establish a series of criteria for determining whether to include these types of clauses in the DTCs.[180]

---

178. In regard to the evolution of the U.S. Model, see Burke 1983, pp. 219-330, Doernberg/Van Raad 1997, pp. 168-185, Berman/Hynes 2000, pp. 697-710 and Kerekes 2016. The DTCs entered into by the U.S. have included similar clauses since the 1945 DTC concluded by the U.S. and the U.K. However, a uniform group of clauses such as those included in the DTCs entered into with EU Member Sate's were not first introduced until the 1989 DTC concluded between the U.S. and Germany.
179. Berman/Hynes 2000, p. 692.
180. Paragraph 12 of the Commentaries on Article 1 of the 2003-2014 OECD Model states the following: (a) the fact that these provisions are not mutually exclusive and that various provisions may be needed in order to address different concerns; (b) *the degree to which tax advantages may actually be obtained by a particular avoidance strategy*; (c) *the legal context in both Contracting States* and, in particular, the extent to which domestic law already provides an appropriate response to this avoidance strategy; (d) *the extent to which bona fide economic activities might be unintentionally disqualified by such provisions*. The sentences in italics are also found in the Commentaries on Article 1 of the 1992-2000 OECD Model.

Chapter 2: Scope of Double Taxation Conventions and Limitation

It should be noted that in both the isolated and the comprehensive approach cases, the basic structure of these clauses is similar in the U.S. Model and in the Commentaries on the OECD Model. This does not mean that there are not some differing aspects due to the distinguishing features of each state and the negotiation process. Even so, it can be sustained that there is a significant degree of uniformity in this regard.

The objective of these clauses, is to limit access to the regime of the DTCs in order to prevent their application in the case of treaty shopping conduct. In accordance with the LOB clauses, tax treaties should only be applied, either in the case where the taxpayer has obtained income from the state of residence for a real business purpose, or where the taxpayer has sufficient nexus to the state of residence.[181]

These are the two basic ideas on which the LOB clauses are founded. The rules make no assumption relating to the actual taxation of the income in the state of residence.[182] Although this criterion may appear in the LOB clauses at times, it is not decisive for the application of the treaty, as long as one of the two previously mentioned conditions are met.

There is no intention to either introduce a general clause of effective liability by means of these rules, or to condition the application of the treaty to the fact that the income obtained at source is taxed, to a certain extent, in the state of residence.[183] This does not mean that tax treaties may not expressly exclude, from their scope of application, those taxpayers that enjoy a 'preferential tax regime' in the state of residence that favours the development of treaty shopping structures. This is called the 'exclusion method' in the Commentaries on the OECD Model. Taxpayers or income enjoying certain regimes will not have the right to treaty protection. The exclusion clause or method will be analysed in the following chapter. At present, it is sufficient to point out that the main problem that arises in this regard entails identifying the 'privileged regimes' which should not be protected under a tax treaty.[184]

However, it should be highlighted that the LOB rule provided for in the 2016 U.S. Model deviates slightly from the rationale of the previous U.S. Models, since some of its tests take into account certain aspects referring to the taxpayer's effective liability in the state of residence. This deviation is due to the inclusion of the so-called special tax regimes clause in the 2016 U.S. Model. This provision denies certain treaty benefits at the source when the corresponding income enjoys a preferential tax regime in the state of residence. This provision will be analysed in Chapter 3 of this study, along with its effects on the LOB rule provided for in the 2016 U.S. Model. The LOB rule provided for in Action 6 of the BEPS project does not contain this provision, as it mainly follows the LOB clauses of the 1996 and 2016 U.S. Models.

Notwithstanding the above, the LOB clauses do not exonerate the taxpayer from meeting the requirement stipulated in Article 1 of the OECD Model, i.e. the taxpayer

---

181. ALI 1992, p. 150 and Doernberg/Van Raad 1997, p. 172.
182. Terr 1989, p. 524.
183. The 1977 and June 1981 versions of the U.S. Model contain provisions in this regard. These provisions have not been included in later versions due to the criticism received and the problems relating to their application. Burke 1983, p. 292.
184. ALI 1992, p. 153.

must be liable to tax on worldwide income in one of the contracting states. Accordingly, first it is necessary to determine if the taxpayer is considered a resident, and subsequently to verify if he meets the requirements of one of the LOB clauses.[185]

In this regard, the LOB clauses do not formally modify the subjective scope of the tax treaties. In spite of these clauses, tax treaties continue to be applied to persons residing in one of the contracting states.[186] Nevertheless, these rules materially affect the personal scope of the treaties. Where such provisions are not made, when only the requirement of residence has been fulfilled, the taxpayer has the right to the full application of a treaty. The LOB clauses greatly limit the part of the treaty applicable to the taxpayer merely due to the fact that he is a resident in one of the contracting states.

From a systematic standpoint, these rules should be included in Article 1 of the treaty, as this is the Article which regulates the personal scope of tax treaties. The 2003–2014 OECD Model implicitly includes these rules in this Article considering that the clauses proposed by the OECD are found in the Commentaries on Article 1. Additionally, the LOB clauses consider those residents who fulfil one of these clauses to be qualified residents. In this respect, it has been pointed out that the effect of these clauses is to 'qualify' the concept of residence provided in the treaties.[187]

In practice, this system has not been followed. In some cases, LOB clauses have been included in the Article prior to the measures for eliminating double taxation in the state of residence, in the protocol to the treaty or in an Article corresponding to the section in which the taxation of the various types of income are regulated.[188] As shall be observed below, this lack of a systematic approach gives rise to difficulties in identifying the rules included under its scope of application. In this respect, it should be highlighted that the BEPS project does not propose to include the LOB rule in Article 1 of the OECD Model. Action 6 of the BEPS project only contains the proposal to introduce a new Article in the Model, but it does not mention which number it will have.

LOB clauses mainly affect the rules of the treaty which exclude or limit taxation in the source state. These provisions will only be applied if the taxpayer complies with one of the LOB clauses provided in the treaty. The scope of the treaty encompassed by

---

185. Jacob 1991, p. 28-12 and Schinabeck 1996, p. 26.
186. Likewise, the requirement of being a beneficial owner is a question which prevails over the fulfilment of the limitation on benefits clauses. Accordingly, prior to examining these rules, it is important to verify that the taxpayer is a resident in accordance with the treaty, and that he is a beneficial owner of the income. Jacob 1991, p. 14 and Berman/Hynes 2000, p. 694.
187. ALI 1992, p. 150.
188. They are included at the end of the chapter which regulates the various types of income in the DTCs with Denmark, Estonia, Latvia, Lithuania, Luxembourg, Ireland, Slovenia and the U.K. In contrast, they are regulated in this chapter, but not at the end, in the DTCs with Finland, Portugal, Spain and Sweden. Lastly, they are regulated following the two methods for eliminating double taxation in the state of residence in the DTCs with the Czech Republic, France, Germany, the Slovak Republic and The Netherlands and in the Protocol in the DTC with Italy. Notwithstanding the above, in general, the Protocols of these DTCs usually add a reference to these types of clauses. *See* section I of Chapter 3.

these rules is definitely relevant. It is the most extensive part of the body of the treaty and the part which most affects international taxation.[189]

As observed in the first chapter, states do not frequently unilaterally waive the right to tax non-residents. On the contrary, most states have unilaterally established rules to eliminate the double taxation suffered by resident taxpayers. Although the treaties provide for measures to eliminate double taxation in the state of residence, the effects of the DTCs are most greatly perceived in relation to the limits on the taxation of non-residents. This is precisely the part of the treaty which is not applied when one of the LOB clauses is not complied with.

In this regard, the type of treaty provisions affected by the LOB clauses has experienced a change.

At first, the scope of the clauses extension was limited to income of a passive nature, i.e. mainly dividends, interest, and royalties.[190] These types of income were included due to their high degree of mobility, or at least due to the mobility of the investments giving rise to this income, which also explains why this income is normally involved in treaty shopping structures.

Subsequently, the tax treaties that included these provisions extended their scope of application to all of the rules which eliminate or reduce taxation in the source state. As evidenced by Article 22 of the U.S. Models, paragraph 20 of the Commentaries on Article 1 of the 2003–2014 OECD Model and Action 6 of the BEPS project, the scope of these rules affect the whole of the tax treaty provisions. However, if the provisions of the treaties entered into by the U.S. and EU Member States are analysed, it can be observed that the extent to which an LOB clause is applied is not the same for all types of income. The main precautions refer mainly to dividends, interest and royalties.

In summary, the main objective of these rules is the limitations on non-resident taxation. It is not clear if the effectiveness thereof affects other provisions of the treaty, since this depends to a large extent on the wording in each case.

In the different versions of the U.S. Model, the 2003–2014 OECD Model and Action 6 of the BEPS project, the LOB clauses include all the provisions established in the treaty which attribute a 'benefit' due to residence in one of the contracting states. 'Benefits' accorded due to residence include limitations on taxation at source, rules to eliminate double taxation in the state of residence and the prohibition of discrimination established in Article 24 of the Model, but only the aspects thereof which relate to taxpayers residing in a contracting state.[191]

Based on this delimitation, the aspects of the prohibition of discrimination which do not refer to residents, i.e. the mutual agreement procedure (Article 25 of both the U.S. Model and the OECD Model) and Article 27 of the U.S. Model and Article 28 of the 2003–2014 OECD Model (members of diplomatic missions and consular posts) would

---

189. In the OECD Model, it is included in Chapter III 'Taxation of income' (Articles 6–21) and in the 1996, 2006 and 2016 U.S. Models (Articles 6–21).
190. Rosenbloom 1983, p. 813. A good example of this is that in the 1977 U.S. Model the provision containing rules in this regard (Article 16) is only applied to dividends, interest and royalties.
191. This is the interpretation sustained by the IRS in the Technical Explanations to the 1996 and to the 2016 U.S. Models. Regarding the LOB clauses of the BEPS project, see OECD 2015a, p. 24.

not be included. The exchange of information procedure (Article 26 of both the U.S. and OECD Models) should also be excluded as it is more of a burden than a benefit to the taxpayer.[192]

Due to the ambiguity in this regard, each treaty will have to be examined to determine the exact scope of the rules affected by the LOB clauses.[193] In any case, the exclusion of the provisions that limit taxation in the source state is common to all of the treaties.

It is our understanding that the above should be interpreted in a restrictive sense. Treaties do not only limit taxation in the source state and establish measures to eliminate double taxation in the state of residence. Tax treaties also provide rules to resolve cases of double residence (tie-break rules) and uniform rules on the economic source of income (source rules). LOB clauses do not affect these aspects, despite the fact that in part, they are also found in the treaty Articles that establish limits on non-resident taxation. As shall be observed, prior to their application, it is essential to determine in which state the taxpayer resides and where the income was generated. Accordingly, if these two aspects are assumptions on which the application of the treaty is based, it would make no sense for the tie break and source rules to be excluded.[194]

The second relevant aspect concerns those taxpayers to which the limitation on benefit clauses are applied.

Generally, LOB clauses are only applied to taxpayers other than individuals. As long as individuals reside in one of the contracting states, they have the right to fully access the benefits provided therein. This is because individuals have few possibilities of directly developing treaty shopping structures. The 'mobility of the taxpayer' is fundamental for the use of such structures. Entities other than individuals, and in particular companies, can easily obtain residence in the state from where they wish to obtain income. This is not the case for individuals.

---

192. Vogel/Shannon/Doernberg/Van Raad 1989, Article 16, pp. 16–23. It should also be taken into account that the rules not included have no potential whatsoever in treaty shopping structures. It would be unlikely for a taxpayer to design a structure of this type simply to benefit from the rules relating to the exchange of information or the mutual agreement procedure.
193. The measures established in the DTC in the state of residence should also be excluded. However, this is not so clear in the light of certain treaties, because from their wording it appears that these measures are not within the subjective scope of the application of the LOB clauses. In our opinion, it is logical that these provisions are not applied if the affected taxpayer does not comply with any of the LOBs. In the case that the source state does not apply the DTC as the taxpayer does not comply with any clause, it would not be justified for the state of residence to have the obligation of applying it. Note that if the state of residence were to have this obligation, it would fully bear the cost generated by the elimination of double taxation. Additionally, the state of residence would not have limited the tax it may levy on the non-resident under its law, as it did not apply the treaty. However, in practice, the fact that the LOBs also include the measures established in the DTC in the state of residence that may not have any material effect due to the fact that the state legislation generally establishes unilateral measures in this regard. ALI 1992, p. 181.
194. The wording of the detailed LOB clauses of the BEPS project follows this approach: 'shall not be entitled to a benefit that would otherwise be accorded by this Convention (other than a benefit under paragraph 3 of Article 4, paragraph 2 of Article 9 or Article 25), unless such resident is a "qualified person", as defined in paragraph 2, at the time that the benefit would be accorded'. OECD 2015a, p. 23.

The criteria based on which the residence of an individual in a state is determined, always require a factual element which attaches the taxpayer to the territory (habitual abode, permanent home, centre of vital interests, etc.). Change in residence to another state for the sole purpose of obtaining income therein can be very costly. Therefore, such a change would not give rise to one of the assumptions on which all tax planning operations are based.

In addition, for a treaty shopping structure to be efficient, it is essential that the income is not effectively taxed in the intermediary state, or, at least, that the tax margin is greatly reduced. The tax regimes which facilitate the above generally relate to the taxation of entities rather than the taxation of individuals.[195] Even so, although within a lesser scope, individuals may take part in certain structures.[196]

Some of these cases may be resolved by applying the concept of beneficial ownership. These would be cases when the individual acts as an agent, fiduciary or trustee (in any trust other than an accumulating trust). On the other hand, additional problems arise in stepping stone structures. There is nothing that prevents these structures from being developed through an individual. However, it is rare for an individual to act as an intermediary in these types of structures.[197] The use of entities is not only logical from a tax standpoint but also from that of corporate law. One of the main characteristics of corporations is the participant's limited liability for corporate debt. This characteristic does not concur in the case of an individual. Therefore, in relation to the prevention of the adverse consequences for the failure of such a structure, it is unlikely that an individual would be used as an intermediary, as he would he held liable for both the tax and the non-tax related negative consequences of the operation with his own equity.[198]

Notwithstanding the above arguments, the individuals' right to apply a treaty where he complies exclusively with the requirement of residence is supported by the grounds for the LOB clauses. As discussed in the beginning of this section, the purpose of these rules is to assure that tax treaties are only applied either in the case where income is obtained in the state of residence for a real business purpose or that the taxpayer has a sufficient nexus to the state of residence. In this respect, the concept of residence is applicable to individuals in accordance with one of the purposes of these clauses.

---

195. Van Weeghel 1998, p. 232.
196. Cases in which an individual transfers his residence to a low tax state are not taken into consideration here. This would give rise to the second step of the structure. The income obtained at source would bear a reduced tax. However, it is important to bear in mind that the treaty network of low tax states is very small, meaning that the main objective of the operation, i.e. to reduce taxation at source, would not be achieved. Additionally, as observed in the first section of this study (section III.B), the majority of states have adopted rules to prevent individuals from transferring their residence to low tax territories. Since this is the case, the second step of the operation would not be reached given that the taxpayer would continue to be taxed as a resident in the source state.
197. Van Weeghel 1998, p. 232.
198. Imagine a stepping stone structure with loans. For a given reason, the individual could be declared bankrupt, in which case he would not be able to fulfil the obligations relating to the loan granted to him.

The criteria established in domestic legislation based on when an individual is considered a resident for tax purposes guarantees that he has a sufficient nexus of a factual nature to the state's territory.[199] As discussed earlier, the same does not occur in the case of entities.[200] From this standpoint, LOB clauses are not applied to individuals because they do not add anything to the concept of residence, which already achieves the purpose underlying this type of rule.

The third aspect of the clauses that must be analysed is their content and the manner in which they function.

LOB clauses contain a series of 'objective tests', the requirements of which must be satisfied in order for the right to apply a treaty to be conferred. It is only necessary to comply with one of these clauses for the provisions of the treaty covered thereby to be applicable.

Although each of the clauses are very different, all of them lead back to the two parameters referred to above, i.e. either income is obtained from the state of residence for a real business purpose, or the taxpayer has a sufficient nexus to the state of residence. One author also pointed out that these rules are characterized by the fact that they evidence a presumptive judgment among the reasons for their creation.[201] The rule assumes that taxpayers who comply with one of the clauses are not making use of a treaty shopping structure.

The two approaches are not in contrast. As observed upon analysing the application of the GAARs, all treaty shopping structures are not considered unlawful but rather only those where no real business purpose is evidenced or where the taxpayer does not have a sufficient nexus to the state of residence. When either of the abovementioned requirements are satisfied, the structure is considered to be 'lawful'. Accordingly, the two approaches lead to the same result. However, we consider it preferable to use the first of these, as fundamentally, the underlying intention thereof is to reinforce the personal scope of the treaties by incorporating the two aforementioned parameters into the definition of the concept of residence.

The wording of the clauses is not expressed in terms as abstract as the parameters on which they are based. Each clause generally defines the requirements which must be satisfied by the taxpayer more precisely.

The main clauses are as follows: the stock exchange clause, the ownership and base erosion clause, the activity clause and the general good faith clause.[202]

The entities listed on secondary markets under the conditions provided for in the treaty satisfy the requirements of the stock exchange clause. In this case, the rule does

---

199. Philips/Collins 1985, pp. 154–156.
200. *See* section II.B.1.B of this chapter.
201. As indicated in the Technical Explanation to the 1996 U.S. Model: 'The assumption underlying each of these tests is that a taxpayer that satisfies the requirements of any of the tests probably has a real business purpose for the structure it has adopted, or has a sufficiently strong nexus to the other Contracting State […] to warrant benefits even in the absence of a business connection, and that this business purpose or connection outweighs any purpose to obtain the benefits of the Treaty' (paragraph 283). Similarly, the 2006 U.S. Model Technical Explanation establishes that 'Article 22 effectively determines whether an entity has a sufficient nexus to the Contracting State to be treated as a resident for treaty purposes'.
202. Berman/Hynes 2000, p. 692.

not take into account who the shareholders are and where they reside as a basis on which to determine whether the treaty is applicable. Although this clause will be studied in depth in Chapter 3, it is important to point out that logically this rule makes no mention of the shareholders. The capital of publicly traded companies tends to be extensively divided, and accordingly from an economic standpoint, it is not appropriate to equate the interests of the company with those of the shareholders. It may also be excessively burdensome to identify the residence of each of the shareholders, especially in publicly traded companies whose capital is extensively divided and in view of the fact that there are ongoing changes to the shares, as a result of trading on the secondary market where they are listed.

The fact that a company is listed on the stock exchange reflects a sufficient degree of nexus to the territory. In addition, due to the extensive stock market requirements which must be met under corporate law in order to be listed on the stock exchange, it is improbable that a publicly traded company would be used for treaty shopping structures. It is not likely that the use of this means to channel such an operation would be efficient from an economic position in view of the pre-operating expenses involved. However, this depends, to a large extent, on the corporate legislation of each state. Legislation that is very flexible in this regard would invalidate the 'presumption' on which this rule is based.[203] Consequently, keeping this premise in mind, some treaties restrict access by this means through the inclusion of additional requirements.

In these terms, the stock exchange clause may appear to be simple. However, the wording of these clauses in the treaties is extremely complex for several reasons. Merely being listed on a secondary market is not sufficient. It is also necessary for the shares to reach a minimum trading volume during each tax period. In some cases, the treaty is very strict with respect to the required trading volume, and in others, it gives rise to uncertainty because this concept is defined using a vague legal concept (substantial and regular trade). Therefore, it is not sufficient for the entity to be formally listed. The listing should be material, an aspect which is evidenced by the actual trade of the shares.

Lastly, in relation to this clause, it should be noted that the U.S. Model and the Action 6 LOB clauses of the BEPS project make it more flexible by also permitting access to companies where entities that comply with this clause have a shareholding (indirect access). In simpler terms, the subsidiaries of the listed companies also have a right to apply the treaty.[204] However, the 2016 U.S. Model has tightened this aspect of the clause by including a base erosion test similar to the one that exists in the ownership and base erosion clause.

The second main clause is that of ownership and base erosion. This clause is aimed at entities not listed on the stock exchange and companies which are listed but do not comply with the stock exchange clause. The main aspect it takes into consideration is the residence of the entity's shareholders. When a certain percentage of the company's capital (normally 50 percent) is held by persons residing in one of the

---

203. Bennett 1991, p. 6.
204. *See* section II.E.3.d, Chapter 3.

contracting states, a sufficient nexus is considered to exist. However, this percentage will not include all residents of any of the contracting states, but rather those considered to be qualified residents.

The concept of 'qualified resident' is not expressly defined in all of the treaties. However, it can be deduced from all of these, and also from the 2006 and 2016 U.S. Models, that the concept includes exclusively individuals, contracting states and the political subdivisions thereof, entities which comply with the stock exchange clause, entities which comply with the ownership and base erosion clause and the other taxpayers expressly indicated in each treaty.[205] The latter case is always of a residual nature and it will be necessary to adhere to that established in each treaty. This group usually includes non-profit organizations and pension funds which satisfy certain requirements.

The concept of qualified resident reinforces the underlying objective of this rule, which is only to apply the treaty where there is sufficient nexus to the contracting states. An effective nexus specifically refers to the requirement that the company shareholders also reside in a state party to the treaty. The main effect of the clause is to exclude those entities whose shareholders are residents in third states. A third state should be understood to be any state which is not a party to the treaty. This clause confers a restricted treatment on companies mainly owned by residents of third states. Such a situation could be admissible from the standpoint of international law. However, there are more doubts in the case of EU Law. This discriminatory treatment may not be justified when the shareholders reside in EU Member States. The compatibility of this concept with EU Law will be addressed in Chapter 4. For the time being, it is sufficient to note that some tax treaties have taken 'the EU factor' into account and have granted entrance to residents of EU Member States in this clause.[206] In this regard, it is worth mentioning that the 2016 U.S. Model and the LOB clause of the BEPS project have loosened this clause by taking into account any resident in any third country as long as it can be qualified as an 'equivalent beneficiary'.[207]

The second part of this clause contains the 'base erosion test'. The ownership requirement does not sufficiently guarantee that no unlawful treaty shopping structures will be developed. Stepping stone structures would have access to the tax treaty benefits by these means if the rule was limited to requiring ownership. Consequently, the clause stipulates that the entity must not allocate more than a certain percentage of the income it has received during the fiscal year to pay beneficiaries that are not considered to be qualified residents. For the purposes of this calculation, only payments of a deductible nature are taken into account. In fact, this structure is only produced where the taxpayer's tax base is effectively eroded.

This second requirement gives rise to the same problems as the first, i.e. the treaty is only applied if a substantial portion of the payments made by the company are

---

205. Rivier 1998, pp. 306–307. The activity clause does not grant the condition of qualified resident.
206. They also provide entrance to the shareholders and other resident taxpayers in member states of the North American Free Trade Agreement (NAFTA) and the European Economic Area (EEA).
207. *See* section III.C of Chapter 3.

to qualified residents. However, as in the case of the ownership clause, the residents of certain third states are taken into account in some treaties and in the 2016 U.S. Model and the Action 6 LOB rule of the BEPS project.

Third is the activity clause. This clause is aimed at taxpayers who do not comply with either of the two previous clauses. The basis of this clause is the existence of a real business purpose which justifies obtaining income from the state of residence.[208] However, the status of qualified resident is not conferred upon those who comply with this clause.

Entities that perform a business activity in the state of residence will have the right to apply the treaty as long as the income obtained at source is directly or incidentally related to the aforementioned activity.

The essential difference between this and the previous clauses are the consequences of complying with the requirements thereof. If the stock exchange clause is complied with, the taxpayer has a right to the full application of the treaty. On the contrary, this provision is applied separately for each item of income obtained. In each case, it will be necessary to verify whether the taxpayer performs a business activity in the state of residence and whether the income obtained at source is either directly or incidentally related to this activity. In the case of the affirmative, the taxpayer will only be enabled to gain access to the treaty in respect of certain income. Therefore, under the regime of this clause, a case may occur where a treaty is only applied to a portion of the income obtained by a company in the source state.

This method is so complex due to the underlying grounds of this rule. It is necessary to verify whether there is a real business purpose for obtaining income. If there is no direct or incidental connection between the income and the business activity, no reason is considered to exist under this rule. Despite the above, it cannot be denied that this clause makes obtaining income through the treaty excessively burdensome, given that the fulfilment of this clause must be verified each time income is obtained.

Lastly is the bona fide clause.[209] Purely speaking, this is not really a limitation on benefits clause. This clause will only be relied on when none of the other clauses are complied with. Such cases will not be rare as the wording of these rules significantly reduces the range of taxpayers who enjoy the protection of the treaty. Where none of the three previous clauses are complied with (stock exchange clause, ownership and base erosion clause and activity clause), the taxpayer must request the application of the treaty by means of the bona fide clause from the source state's tax authorities. If the request is approved, the treaty will be applied. Note that treaty benefits are applied by virtue of the authorities' decision and not the direct application thereof. In order to make this decision the authorities will assure that 'the establishment, acquisition, and maintenance of such person and the conduct of its operations did not have as one of its principal purposes the obtaining of benefits under the Convention'. In summary, the

---

208. Berman/Hynes 2000, p. 695.
209. In this case, we have given this provision a name similar to the one used in the Commentaries on Article 1 of the 2003–2014 OECD Model (paragraph 19.a). However, it should be noted that this clause is also known by the name of the discretionary provision.

taxpayer has to prove that he is not in the state of residence solely to benefit from the treaty by evidencing that there is a real business purpose for his presence.

As can be verified, in view of the wording of these clauses, little margin is left for the development of artificial treaty shopping structures. This is a result of the significant reduction in the subjective scope of the DTCs. The consequences of not complying with either the stock exchange or the ownership and base erosion clause are quite burdensome for the taxpayer. The taxpayer will either have to prove that he complies with the activity clause for each amount of income, or demonstrate that he is acting in good faith in the terms discussed above (bona fide clause). It is likely that among the taxpayers who are excluded from these clauses, there are many whose situation is not at all reprehensible. However, the burden of proof lies with them and not the tax authorities to prove that they actually have a sufficient business purpose that justifies their presence in the state of residence.

In this respect, from a material point of view, the main effect of the clause includes placing the burden of proof on the taxpayer. This effect will be better understood if the two possible forms that can be used to formulate the LOB clauses are briefly examined.

In the first form, the application of the treaty is only subordinate to the concept of residence. The taxpayer must be liable to tax on worldwide income in one of the contracting states. The treaty will include a general clause which authorizes the tax authorities to deny its application where the presence in the state of residence is for merely tax-related reasons and there is no real business purpose. However, the taxpayers who comply with any of the clauses discussed above (stock exchange, ownership and base erosion and activity clauses) will not be affected by the general clause. The limitation on benefit clauses should act as 'safe harbour rules'. Taxpayers on the correct side of the line will be safe and will not have to fear a qualification of tax avoidance.[210]

It should be noted that this formulation of the LOB clauses does not deprive the concept of residence from carrying out its function in the treaties drawn up in accordance with the OECD Model. The right to apply the treaty will be conferred upon taxpayers with residence in one of the contracting states. LOB clauses only prevent taxpayers from suffering the consequences of the application of the general anti-avoidance clause provided in the treaty, but they do not directly open the door to the treaty benefits.

The 'burden of proof' lies with the tax authorities for the denial of the treaty's regime. The taxpayer is only required to prove that he resides in one of the contracting states, which as has been observed, is relatively simple. On the contrary, the tax authorities have the difficult task of applying GAARs in order to deny treaty benefits.

The second alternative is the final approach used by the treaties being studied, the 1996, 2006 and 2016 U.S. Models and Action 6 of the BEPS project.[211] The taxpayer only has the right to the treaty regime if he resides in one of the contracting states and

---

210. Palao 1996, p. 9.
211. This is also found in paragraph 20 of the Commentaries on Article 1 of the 2003–2014 OECD Model.

also complies with one of the clauses provided for in the treaty. In this case, the regime of the treaty is directly accessed by complying with one of the clauses set forth in the treaty, notwithstanding the fact that the taxpayer must also satisfy the requirement of residence. Accordingly, in this case the LOB clauses are not actually safe harbour rules, as they are an assumption on which the application of the treaty is based and do not prevent the denial of the treaty's application.

Given the restrictive wording of the main clauses, it is not uncommon for many taxpayers to be excluded from the subjective scope of the treaty, even though their presence in the state of residence is not at all reproachable.[212] These taxpayers are required to request the application of the treaty through the bona fide clause. As opposed to the case of the first alternative, the burden of proof lies with the taxpayer and not the tax authorities, although in this case, as is logical, this burden is required to access the treaty regime rather than to deny its application. The taxpayer must prove that the grounds for his presence in the state of residence are not exclusively tax related because he has a real business purpose.

The most restrictive option was chosen in the wording of the LOB clauses used in the treaties, the U.S. Models and Action 6 of the BEPS project. The main effect of these clauses is the reversal of the burden of proof.[213] The clauses free the tax authorities from the complex and difficult tasks involving the application of the GAARs by transferring the burden of proving 'that his actions are not improper or abusive' to the taxpayer. This is evidenced more clearly where the taxpayer must access the treaty through the bona fide clause.

Furthermore, under this system the source state's tax authorities may verify the situation of all the state of residence's taxpayers which do not comply with any of the main clauses, as these taxpayers will seek access through the bona fide clause.[214] The first alternative was not chosen precisely to prevent certain operations from benefiting from a treaty due to the lack of means available to the tax authorities to verify all transactions. Additionally, the tax authorities avoid dealing with all the application problems intrinsic to all general anti-avoidance clauses. The burden of proof now lies with the taxpayer.

The treaties have chosen the second alternative which is the most restrictive. It is important not to lose sight of the fact that the main driving force behind the inclusion of these rules in the treaties is the U.S.[215] The inclusion of a uniform set of limitations on benefits clauses in all tax treaties is not a practice carried out by the rest of the states, at least not until the OECD/G20 BEPS project. Additionally, as it was analysed in section II.A, it should be highlighted that according to Action 6 of the BEPS project approach, a person who complies with the LOB rule could be deprived of treaty

---

212. ALI 1992, pp. 176-178.
213. Dahlberg 1997, p. 296.
214. Isenbergh 1996, pp. 62-24 and 62-25.
215. Tomsett 1986, p. 1785 and Berman/Hynes 2000, p. 692. India and Japan have also introduced in some of their tax treaties provisions similar to the LOB clauses of the U.S. Model. *See* OECD 2015a, p. 20 and Kerekes 2016, pp. 172-173.

benefits under the PPT rule or a domestic general anti-abuse rule.[216] It is our understanding that this proposition is debatable, at least under some of the LOB clauses, especially in regard of the activity clause and the bona fide clause.

As stated by the American Law Institute (ALI), the reaction of the U.S. to treaty shopping has been disproportionate.[217] The treaty shopping structures do not depend exclusively on the subjective scope of tax treaties, but rather on the intermediary state's tax regime. Stepping stone structures are technically more difficult to develop in states whose legal orders provide for strict rules in relation to transfer pricing, thin capitalization and interest deductions.[218] The other aspect which should be borne in mind is that the intermediary state does not subject the payments made to non-residents to non-resident taxation.

Since these structures depend on the tax regime in the intermediary state, it does not appear reasonable to apply the same measures to all states. The severity of the LOB clauses should be balanced with the possibilities offered under the legislation of the state with which a treaty is entered into.[219] In fact, the rest of the states act in this manner, precisely following the indications provided for in the Commentaries on Article 1 of the 2003-2014 OECD Model: when seeking a solution, treaty negotiators should take into account 'the legal context in both Contracting States and, in particular, the extent to which domestic law already provides an appropriate response to this avoidance strategy' (paragraph 12).[220]

However, the position of the U.S. which is expressed in the 1996, 2006 and 2016 Models is altogether different. The policy of the U.S. in relation to tax treaties does not show signs of changing as evidenced by the latest version of the U.S. Model and U.S.

---

216. The U.S. approach is similar to the BEPS approach, at least according to the wording of the Technical Explanations to the 1996 and 2006 U.S. Models. These Technical Explanations state the following: 'Article 22 and the anti-abuse provisions of domestic law complement each other, as Article 22 effectively determines whether an entity has a sufficient nexus to the Contracting State to be treated as a resident for treaty purposes, while domestic anti-abuse provisions (e.g. business purpose, substance-over-form, step transaction or conduit principles) determine whether a particular transaction should be recast in accordance with its substance. Thus, internal law principles of the source Contracting State may be applied to identify the beneficial owner of an item of income, and Article 22 will then be applied to the beneficial owner to determine if that person is entitled to the benefits of the Convention with respect to such income.'
217. 'As a general proposition, the Institute believes that the United States appears to have over-reacted to the treaty shopping problem'. ALI 1992, p. 165. From the report by ALI it is deduced that the formulation of the LOBs should be the opposite of that provided in the 1996 U.S. Model, i.e. they should simply be safe harbour rules with regards to the general anti-avoidance rule. According to Rosenbloom 1991, p. 92, 'But on the usual U.S. principle that anything worth doing is worth overdoing, recent formulations of these provisions have taken the limitation on benefits article to new heights, or depths, of detail and complication'.
218. In this regard, Action 4 of the BEPS project contains recommendations regarding best practices in the design of rules to prevent base erosion through the use of interest expense. *See* OECD 2015d.
219. Loengard 1993, pp. 284-285. As stated by Spector/Salou 1995, p. 97, it is not comprehensible that the DTC between the U.S. and France includes clauses which are as complex as those included in the DTC between the U.S. and the Netherlands, when France is not a state used for treaty shopping operations.
220. Although it is less exact terms, this criterion is also found in the Commentaries on Article 1 of the 1992-2000 OECD Model (paragraph 12).

tax treaties. In addition, the U.S. treaties which do not contain such clauses, or at least do so to a lesser extent, are being renegotiated. Furthermore, the position of the U.S. has received support from the OECD based on the changes included in the Commentaries to Article 1 of the 2003 OECD Model and especially on Action 6 of the BEPS project, as long as one of its recommendations is to include a 'specific anti-abuse rule [in the Model] based on the limitation-on-benefits provisions included in treaties concluded by the United States and a few other countries (the "LOB rule")'.[221] However, it should also be highlighted, that 2016 BEPS Multilateral Instrument is somewhat different, as it provides a simplified version of the LOB rule and its application is not mandatory, at least according to its Article 7(6).[222]

The LOB clauses, as worded in the 1996, 2006 and U.S. Models and the BEPS project, significantly limit the subjective scope of DTCs. This effect may undermine the objectives assigned to DTCs, i.e. to eliminate the obstacle of international double taxation on the international movement of persons and services. As one author has pointed out, if these rules have not yet materially had significant repercussions on these scopes, it is due to the fact that they are not being applied.[223] It is difficult to prove whether this statement is true. However, as shall be observed in section VI of Chapter 3, administrative procedures for their application have made the immediate consequences of these rules more flexible.

In addition, the policy of the U.S. in this regard is difficult to understand since this state is a net exporter of capital, whose system is based on the CEN model (capital export neutrality). These rules do not contribute to the affirmation of the principle of residence chosen by the U.S. tax system, as they also affect residents in the U.S.[224] The cost borne by the state of residence in relation to the elimination of international double taxation increases by the same degree as taxation at source. Therefore, if the source state strictly applies these rules, the number of taxpayers excluded from the subjective scope of the treaty, and correspondingly, the tax costs borne by the state of residence will increase. This same criticism can also be applied to Action 6 of the BEPS project and to the changes made to the Commentaries on Article 1 of the OECD Model in 2003, and in particular, to paragraph 20, which proposes a group of clauses similar to those included in Article 22 of the U.S. Models.

Surely, the reason that the LOB clauses have been worded in the manner discussed relates to the fact that they were drawn up by the U.S. without bearing in mind that a state not only acts as the source state but also as the state of residence. These measures have failed to maintain a due balance in this conflict of interests.[225]

---

221. OECD 2015a, p. 18.
222. Article 7(6) of the 2016 BEPS Multilateral Instrument reads as follows: 'A Party may also choose to apply the provisions contained in paragraphs 8 through 13 (hereinafter referred to as the "Simplified Limitation on Benefits Provision") to its Covered Tax Agreements by making the notification described in subparagraph c) of paragraph 17. The Simplified Limitation on Benefits Provision shall apply with respect to a Covered Tax Agreement only where all Contracting Jurisdictions have chosen to apply it'.
223. Loengard 1993, p. 282.
224. Burke 1983, p. 285. According to Sheppard 2016, p. 728, 'The new [2016 U.S.] model looks at the United States from the standpoint of a source country'.
225. Vogel/Shannon/Doernberg/Van Raad 1989, Article 16, p. 4.

Despite the above, in principle, the assumption on which they are based is positive. The concept of residence set forth in the OECD Model does not stop these types of structures from being developed. The scope of tax treaties needs to be reinforced to prevent their application in purely tax driven transactions, although perhaps it would not be necessary to do so in such restrictive terms. In this respect, these clauses could have been introduced without reversing the burden of proof. Obviously, it would also be necessary to determine the mechanisms required to facilitate the application of the GAAR, whose formulation should be included in the treaty.[226] In this manner, compliance with the LOB clauses, formulated in the reverse sense, would serve to prevent the denial of the treaty and not to obtain its application. In these terms, the concept of residence would continue to be the only requirement that would have to be satisfied for the treaties to be applicable.

Furthermore, the actual position of the U.S. and the OECD in this regard does not seem to consider the measures adopted on harmful tax competition. As discussed at the end of section I.C of this chapter, some of the regimes affected by the actions of the OECD and the EU on harmful tax competition are precisely those which allow for the elimination of tax in the intermediary state. In this respect, since these actions were taken on an international level, limiting the inclusion of these types of clauses could have been considered.[227]

It is likely that this was not the case because the U.S. was not confident in the fact that these actions would finally lead to positive results. In any case, it should also be borne in mind that whereas the U.S. may force a state to accept the inclusion of LOB clauses in a treaty, it is unlikely that it can force a state to eliminate the measures which facilitate treaty shopping under its law.[228] The only option in this case is try to force the inclusion of a provision similar to the exclusion clause in the tax treaty, as the U.S. have done in the 2016 U.S. Model by including the so-called STRs clause.

The position finally adopted by the U.S. consisted of including these LOB clauses in the treaties that it enters into, in a general manner, in order to assure that only taxpayers with a sufficient nexus to the contracting states or a real business purpose for obtaining income from the state of residence benefit from the treaty.

The OECD seems to have also adopted the latter approach. However, unlike the U.S. Model, the OECD does not require the inclusion of an LOB clause in all tax treaties. Action 6 of the BEPS project only requires adopting a minimum standard to address treaty abuse. The LOB rule proposed in Action 6 of the BEPS Model does not form part

---

226. The 1988 OECD report, p. 68, states that the problems relating to the application of the general anti-avoidance rules within the scope of the DTCs should be clarified. To a lesser or greater extent, the Commentaries on Article 1 of the 2003–2014 OECD Model (paragraphs 7–10.2) include its position in this respect.
227. However, these actions do not appear to be incompatible with the inclusion of LOB clauses in the DTCs, since recommendation no. 9 of the 1988 OECD report, p. 47 invites the introduction thereof. The Commentaries on Article 1 of the 2003–2014 OECD Model also precisely adopt this approach, i.e. to bear in mind the tax regime provided in the intermediary state. It is stated that the exclusion method should be used in these cases.
228. Even where the U.S. could force the elimination of these regimes, it has no means to prevent them from being included in the future.

of the minimum standard described in this Action, as it does not require LOB clauses to be included in any event. In effect, according to the final document of Action 6:

> at a minimum [...] countries should agree to include in their tax treaties an express statement that their common intention is to eliminate double taxation without creating opportunities for non-taxation or reduced taxation through tax evasion or avoidance, including through treaty shopping arrangements [...]; they should also implement that common intention through either the combined approach described in paragraph 19 (subject to the necessary adaptations referred to in paragraph 6 above), the inclusion of the PPT rule or the inclusion of the LOB rule supplemented by a mechanism (such as a treaty rule that might take the form of a PPT rule restricted to conduit arrangements or domestic anti-abuse rules or judicial doctrines that would achieve a similar result) that would deal with conduit arrangements not already dealt with in tax treaties.[229]

II.C Domestic Specific Anti-treaty Shopping Measures

This last section refers to the adoption of specific rules against treaty shopping structures in domestic legislation. Accordingly, it does not address the problems discussed earlier relating to the application of the domestic law's GAARs to counter cases of tax avoidance within the scope of the DTCs, but rather analyses the problems arising in relation to the rules unilaterally adopted by states specifically to deny the benefits provided under the DTCs where treaty shopping structures are developed.

First, it should be noted that these rules are unilaterally adopted by a contracting state in order to limit the scope of application of the treaty. The grounds for such a limitation are fundamentally to prevent treaties from being applied in cases of treaty shopping. The states that have adopted these types of rules have worded them in terms similar to the LOBs. Where they are included in a treaty, these rules materially reduce the subjective scope of the treaty. The main characteristic of these rules is that they have been unilaterally adopted by one of the states that has entered into the treaty.

As pointed out by the OECD, these measures give rise to a tax treaty override.[230] In accordance with Articles 26 and 27 of the VCLT, all treaties in force obligate the parties thereto and should be complied with by these parties in good faith. The parties may not appeal to the provisions of their domestic law as justification for the breach of a treaty. According to the OECD, at least in principle, when an abusive use of a treaty is disclosed, the reaction should not be to adopt rules of this nature.[231] Bear in mind that this is a generalized limitation to the terms of access to the treaty, which differs greatly from the GAARs to deny the application of a treaty in a specific case where abuse has been disclosed. In these cases, there is no generalized modification in the

---

229. OECD 2015a, p. 19.
230. OECD 1990, p. 28.
231. OECD 1990, p. 31 and Becker 1988, p. 385. However, it should be borne in mind that the Commentaries on Article 1 of the 2003–2014 OECD Model state that, as a general rule, there will be no conflict between specific domestic anti-avoidance rules and the provisions of tax conventions (paragraph 9.2). Action 6 of the BEPS project has developed this approach. *See* OECD 2015a, pp. 78–85.

terms of the treaty, but rather a simple non-application of the treaty for a specific reason. Despite the reservations in relation to them, and as long as they are used with due precaution, these rules seem to be accepted on an international level.

In contrast, the adoption of a regulation in the respect discussed earlier would give rise to a substantial unilateral change in the terms of the treaty and accordingly, cannot be accepted. The method of correction should involve the renegotiation of the treaty, or where appropriate, the withdrawal therefrom. In this respect, Article 60 and the subsequent VCLT Articles recognize the right to terminate a treaty when there is an unjustified breach thereof in accordance with international law or when there is a fundamental change in circumstances.

However, the above has not prevented specific unilateral rules from being adopted by the states. The possibility of adopting these provisions largely depends on the international law of each state.

From the international law viewpoint, the superiority of the treaties is accepted without argument.[232] In contrast, from the domestic law point of view, the matter is notably more complex. The position of the treaties with respect to domestic law in the various legal orders varies greatly.

First, there are legal systems that recognize the prevalence of the treaties with respect to domestic legislation. In this case, the legal order guarantees the observance of international rules and obligations. The previous and subsequent domestic rules which are contrary to a treaty will not be applicable. This is the case, for example of the Spanish legal order (Article 96 of Spain's Constitution). Consequently, it is impossible for cases of treaty override to arise as no rule, previous or subsequent to a DTC, may alter that which is agreed upon in this treaty. The tax treaty will remain in force until it is modified or denounced.

Second, there are legal orders under which domestic and conventional rules are considered to be comparable and are given the same rank. Where there is a concurrence of both rules, it is resolved based on the *lex posterior derogat lex anterior* rule. In accordance with these systems, a later rule prevails over the treaty.

In these legal orders, cases of a treaty override are possible. A paradigmatic example is the legal order of the U.S. As Borrás notes, on the basis of current practice and the U.S. Constitutions, the Restatement of the Law Third (1986), stipulates in section 115, that an Act of Congress shall prevail over the pre-existing treaty if it is clear that this is the intention of Congress and both rules cannot be applied in conjunction.[233]

---

232. Borrás 1991, p. 57.
233. Borrás 1991, pp. 59–60. Following its amendment in 1988, paragraph 7852(d) of the U.S. Internal Revenue Code (IRC) states that 'for purposes of determining the relationship between a provision of a treaty and any law of the United States affecting revenue, neither the treaty nor the law shall have preferential status by reason of its being a treaty law'. Paragraph 894(a) establishes that the provisions of the IRC will be applied with due regard to any conventional obligation of the Unites States which is applicable to the taxpayer. This declaration of the American legislation does not guarantee that cases of treaty override will not arise, based on that which was discussed with respect to its Constitution. Moreover, it can be perceived that the U.S. intention is not to truly comply with its international obligations, given that the text prior to the 1988 version of paragraph 7852(d) established that no provision of the IRC shall apply in any case where its application would be contrary to any treaty obligation of the U.S.

Despite the fact that the Restatement states that the domestic rule prevails, this does not mean that the U.S. is freed from complying with its internationally assumed obligation and the consequences of the breach of this obligation. Nevertheless, in practice it is impossible to require the U.S. to fulfil its obligation to respect the treaty, because international law does not provide sufficient means for this purpose.[234]

The U.S. has not hesitated in adopting provisions that involve a breach of the DTCs entered into.[235] The most relevant case of treaty override in U.S. law is the legislation on branch profit tax approved in 1986.[236] The U.S. Congress justifies this tax alleging the need to prevent discrimination between the companies residing in the U.S. and the branches of non-resident companies operating within American territory. In principle, the profit obtained by these two bodies is taxed in similar terms. In the opinion of the American tax authorities, the different regime materializes when the profit obtained is distributed. A non-resident in the U.S. that receives a dividend from a company residing in the U.S. is liable to non-resident tax. On the contrary, the head office of a branch located in the U.S. is not liable to any tax when the branch transfers the income it has generated within U.S. territory to this office.

In order to make both regimes comparable, a tax amounting to 30 percent of the gross amount was established on the income transferred to the non-resident companies owning the branches located in the U.S. When adopting this regulation, the U.S. considered that this rule might be contrary to some of the DTCs concluded prior to its adoption. To avoid this conflict, the U.S. stated that it planned to renegotiate these treaties. With respect to subsequent treaties, the required provisions were included to allow for this regulation. These treaties normally establish limits on domestic law in this regard. First, the amount of tax is limited, and is normally comparable to the limit provided for dividends from company shares. Second, limits are established with respect to the determination of the income which is to be taxed.

The intention of the U.S. was to respect the DTCs that do not allow for this tax, and also to adhere to the limits expressly regulated in the treaties. However, in both cases, respect for the limits of the DTCs was conditional on the fact that the non-resident was considered to be a qualified resident. This is the point that gave rise

---

in effect on the date of enactment. However, the previous wording did not have relevant effects. It is always possible that a subsequent rule, the intention of which was to fail to comply with a treaty, would revoke it in general or in a specific case. However, if the intention thereof was evidenced to be compliant with the treaties concluded, this intention is not evidenced in the subsequent version of the text or paragraph 894 of the Code. *See* Becker/Wurm 1988, p. 261, Van Weeghel 1998, p. 192, footnote 4 and Doernberg 1999, pp. 106 and 107.

234. Becker/Wurm 1988, p. 262. As pointed out by these authors, the only possible reaction would be for the other contracting state to fully or partially terminate the treaty.
235. Van Weeghel 1998, p. 193.
236. *See* paragraph 884 of the Internal Revenue Code and Treasury Regulations 1884-4 (in *International Income Taxation. Code, & Regulations. Selected Sections*, Commerce Clearing House, Inc., Chicago, 1993, pp. 1083–1097). In regard to the reasons justifying the inclusion of these rules and their wording, *see General Explanation of the Tax Reform Act of 1986*, Prentice Hall, Inc., Englewood Cliffs, 1987, pp. 1035–1047. This regulation establishes an additional tax on income distributed by the branch to its head office (branch profit tax) and on the interest paid to non-resident entities by the branch (branch interest tax). In this study, reference is only made to the additional tax on distributed profits. *See* Infanti 2001, p. 682, for the cases of U.S. domestic rules which involve treaty override.

to a case of treaty override. Only in cases in which the non-resident is considered to be a qualified resident, will the U.S. apply or refrain from applying the branch tax in accordance with the limits of the treaties entered into. Where the resident is not considered to be a qualified resident, branch tax will be fully applied.

The purpose of this requirement was to prevent treaty shopping,[237] but not any case of treaty shopping, only structures that entailed placing the company that owned the branch established in the U.S. in a state where the treaty with the U.S. does not allow for the application of branch tax or significantly limits its scope.

The condition of qualified resident is acquired, in accordance with American law, by complying with any of the following clauses: stock exchange clause, ownership and base erosion clause and the activity clause. Taxpayers who do not comply with any of these clauses may request that this condition be granted to them by the U.S. tax authorities. These clauses are worded in terms similar to those discussed in the previous section. In fact, the LOBs laid down in the 1996, 2006 and 2016 U.S. Models and the DTCs are based on those established in the American regulation on branch tax.[238]

The specific legal regime of the American law clauses will not be an object of this study. However, reference to this regime will be made in reference to the study of the clauses included in the DTCs. It should only be noted that the branch tax clauses scope of application is different. The concept of qualified resident is only required to prevent the application of the branch tax regulation, or in other words, to prevent the U.S. from not respecting the limits established by the DTC in question. As can be observed, it is clear that these American laws are in breach of the international obligations assumed by the U.S. as a consequence of having entered into DTCs. The concept of qualified resident significantly affects the subjective scope of the DTCs with respect to a certain type of tax, i.e. the tax on income transferred from branches to their head offices.

The practice of treaty override gives rise to serious consequences in relation to the DTCs. One of the treaties purposes is to introduce an element of certainty into the tax regime applied to non-residents in the source state. The practice of treaty override undermines the legal security that tax treaties aim to develop. Also, it may be a disincentive for future investments in the state that practices the treaty override, precisely due to the insecurity that this phenomenon generates in regard to the tax burden finally borne by these investments. Also, from a political standpoint, states that continually carry out such practices will be discredited on an international level. These state's loss of credibility may seriously hinder the conclusion of treaties in the future.[239]

The latter did not occur in the case of the U.S. The U.S. continues to enter into DTCs. Moreover, following the adoption of the branch tax law, the inclusion of clauses similar to those provided in this law has become generalized. On the contrary, the treaty override by the U.S. did lead to the aforementioned uncertainty. Consequently,

---

237. Van Herksen 1996, p. 21.
238. Lerner/Lebovitz/Pridjian 1992, p. 31.
239. Becker/Wurm 1988, pp. 262–263. However, as pointed out by Phillips 1995, p. 15, despite the fact that the U.S. continually engages in these practices, its international position has not changed. The countries which have entered into treaties with the U.S. have not terminated any treaty.

Chapter 2: Scope of Double Taxation Conventions and Limitation

it is understandable that in treaties such as that entered into by the U.S. and the Netherlands, the latter state expressed its concern in regard to the treaty override phenomenon, and established the obligation to communicate any change in domestic law which might give rise to a breach of the treaty within the text of the treaty.[240] In this case, the provision is clearly directed to the U.S. under Dutch law; treaties prevail over domestic legislations, meaning that cases of treaty override are not possible.

Lastly, some of Switzerland's actions in this regard shall be discussed. On 14 December 1962, Switzerland approved a Decree to prevent treaty shopping. With the adoption of this piece of law, Switzerland intended to demonstrate to the rest of the states that it did not intend to favour the establishment of companies in its territory for the purpose of channelling the obtainment of all types of income by means of its network of treaties.[241]

The rules adopted by Switzerland against treaty shopping were aimed at preventing certain taxpayers from benefiting from the limits on taxation at source established by the treaties. The application of these rules normally corresponds to the source state and not to the state of residence. The rules intend for a treaty to not be applied by the source state where there is an abusive use of the treaty by an entity residing in the other state.

Accordingly, the Swiss rules protected taxation at source in the face of treaty shopping structures but from the position of the state of residence. In this respect, the 1962 Decree provided for a series of measures to prevent entities residing in Switzerland from benefiting from the reductions at source under the treaties entered into by this state. These measures were applied when the presence in Swiss territory is considered to be abusive.

The Decree established that an abuse of the treaty will generally be considered to exist if through such claim, a substantial part of the tax relief would benefit, directly or indirectly, persons not entitled to a tax convention, mainly residents in third states. The Decree subsequently clarified the general rule by means of a series of essentially three cases: (a) entities where a substantial part of the income is used, directly or indirectly, to satisfy the rights or claims of persons not entitled to a tax conventions (base erosion); (b) entities resident in Switzerland, in which persons not entitled to a DTC have, directly or indirectly, a substantial interest by way of participation in the financial structure or otherwise, and which do not make appropriate profit distributions; (c) income which benefits, by virtue of a fiduciary relationship, a person not entitled to a tax convention.[242] The rule considered that the taxpayers who fell under one of the

---

240. *See* Article 29(6) of the DTC between the U.S. and The Netherlands (1992). In this manner, the contracting states are expected to take the necessary measures to allow for the full application of the DTC. In an exchange of letters between both governments on 18 December 1992, it was indicated that where the full application of the treaty was not possible due to the domestic legislation adopted, the contracting states would renegotiate the treaty.
241. The English version of the Decree is found in the article 'Swiss Measures against the Abuse of Tax Conventions', Publications of the IBFD, n° 19, 1963, pp. 33–36. The tax authorities sent out a circular to clarify some aspects of the application of the rules of this text, which are also contained in the cited publication (pp. 37–41). This circular was partially modified in 1998. *See* Reinarz 1999 and Jung 2011.
242. Lüthi 1989, p. 338.

above cases, is using the treaty in an abusive manner. However, there were a series of exceptions in relation to the first two cases. A taxpayer is not considered to have used a DTC abusively when he carries on a business activity (activity clause) or is listed on the stock exchange (stock exchange clause).[243] As can be observed, in some respects, this rule was similar to the LOB clauses.

The peculiarity of these rules lies in the fact that it is the state of residence and not the source state that denies the entities residing in its territory from gaining access to the treaty benefits with respect to taxation at source. For this purpose, the Swiss rule stipulated that the Swiss certificates of residence shall not be granted or the certificates already held shall be revoked and the source state shall be informed of the abusive use of the treaty by a taxpayer residing in its territory in accordance with its laws. This provision even provided that where abuse arises, the Swiss tax authorities will claim the tax revenues that the taxpayer failed to pay in the source state in accordance with the application of the treaty. The amounts collected will be turned over to the source state.

As can be observed, although the state that adopts the measures against treaty shopping varies, the wording of the rule is substantially the same as that of the LOBs. The unilateral nature of these rules creates the same problems as the treaty override by the U.S. However, on a positive note, these rules directly involve the state of residence in the phenomenon of treaty shopping. In fact, it is not the source state that denies the application of the DTC because its considers the presence of the taxpayer in the state of residence to be abusive, but rather the state of residence which uses the mechanisms deemed appropriate to assure that the entities residing in its territory do not benefit from the DTCs at source when its actions are qualified as abusive. From this standpoint, the Swiss rule should be considered positively.

---

243. Reinarz 1999, p. 117.

CHAPTER 3
Legal Framework and Application of Limitation on Benefits Clauses

I PRELIMINARY REMARKS

The purpose of this chapter is to analyse the legal framework and application of LOB clauses. This analysis will be performed based on the U.S. Model, the OECD Model, the LOB rules proposed in the BEPS project and the tax treaties concluded between the U.S. and EU Member States.[1] The scope of the DTCs studied has been limited to those entered into by the U.S. with the EU; the compatibility of these treaties with EU law will be analysed in Chapter 4.

The analysis of the tax treaties concluded between the U.S. and EU Member States will be based on the legal framework established in Article 22 of the 1996[2] and

---

1. Reference will also be made to the LOB clauses provided for in the Commentaries on Article 1 of the OECD Model (paragraphs 13-19 and paragraph 20), insofar as the LOB clauses proposed in Action 6 of the BEPS project have not yet been included in the OECD Model and its Commentaries. The tax treaties which will be analysed are as follows: Austria-U.S. DTC (1996, Article 16), Belgium-U.S. DTC (2006, Article 21), Bulgaria-U.S. DTC (2007, Article 21), Cyprus-U.S. DTC (1984, Article 26), Czech Republic-U.S. DTC (1993, Article 17), Denmark-U.S. DTC (1999, as amended through 2006, Article 22), Estonia-U.S. DTC (1998, Article 22), Finland-U.S. DTC (1989, as amended through 2006, Article 16), France-U.S. DTC (1994, as amended through 2009, Article 30), Germany-U.S. DTC (1989, as amended through 2006, Article 28), Greece-U.S. DTC (1950), Hungary-U.S. DTC (1979), Italy-U.S. DTC (1999, Article 2 of the Protocol), Ireland-U.S. DTC (1997, Article 23), Latvia-U.S. DTC (1998, Article 23), Lithuania-U.S. DTC (1998, Article 23), Luxembourg-U.S. DTC (1996, Article 24), Malta-U.S. DTC (2008, Article 22), the Netherlands-U.S. DTC (1992, as amended through 2004, Article 26), Poland-U.S. DTC (1974), Portugal-U.S. DTC (1994, Article 17), Romania (1973), the Slovak Republic-U.S. DTC (1993, Article 17), Slovenia-U.S. DTC (1999, Article 22), Spain-U.S. DTC (1990, Article 17), Sweden-U.S. DTC (1994, as amended through 2005, Article 17) and United Kingdom-U.S. DTC (2001, as amended through 2002, Article 23). Finally, it should be mentioned that the U.S. has still not signed a tax treaty with Croatia.
2. The following U.S. tax treaties follow the 1996 U.S. Model LOB rule: Austria, Estonia, Italy, Ireland, Latvia, Lithuania, Luxembourg, Portugal, Slovenia, Spain and the U.K. It should be noted

2006 U.S. Models,[3] as most of those tax treaties follow the mentioned U.S. Models.[4] However, reference will also be made to the modifications introduced by the 2016 U.S. Model. In this regard, all the treaties referred to follow the structure provided for in Article 22 of the different versions of the U.S. Model, notwithstanding the special features of each treaty resulting from the negotiation process. These special features will be mentioned in connection with the study of each clause.

It is important to note that although the regime of these clauses is always regulated under a single rule, the placement thereof varies in each treaty. In most of the treaties, the protocols add or clarify some aspects of these clauses, and, accordingly, should also be taken into account.

Additionally, many tax treaties include a Memorandum of Understanding which also affects the LOB clauses. These documents include an agreement made by the competent authorities of the contracting states regarding the interpretation and application of its provisions. Technically, the Memorandum does not form part of the treaty. However, in accordance with Article 31 of the VCLT, it does form part of the treaty's context, and, accordingly, should be taken into account for the purposes of the treaty's interpretation and application.[5]

The Technical Explanations issued by the U.S. IRS do not form part of the treaties context within the meaning of Article 31 of the VCLT, because they include an exclusively unilateral interpretation.[6] However, there is no doubt that they are somewhat relevant because they evidence the U.S. IRS's interpretation of these rules.

The LOB clauses incorporate a number of concepts (substantiality, disproportionate class of shares, etc.) which are unknown under the law of many states and for which the treaty does not provide a definition. Pursuant to Article 3(2) of the OECD Model and the U.S. Model, in this case, any other term not defined therein shall, unless the context otherwise requires, have the meaning that it is given under the law of the state to which the convention applies.

In many cases, a referral to domestic law will not resolve the problem relating to the definition of a term, especially if the state applying the treaty is not the U.S. This is because most of these rules are taken from U.S. law. Nevertheless, it is important to note that certain tax treaties provide some definitions in this respect. Materially, these definitions are not substantially different from those provided under U.S. law. Even so,

---

that the tax treaties with Hungary (2010, Article 22), Luxembourg (2009 Protocol) and Spain (2013 Protocol) have been amended. These modifications have not yet entered into force. In all cases, a new LOB rule is envisaged in these tax treaties, which follows the 2006 U.S. Model.

3. The following U.S. tax treaties follow the 2006 U.S. Model LOB rule: Belgium, Bulgaria, Denmark, Finland, France, Germany, Malta, the Netherlands and Sweden.
4. The following U.S. tax treaties follow previous versions of the U.S. Model: Cyprus, the Czech Republic, Greece, Hungary, Poland, Romania and the Slovak Republic. It should be noted that in 2013 the U.S. and Poland have signed a new treaty. This treaty still has to be ratified. The LOB rule provided in Article 22 of this tax treaty follows the 2006 U.S. Model.
5. Soler/Ribes 2001, p. 315.
6. The 1996 and the 2006 U.S. Models have their own Technical Explanation. The Technical Explanation of the 2016 U.S. Model is yet to be published, nonetheless such release had been scheduled for spring 2016.

it should be borne in mind that they guarantee that the meaning of the concept remains unchanged. This is not the case however, when there is a referral to domestic law.

These definitions can also be useful in determining the meaning of a concept in DTCs where no definition is provided. Additionally, they facilitate the development of autonomous concepts which contribute to the interpretation of the treaties more so than the referral technique.

Without prejudice to Article 3(2) of the OECD Model, the source state's domestic law lacks the sufficiency required to resolve all problems relating to the application of these clauses. As shall be observed, it is essential to rely on the state of residence's legislation to assure that the requirements of these clauses are satisfied. As we are most familiar with Spanish law, some references thereto and to the DTC between Spain and the U.S. will be made for illustrative purposes.

This study will be organized as follows: First, the clauses that entitle taxpayers to the full application of a convention will be analysed. These are the clauses that confer the status of qualified resident upon the taxpayers. Second, the clauses that entitle taxpayers to apply the conventions but do not confer the status of qualified resident upon them will be examined. Such taxpayers will be referred to as non-qualified residents entitled to the application of a convention. Third, the clauses which grant access to certain benefits of the convention will be discussed. Such taxpayers will be referred to as non-qualified residents entitled to the partial application of a convention. Partial application usually refers to the following categories of income: dividends, interests, royalties and the branch tax.

Fourthly, exclusion clauses will be studied. These clauses deny the application of the convention (the exclusion clause and the PE clause) although the taxpayer is eventually classified as one of the previously mentioned categories of residents. Concepts used in the exclusion clause will be easier to comprehend following the examination of the aforementioned types of provisions. Additionally, in some cases verification of the application of the exclusion clause may only be made if the taxpayer has previously satisfied the requirements of one of the clauses which entitles them to claim the treaty benefits. Taxpayers who do not comply with any of the above clauses or are within the scope of application of the exclusion clause, may resort to the bona fide clause. Lastly, the procedural aspects of the application of these clauses will be examined.

Following is an outline of the way in which the conventions with LOB clauses function:

Structure of the conventions with LOB clauses:

1. Required to be a resident in one of the contracting states
2. Required to be the beneficial owner of the income
3. Required to comply with one of the LOB clauses (general outline)

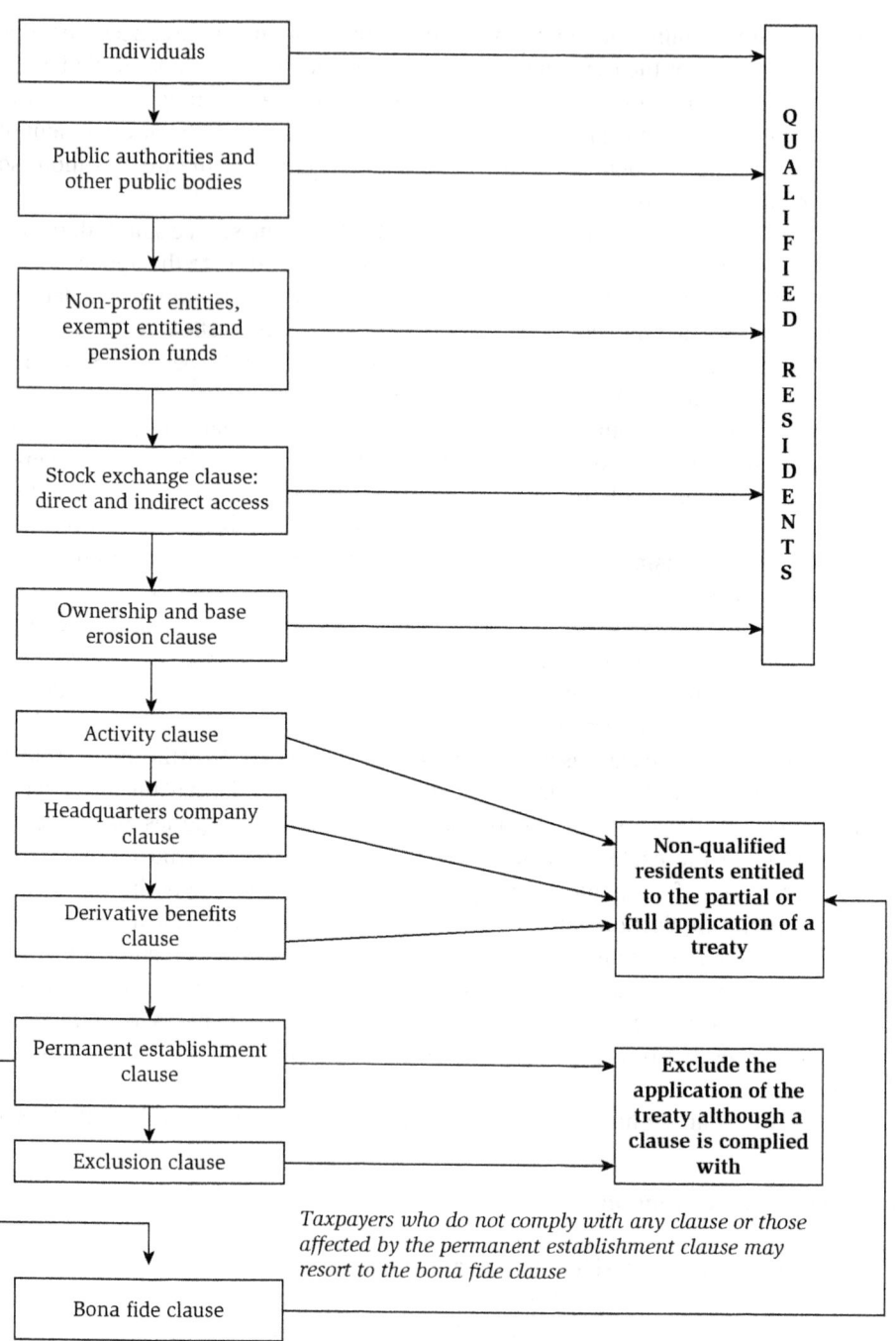

II CLAUSES THAT CONFER THE STATUS OF QUALIFIED RESIDENT

II.A Individuals

Individuals are only required to reside in one of the contracting states to be considered a qualified resident. As observed in Chapter 2 (section III.B.3), the concept of residence applicable to individuals includes the assumptions on which the LOB clauses are based.

Although citizenship is not an accepted liability criterion under Article 4(1) of the OECD Model, it is expressly mentioned in Article 4(1) of the U.S. Model (1996, 2006 and 2016). The DTCs entered into by the U.S. follow Article 4(1) of the U.S. Model, meaning that where citizenship gives rise to liability to tax in a state on worldwide income, the taxpayer will be considered as a resident for the purposes of the treaty.

Citizenship is a criterion based on which taxpayers are liable to tax in the U.S. on worldwide income. In principle, U.S. citizens are considered as residents for the purpose of the DTCs concluded by this state, even though they have no nexus of a factual nature to the U.S. territory.[7]

As can be observed, this liability criterion does not follow either of the two assumptions on which these clauses are based. Citizenship alone does not give rise to any nexus of a factual nature to the territory. This criterion will only be justified by the fact that the taxpayer bears tax on worldwide income in the state where he is a citizen. Therefore, the means by which to eliminate double taxation must be agreed upon.

Even so, this argument does not justify the application of the treaty from the standpoint of the assumptions on which the LOB clauses are based. Likewise, as pointed out by experts in this field,[8] the criterion of citizenship within the scope of the DTCs triggers multiple application problems. It increases the cases of double residence and gives rise to triangular situations which are difficult to resolve.[9]

For these reasons, it was proposed that as in the case of the OECD Model, citizenship should not be considered for the purposes of the application of tax treaties.[10] Despite this fact, the criterion of citizenship continues to be applied in the DTCs entered into by the U.S.

---

7. The tax treaties entered into by the U.S. also include the so-called saving clause. In accordance with this clause, the U.S. saves the right to tax its own citizens and residents as if the treaty had not come into effect. However, this clause excludes certain categories of income regulated by the treaty from its application. See Doernberg/Van Raad 1992 and Doernberg/Van Raad 1997, pp. 11-12.
8. Shannon 1988, p. 208.
9. Imagine a U.S. citizen who resides in Spain and obtains dividends in France. Should France consider the limit provided in the DTC between Spain and France or the one established in the DTC between the U.S. and France?
10. Kaplan 1993, p. 179. As stated by Shannon 1988, p. 208, in order to retain the right to tax its citizens on the worldwide income obtained, the U.S. only has to include a 'saving clause' in the DTC. The U.S. is not required to allow U.S. citizens residing in a third state to claim access to the treaties entered into by the U.S.

However, the scope of this criterion has been changed, particularly in the DTCs entered into by the U.S. which include LOB clauses. For example, in the case of the DTC between the U.S. and Spain, a provision with the following wording was introduced:

> A United States citizen or an alien admitted to the United States for permanent residence (a 'green card' holder) is considered to be a resident of the United States only if the individual has a substantial presence in the United States or would be a resident of the United States and not of another country under the principles of sub-paragraphs (a) and (b) of paragraph 2 of that Article.[11]

This provision effectively converts the criterion of citizenship into one of a factual nature.[12] A U.S. citizen will only be considered as a resident for the purposes of the treaty in two cases. First, he or she must have a substantial presence in the U.S. Under U.S. law, an individual is understood to have such a presence if he or she has been present in the U.S. for at least thirty-one days during the current year and for an average of 183 days during the previous three-year period.[13] Second, if the U.S. citizen is also considered to be a resident in a third state, the convention will only be applicable if the conflict of dual residence between the third state and the U.S. is resolved in favour of the U.S. Of course, the problem of dual residence should only be resolved in this manner since the individual has either his permanent home, centre of vital interests or habitual abode in the U.S. For example:

> A U.S. citizen obtains dividends in Spain. Since he has a home in France and is considered to be a resident under French law, this taxpayer is taxed in France on worldwide income. However, as he is a U.S. citizen (and also has a home in the U.S.) he is also taxed in the U.S. on worldwide income. In view of the application of the France-U.S. DTC, this case of dual residence is resolved in favour of the U.S. Although the citizen has a home in both the U.S. and in France, his centre of vital interests is considered to be in the U.S. In this case, the U.S. citizen is considered to be a resident for the purposes of the DTC between Spain and the U.S., and accordingly, the tax levied on the dividends obtained in Spain may not be higher than the limit established in the treaty. If the conflict of dual residence between France and the U.S. had been resolved in favour of the U.S. based on the criterion of citizenship, this U.S. citizen would not be considered to be a resident for the purposes of the DTC between Spain and the U.S.

These provisions significantly limit the criterion of citizenship within the scope of the DTCs entered into by the U.S.[14] From the standpoint of our study, they trace the

---

11. Article 5 of the Spain-U.S. Protocol. Note that no similar rule adapted to entities is included to clarify the scope of the place of incorporation criterion.
12. The LOB clauses provided for in paragraph 20 of the Commentaries on Article 1 of the OECD Model do not contain a similar provision. The same applies to the LOB rule provided in Action 6 of the BEPS project. Obviously, in this case this provision is not required as citizenship is not an admissible criterion under Article 4 of the OECD Model.
13. *See* McDaniel/Ault 1998, pp. 61–63 and Doernberg 1999, pp. 19–22.
14. The following tax treaties contain similar provisions: Austria (Article 4(1)(c)), Belgium (Article 4(2)), the Czech Republic (Article 4(2)(c)), Denmark (Article 4(4)), Estonia (Article 4(2)(c)), Finland (Article 4(1)(b)), France (Article 4(2)(a)), Germany (Article 2 of the Protocol), Ireland (Article 4(1)(a)), Italy (Article 1(5)(c) of the Protocol), Latvia (Article 4(2)(c)), Lithuania (Article 4(2)(c)), Luxembourg (Article 4(1)(c)), the Netherlands (Article 4(1)), Portugal (Article 3(c) of the Protocol), the Slovak Republic (Article 4(2)(c)), Slovenia (Article 4(1)), Sweden

concept of residence back to the assumptions on which the LOB clauses are based. With the changes discussed above, the criterion of citizenship, is converted into a criterion of a factual nature which reveals that the individual has a sufficient nexus to the state's territory.

Therefore, U.S. citizens will only be considered as qualified residents if they are previously deemed to be residents within the meaning of the convention. In order to be deemed as such, the citizen must have a substantial presence, permanent home or habitual abode in the U.S.[15]

II.B Governmental Entities and Other Public Agencies

Pursuant to Article 22 of the 1996 U.S. Model 'qualified governmental entities' are automatically considered as qualified residents. Article 3(1)(i) of the 1996 U.S. Model defines this concept as follows:

> the term 'qualified governmental entity' means:
>
> (i) any person or body of persons that constitutes a governing body of a Contracting State, or of a political subdivision or local authority of a Contracting State;
> (ii) a person that is wholly owned, directly or indirectly, by a Contracting State or a political subdivision or local authority of a Contracting State, provided (A) it is organized under the laws of the Contracting State, (B) its earnings are credited to its own account with no portion of its income inuring to the benefit of any private person, and (C) its assets vest in the Contracting State, political subdivision or local authority upon dissolution; and
> (iii) a pension trust or fund of a person described in subparagraph (i) or (ii) that is constituted and operated exclusively to administer or provide pension benefits described in Article 19;
>
> provided that an entity described in subparagraph (ii) or (iii) does not carry on commercial activities.

The 2006 U.S. Model does not provide for the concept of 'qualified governmental entities'. However, its Article 22(2)(b) provides that 'a Contracting State, political subdivision or local authority thereof' are considered 'qualified persons'. The wording

---

(Article 4(1)(b)) and the U.K. (Article 4(2)). The tax treaties with Cyprus (1984), Bulgaria (2007), Greece (1950), Hungary (1979), Malta (2008), Poland (1974) and Romania (1973) do not contain a similar provision. In this regard, except in the cases of the 2007 Bulgaria-U.S. DTC and the 2008 DTC Malta-U.S., this is due to the fact that these treaties do not include LOB clauses similar to those provided for in Article 22 of the 1996 and 2006 U.S. Models. There is no explanation for the omission of a clause similar to the ones mentioned at the beginning of this chapter (see footnote 1) in the treaties with Bulgaria and Malta. Moreover, the DTCs with Greece, Hungary and Poland do not include any type of LOB rule. The clauses contained in the DTC with Cyprus are similar to those provided for in the 1977 U.S. Model. These provisions are based on the assumption that the taxpayer is effectively taxed in the state of residence. There is no rule similar to the one examined since, although there is no nexus of a factual nature to the state of residence, taxation still arises given that the taxpayer is liable to tax in accordance with the criterion of citizenship.

15. However, as shall be observed, LOB clauses allow access to U.S. citizens by means of another type of clause.

of Article 22(2)(b) of the 2016 U.S. Model is slightly different in comparison to the mentioned Article of the 2006 U.S. Model, insofar as it adds 'any agency or instrumentality of any such Contracting State, political subdivision or local authority'.

As can be seen, the three mentioned U.S. Models, the OECD Model and Action 6 BEPS project consider 'a Contracting State, political subdivision or local authority thereof' qualified persons. In view of the characteristics and functions assigned to these types of entities, the automatic concession of the status of qualified resident is fully justified. These entities have a sufficient nexus to the territory and it is unlikely that they will be used for the development of treaty shopping structures.[16]

The first problem which arises in relation to the application of this clause is the consideration of these public bodies as residents. In Spain, for example, this problem does not arise. The state and other regional governments (autonomous regions and municipalities) are subject to corporate income tax on worldwide income as long as all the above are legal entities, notwithstanding the fact that they may enjoy full exemption in the Spanish corporate tax. As they are liable to tax on worldwide income, they are considered to be residents for the purposes of the treaty.

To avoid the complications that may result from the consideration of these entities as residents when they are not formally subject to taxation, the OECD Model and the three mentioned U.S. Models directly classify them as such.[17] Accordingly, it is not necessary for 'qualified governmental entities' to be liable to tax on worldwide income.

The second matter of significance in relation to this clause concerns the entities included within the concept of 'qualified governmental entities' provided in the 1996 U.S. Model. In this regard, Article 3.1.i) of the 1996 U.S. Model defines the taxpayers that are classified as qualified governmental entities. A requirement common to all three cases described below is that the entities may not engage in commercial activities.

First, this concept includes those entities that constitute public authorities in a strict sense, regardless of their level of government (central, subdivision and local). As noted above, these public bodies are also included in the 2006 and 2016 U.S. Model.

Second, the 1996 U.S. Model includes entities wholly owned, directly or indirectly, by a contracting state or a political subdivision or local authority of a contracting state, providing that the following requirements are satisfied: the entity is organized under the laws of the contracting state; its earnings are credited to its own account with no portion of its income inuring to the benefit of any private person; its assets vest in the contracting state, political subdivision or local authority upon dissolution. Since these entities are not included in the 2006 and 2016 U.S. Models, they will have to gain access to treaty benefits through the rest of the LOB rule tests. Nevertheless, we must not overlook the fact that the 2016 U.S. Model includes in this

---

16. Strauch 1997, p. 40 and Van Weeghel 1998, p. 233.
17. The LOB rule provided for in paragraph 20 of the Commentaries on Article 1 of the OECD Model also considers qualified governmental entities to be qualified residents. However, as opposed to the 1996 U.S. Model, it does not define this concept. The detailed version of the LOB rule proposed in Action 6 BEPS project reads as follows: 'a Contracting State, or a political subdivision or local authority thereof, or a person that is wholly owned by such State, political subdivision or local authority'.

LOB rule test 'any agency or instrumentality of any such Contracting State, political subdivision or local authority'. As the 2016 U.S. Model does not provide a definition of those terms, it may be useful to rely on the 1996 U.S. Model to determine which entities have such status.

Lastly, under the concept of 'qualified governmental entities' the 1996 U.S. Model includes pension funds and trusts constituted by public authorities or any entity referred to above, in order to administer or provide pension benefits to public servants within the meaning of Article 19 of the treaty.

As can be observed, the definition provided in the 1996 U.S. Model is broader than that provided for in the OECD Model and the 2006 and 2016 U.S. Models. These Models only include entities that constitute public authorities in a strict sense and, in the case of the 2016 U.S. Model, any agency or instrumentality of such public authorities.[18] In this regard, not all of the treaties being studied include a concept of 'qualified governmental entity' similar to that provided in the 1996 U.S. Model. Therefore, in each case it will be necessary to examine the concept provided in order to determine which entities are included. Those which are excluded must follow the general regime, i.e. residence and compliance with an LOB test different to the one that is being analysed in this section.

Without a doubt, in certain cases it may be rather complicated to determine which entities are included. To resolve this problem, some tax treaties have used the technique of identifying certain entities individually.[19] This technique facilitates the resolution of problems arising in relation to a general concept whose limits are not sufficiently specified within the body of the treaty. Even so, another possibility would be to resort to a mutual agreement procedure to resolve the problems relating to the interpretation and application of this rule. In any case, the fact that an entity may not obtain access to a treaty by this means does not prevent it from doing so by any other means.

Lastly, reference should be made to one aspect of the DTCs entered into by the U.S. with France – prior to its amendment in 2009 – and Ireland which is not found in any other treaty. As shall be observed in a later section, under the stock exchange clause, indirect access to a treaty is also provided to entities whose shareholders directly comply with this clause. The stock exchange clauses in the treaties with France and Ireland also take into consideration the shareholdings of public authorities and companies in which public authorities have a shareholding.

As pointed out by experts in this field, this consideration was included due to the fact that public companies were in the process of being privatized when the treaty was concluded.[20] Obviously, following the privatization, these companies lost this regime of special access to the stock exchange clause.

---

18. Doernberg/Van Raad 1997, p. 35.
19. This is the case, for example, in the Italy-U.S. DTC. Article 4 of the Protocol mentions *La Banca d'Italy*, *L'Istituto per il Commercio con l'Estero* and *L'Istituto per l'Assicurazione del Credito*.
20. Spector/Salou 1995, p. 98, footnote 59.

II.C Tax-Exempt Organizations

In accordance with Article 22 of the 1996 U.S. Model, by means of referral to Article 4(1)(b)(i), entities established and maintained exclusively for a religious, charitable, educational, scientific, or other similar purpose, that have been organized under the laws of a contracting state and that are generally exempt from tax on the income obtained, are considered to be qualified residents. The entities must continue to have a religious, charitable, or other similar purpose at the time the treaty application is requested.[21]

The 2006 U.S. Model provides the same provision.[22] The same occurs in the 2016 U.S. Model. In this regard, according to the Technical Explanation of the 1996 U.S. Model, these entities are automatically considered to be qualified residents as it is unlikely that they will be used for treaty shopping structures. The Technical Explanation of the 2006 U.S. Model does not contain the latter mention.

Most state laws provide favourable regimes for these types of entities.[23] Tax relief techniques of various types (reduced tax rates, tax credits, etc.) are used in this regard. With this in mind, it should be highlighted that income related to the entity's object or specific purpose is usually declared exempt.

In our opinion, these entities are included within the concept of qualified resident in order to maintain this special regime on an international level. Given the structure of these types of entities, it would be difficult for them to gain access to a treaty by means of another clause.[24]

Entities which enjoy the preferential tax regime applied to tax-exempt organizations are normally subject to administrative controls. The control that these entities are subjected to exclude the development of treaty shopping structures. Additionally, it should be borne in mind that the exemption regime is only granted if the income obtained is derived from activities relating to the entity's specific purpose. Unrelated business income is taxed in accordance with general rules.[25] In principle, in view of this characteristic of the regime being applied to tax-exempt organizations, such entities are excluded from treaty shopping structures. It would be difficult to connect the income generated by these structures to the non-profit related purpose of such an entity.

The Technical Explanations to the 1996 and 2006 U.S. Models do not clarify whether all income obtained by tax-exempt organizations is comprised within the

---

21. As in the case of the previous clause, the U.S. Models directly classify these entities as residents to facilitate compliance with the residence requirement, as these entities are not formally subject to corporate income tax in all states. *See* Doernberg/Van Raad 1997, p. 33.
22. *See* Articles 4(2)(b) and 22(2)(d) of the 2006 U.S. Model.
23. Gliksberg 1999, p. 159.
24. These types of entities often adopt the form of a foundation. A foundation's structure prevents it from obtaining access to a treaty by means of the stock exchange clause, as entities are normally required to be incorporated to be listed on a stock exchange. It is also impossible for such entities to comply with the ownership and base erosion clauses as there are normally no shares in these types of entities. Finally, such entities would not be able to comply with the activity clause. The special tax regime for these entities is conditional upon the fact that the main object of these entities does not consist in the performance of an active business or trade.
25. Godfrey 1983, p. 6.

scope of the concept of qualified resident. The text of the 1996, 2006 and 2016 U.S. Models do not stipulate anything in this respect, meaning that in principle, it would apply to all income that might be obtained.

In our opinion, this aspect should be clarified. Generally, the exemption regime used under the states' domestic laws is not subjective. Not only is a specific legal form required (e.g. foundation, public interest association) to enjoy the exemption, but also a direct connection between the income and the entity's welfare oriented purpose.[26] This LOB clause should have been worded in terms similar to the domestic regimes in this regard, i.e. an entity is only deemed to be a qualified resident in respect of the income to which the regime for tax exempt organizations applies in the state of residence.

Although the U.S. Models do not provide anything in this respect, it must be borne in mind that this clause is taken from U.S. tax law. The exemption regulated in section 501(c) of the Internal Revenue Code (IRC) does not include income that is not related to the entity's object or specific purpose.[27] In this respect, it may be sustained that this is also a requirement within the scope of a treaty. Like on a domestic level, the income that is unrelated to the entity's object or specific purpose should not benefit from the status of qualified resident conferred upon these entities. Without a doubt, this additional requirement complicates the terms of application of this clause. In each case, it will be necessary to determine whether the income obtained relates to the entity's purpose.

Notwithstanding the above, it is important to bear in mind that this requirement is not expressly provided for in the mentioned U.S. Models. Perhaps this is due to the fact that based on the wording of this LOB test, it only includes entities engaged exclusively in activities relating to the aforementioned purposes. In principle, it could be concluded that if this is their only purpose, it is not possible for them to obtain income not connected thereto. However, the fact that this is their only purpose does not mean they may not obtain unrelated income. Therefore, we consider that the above referred to requirement should have been expressly included.

Additionally, it should be noted that all of the DTCs include a similar clause. In some DTCs the following requirement is added: more than half of the beneficiaries, members, or participants, if any, in such an organization are required to be qualified residents (see, for example, DTCs with the Czech Republic, Estonia, Latvia, Lithuania and the Slovak Republic). There is no doubt that this requirement complicates the application of the clause and makes it similar to the ownership and base erosion clause which will be analysed later.

---

26. Gliksberg 1999, p. 183 and Bravo 2016, p. 198.
27. *See* paragraph 55 of the Technical Explanation of the 1996 U.S. Model and Godfrey 1983, pp. 23–26. The 2006 U.S. Model Technical Explanation contains no reference to the Internal Revenue Code.

II.D Pension Funds

In accordance with Article 22 of the 1996 U.S. Model, which also refers to Article 4(1)(b)(ii), generally exempt entities organized under the laws of a contracting state to provide pensions or other similar benefits to employees pursuant to a plan are considered to be qualified residents provided that more than 50 percent of the person's beneficiaries, members or participants are individuals resident in either contracting state.[28]

The wording of the 2006 U.S. Model is similar to that found in the 1996 U.S. Model, although the concept of 'pension fund' is defined in broader terms in its Article 3(1)(k):

> [T]he term 'pension fund' means any person established in a Contracting State that is:
> i) generally exempt from income taxation in that State; and
> ii) operated principally either:
>   A) to administer or provide pension or retirement benefits; or
>   B) to earn income for the benefit of one or more persons described in clause A).

In the 2006 U.S. Model, as in the case of the 1996 U.S. Model, a pension fund is a qualified person if 'more than 50 percent of the person's beneficiaries, members or participants are individuals resident in either Contracting State'. The equivalent proviso in the 2016 U.S. Model provides relevant deviations, which will be analysed at the end of this section.

The requirements of this clause influence three aspects: taxation of the entity that obtains the income, the activity it performs and the classification of its beneficiaries, members and participants.

The clause places most emphasis on pension funds. Under the 1996 and the 2006 U.S. Models, they are directly classified as residents to guarantee compliance with the residence requirement. In some states, these entities are not subject to taxation, and in other cases, for example under Spanish domestic law, although they are not legal entities, they are subject to corporate income tax, but at a reduced tax rate.

In our opinion, full exemption is not essential in all cases. The 1996 and 2006 U.S. Models only mention this aspect to justify the direct classification of these entities as residents, or in other words, to resolve the problems that could result from considering these entities as residents even though they are fully exempt from taxation. Mention of this aspect was not made to establish an additional requirement for compliance with this clause. It would not make sense for the tax treatment of these pension funds to be worse than if they were effectively taxed. In summary, the clause is not meant to

---

28. Paragraph 20 of the Commentaries on Article 1 of the OECD Model contains a similar clause in section 2(b).

exclude pension funds that are effectively taxed, but rather only to clarify that fully exempt pension funds are considered to be residents.

As in the case of the previous clause, the activity engaged in by the entity must be one of those mentioned in the 1996 and 2006 U.S. Models. This case has been included because, with regards to pension funds, the legislator only intends to tax the shareholder on the income obtained.[29] The preferential tax regime which pension funds usually enjoy (no liability, exemption or a reduced tax rate) is structured to assure that double taxation does not arise. Income should only be taxed when attributed to the beneficiary.

The 1996 and 2006 U.S. Models also guarantee that there is a sufficient nexus to the fund's state of residence, requiring that more than 50 percent of the person's beneficiaries, members or participants are individuals resident in either contracting state. As pointed out by one author, this requirement is unnecessary.[30] The legal and financial structure of pension funds technically makes the channelling of treaty shopping structures impossible.

The 50 percent requirement also gives rise to an important limitation on the creation of pension funds in which, individuals residing in other states, participate. It is not rare for this to occur, especially in the case of multinational enterprises.[31] This requirement forces them to create a fund for each state in which the multinational enterprise operates. Nevertheless, some DTCs have substituted this requirement. When this occurs, the pension fund's sponsor is only required to be entitled to claim the treaty benefits. It should be noted that the DTC is only required to be applicable, and accordingly, it is not necessary for the sponsor to be a qualified resident.

U.S. tax treaties have generally followed the U.S. Models, although there are some differences which will be pointed out below.

The DTC between Spain and the U.S. provides this clause in the following terms: persons considered to be 'a tax-exempt organization, other than those described in sub-paragraph (c), provided that more than half of the beneficiaries, members, or participants, if any, in such organization are entitled to the benefits of this Convention'. The protocol to the treaty clarifies this clause by stating the following:

> The tax-exempt organizations described in paragraph 1(d) of Article 17 include, but are not limited to, pension funds, pension trusts, private foundations, trade unions, trade associations, and similar organizations. In all events, a pension fund, pension trust, or similar entity organized for purposes of providing retirement, disability, or other employment benefits that is organized under the laws of a Contracting State shall be entitled to the benefits of the Convention if the organization sponsoring such fund, trust, or entity is entitled to the benefits of the Convention under Article 17.

As can be observed, the clause provided in the DTC between Spain and the U.S. does not limit the scope of activities in which the entities may engage. However, based on the clarification in the Protocol, this rule is essentially provided for pension funds.

---

29. ALI 1992, p. 142.
30. Van Weeghel 1998, p. 235.
31. Van Weeghel 1998, p. 235.

The 50 percent requirement is not applied to these entities as long as the organization sponsoring the fund is entitled to apply the treaty. It should be noted that the treaty establishes that the sponsors are only required to be entitled to the treaty benefits under Article 17. In this respect, the DTCs do not limit this clause to qualified residents. It is sufficient to comply with any of the clauses provided, and not only those by which the entity is deemed to be a qualified resident.

In addition to the treaty with Spain, the tax treaties with France (Article 30(2)(d)), Germany (Article 28(2)(e)) and the Netherlands (Article 26(2)(d)) provide for this possibility.

Finally, the pension funds test provided for in the 2016 U.S. Model will be briefly analysed. The term 'pension fund' means any person established in a contracting state that is:

(i) generally exempt from income taxation in that Contracting State; and
(ii) operated exclusively or almost exclusively:
    (A) to administer or provide pension or retirement benefits; or
    (B) to earn income for the benefit of one or more persons established in the same Contracting State that are generally exempt from income taxation in that Contracting State and that are operated exclusively or almost exclusively to administer or provide pension or retirement benefits.

The definition of pension funds is somewhat different in comparison to the one provided for in the 2006 U.S. Model, insofar that the 2016 Model uses the expression 'exclusively or almost exclusively', whereas the 2006 Model provides the term 'principally'. Although it is difficult to assess the difference between both terms, it seems that the main objective of this modification is to restrict the activities carried out by the entity, which are not related to the administration or provision of pensions or retirement benefits.

The provision, as in the 2006 U.S. Model, embraces both pension funds (letter 'A') and the so-called fund of funds (letter 'B'). These entities do not directly provide pension benefits to individuals but are constituted and operated to invest the funds of pension funds. In both cases, in order to be a qualified resident, more than 50 percent of the beneficiaries of the pension fund, or the pension funds of the 'fund of funds' must be individuals resident in either contracting state.

The detailed version of the LOB rule provided in Action 6 of the BEPS project contains a pension funds test similar to the one found in the 2016 U.S. Model. However, in Action 6 individuals that are resident in third states are also eligible for the 50 percent requirement, to the extent that they 'are entitled to the benefits of a comprehensive [tax treaty] between [the country where they reside] and the State from which the benefits of this Convention are claimed'. In addition, Action 6 establishes that with respect to dividends and interest, the tax treaty between the 'third state beneficiary' and the source state should provide for a tax rate that is at least as low as the rate applicable under the convention between the source state and the state where the pension fund resides. The rationale behind this provision is similar to the rationale behind the derivative benefits clause, which will be analysed in section III.C of this chapter.

II.E Stock Exchange Clause

II.E.1 Preliminary Remarks

The stock exchange clause is worded in the following way in Article 22(2)(c) of the 1996 U.S. Model:

> 2. A resident of a Contracting State shall be entitled to all the benefits of this Convention if the resident is: [...]
> c) a company, if
>
> (i) all the shares in the class or classes of shares representing more than 50 percent of the voting power and value of the company are regularly traded on a recognized stock exchange

The wording of Article 22(2)(c) of the 2006 U.S. Model is slightly different:

> A resident of a Contracting State shall be a qualified person for a taxable year if the resident is: [...]
> c) a company, if:
>
> i) the principal class of its shares (and any disproportionate class of shares) is regularly traded on one or more recognized stock exchanges, and either:
> A) its principal class of shares is primarily traded on one or more recognized stock exchanges located in the Contracting State of which the company is a resident; or
> B) the company's primary place of management and control is in the Contracting State of which it is a resident; or

Finally, the wording of Article 22(2)(c) of the 2016 U.S. Model coincides with the wording of the clause provided in the 2006 U.S. Model. The detailed version of the LOB rule proposed in Action 6 of the BEPS project follows the stock exchange clause provided in the 2006 U.S. Model.

This part of the stock exchange clause provides the alternative of gaining direct access to the status of qualified resident.

Under the mentioned Models, a company's shares must comply with three requirements: (a) a number of shares representing more than 50 percent of the company's capital stock and voting power must be traded on a secondary market; (b) These shares must be traded substantially and regularly on a stock exchange; (c) the stock exchange on which the shares are listed and traded must be recognized by the treaty. The only substantial difference between the 1996 and the 2006/2016 U.S. Models refers to the fact that when the principal class of shares is not primarily traded in the state where the company resides, in order to comply with this rule the company must prove that the primary place of management and control is in the contracting state of which it is a resident.

The 1996, 2006 and 2016 Models also allow for indirect access to this clause by those entities in which, companies that comply with this clause, have a shareholding, or in simpler terms, by the subsidiaries of publicly traded companies. This alternative is expressed in the following terms in the 1996 U.S. Model:

> (c) a company, if [...]
>   (ii) at least 50 percent of each class of shares in the company is owned directly or indirectly by companies entitled to benefits under clause (i), provided that in the case of indirect ownership, each intermediate owner is a person entitled to benefits of the Convention under this paragraph;[32]

The 2006 U.S. Model, in comparison with the 1996 U.S. Model, adds two further requirements. First, the mentioned 50 percent must include, likewise, 50 percent of any disproportionate class of shares. Second, it limits the number of companies which directly or indirectly own the company requesting the application of the treaty. That company must be owned directly or indirectly by five or fewer companies.

Finally, the 2016 U.S. Model has introduced more complexity: insofar as it has introduced a base erosion prong in this clause. This additional prong will be analysed in sections II.E.3.d and II.F.3 of this chapter.

On first consideration, the terms of the stock exchange clause are simple. The clause includes publicly traded companies and their subsidiaries. However, its meaning is actually much more complicated. As observed in the previous chapter, one of the assumptions that the clause was based on is that it excludes treaty shopping, because a separation arises between the economic interests of the company and its shareholders.[33] This separation mainly arises due to the fact that the shares of the publicly traded company are traded on secondary markets without the involvement of the company. To guarantee that this is actually the case, the clause requires that the listed shares are traded in a substantial and regular manner. The meaning of this concept, the terms of which are very strict, shall be discussed later.

In this respect, it should be noted that if the stock market on which the shares are traded were to function correctly, it would not be necessary for any requirement under tax law to be established in this respect. For example, under Spanish domestic law, the Spanish Securities Market Commission is authorized to exclude from trading, those

---

32. The isolated stock exchange clause proposed in the Commentaries on Article 1 of the OECD Model (paragraph 19.d) also provides for direct and indirect access thereto. Additionally, the stock exchange clause provided in paragraph 20 of the Commentaries on Article 1 of the OECD Model is similar to the clause included in the U.S. Model, notwithstanding some differences, which will be pointed out. Finally, the stock exchange test envisaged in the detailed version of the LOB rule of Action 6 of the BEPS project is similar to the 2006 U.S. Model. *See* OECD 2015a, p. 26.
33. Van Weeghel 1998, p. 234.

securities that do not meet the regulatory requirements established relating to publicizing, trading volume and frequency. Pursuant to the 1993 Spanish Securities Market Commission Annual Report:

> the ongoing listing on the stock exchange of companies which lack actual stock market activity is counterproductive for the market as a whole. The listing of inactive companies causes a negative image of the market as a whole to be transmitted to investors, thereby harming companies willing to actively participate in the market.[34]

Therefore, if the stock exchange on which the shares are traded functions correctly, it is not necessary for requirements to be established under tax law in relation to the shares' trading volume and frequency. If this is the case, only companies with effective stock market activity will be listed on the market.

Likewise, the rationale on which the rule is based is related to the fact that the company's capital is widely distributed. Where this is the case, in accordance with the rule of convenience, the treaty declines to require the identification of each of the shareholder's residence, as in the case of the ownership and base erosion clause.[35] Furthermore, if the publicly traded company's shares are actually traded, it would be very burdensome to verify the identity and residence of each of the shareholders.

As previously mentioned, it should also be borne in mind that given the extensive stock market requirements which must be met under corporate law in order to be listed on the stock market, it is improbable that a publicly traded company would be used for treaty shopping structures. It is not likely that the use of this means to channel such an operation would be efficient from an economic standpoint in view of the pre-operating expenses involved. However, this depends, to a large extent, on the corporate legislation of each state. Very flexible legislation in this regard would invalidate the 'presumption' on which this rule is based.[36]

In summary and in view of the above, it can be verified that this clause classifies entities as qualified residents on the basis of subjective elements. The rule sets forth a number of precautions to guarantee that the assumptions on which the clause is based are effectively fulfilled.

---

34. Spanish Securities Market Commission, *Annual Report 1993*, pp. 263 y 264 (information taken from this body's web page http://www.cnmv.es). Therein, information is provided regarding how the Spanish Securities Market Commission has initiated exclusion procedures to guarantee that only entities with actual stock market activity are listed.
35. ALI 1992, p. 158 and De Broe/Luts 2015, p. 129. According to Bates/Berman/Gani/Gutmann /Imamura/Klugman/Rust 2013, p. 395, 'Both the burden of securities regulation and the attendant glare of public scrutiny make publicly traded companies a poor choice for treaty shopping. Inasmuch as the likelihood of abuse is relatively low, the residence of the shareholders is less relevant'.
36. An example of this is the Netherlands-U.S. DTC. To comply with the stock exchange clause, the entity is also required to have a substantial presence in the state where it is a resident. Whether a company has a substantial presence in a contracting state is determined by the trading volume of its stock on the recognized stock exchanges in its primary economic zone or by reference to its primary place of management. These requirements are meant to guarantee that the entity actually has a factual nexus to the state of residence, which may not always be demonstrated by the fact that it is listed on the stock market. *See* Van der Weijden/Doets 2004, pp. 305-307.

There are essentially four aspects of this clause which are to be addressed. For the clause to be applicable, the company's principal class of shares are required to be listed and to be regularly and substantially traded. The first two aspects to be analysed refer to the meaning of these two concepts.

In order to be taken into account, the shares must be listed and traded on the secondary markets included in the treaty. The 1996 U.S. Model limits these to the stock exchanges existing in any of the contracting states. As shall be observed, some tax treaties and the 2006 and 2016 U.S. Models allow the shares to be listed on certain stock exchanges established in third states, i.e. states that are not party to the treaty. In these cases, the treaties are recognizing that the contracting states are included in certain international organizations, and the actual nexus of the publicly traded company is not limited to the territory of the state where it resides, but rather extended to the states which form part of the international organization to which the contracting states belong. However, the 2006 and 2016 U.S. Models require that when the company's principal class of shares are regularly traded on one or more recognized stock exchanges located in a state different from the state where the company resides, the company's primary place of management and control should be located in the contracting state where it is a resident.

Finally, reference must be made to the requirements for indirect access to the clause. Most relevant in this respect is the concept of indirect shareholdings. In this regard, it should be noted that the stock exchange clause does not establish any obligation to comply with the base erosion prong of the ownership and base erosion clause. However, the 2016 U.S. Model and some treaties (Luxembourg and Malta) include the latter prong in cases of indirect access.

II.E.2   Direct Access

II.E.2.a   Principal Class of Shares (and Disproportionate Class of Shares)

The 1996 U.S. Model does not use this term. It only establishes that all the shares in the class or classes of shares representing more than 50 percent of the voting power and value of the company must be regularly traded on a recognized stock exchange.

The 2006 and 2016 U.S. Models, and most U.S. tax treaties, provide the expression 'principal class of shares'. In principle, there is no material difference because the 2006 and 2016 U.S. Models define this concept in the same terms as the 1996 U.S. Model. The concept of 'principal class of shares' is defined in both Models as follows:

> The term 'principal class of shares' means the ordinary or common shares of the company, provided that such class of shares represents the majority of the voting power and value of the company. If no single class of ordinary or common shares represents the majority of the aggregate voting power and value of the company,

the 'principal class of shares' are those classes that in the aggregate represent a majority of the aggregate voting power and value of the company[37]

Therefore, the result is the same in both cases, i.e. the principal class of shares representing this figure must be traded on a recognized stock exchange.

Nevertheless, the DTC between Luxembourg and the U.S. (Article 24(2)(d)) does give rise to some doubts, as it does not define this concept. This treaty only requires that the class of shares representing the majority of capital and voting power be traded. Therefore, a doubt arises as to whether it is necessary for the principal class of shares (in reference to capital stock and voting power) to exceed a percentage of 50 percent. If this were not necessary, only the class of shares representing the majority of capital and voting rights would be required to be traded, as opposed to any other class of shares. However, this class of shares would not have to represent more than 50 percent of both parameters. The above interpretation is not that adopted by the U.S. tax authorities. According to the Technical Explanation of the DTC with Luxembourg, the shares are always required to represent more than 50 percent of the company's capital stock and voting power.

In any case, this requirement is significantly more flexible in the different versions of the U.S. Model and the tax treaties being examined than in the December 1981 version of the U.S. Model and the U.S. branch tax law. In the first case, all shares were required to be traded and, in the second, at least 80 percent thereof.[38]

The different versions of the U.S. Model are based on the assumption that there are different classes or types of shares in a company. When there is only one type of share, it is not difficult to calculate the percentage traded. However, problems arise when the company has various classes of shares and none of these account for a percentage of 50 percent, or at least not in the case of capital stock nor voting power. The solution provided in both the Technical Explanation of the 1996 and 2006 U.S. Models and the Technical Explanations of the specific treaties entails adding together as many classes of shares required to exceed the established percentage. As previously mentioned, the calculation of the required percentage becomes increasingly more complex to the extent that the company has various classes of shares with different values and voting power.[39]

In regard to the concept of 'principle class of shares', some U.S. tax treaties, before the 2006 U.S. Model was released, mentioned the 'disproportionate class of shares'.[40] This concept was incorporated into the 2006 U.S. Model. All tax treaties that

---

37. *See* Article 22(5)(b) 2006 U.S. Model and Article 22(6)(b) 2016 U.S. Model.
38. *See* Vogel/Shannon/Doernberg/Van Raad, 1989, Article 16, p. 41 and Morrison/Bennett 1993a, p. 335.
39. Bennett/De Hosson/Morrison 1993, p. 56.
40. For example, the treaties between the U.S. and Ireland (Article 22(8)(d)(ii)), Luxembourg (Article 24(6)), the Netherlands (Article 26(8)(a), before it was amended in 2004) and the U.K. (Article 23(5)). The Technical Explanation of the DTC between Austria and the U.S. (paragraph 197) also mentions these shares, but postpones taking them into consideration until there is a mutual agreement procedure between the two contracting states (*see* Strauch 1997, p. 82). Paragraph 20 of the Commentaries on Article 1 of the OECD Model provide this concept and define it in terms similar to the 2006 and 2016 U.S. Models.

were negotiated taking into account the 2006 U.S. Model contain the term 'disproportionate class of shares'. It is also provided for in the 2016 U.S. Model.

A 'disproportionate class of shares' is one which grants the shareholder the right to participate in a higher proportion of the income obtained by the entity in the source state than that which corresponds based on the value of the shares. This disproportionate right does not necessarily have to materialize at the time dividends are paid, but rather can be granted by other means, such as by the write-off of the shareholders' debts to the company. The disproportion consists in the right to a higher profit than that which corresponds based on the value of the share. In this individual case, the higher profit received is charged to the income obtained by the company in the other contracting state.

A treaty shopping structure may be developed by means of such shareholdings, as long as the company complies with the stock exchange clause. However, the development of this type of structure depends on whether the corporate law applicable to the company allows it to assign disproportionate economic rights to the shares in the manner discussed above.[41]

The term 'disproportionate class of shares' has the following effects in the 2006 and 2016 U.S. Models. These Models require that these types of shares be added together with the principal class of shares in order to assure that they also comply with the trading requirement. Based on the wording of the stock exchange clause in the 1996 U.S. Model, not all shares are required to satisfy the aforementioned requirement, meaning that a disproportionate class of shares may be excluded. By including this type of share, the development of a treaty shopping structure is prevented, as these shares must also meet the substantial and regular trading requirements. As mentioned earlier, this requirement guarantees that there is an actual separation between the company's and the shareholders' interests.

However, in some treaties negotiated before the 2006 U.S. Model, the term 'disproportionate class of shares' has different effects. That occurs in the DTCs with Luxembourg and the U.K. In the case where there is a disproportionate class of shares, these treaties limit the application of the tax reduction in the source state to the portion of income that corresponds to the percentage of shares, which would be held in the case where there were no disproportionate economic right.[42] However, this only occurs when more than 50 percent of the capital stock and voting power is owned by persons that are not qualified residents or to persons residing in EU, North American Free Trade Agreement (NAFTA) and European Economic Area (EEA) (only in the U.K.-U.S. DTC) Member States.[43] For example:

> A company residing in the U.K. obtains dividends in the U.S. for a value of 1000 units of account. The company complies with the stock exchange clause. 60 percent of the company's capital stock is owned by a company residing in Switzerland. The rest belongs to qualified residents. The shares held by the

---

41. Cohen/Pollack/Scherer 1997, p. 62.
42. Schaffner 1997, p. 169 and Winandy 1996, p. 25.
43. Later the meaning of the concept of residence in EU, NAFTA and EEA states will be analysed. As shall be observed, it is not sufficient to be a resident in one of these states.

company in Switzerland give it the right to obtain the profits corresponding to the shares' value in addition to 100 percent of the dividends obtained in the U.S. In this case, only 60 percent of the dividends obtained in the U.S. (600 units of account) benefit from the treaty's tax ceiling.

In our opinion, in these treaties, it would be only be logical to apply this clause in the case that the disproportionate class of shares belonged to non-qualified residents, as in this case the person who effectively benefited from the treaty would not have a sufficient nexus to the contracting states. Where the disproportionate class of shares belongs to qualified residents, the application of the treaty is justified since they do have a sufficient nexus. However, it should be pointed out that it would be very burdensome to determine whether or not the taxpayers who own these shares are qualified residents.

Based on the wording of Article 24(6) of the DTC between Luxembourg and the U.S., it is not clear whether this limit applies to all income obtained in the source state or only to income related to the disproportionate class of shares. It would be most reasonable for the normal regime to be applied to the unrelated income, i.e. the full application of the treaty.

II.E.2.b Substantial and Regular Trading

This concept is not defined in any of the U.S. Models.[44] However, some treaties, for example, in the DTCs with Denmark, Ireland, Luxembourg, the Netherlands and the U.K., do provide a definition.

This requirement excludes those companies that lack stock market activity, because the trading of the shares of these companies is inactive. For the assumption on which the rule is based to arise, the company must be effectively quoted. The company is considered to be 'effectively quoted' when its shares are actually traded on the market. Therefore, a certain trading frequency and volume is required. When this trading frequency and volume are reached, the assumption underlying the rule is adhered to. With respect to this concept, the problem relates to defining the required trading volume and frequency.

When a treaty does not expressly define the concepts used and a different interpretation is not derived from the context of the treaty, the definition it has under domestic law should prevail.[45] In the event that the U.S. is the source state, a definition of this concept is provided under domestic law. This concept is defined under U.S. branch tax legislation (Treasury Regulations section 1.884-5(d)(4)(i)(B)).[46] The same is not true when the opposite occurs. There is no definition of this concept under the tax

---

44. This concept is not defined in paragraph 20 of the Commentaries on Article 1 OECD Model either.
45. See Article 3(2) of the OECD and the U.S. Models.
46. The Technical Explanations of the 1996 and 2006 U.S. Models establish that the term 'regularly traded' will be 'defined by reference to the domestic tax laws of the state where treaty benefits are sought, generally the source state. In the case of the U.S., this term is understood to have the meaning it has under Treas. Reg. section 1.884-5(d)(4)(i)(B), relating to the branch tax provisions of the Code'.

law of the EU Member States. However, it would be possible to refer to corporate law to determine the minimum trading volume and frequency required, in the case that such a requirement were made.[47]

Under U.S. law, a class of shares satisfies this requirement if, during a tax period, it has been traded for a minimum of sixty days more than the usual minimum on that stock exchange (trading frequency). It is also necessary for each class of traded shares to exceed, by at least ten percent, the number of issued and fully paid shares of each class (trading volume). In simpler terms, if there are a hundred fully paid shares in a class, at least ten of these shares must have been traded.[48] For example:

> Company A resides in Spain. It has three classes of shares: A, B and C. Classes A and B are the principal shares because they represent over 50 percent of the voting power and capital stock. These shares, as a whole, must comply with the trading requirement. Only 30 percent of the issued A and B shares are listed. They are quoted on both a Spanish and a U.S. secondary market. Trading was as follows:

	Madrid	NASDAQ	
Class A	14%	12%	26%
Class B	14%	11%	25%
Total	28%	23%	51%

In this case the requirement is met, because 15.3% of the principal shares were traded (51% × 30%/100 = 15.3%).[49]

When the U.S. is the source state, in principle, the company listed on the stock exchange in the state of residence must satisfy this requirement. However, experts in this field have pointed out that the requirements under U.S. law should not be applicable within the scope of treaties that include a set of LOB clauses similar to those provided in the 1996, 2006 and 2016 U.S. Models, since the 1986 branch tax rules are provided for those treaties that do not contain these types of rules.[50]

The alternative would be to introduce an autonomous concept. In this respect, it would be useful to refer to the definitions provided in the treaties discussed at the beginning of this section. These treaties define this requirement in similar terms. In some respects, these definitions make the requirements more flexible than under U.S. law. However, in other respects the requirements are stricter. In treaties where this concept is not expressly defined, it is likely that the U.S. tax authorities will recognize that this requirement of the clause has been met if the shares are quoted under the terms provided in the treaties that do contain a definition. On the other hand, it would

---

47. Cohen/Pollack/Scherer 1997, p. 62.
48. Berman/Hynes 2000, p. 693. Not all of the principal shares must be listed on a stock exchange. However, at least 10 percent of the issued shares must be effectively traded. Therefore, if only 30 percent of the company's shares are quoted, at least 33 percent of the 'quoted shares' must have been traded (30 × 33 / 100 = 10). See Bennett/Morrison/Daniels/De Hosson 1995, p. 71.
49. Strauch 1997, pp. 83–84.
50. Jacob 1991, p. 28.

be unlikely for the requirements of the U.S. tax authorities to be more burdensome than those provided under its own domestic law.[51]

The treaties that define this concept present two fundamental deviations from the concept provided under U.S. law.

On one hand, all of the treaties contain stricter trading frequency requirements. In the DTCs entered into by the U.S. with the Netherlands and the U.K., the shares must be traded every month of the taxable year and must exceed the normal minimum quantities on the stock exchange where the shares are traded. In the DTCs with Denmark and Ireland, trading is only required each quarter.[52] Under U.S. law, the requirement is sixty days.

On the contrary, the trading volume requirement is less burdensome. In the five treaties (Denmark, Ireland, Luxembourg, the Netherlands and the U.K.), the volume of shares traded is reduced from 10 percent to 6 percent.

Based on its wording, a company will only be able to verify its compliance with the clause at the end of the taxable year since it will only be possible to verify whether the shares' trading frequency and volume has reached the required level once the tax period has ended. Nevertheless, with respect to trading volume, these treaties differ from U.S. legislation insofar as they establish that the percentage from the previous year will be taken into account. Therefore, to some extent, the companies will be aware of whether they have complied with this requirement in advance.[53]

II.E.2.c Recognized Stock Exchanges

The 1996, 2006 and 2016 U.S. Models only authorize a company to be listed and for its shares to be traded on one of the stock exchanges located in the contracting states. If the company's shares are traded on a stock exchange that is not recognized, it will not be deemed to be a qualified resident.

According to the U.S. Models and all its treaties, the term 'recognized stock exchange' means the NASDAQ System owned by the National Association of Securities Dealers, Inc. and any stock exchange registered with the U.S. Securities and Exchange Commission as a national securities exchange under the U.S. Securities Exchange Act of 1934.

Most tax treaties establish that any other stock exchange agreed upon by the competent authorities of the contracting states will also be recognized. In this regard, it should be taken into account that the U.S. basically requires three conditions to be fulfilled in order to agree on the recognition of other stock exchanges: (a) serious listing requirements; (b) broad ownership; and (c) a significant amount of trading.[54] As can be observed, these three requirements are exactly those which guarantee that the listing of a company on a stock exchange fulfils the assumptions on which this clause is based. The latter essentially depends on the structure of the stock exchange.

---

51. Schinabeck 1996, p. 28.
52. The Luxembourg-U.S. DTC makes no requirement relating to trading frequency.
53. Winandy 1996, p. 23.
54. Muntendam 1996, p. 389.

Most of the tax treaties signed by the U.S. with EU Member States recognize other stock exchanges.[55] These stock exchanges are different because none of them are located in one of the contracting states. Practically all of the LOB clauses contained in these treaties include certain clarifications in order to take into account that these states form part of certain international organizations. It should be noted that most of the recognized stock exchanges are located within the territory of EU, NAFTA and EEA Member States.

Accordingly, in the DTCs in which other stock exchanges are recognized, the aforementioned requirements may be satisfied either in the stock exchanges located in each contracting state or in these other stock exchanges.

The DTC with Luxembourg lays down certain restrictions.[56] As is known, this clause authorizes the application of the treaty because it assumes that the capital stock is widely distributed. This circumstance contributes to the fact that the company's and the shareholders' interests do not coincide.

This tax treaty limits the stock exchanges on which the shares of the closely held companies can be traded, and also exclude some of those mentioned. Specifically, the DTC between Luxembourg and the U.S. excludes the Luxembourg stock exchange, the NASDAQ System and any other stock exchange agreed upon by the competent authorities.

Closely held companies are defined in the following terms: a company of which 50 percent or more of the principal class of shares is owned by persons, other than qualified persons or residents of an EU Member State,[57] each of whom beneficially owns, directly or indirectly, alone or together with related persons, more than 5 percent of such shares for more than thirty days during a taxable year. In summary, these are publicly traded companies whose capital stock is not widely distributed, since 50 percent of the principal shares are held by a maximum of ten taxpayers ($50/5 = 10$). These taxpayers are not considered to be qualified residents.[58]

As pointed out by experts in this field, the stock exchange clause assumes that the company's capital stock is widely distributed, meaning that a significant shareholding of more than 5 percent in publicly traded companies, that is owned by a person not entitled to the treaty benefits, is not in line with the assumptions on which this clause is based.[59] In these cases, in order to guarantee that there is a sufficient nexus to the

---

55. For example, the tax treaties with France, Luxembourg and the U.K. recognize the following stock exchanges: Amsterdam, Brussels, Frankfurt, Hamburg, London, Madrid, Milan, Paris, Sydney, Tokyo and Toronto. The Netherlands-U.S. DTC adds to the latter list the following stock exchanges: the Irish Stock Exchange, the Swiss Stock Exchange and the stock exchanges of Johannesburg, Stockholm and Vienna (*see* new Article 26(8)(a)). The DTC between Ireland and the U.S. encompasses Amsterdam, Brussels, Frankfurt, Hamburg, London, Madrid, Milan, Paris, Stockholm, Sydney, Tokyo, Toronto, Vienna and Zurich.
56. With respect to the DTC between the Netherlands and the U.S., the 2004 amendment eliminated the restriction being commented on. It is likely that this restriction was eliminated as a result of the inclusion of the requirement whereby the entity must have a substantial presence in the state in which it is a resident.
57. In the DTC between Luxembourg and the U.S., residents in NAFTA Member States are added.
58. DeCarlo/Granwell/Van Weeghel 1993, p. 275.
59. Muntendam 1996, p. 389.

Chapter 3: Limitation on Benefits Clauses

contracting states, this treaty only deems a company to be a qualified resident if its shares are traded on a stock exchange located within the state's territory.

Experts have also pointed out that by this means, the intention is to prevent another type of treaty shopping, the so-called stock exchange shopping.[60] With respect to the excluded stock exchanges, and particularly in the case of the treaty entered into with Luxembourg, the contracting states have considered it to be relatively simple for a company to be listed on the NASDAQ or the Luxembourg stock exchange, which could cause its shares to be held by a reduced number of persons who are not qualified residents or residents in any of the states belonging to the aforementioned international organizations.[61]

II.E.2.d   Primary Place of Management and Control

As seen in the previous chapter, U.S. tax treaties have extended the number of recognized stock exchanges. In fact, many of the recognized stock exchanges are not located in any of the territories of the contracting states. Nevertheless, in order to prevent the so-called stock exchange shopping, the 2006 U.S. Model introduced a new requirement in the stock exchange clause. This requirement is also provided for in the 2016 U.S. Model.

This requirement applies when the company's principal class of shares is primarily traded on one or more recognized stock exchanges located outside of the contracting state of which the company is a resident. Where the latter occurs, the company will only be entitled to the treaty benefits under the stock exchange clause if its primary place of management and control is in the contracting state of which it is a resident.

The term 'primary place of management and control' is defined in the 2006 U.S. Model as follows:

> a company's 'primary place of management and control' will be in the Contracting State of which it is a resident only if executive officers and senior management employees exercise day-to-day responsibility for more of the strategic, financial and operational policy decision making for the company (including its direct and indirect subsidiaries) in that State than in any other state and the staff of such persons conduct more of the day-to-day activities necessary for preparing and making those decisions in that State than in any other state.

According to the 2006 U.S. Model Technical Explanation, this term should be distinguished from the 'place of effective management' test which is used in Article 4(3) of the OECD Model and by many other tax treaties to establish residence. In some cases, the place of the effective management test has been interpreted to mean the place where the board of directors meets. By contrast, under the U.S. Model, the primary place of management and control test looks at where the day-to-day responsibility for the management of the company (and its subsidiaries) is exercised. In

---

60. Chica/Johnson 1993, p. 1515.
61. Schaffner 1997, p. 167.

this regard, the company's primary place of management and control will be located in the state where the company is a resident only if the executive officers and senior management employees exercise the day-to-day responsibility for more of the company's strategic, financial and operational policy decision making (including direct and indirect subsidiaries) in that state than in the other state or any third state, and the staff that support the management in making those decisions are also based in that state. Thus, the test looks at the overall activities of the relevant persons to see where those activities are conducted.

In most cases, it will be a necessary, but not a sufficient condition that the headquarters of the company be located in the contracting state where the company is a resident. To apply the test, it will be necessary to determine which persons are to be considered 'executive officers and senior management employees'. In most cases, it will not be necessary to look beyond the executives who are members of the Board of Directors (the 'inside directors') in the case of a U.S. company. That will not always be the case, however; in fact, the relevant persons may be employees of subsidiaries if those persons make the strategic, financial and operational policy decisions. Moreover, it would be necessary to take into account any special voting arrangements that result in certain board members making certain decisions without the participation of other board members.

As can be observed, this requirement tries to guarantee a sufficient nexus between the company and the contracting state where it is a resident; the 1996 U.S. Model did not require a company to satisfy a 'same country' listing or trading requirement or to have any other connection (apart from residency) to its own contracting state.[62] This assumption does not necessarily concur when its principal class of shares is primarily traded in other territories. The latter explains why this new requirement was introduced in the 2006 U.S. Model. In this regard, the U.S. policy has been clear on this issue: it has been accepted to broaden the number of recognized stock markets, provided that the company has a substantial presence in the state where it is a resident.[63] A number of treaties and protocols signed before and after 2006 provide a 'stock exchange test' similar to the one provided for in the 2006 U.S. Model.[64]

II.E.3 Indirect Access: Subsidiaries of Publicly Traded Companies

Through this alternative, the stock exchange test deems companies which are not listed, or which cannot directly access the treaty benefits by this means, to be qualified residents in the case where they are controlled by companies that do comply with the stock exchange test. In simpler terms, this alternative gives the subsidiaries of companies that comply with the stock exchange clause access to the treaty.

---

62. Miller/Stone 2008, p. 2.
63. U.S. Department of the Treasury 2007, p. 80.
64. *See*, among others, Articles 22(6)(c)(i) and 22(8)(d) of the 1992, as amended through 2004, the Netherlands-U.S. DTC and Article 28(2)(c) of the 1989, as amended through 2006, Germany-U.S. Model.

Article 22(2)(c)(ii) of the 1996 U.S. Model defines indirect access in the following terms:

[a company, if:]
at least 50 percent of each class of shares in the company is owned directly or indirectly by companies entitled to benefits under clause (i), provided that in the case of indirect ownership, each intermediate owner is a person entitled to benefits of the Convention under this paragraph;

The equivalent proviso provided for in Article 22(2)(c)(ii) of the 2006 U.S. Model reads as follows:

[a company, if:]
at least 50 percent of the aggregate vote and value of the shares (and at least 50 percent of any disproportionate class of shares) in the company is owned directly or indirectly by five or fewer companies entitled to benefits under clause i) of this subparagraph, provided that, in the case of indirect ownership, each intermediate owner is a resident of either Contracting State;[65]

The concept of control used by the U.S. Models is based on the existence of a substantial shareholding in a company which does not directly comply with the stock exchange clause.

Under the 1996 U.S. Model, the company that exercises this control is required to hold at least 50 percent of each class of shares. It should be noted that this Model does not require the shares to represent a certain percentage of capital stock and voting power as in the case of direct access. Although the shares owned by the controlling company represent more than 50 percent of the capital and voting power, this requirement is not satisfied unless the company owns at least 50 percent of each class of shares. In this regard, a company may have control over another company even though it does not own a significant number of its shares. The concept of control comprises all cases where the possibility of influencing the other company's decisions exists.[66] Despite this fact, the 1996 U.S. Model has defined this concept in the limited manner discussed above.[67] The latter explains why this aspect was modified in the 2006 U.S. Model, in order to require that the company or companies which exercise the control hold at least 50 percent of the aggregate vote and value of the shares.

Practically all of the treaties have followed the 1996 and 2006 U.S. Models. However, the DTC between Luxembourg and the U.S. only requires that the company 'be controlled' by entities that comply with the stock exchange clause. In principle,

---

65. Paragraph 20 of the Commentaries on Article 1 of the OECD Model formulates the alternative of indirect access in the same terms as the 2006 U.S. Model.
66. Schaffner 1997, p. 167.
67. Some treaties negotiated under the 1996 U.S. Model require, as in the 2006 U.S. Model, the shares in the controlled company to represent 50 percent of the capital stock and voting power. See the DTCs with Ireland (Article 23(2)(e)(ii)) and the U.K. (Article 23(2)(c)(ii)). Moreover, the Austria-U.S. DTC only states that 90 percent of the company should be owned by a publicly traded company (Article 16(1)(f)). The DTCs with the Czech Republic (Article 17(1)(d)) and the Slovak Republic (Article 17(1)(d)) state that all of the shares must be owned by entities that comply with the stock exchange clause. The DTCs which follow the 1996 U.S. Model in this regard are those entered into with Estonia, Latvia, Lithuania, Portugal, Slovenia and Spain.

more cases than those provided for in the Model itself should be admissible under this concept. In this respect, it is also important to mention the concept used by the 1996 tax treaty between Switzerland and the U.S., although it is not one of the treaties being studied herein.

In the DTC with Switzerland, companies in which a predominant interest is owned by an entity that complies with the stock exchange clause will have direct access to the clause.[68] The Memorandum of Understanding of this convention includes a number of examples in this respect. In most of the examples, a company is determined to have a predominant interest in another company due to fact that it owns a significant number of shares in this company. However, there are other examples in which this interest is not necessarily derived from the ownership of shares.[69]

This concept will not be analysed in depth. However, it is important to note that this definition is more flexible as the control is not limited to the fact that a certain percentage of shares are owned. However, although this definition is more flexible, it is less precise and may give rise to uncertainty regarding whether the clause has been complied with.

The second aspect of this clause refers to the taxpayers that exercise control. The 1996 and 2006 U.S. Models require the controlling company to comply with the stock exchange clause. It is necessary for these companies to reside in one of the contracting states, because, on the contrary, they would not comply with the stock exchange clause.[70]

Due to the wording of the DTC between Luxembourg and the U.S., in the case of indirect access, some authors have questioned whether it was sufficient for the controlling company to be listed on one of the recognized stock exchanges, regardless of where it resides.[71] This convention does not expressly state that the controlling company must reside in one of the contracting states. It is perfectly acceptable for the company to be listed on one of these stock exchanges but to have its residence for tax purposes in a different state.

In our opinion, this doubt does not really exist. If the convention were to be interpreted systematically, this requirement would still have to be complied with. The controlling company is always defined by referral to the section regulating direct access to this clause. Therefore, the referral would not be to any type of company, but rather exclusively to companies residing in one of the contracting states, that are listed on one of the stock exchanges recognized by the conventions and under the terms provided therein (regular and substantial trading of the principal shares). Consequently, although not expressly indicated, in view of the referral used to define this form of access in the stock exchange clause, it is assumed that the controlling companies

---

68. McCarthy 1997, p. 112.
69. Reinarz 1996, p. 3.
70. The Spain-U.S. DTC is more restrictive than the Model, because the controlling company must reside in the same state as the controlled company. Therefore, a company residing in Spain controlled by a company residing in the U.S., whose shares are substantially and regularly traded on the NASDAQ, would not comply with this clause. The same occurs in the case of the DTC between the Czech Republic and the U.S.
71. Cohen/Pollack/Scherer 1997, p. 63.

actually comply with the stock exchange clause, meaning that they are previously required to be residents in one of the contracting states.[72]

Based on the above, an interpretation to the contrary does not seem admissible. Furthermore, it is unlikely that it would be accepted by the U.S. tax authorities because it would clearly contradict the position taken in both U.S. Models.[73] However, although the text of the treaty may lead to an interpretation to the contrary, such an interpretation would have no practical effect in the event that the U.S. tax authorities refused to accept it, as they would use domestic treaty override mechanisms to maintain this requirement.

As observed, the 1996 and 2006 U.S. Models do take indirect shares into account in this calculation. Not all treaties follow the Model's structure. For calculation purposes, the main difference consists in determining which entities may form part of the indirect ownership chain. A question arises as to whether only qualified residents are admissible, or if non-qualified residents are also entitled to apply the convention.

Finally, this clause differs from the ownership and base erosion clause, precisely because it does not require that the 'base ownership test' be passed. This is true in the case of all the DTCs except those entered into with Luxembourg and the Netherlands. In this regard, it must be pointed out that the 2016 U.S. Model has introduced a base erosion prong in this test.

II.E.3.a Percentage of Ownership Interest and Controlling Entities

Except for the DTCs with Austria (90 percent) and the Czech Republic (100 percent), all treaties that authorize this form of access require a percentage of 50 percent as proposed in the 1996 and 2006 U.S. Models.

The 2006 U.S. Model, and many treaties, lay down a restriction for which in our opinion, there are no strong grounds.[74] The percentage of the company's shares indirectly accessing the treaty may not be owned by more than five companies residing in one of the contracting states that comply with the stock exchange clause.[75] This means, for example, that a company residing in Italy whose capital stock is equally distributed among ten companies residing in the U.S., and whose shares are substantially and regularly traded on a recognized stock exchange may not indirectly access this clause.[76]

The Technical Explanation of the 2006 U.S. Model, as well as the mentioned treaties, do not explain the reason for this requirement. In our opinion, there are no

---

72. In order to avoid doubts of any kind, the DTC between Ireland and the U.S. expressly states that the controlling company must reside in one of the contracting states and comply with the stock exchange clause. *See* Crowdus 1997, p. 562.
73. Cohen/Pollack/Scherer 1997, p. 63.
74. *See*, among others, the treaties with Austria, Bulgaria, Denmark, Germany, Italy, Slovenia, the Netherlands and the U.K. However, according to Rust 2015, p. 132, 'The limitation to five publicly traded companies as shareholders was chosen to enable joint ventures without completely watering down the publicly traded test'.
75. Paragraph 20 of the Commentaries on Article 1 of the OECD Model also lays down this requirement.
76. Valente/Magenta 2000, p. 44.

grounds whatsoever for this limit on the number of shareholders. The control exercised by the shareholders as well as the possibility that the company be used for treaty shopping structures decreases in proportion to the dispersion of the company's capital stock.

In addition to the possibility included in the 1996 and 2006 U.S. Models, the tax treaty with Ireland provides for other forms of access.

The Ireland-U.S. tax treaty (Article 23(2)(e)(ii)) states that not only companies that comply with the stock exchange clause are authorized, but also 'qualified governmental entities', and companies in which the latter have a shareholding, when these shares represent more than 50 percent of the company's capital stock and voting power. For example:

> The shares of a company residing in Ireland are distributed in the following manner. 30 percent of the capital stock and voting rights belong to a company residing in Ireland that complies with the stock exchange clause (shareholding A). 5 percent is owned by a company residing in the U.S. (shareholding B). 15 percent belongs to a qualified governmental entity in Ireland (shareholding C). 20 percent belongs to a company residing in Ireland which is fully owned by a U.S. qualified governmental entity (shareholding D). The other 30 percent is owned by a company residing in Italy (shareholding E). The company residing in Ireland has indirect access because 65 percent of its capital stock and voting power are owned by the taxpayers stated in the treaty (shareholdings A, C and D). In accordance with the 1996 and 2006 U.S. Models, it does not indirectly comply with the stock exchange clause because only shareholding A, which is of less than 50 percent, would be considered in the percentage calculation.

This treaty significantly facilitates access to the benefits thereof to companies where public entities have a direct or indirect ownership interest. In the ownership and base erosion clause, the shares belonging to public entities are also considered in the calculation of the percentage of shares as they are qualified residents. However, not only does this clause require compliance with the ownership requirement, but also with the 'base erosion test'. In the majority of cases, the DTC with Ireland frees publicly owned companies from complying with these requirements and allow these companies indirect access through the stock exchange clause.

Second, the DTC with France (Article 30(1)(c)(iii)), before it was amended by the 2009 Protocol, also allowed companies controlled by residents in EU Member States to indirectly access this clause in the case that they satisfy a group of requirements.[77]

Two observations should be made prior to analysing its legal framework. First, a certain percentage of the controlled company's capital stock and voting power is required to be owned by companies residing in one of the contracting states that comply with the stock exchange clause. Second, this special rule only applies when the company given indirect access is a resident of France. Companies residing in the U.S. may only indirectly access the clause in the previously discussed general form.

The ownership interest should be structured in the following manner. At least 30 percent of the voting power and capital stock must be directly or indirectly owned by

---

77. This alternative was also provided in the tax treaty between the Netherlands and the U.S. before it was amended in 2004. *See* Van der Weijden/Dotes 2004, p. 307.

companies that reside in the same state (France) and comply with the stock exchange clause. Therefore, contrary to the general case, the shares of companies residing in the U.S. that comply with the stock exchange clause will not be taken into account. This treaty also allows shares to be owned by public entities and subsidiaries, under the terms provided.[78]

Furthermore, at least 70 percent of the company's voting power and capital stock must be directly or indirectly owned by companies residing in one of the contracting states that comply with the stock exchange clause, and to companies residing in EU Member States whose principal class of shares is substantially and regularly traded on one of the stock exchanges recognized by the treaty, i.e. which comply with the stock exchange clause. In this respect, this treaty considered in this calculation, the contracting states public entities and companies in which they have a shareholding, as well as public entities of EU Member States and the companies in which these entities have a shareholding.[79]

As can be observed, these taxpayers are considered in the calculation of the 30 percent requirement and the 70 percent requirement. On the contrary, it would be practically impossible to comply with this clause in the event that the taxpayers referred to in the case of the 30 percent requirement were to own a shareholding exceeding this percentage. For example:

> 35 percent of the capital stock of company A, which is a resident of France, is owned by company B, which is also a resident of France, and complies with the stock exchange clause. The other 65 percent is distributed in the following manner: 40 percent belongs to company C, which is a resident of Spain. The shares of company C are traded substantially and regularly on the Madrid stock exchange. The remaining 25 percent is owned by company D, which is a resident of Switzerland. The 30 percent requirement is met because company B, which complied with the stock exchange clause and resides in the same state as company A (France), has a shareholding which exceeds this amount. The 70 percent requirement is also met, as company C, which resides in the EU, owns shares of company A, and this company's shares are substantially and regularly traded on a recognized stock exchange. If the shareholdings of company C (40 percent) and B (35 percent) are added together the 70 percent requirement provided in the treaty is also met.

The wording of the clause was quite complicated, but at least it allowed for an increase in the number of companies who may access the treaty. By taking into account the EU Member States, the treaty materially broadened the nexus that the company must have to the state of residence. The treaty may be applied if there was a sufficient nexus in EU Member States. Even so, it should be taken into consideration that the taxpayer's nexus to the state of residence's territory was not completely disregarded in the case of the 30 percent requirement. However, the required percentage was significantly reduced with respect to the general percentage required for indirect access to the treaty by means of the stock exchange clause (50 percent).

---

78. *See* Schinabeck 1996, p. 30.
79. Spector/Salou 1995, p. 99.

II.E.3.b The Concept of European Union, North American Free Trade Agreement and European Economic Area Member State Resident

The concept of EU, NAFTA and EEA Member State resident also appears in other LOB clauses, particularly in the ownership and base erosion and derivative benefits tests. In this section, the meaning of this concept shall be analysed, and shall then be referred to in subsequent sections in connection with the study of the rest of the clauses.

In various clauses, this concept is used to calculate the shares held by taxpayers which are residents in one of the states forming part of the aforementioned organizations or international agreements. As shall be observed, this concept requires more than simply being a resident in accordance with the Member States legislation in the international organizations referred to.

Generally, two requirements must be met. First, the shareholder's state of residence is required to have entered into a DTC with the state where the income is generated. The U.S. has concluded tax treaties with all EU –with exception of Croatia-, NAFTA and EEA Member States, meaning that compliance with this requirement will not give rise to any problem when the U.S. is requested to apply the convention as the source state.

Second, the treaty entered into with the U.S. by the shareholder's state of residence must contain a general LOB rule similar to that provided in Article 22 of the 1996, 2006 and 2016 U.S. Models. In addition to being considered a resident for the purposes of this treaty, the taxpayer exercising control (shareholder) must comply with one of the clauses provided in the treaty concluded with the U.S., by which, it is deemed to be a qualified resident. Therefore, the taxpayer may not just comply with any clause conferring the right to apply the treaty, but rather with those clauses by which it is deemed to be a qualified resident.

The second requirement may give rise to the following problem; although the U.S. has concluded DTCs with almost all states forming part of the EU, NAFTA and EEA, not all of these treaties contain a set of LOB clauses similar to those provided in the different versions of the U.S. Model. The treaties in force with Greece and Hungary do not include any such clause and the DTC with Cyprus only contains a limited form of these clauses, as they were both negotiated in accordance with the 1981 U.S. Model. Additionally, the U.S. has still not signed a tax treaty with Croatia.

To resolve the problem which might arise as a result of the second requirement, the treaties lay down the following legal fiction. The shareholder will be considered to be a resident in an EU, NAFTA or EEA Member State if it would have complied with one of the LOB clauses, by which the status of qualified resident would have been conferred upon it, in the event that it had been considered to be a resident[80] in the state that entered into a treaty with the U.S. whose application is desired (i.e. in the state where the company in which it has a shareholding resides). For example:

---

80. This not only requires compliance with the LOB clauses but also tax liability on worldwide income, because on the contrary, the taxpayer is not a resident within the meaning of the treaty and may not take the next step, i.e. verification as to whether it complies with one of the LOB tests.

The DTC involved is the treaty concluded between France and the U.S. A company residing in France requests the U.S. tax authorities to apply the treaty in respect of certain income obtained in the U.S. The French company is 50 percent controlled by a company residing in Greece. The treaty concluded between the U.S. and Greece does not contain LOBs. However, if the company residing in Greece were to reside in France, it would have complied with the ownership and base erosion clause (by which it would be deemed to be a qualified resident). As this is the case, the Greek company's shareholding is considered in the percentage calculation given that it meets the previously discussed requirements of the concept.[81]

The concept of an EU, NAFTA and EEA Member State resident is defined in similar terms in all the treaties in which it is provided.

II.E.3.c Indirect Shareholding

All of the treaties that allow for indirect access calculate both direct and indirect shareholdings. However, for the indirect shareholding to be taken into account, all the entities included in the 'chain of ownership' must comply with certain requirements. These requirements have changed over time in the different versions of the U.S. Model.

In the 1996 U.S. Model, all entities included in the 'chain of ownership' had to be considered as qualified residents.[82] This is the interpretation derived from Article 22 of the 1996 U.S. Model and from the Technical Explanations of some tax treaties.[83] Therefore, the entities that form part of the 'indirect chain of ownership' are not also required to comply with the stock exchange clause, but, they must at least be considered qualified residents. Indirect shareholdings will not be considered if any of the entities included in the chain of ownership is not a qualified resident. When the chain is broken, the indirect ownership interest is not considered in the calculation of shares.

The 2006 U.S. Model does not require all entities forming part of the 'indirect chain of ownership' to be qualified residents. It is sufficient that each intermediate owner is a resident of either contracting states.[84] In this regard, the 2006 Model appears to be more flexible than the previous one, as it is not necessary for the intermediate owners to comply with an LOB clause in order to be considered.

The 2016 U.S. Model has tightened up this requirement, as intermediate owners can no longer reside in either of the contracting states. According to Article 22(2)(d)(ii)

---

81. Spector 1993, pp. 163–164.
82. Berman/Hynes 2000, p. 694. However, according to paragraph 20 of the Commentaries on Article 1 of the OECD Model, taxpayers are required to be residents in one of the contracting states, but not to be qualified residents.
83. The Models and DTCs do not define how indirect ownership is determined. Schinabeck 1996, p. 29, states that under the U.S. domestic law (the branch tax), the shares are calculated through the corresponding prorating based on the shares held by those forming part of the chain of ownership. Accordingly, for example, if a company residing in France is 80 percent owned by company A, which in turn is 75 percent owned by company B, which complies with the stock exchange clause, then following the corresponding prorating, compliance with the percentage requirement, i.e. 50 percent, (which is the result of multiplying 80 by 75 and dividing the sum by 100) may be verified.
84. Julien/Koch/Szudoczky 2017, p. 14.

of the 2016 U.S. Model, intermediate owners must reside in the same contracting state from which a benefit under the tax treaty is being sought, i.e. the source state. However, at the same time, the 2016 U.S. Model has added a new set of eligible intermediate owners, i.e. the so-called qualifying intermediate owners. This is a completely new term, which is defined in Article 22(7)(f) of the 2016 U.S. Model as follows:

> the term 'qualifying intermediate owner' means an intermediate owner that is either:
>
> (i) a resident of a state that has in effect with the Contracting State from which a benefit under this Convention is being sought a comprehensive convention for the avoidance of double taxation that includes provisions addressing special tax regimes and notional deductions analogous to subparagraph (l) of paragraph 1 of Article 3 (General Definitions) and subparagraph (e) of paragraph 2 of Article 11 (Interest), respectively; or
> (ii) a resident of the same Contracting State as the company applying the test under subparagraph (d) or (f) of paragraph 2 or paragraph 4 of this Article to determine whether it is eligible for benefits under the Convention;

According to the above, the 2016 U.S. Model admits third country's residents as intermediate owners if they are residents of a country that has in effect a comprehensive tax treaty with the source state that contains rules addressing special tax regimes and notional interest deductions.[85] Moreover, intermediate owners who reside in the same contracting state as the company requesting treaty benefits through the indirect stock exchange test are only eligible if they comply with any of the following LOB rule tests: indirect stock exchange, ownership and base erosion test and derivative benefits.

As can be seen, the 2016 U.S. Model has introduced a high degree of complexity in determining which intermediate owners are eligible. That is why it is difficult to agree with the reasoning of the Preamble of the 2016 U.S. Model to introduce this modification,[86] since the draft of the Model released for public comment in May 2015

---

85. The special tax regimes provision is provided for in Article 3(1)(l) of the 2016 U.S. Model. There is not a similar provision in the previous versions of the U.S. Model nor in the OECD Model. The main purpose of this provision is to deny treaty's benefits at source when the person claiming the benefits enjoys a preferential tax regime in the state of residence. This rule will be analysed in section IV.B.2 of this chapter. Moreover, 'notional interest deduction' is a measure in international tax law enabling a company to deduct from their taxable income a fictitious interest calculated based on their shareholder's equity (net assets). The 2016 U.S. Model does not define this term. This new rule allows a treaty partner to tax interest arising in that country in accordance with the domestic law if the interest is beneficially owned by a related person that benefits from a notional interest deduction.
86. The Preamble states as follows: 'Comments requested that the rules for intermediate ownership contained in the various ownership-based LOB tests in the May 2015 draft be relaxed. In response to these comments, the intermediate ownership rules in the LOB test for subsidiaries of publicly traded companies (paragraph 2(d) of Article 22) and the general ownership-base erosion test (paragraph 2(f) of Article 22) in the 2016 Model LOB have been revised to permit as an intermediate owner any company that is a resident of a country that has in effect a comprehensive tax treaty that contains rules addressing special tax regimes and notional interest deductions.'

followed the 2006 U.S. Model. In this regard, although the 2006 Model did not admit persons residing in third states as intermediate owners, it admitted all residents of either contracting state, even if they did not comply with any of the LOB tests. In addition, this provision of the 2016 U.S. Model, along with others, somewhat distorts the original rationale of the LOB rule, since, to a certain extent, it takes into account the effective liability of the taxpayer in the state of residence in order to decide if treaty benefits should be applicable. It is somewhat striking that this new rationale is taken into account in some of the LOB rule tests but not others.

II.E.3.d Base Erosion

As previously mentioned, one characteristic of the stock exchange clause is that it does not require compliance with the base erosion prong of the ownership and base erosion test. However, the 2016 U.S. Model has included this prong of the ownership and base erosion clause in the indirect stock clause. However, the latter is not a totally new provision, as some U.S. tax treaties, such as the ones signed with Luxembourg and Malta (also in the case of direct access), lay down this additional requirement.

Here, only the base erosion prong introduced by the 2016 U.S. Model in the indirect stock exchange clause will be analysed, since the tax treaties with Luxembourg and Malta refer to the general ownership and base erosion test provided therein. The 2015 U.S. Draft does not give any clue as to why this additional requirement has been included in the indirect stock exchange test.

Article 22(2)(d)(ii) of the 2016 U.S. Model reads as follows:

> (ii) with respect to benefits under this Convention other than under Article 10 (Dividends), less than 50 percent of the company's gross income, and less than 50 percent of the tested group's gross income, is paid or accrued, directly or indirectly, in the form of payments that are deductible for purposes of the taxes covered by this Convention in the company's Contracting State of residence (but not including arm's length payments in the ordinary course of business for services or tangible property, and in the case of a tested group, not including intra-group transactions):
> (A) to persons that are not residents of either Contracting State entitled to the benefits of this Convention under subparagraph (a), (b), (c) or (e) of this paragraph;
> (B) to persons that are connected persons with respect to the company described in this subparagraph and that benefit from a special tax regime with respect to the deductible payment; or
> (C) with respect to a payment of interest, to persons that are connected persons with respect to the company described in this subparagraph and that benefit from notional deductions described in subparagraph (e) of paragraph 2 of Article 11 (Interest);

The first thing that must be highlighted is the fact that the base erosion prong does not affect dividends. However, in the base erosion prong established in the ownership and base erosion clause and in the derivative benefits clause, dividends are not excluded from this requirement.

When dividends are not involved, the company must provide evidence that less than 50 percent of the company's gross income, and less than 50 percent of the tested group's gross income, is paid, in the form of deductible payments, to certain persons. Those 'disapproved payees'[87] are residents in third states, residents in either contracting state which are not entitled to treaty benefits under certain LOB tests (individuals, public bodies, direct stock exchange, tax-exempt organizations and pension funds) and connected residents of either contracting state entitled to treaty benefits under the mentioned LOB tests that benefit from a special tax regime with respect to the deductible payments.[88] When interest is involved, a further requirement is introduced. The recipients of the interest must be connected residents of either contracting state entitled to treaty benefits under the mentioned LOB tests that benefit from notional deductions.

To carry out these calculations, this test requires assessing not only the company's gross income but also the tested group's gross income. The latter term ('tested group') is another novelty introduced by the 2016 U.S. Model, which is also provided in the general ownership and base erosion clause and the derivative benefits clause.

Under the 2016 U.S. Model, a company's gross income and payments would be measured not only for those items, but also on any tested group basis of which the company forms a part. Thus, in a tested group scenario, two base erosion tests must be met: the first with the resident entity claiming treaty benefits and separately with all members of the tested group. As Stone has pointed out, 'in both tests, the gross income and deductible payments are measured on a resident company and tested group basis'.[89]

The entities that may be included are the ones with which the entity requesting treaty benefits participates as a member of a tax consolidation fiscal unity or a similar regime that requires members of the group to share profits and losses. Entities which share losses with the company, pursuant to a group relief or other loss sharing regime in the taxable year, may also be included. The aim of this provision, which is significantly complex, seems to be avoiding base erosion through the offset of losses generated by other entities.

Clearly, the base erosion requirement added to the indirect stock exchange test prompts that this test has 'no advantage' with respect to the ownership and base erosion test.

II.F Ownership and Base Erosion Clause

II.F.1 *Preliminary Remarks*

The last clause which confers the classification of qualified resident upon a taxpayer is the ownership and base erosion clause. This clause provides two requirements: the

---

87. Sheppard 2016, p. 730.
88. The special tax regimes rule provided for in the 2016 U.S. Model is analysed in section IV.B.2 of this chapter.
89. Stone 2015, p. 628.

Chapter 3: Limitation on Benefits Clauses

ownership and the base erosion requirements. Simultaneous compliance with both clauses is required to be deemed a qualified resident.

This clause has undergone several changes in the different versions of the U.S. Model. Hereafter, the main features of the two prongs of this test will be briefly explained.[90] The detailed version of the LOB rule proposed in Action 6 of the BEPS project contains an ownership and base erosion clause identical to the one provided for in the 2006 U.S. Model.

To comply with the ownership clause, the 1996 U.S. Model requires that at least 50 percent of each class of an entity's shares must be directly or indirectly owned by qualified residents during at least half of the days in the tax period. The owners must be residents of the same contracting state as the taxpayer.[91] Therefore, is it not sufficient that the qualified owners are resident in the other contracting state, i.e. the source state.

The 2006 and 2016 U.S. Models contain two remarkable differences. First, here not all qualified residents are eligible, as persons that are qualified persons under the indirect stock exchange clause (subsidiaries of public-traded companies) are excluded. Therefore, the shares must be owned only by individuals, governmental bodies, public traded companies, tax-exempted organizations and pension funds. Second, a different terminology is used, the ownership requirement refers to shares or other beneficial interests representing at least 50 percent of the aggregate voting power and value. As it has been observed, the 1996 U.S. Model only required a 50 percent ownership of each class of shares.

In the case of indirect ownership, the 1996 U.S. Model established that indirectly owned shares would only be taken into account in the calculation of this percentage if all the taxpayers that formed part of the chain of ownership were also qualified residents. The 2006 U.S. Model has simplified this requirement and it is sufficient if the intermediate owners are residents of the same contracting state as the taxpayer. Finally, the 2016 U.S. Model has modified this requirement, and only qualifying intermediate owners are eligible. The latter term, i.e. 'qualifying intermediate owner', is also included in the stock exchange test of the 2016 U.S. Model. Since the meaning of the term 'qualifying intermediate owner' was analysed in section III.E.3.c), we will not analyse it again in depth here.

As can be verified, the requirements provided in the ownership prong of this LOB test are of a qualitative (who are the shareholders?), quantitative (what percentage of shares must be held?) and temporal (for how long must the shares be held?) nature.

Moreover, in respect of the base erosion text, the U.S. Models and the treaties entered into by the U.S. always link the 'base erosion test' to the ownership clause. The ownership clause alone is not sufficient to deny the application of the treaty in cases of stepping stone structures.[92] The structure redirects the income obtained in the source

---

90. The Commentaries on Article 1 of the OECD Model contain a similar isolated clause (paragraph 17). Together with this isolated clause is the clause provided in paragraph 20(2)(e). The latter is similar to the clause provided in U.S. Model, although there are some differences which will be noted later.
91. Rust 2015, p. 134.
92. Wurm 1992, p. 662, Cavestany 1993, p. 99 and Goossen 1993, pp. 24–25.

state to the last investor, thereby transforming the income obtained at source into an expense in the intermediary company's state of residence. The income flows by means of an expense to a third state. Although this structure is normally developed by means of a company owned by non-residents, this is not necessarily the case.

The ownership clause only denies the application of the treaty when the majority of the capital stock of the company located in the state of residence is owned by non-residents. This clause does not allow for the denial of the treaty's application when the stepping stone structure is channelled by means of a company, which has most of its capital stock owned by residents. Therefore, the ownership clause is linked to the base erosion clause to prevent the application of the treaty in the event that this type of structure is used.

Among the clauses provided in the Commentaries to the OECD Model, is the isolated ownership clause (the 'look-through approach'), although as in the case of the U.S. model, an isolated clause linked to the base erosion clause ('the channel approach.') is also provided.[93] The Commentaries on the OECD Model state that problems arise in relation to this clause in the event that it is not linked to the base erosion clause in order to prevent stepping stone structures. However, it should be pointed out that the ownership or transparency clause is the only limitation on benefits clause that has been used to a certain extent by contracting states other than the U.S., such as Spain.[94]

The second phase of the clause consists in verifying whether or not the 'base erosion test' has been passed. According to the 1996 U.S. Model, less than 50 percent of the taxpayer's gross income may be paid to persons who are not residents of either contracting state, in the form of payments that are deductible from its tax base. Payments made to non-residents, that are attributable to a PE located in either of the contracting states, are not considered in this percentage. As can be observed, this requirement aims to prevent the company's tax base from eroding, or in other words, to assure that a treaty is only applied to entities that do not erode their tax base.

In this regard, the 2006 U.S. Model has tightened the base erosion prong of this test, in order to comply with the 50 percent requirement, payments to persons who are not qualified residents must also be taken into account. Additionally, the 'PE exclusion' laid down in the 1996 U.S. Model has been eliminated. Hence, payments attributable to a PE situated in either contracting state must also comply with this requirement. As will be outlined below, the 2016 U.S. Model has introduced further requirements, which make it even more difficult to comply with this part of the ownership and base erosion clause.

The two requirements of this clause aim to guarantee that a company is only entitled to apply a treaty when it and the income obtained at source maintain a sufficient factual nexus to one of the contracting states. Therefore, the clause limits the

---

93. Between the parentheses is the terminology used by OECD with respect to the names of these clauses. It should be borne in mind that this clause was isolated and not included within the context of the group of LOB tests provided in paragraph 20 of the Commentaries on Article 1 of the OECD Model.
94. Raventós 1995a, p. 71 and Vega 2003, pp. 244–245.

application of the treaty to companies owned by residents in one of the states that is party to the treaty. It also assures that the income generated at source is not obtained indirectly by residents in third states by means of the base erosion test.[95]

The problems relating to each of these clauses will be analysed separately, in light of how they are included in the DTCs being studied. It is important to note that the treaties generally intend to clarify some of the questions relating to their application, in addition to adding elements so they take into account that some of the contracting states are members of certain international organizations. With respect to the latter, the territorial boundaries to which there should effectively be a material nexus are extended.

II.F.2 Ownership Test

II.F.2.a Negative or Positive Wording of the Test

Whether the ownership test is worded positively or negatively may have significant consequences on the number of taxpayers that are able to comply with it.

The U.S. Models and most tax treaties word this requirement in a positive manner. The Models state that at least 50 percent of shares in the company should be directly or indirectly owned by certain qualified residents.[96] For example:

> Company A, a resident in Spain, is 45% owned by company B, a resident in Morocco, and 55 percent owned by company C, a resident in Spain that complies with the stock exchange clause. Company B has a 40 percent shareholding in company C. Company A complies with the ownership clause because 55 percent of each class of shares is owned by a qualified company (company C). However, it should be noted that company B has an ownership interest of 67 percent, if both its direct shareholding (45 percent) and indirect shareholding through company C (55 x 40 / 10 = 22) are taken into account. This shareholding has no effect when the clause is worded positively, since the indirect shares held by non-qualified residents are not taken into account.

This same clause was worded negatively in the tax treaty between France and the U.S. (Article 30(1)(d)(i), prior to its amendment in 2009), and stated that non-qualified residents may not directly or indirectly own 50 percent or more of a company's capital stock. In accordance with this wording, company A from the previous example would

---

95. Kim 1990, p. 993.
96. Although not provided in the text of the Model, the Technical Explanation of the 1996 U.S. Model (paragraph 303) includes the expression 'beneficial interest'. In the event that 50 percent of the persons with a beneficial interest in the company are qualified residents, the company will be entitled to apply the treaty. Some entities such as trusts do not technically have any shareholders. This concept is used to prevent these entities from being excluded from the treaty. In this case, it will be necessary to determine the proportion of the trust beneficiaries who meet this condition. In the 2006 and 2016 U.S. Models the term 'beneficial interest' is provided for in the wording of the ownership and base erosion clause.

not comply with the ownership clause, since company B, a non-qualified resident, had a shareholding of more than 50 percent, in the event that both direct and indirect ownership are considered.

Materially, the negative wording of this clause does not have as many effects as it may first appear. In the above example, company A would be entitled to the treaty benefits by means of indirect access to the stock exchange clause, given that the company is more than 50 percent owned by a company that does comply with the clause. However, in exceptional cases when the clause is worded negatively, the taxpayer may not be able to access the treaty by means of any clause which confers the status of qualified resident upon it. In these cases, if the clause had been worded positively, the ownership clause would have been complied with without any type of problems. For example:

> The shares in company A, a resident in France, are owned by the following taxpayers as follows: Six companies (companies B) residing in France which, as they comply with the indirect access form of the stock exchange clause, are qualified residents. Each company has a 9 percent shareholding. The total shareholding amounts to 54 percent. Company C, a non-qualified resident, has a 46 percent shareholding in company A. It also has shareholdings of 49 percent in two of the companies (companies B) that access the treaty by means of the indirect form of the stock exchange clause. If the wording of the clause were positive, company A would access the treaty, as more than 50% of this company is owned by qualified residents (companies B). If the wording of the clause were negative, company A would not be able to access the treaty as more than 50 percent of the company is owned by a non-qualified resident. It should be noted that company C has an ownership interest of more than 50 percent in company A if both direct and indirect ownership (by means of the companies B) are taken into consideration. In this case, company A may not access the treaty by means of the stock exchange clause because the companies which control its capital stock only access the stock exchange clause indirectly.

Accordingly, it may be asserted that a positive wording is more flexible and facilitates compliance with the ownership clause.[97]

II.F.2.b   Percentage and Indirect Ownership

The U.S. Models provide that the percentage which must be reached by qualified residents is at least 50 percent (positive wording).[98] Therefore, these taxpayers are only required to own at least 50 percent of the shares. However, some tax treaties have

---

97. De Lignie 1995, p. 72.
98. In this respect, the U.S. Models follow the proposal of ALI 1992, p. 168. In some treaties, as in the 2006 and 2016 U.S. Models, the disproportionate class of shares must also be taken into account. The definition and wording of this concept is exactly the same as in the stock exchange clause. Therefore, reference is made to section II.E.2.a., Chapter 3, in which this matter was discussed. Some treaties, as in the Ireland-U.S. DTC, this requirement only applies in the stock exchange clause.

Chapter 3: Limitation on Benefits Clauses

worded this requirement in slightly stricter terms.[99] In these treaties, it is stated that 'more than 50 percent must be owned by qualified residents'. Although there is a difference of only decimal points and a company with a percentage of 50.1 percent would comply with the clause, this is not a trivial matter.

One of the usual forms of business integration is the joint venture. A paradigmatic case of this figure is that of joint subsidiaries. Most typically, a joint subsidiary is a company formed by two enterprises or groups of enterprises, each of which own 50 percent of the company, in order to achieve a common purpose. These types of companies would not comply with the ownership clause in the event that one of the shareholders were not a qualified resident.[100] Nevertheless, each company's percentage of ownership interest may be corrected in order to comply with this clause. Even so, we consider this correction to be difficult to make as the position of each company in the joint venture would be seriously altered, considering that the company owning more than 50 percent of the company would mostly likely have a majority vote in the general meeting of shareholders. It is unlikely that one of the two companies would agree to be a minority shareholder merely for tax purposes.

Furthermore, the U.S. Models take indirect shareholdings into account to reach the percentage of 50 percent. As in the case of the stock exchange clause, all taxpayers forming part of the chain of ownership are required to meet certain requirements. In this regard, under the 1996 U.S. Model all intermediate owners were required to be qualified residents. As shall be observed below, this requirement makes no sense in the ownership clause, and this is surely the reason that few treaties have followed the 1996 U.S. Model.[101] In fact, this requirement was removed in the 2006 U.S. Model, where intermediate owners are only required to be residents.

In the stock exchange clause, it makes sense to require that indirectly owned shares only be taken into account when all of the taxpayers that form part of the chain of ownership are qualified residents. In this case, a company is able to obtain the status of qualified resident by means of indirect access to this clause, when the company that complies with the stock exchange clause directly or indirectly owns shares representing a certain percentage of a company's capital stock and voting power.

However, it does not make sense to include this requirement in the ownership clause because if all the taxpayers are required to be qualified residents, there is no need to take any indirectly owned shares into account. Only the shares of the first person in the chain would be calculated and there would be no need to continue forward since this person would have a direct ownership interest. In the ownership clause, almost all qualified residents serve for compliance with the 50 percent requirement.[102] By contrast, in the stock exchange clause, only a certain qualified

---

99. *See*, among other, the tax treaties with Austria and Spain. They are treaties mainly negotiated before the 1996 U.S. Model.
100. Vogel/Shannon/Doernberg/Van Raad 1989, Article 16, p. 24.
101. The DTCs with Estonia (Article 22(2)(c)(i)), Italy (Article 2(2)(f)(ii) of the Protocol), Latvia (Article 23(2)(c)(i)), Lithuania (Article 23(2)(c)(i)) and Slovenia (Article 23(2)(f)(i)). DeCarlo/Granwell/Van Weeghel 1998, p. 276.
102. As it has been already mentioned, the 2006 and 2016 U.S. Models exclude qualified residents under the indirect stock exchange test.

resident, i.e. the one who complies with the stock exchange clause, is considered. Accordingly, it makes no sense for the 1996 U.S. Model to require that all owners be qualified residents, as this requirement excludes the possibility of indirect ownership. In the case that the person is a qualified resident, the first person in the chain of ownership would directly own shares, meaning that it would not be necessary to continue forward in the chain.

In summary, we consider the requirement laid down in the 1996 U.S. Model to have little sense, since it eliminates the possibility of indirect ownership of shares. In the tax treaties that follow the 1996 U.S. Model, indirectly owned shares are not taken into account. However, in the rest of the treaties, they are considered, as in the 2006 U.S. Model. Nevertheless, in the following section, it shall be observed that in some cases, the U.S. Model's concept of indirect ownership does make sense.

To determine how the indirect ownership interest is calculated, and disregarding the 1996 U.S. Model's requirement, it is useful to refer to the wording of the treaty between Ireland and the U.S. (Article 23(2)(c)(1)). This treaty establishes that the indirectly owned shares will only be considered 'provided that such ownership test shall not be satisfied in the case of a chain of ownership unless it is satisfied by the last owners in the chain'. Technically, the chain of ownership only really reaches its end when there is an individual, which, obviously, cannot be owned by anyone. It would also be possible to consider taxpayers, such as foundations, which have no shareholders. Accordingly, advancing forward in the chain of ownership until a qualified resident were found would not be sufficient in the event that this company were also owned by a non-qualified resident, because in this case 'it would not be the last owner'.

Based on the wording of the rule, it would be excessively burdensome to analyse whether there is an indirect shareholding which may be taken into account, especially when many steps would be required to find such an individual. However, in some cases, it does allow for the consideration of indirect ownership interests, which is not possible under the DTCs that follow the 1996 U.S. Model's rule.

The rest of the treaties make no reference whatsoever to the requirements that must be satisfied by indirectly owned shares. In our opinion, it could be sustained that in this case, it is only necessary to analyse the chain of ownership until a qualified resident is found. It should not be necessary, as stipulated in the Irish treaty, for it to be 'satisfied by the last owner in the chain'.

Finally, as it was explained in section III.E.3.c, in the 2016 U.S. Model only 'qualified intermediate owners' are eligible. Therefore, as in the 2006 U.S. Model, it is not enough for intermediate owners to be residents of the same contracting state where the entity requesting treaty benefits resides.

II.F.2.c Qualified Residents

The U.S. Models do not use the concept of qualified resident when stipulating which taxpayers are required to own at least 50 percent of the shares. According to the 1996 U.S. Model, only the shares owned by taxpayers that comply with one of the following

Chapter 3: Limitation on Benefits Clauses

clauses should be considered: individuals, qualified governmental entities, both the direct and indirect forms of the stock exchange clause, tax-exempted organizations and pension funds. The 2006 and 2016 U.S. Models mention the same clauses with the exception of the indirect stock exchange clause.

As can be observed, the U.S. Models make no mention of the ownership and base erosion clause. However, some tax treaties, like the ones signed with Ireland, Luxembourg and Portugal also consider the shares owned by taxpayers who are deemed to be qualified residents by means of the ownership and base erosion test. The consequences of this difference are significant. In the tax treaties that follow the U.S. Models, it will be more difficult to comply with the ownership clause.[103] For example:

> Company A, a resident in Spain, is 60 percent owned by company B, which is also a resident in Spain. The rest of the company is owned by a company residing in Venezuela. Company B complies with the ownership and base erosion clause, because it is 60 percent owned by an individual residing in Spain. According to the U.S. Models, company A does not comply with the ownership clause as company B is not taken into account. Even if the indirect shareholding held by the individual controlling company B were taken into account, company A would not have a right to apply the treaty because its indirect ownership interest in A is less than 50 percent (it is 36%, 60 x 60/100 = 36). If the U.S. Models were not followed, company A would comply with the clause, because it is more than 50 percent owned by a qualified resident.

In our opinion, it makes little sense to exclude the entities that comply with the ownership and base erosion test. By satisfying these two requirements, these companies have already demonstrated that they have a sufficient factual nexus to the territory, meaning that they can also be taken into account to 'qualify' other entities.[104]

In this respect, although a taxpayer may be deemed to be a qualified resident by means of the ownership and base erosion clause, this is not always the case, since the clause does not also serve for the purpose of qualifying other entities.[105] However, the wording of the U.S. Models explains the meaning of indirect shares in this clause.

As observed in the previous section, it makes no sense to require all those included in the chain of ownership to be qualified residents, if, for the purpose of having its ownership interest taken into account in the percentage of shares, it is sufficient to be a qualified resident. However, in the U.S. Models, not all qualified residents are considered in the calculation of this percentage, as those who comply with the ownership and base erosion clause are not taken into account. Accordingly,

---

103. The clause provided in paragraph 20 of the Commentaries on Article 1 of the OECD Model follows the 2006 and 2016 U.S. Model. Hence, its ownership and base erosion clause does not consider either residents who comply with the ownership and base erosion clause or taxpayers that access the treaty by means of the indirect form of the stock exchange clause in the calculation of the required percentage of shares.
104. As stated by Winandy 1996, p. 20, being deemed a qualified resident does not only serve for obtaining access to the treaty's regime, but rather also to facilitate access to others. However, Bates/Berman/Gani/Gutmann/Imamura/Klugman/Rust 2013, p. 398, consider that 'presumably the rationale for treating companies that qualify under the ownership/base-erosion test as tainted payees is preventing indirect base-erosion'.
105. Goossen 1993, p. 28.

there could effectively be shares indirectly owned in full by qualified residents, where those in the middle of the ownership chain are considered to be qualified residents in accordance with the ownership and base erosion clause. As in the case of the stock exchange clause, not just any qualified resident would be considered, but rather a qualified resident that accessed the treaty by means of a clause other than the ownership and base erosion clause. Even so, as observed in the above example, the exclusion of these taxpayers makes it difficult to access the treaty.

This problem does not arise in the case of the tax treaties that do not follow the 1996 U.S. Model. However, as previously discussed, in these treaties it would not make sense to include a concept of indirect ownership interest such as that provided in the 1996 U.S. Model.

The second matter which should be addressed in relation to the qualitative aspects of the ownership clause, is that some treaties provide that the shares owned by U.S. citizens will also be taken into account in the calculation of this percentage.

In accordance with the LOB rule, individuals with U.S. citizenship will not be considered to be residents within the scope of the treaty if they do not have a substantial presence in one of the contracting states. When there is no factual nexus to the U.S. or the other contracting state, a U.S. citizen is not considered to be a resident nor a qualified resident. In summary, a person may not request the application of the convention merely due to the fact that he or she is a U.S. citizen.

However, the shares owned by U.S. citizens, even those who are not considered to be qualified residents, are taken into account to determine whether there is compliance with the ownership clause in some treaties.[106] In this respect, these treaties are not materially different to the U.S. Models. The U.S. Models do not mention U.S. citizens, but this is due to the fact that the U.S. Models do not contain a rule, whereby a U.S. citizen is not considered to be a resident when it does not have a nexus of a factual nature to one of the contracting states. Therefore, there is no need to expressly mention U.S. citizens in this clause, given that the individuals considered to be residents are automatically considered to be qualified residents according to the U.S. Models.

To a certain extent, the mention of individuals with U.S. citizenship undermines the factual assumption on which this clause is based, i.e. the existence of a factual nexus to the territory, and a nexus which is based on the residence of the company's shareholders. In accordance with the above, the treaty may be applied to companies whose shareholders have no effective nexus to any of the contracting states.

It has been pointed out, that taking these persons into account in the calculation of shares is justified as there is no danger of tax avoidance.[107] U.S. citizens are liable to

---

106. *See*, among others, the tax treaties with Austria (Article 16(1)(d)(i)), Estonia (Article 22(2)(c)(i)), Ireland (Article 22(2)(c)(i)), Latvia (Article 22(2)(c)(i)), Lithuania (Article 23(2)(c)(i)), Luxembourg (Article 24(2)(c)(i)), Portugal (Article 17(1)(e)(i)) and Spain (Article 17(1)(g)(i)). In this respect, although they may not directly claim the benefits of the treaty since it is still necessary to satisfy the substantial presence requirement, they will be taken into account not only to calculate the shares owned in the case of the ownership clause, but also in any other case that the treaty refers to the concept of qualified resident. Kaplan 1993, p. 179.
107. Vogel/Shannon/Doernberg/Van Raad 1989, Article 16, p. 40 and Jacob 1991, p. 31.

tax in the U.S. on worldwide income by virtue of their citizenship. Therefore, for example, although a U.S. citizen incorporates a company in the Netherlands to obtain the income generated in the U.S. from this state, this income will ultimately be taxed in the U.S. This is due to the fact that the saving clause provided in the treaty authorizes the taxation of this income in the U.S.

In our opinion, the fact that U.S. citizens are always taken into account is not at all justified from the standpoint of the assumptions on which the LOB clauses are based. A closer inspection reveals that they are not mentioned to prevent treaty shopping in the U.S., but rather to foster the development of treaty shopping structures by U.S. citizens in third states, so that they repatriate their income to the U.S. with the least tax cost possible. This would lead to higher tax revenue in the U.S., because the lesser tax levied abroad, the lesser tax revenue lost due to the application of the credit method in the state of residence.[108]

U.S. companies usually use certain states to channel their investments abroad. Access to the treaties entered into by the state used is not complicated, since these treaties do not usually contain LOB clauses. Subsequently, repatriation to the U.S. will not give rise to any problem relating to compliance with the LOB rule, as U.S. citizens are taken into account in the ownership clause.

To guarantee the consistency of the LOB rule, the inclusion of U.S. citizens should be reconsidered. U.S. citizens should only be taken into account when they effectively reside in one of the contracting states. In this respect, as in the case where a U.S. citizen directly claims the benefits of a treaty, their shares will only be taken into account if they have a substantial presence in one of the states that is party to the treaty. An interpretation to the contrary would give rise to situations that are not at all consistent. For example, a U.S. citizen residing in Venezuela may not request the direct application of the treaty between Spain and the U.S. However, if it incorporates a company in Spain it may indirectly obtain its application. We consider these situations to be undesirable for the contracting state, or at least for a contracting state other than the U.S., especially since this other contracting state has requested the inclusion of the rule limiting the criterion of citizenship.

II.F.2.d   Holding Period

With respect to the holding period, the 1996 and 2006 U.S. Models follow the domestic branch tax law: at least half of the days of the taxable year, the entity must be owned by qualified residents in the terms previously discussed.[109] Based on the wording of this requirement, it is not essential to comply with the ownership clause for the whole tax period, but rather for the period of time stipulated.

---

108. Kaplan 1993, p. 179.
109. Vogel/Shannon/Doernberg/Van Raad 1989, Article 16, p. 23. The same holding period is provided in paragraph 20 of the Commentaries on Article 1 of the OECD Model. The wording of the 2016 U.S. Model is slightly different: 'on at least half of the days of any twelve-month period that includes the date when the benefits otherwise would be accorded'.

In the case that a period of time is not established, a doubt arises in regard to whether the taxpayer is required to comply with this clause for the full taxable year, for just one day in this year, on the date the tax becomes due or each time income is obtained in the source state.

The last option seems to be most sustainable from the standpoint of the OECD Model. Article 10 of the OECD Model provides for two regimes in relation to dividends, depending on whether or not they are from a significant percentage of shares. The Commentaries (see paragraph 16 on Article 10) state that a determination as to whether the percentage of shares has been complied with, is to be made on the date that the tax is payable in the source state. If by analogy, this rule were applied to the case of this LOB test, each time the taxpayer obtained income in the source state, it would be necessary to determine whether the requirements were satisfied on the date the tax became payable. However, this option is the most burdensome, since compliance with this clause is required to be verified each time income is obtained.

This tax payable at source rule is hardly practical because an entity does not normally know whether it has complied with this clause until the end of the taxable period. Based on the terms of the base erosion clause, it would be impossible to determine if the entity has allocated more than 50 percent of its full income to non-qualified residents until the end of the tax period.

In this respect, it would be logical to make the date, on which compliance with the clause is verified, coincide with the final date of the tax period for the tax levied on the taxpayer in the state of residence. This date is also the same as the date on which the tax must be paid by the company that has obtained income, as in the case of periodical taxes, the date on which the tax is payable is generally the last day of the tax period. Based on this rule, it will only be necessary to comply with the ownership clause on the date on which the tax is payable in the state of residence.

This solution significantly facilitates the application of the clause, but may also give rise to cases of tax avoidance. In order to meet this requirement, it would not be unimaginable for taxpayers to reach agreements with qualified residents by which the shares are transferred on the same date as that on which the tax is payable. To prevent this avoidance conduct, tax rules which establish a minimum holding period are usually provided, and this is exactly what has been done in the case of the U.S. Models.

These problems would not arise if all the tax treaties being studied had followed the U.S. Models. However, some treaties do not provide any rule in this respect.[110]

This omission gives rise to a doubt in regard to the criteria which should be used in the case of the latter treaties. When the U.S. acts as the source state, it would only be reasonable not to require compliance with a holding period which is longer than the period required under its own domestic law. However, it is difficult to determine how this matter is treated in the other states when they act as the source state. In the case of Spain, for example, it is likely that the criterion used is the date on which the tax on

---

110. See, among others, the tax treaties signed by the U.S. with the following countries: Austria, Cyprus, the Czech Republic, Ireland, Luxembourg, Portugal, the Slovak Republic and Spain.

the income obtained by the non-resident is payable. Each time a non-resident obtains income, compliance with the clause will have to be previously verified.[111]

In our opinion, domestic law should not be relied on to resolve this problem as this would most likely give rise to a non-uniform application of the treaty. A common solution should be adopted and it could very well be that provided for under U.S. law. This solution is flexible, as it is not necessary to hold the shares for the full taxable year or each time income is obtained. At the same time, it is strict enough to prevent avoidance conduct. A minimum holding period prevents these situations.

II.F.3 Base Erosion Test

This test is useful in preventing stepping stone structures from claiming the benefits of a treaty.[112] The income obtained at source is transferred to a third state, transforming it into an expense which is billed to the intermediary company. This system allows the income obtained at source to not be taxed, or only to be minimally taxed in the intermediary company's state of residence.

To prevent this type of structure from claiming the benefits of a treaty, the rule requires the examination of the entity's tax base. When a significant percentage of the income received is used to meet liabilities to non-qualified residents, the application of the treaty is denied. In this respect, the rule is based on the presumption that if a certain level of expenses is billed by non-residents, the company ceases to have a sufficient nexus to the state of residence, because the majority of the income obtained is indirectly transferred to taxpayers that are not qualified residents. Accordingly, to comply with this clause and for the treaty to be applied, the taxpayer must not erode his tax base.

According to the 1996 U.S. Model, a taxpayer complies with the base erosion clause if:

> less than 50 percent of the person's gross income for the taxable year is paid or accrued, directly or indirectly, to persons who are not residents of either Contracting State (unless the payment is attributable to a permanent establishment situated in either State), in the form of payments that are deductible for income tax purposes in the person's State of residence.[113]

The wording of the base erosion test is slightly different in the 2006 U.S. Model:

---

111. This solution is similar to that derived through the application, by analogy, of the solution provided in the Commentaries on Article 10 of the OECD Model. Therefore, the same criticism made previously when discussing this solution also applies in this case.
112. Dahlberg 1997, p. 296.
113. The DTC between Spain and the U.S. does not mention a specific percentage. It only states that gross income may not be used in substantial part, directly, or indirectly, to meet liabilities to non-qualified residents. The Technical Explanation of the DTC with Spain states that when this term is used, reference is being made to the 50 percent requirement. However, under this concept it adds that 'in appropriate circumstances a lower percentage of income may be considered substantial'. See Cavestany 1992, p. 6.

less than 50 percent of the person's gross income for the taxable year, as determined in the person's State of residence, is paid or accrued, directly or indirectly, to persons who are not residents of either Contracting State entitled to the benefits of this Convention under subparagraph a), subparagraph b), clause i) of subparagraph c), or subparagraph d) of this paragraph in the form of payments that are deductible for purposes of the taxes covered by this Convention in the person's State of residence (but not including arm's length payments in the ordinary course of business for services or tangible property).

The 2016 U.S. Model has introduced further modifications, which will be referred to below.

Moreover, the isolated ownership and base erosion clause provided in the Commentaries on Article 1 of the OECD Model (paragraph 17) does not follow the clause provided in the U.S. Model in this regard. However, the clause provided for in paragraph 20 of the Commentaries on Article 1 of the OECD Model almost completely follows the 2006 U.S. Model. The isolated clause of the Commentaries on the OECD Model requires a correlation between the income obtained in the source state and the amounts used to meet liabilities to residents in third states. Consequently, although a similar percentage is established, it may not apply on the total gross income obtained by the company, but rather exclusively on the income obtained in the source state. Likewise, the rule only considers the payments made to non-residents with which the company is associated.

In this study, only the problems relating to the legal regime of the clause provided in the U.S. Models and the treaties will be analysed, by means of the different elements which it comprises: concept of gross income, beneficiaries of the payments and the concept of deductible expenses.

II.F.3.a Tax Base: Concept of Gross Income

According to the U.S. Models, to comply with this clause, the entity must not pay more than 50 percent of its gross income for the taxable year to 'certain persons' (mainly persons who are not residents of either contracting state), in the form of payments that are deductible from the tax base. The 1996 and 2006 U.S. Models do not define the meaning of this concept. Moreover, the 2016 U.S. Model provides a definition of the term gross income in its Article 22(7)(h):

> h) the term 'gross income' means gross receipts as determined in the person's Contracting State of residence for the taxable year that includes the time when the benefit would be accorded, except that where a person is engaged in a business that includes the manufacture, production or sale of goods, 'gross income' means such gross receipts reduced by the cost of goods sold, and where a person is engaged in a business of providing nonfinancial services, 'gross income' means such gross receipts reduced by the direct costs of generating such receipts, provided that:
>
> > (i) except when relevant for determining benefits under Article 10 (Dividends) of this Convention, gross income shall not include the portion of any dividends that are effectively exempt from tax in the person's Contracting State of residence, whether through deductions or otherwise; and

(ii) except with respect to the portion of any dividend that is taxable, a tested group's gross income shall not take into account transactions between companies within the tested group.

If a tax treaty does not provide a definition of this concept and it cannot be determined from the context, it shall have the meaning that it has under the domestic law of the state applying the treaty (Article 3(2) OECD and U.S. Models). As in the case of other concepts not defined by the treaty, referring to domestic law may jeopardize the uniform application of the treaty, since each law may provide a different definition. An autonomous concept would eliminate the problems caused by referring to domestic law. The meaning of the term may be determined based on the treaties that do define it.[114]

Only some treaties, like the ones signed with the Czech Republic, the Netherlands, the Slovak Republic, Spain and the U.K., define the concept of gross income. These treaties basically use the definition of this concept provided under U.S. law. For example, in the DTC with Spain, the concept of gross income is defined in the following terms:

> the term 'gross income' means gross receipts or where an enterprise is engaged in a business which includes the manufacture or production of goods, gross receipts reduced by the direct costs of labour and materials attributable to such manufacture or production and paid or payable out of such receipts.

Gross income is the same as the full income obtained, except when the entity is engaged in the manufacture or production of goods. In this case, the taxpayer may deduct direct manufacturing costs. To determine what these items are, it may be useful to refer to the principles of cost accounting, since these concepts are taken therefrom.[115]

The higher the volume of deductible expenses, the lower the volume of payments, which may be made to non-qualified residents, will be, as the consideration of these costs will reduce the amount of gross income. The percentage of 50 percent is applied on gross income, and accordingly, the lower the amount of this income, the lower the volume of payments that will be covered by this rule. It is likely that it will be in the taxpayer's interest to interpret the application of these deductible expenses restrictively in order to facilitate access to the treaty.

To carry out these calculations, the 2016 U.S. Model requires that not only the company's gross income is assessed but also the tested group's gross income. The latter term ('tested group') is another novelty of the 2016 U.S. Model, which is also provided for in the indirect stock exchange clause. In this regard, the Model obliges those affected to take other entities gross income into account. The entities that may be included are those with which the entity requesting treaty benefits participates as a member of a tax consolidation fiscal unity or a similar regime that requires members of

---

114. Chica/Johnson 1993, p. 1514.
115. Strauch 1997, p. 63. The Technical Explanation of the DTC between Austria and the U.S., despite the fact that this treaty does not define the concept, it does clarify which items may be included within the scope of the concept of direct costs.

the group to share profits and losses. Entities which the company share losses with pursuant to a group relief or other loss sharing regime in the taxable year may also be added. The aim of this provision, which is significantly complex, seems to be avoiding base erosion through the offset of losses generated by other entities.

Moreover, the gross income which must be considered to determine if the base erosion test is complied with, will be the income obtained in the current taxable year. As previously discussed, this will delay the knowledge of whether the clause has been complied with until the end of the taxable year.

The tax treaties with Denmark, France and the Netherlands, before they were amended in 2006, 2009 and 2004 respectively, laid down a special rule which eliminated this drawback. This rule effectively brings forward the date on which the taxpayer knows whether it has complied with this clause. The taxpayer will take the higher of the following aggregates; the gross income for the previous taxable year or the average of the previous four years. According to this rule, from the first day of the tax period, the taxpayer will be aware of the volume of deductible expenses to which the transactions with non-qualified residents may amount.[116] In our opinion, this rule actually allows the taxpayer to determine when it has not complied with the law, rather than if it has complied therewith. It should be noted that although the income from previous years is taken into account, the expenses with which this aggregate are compared are those incurred in the current year. Consequently, until the tax period has ended, deductible expenses may continue to be generated for the entity. When these expenses exceed the stipulated percentage, an entity will know that it has not complied with the clause. On the contrary, until the tax period has ended, the entity will not be certain that it has complied with the clause, given that until the tax year ends it is possible for expenses to be generated that exceed the authorized amount. Even so, at least this rule gives rise to a higher degree of certainty as it allows the taxpayer to be aware of when the clause has been breached.

II.F.3.b Beneficiaries of the Payments: Qualified Residents

The 1996 U.S. Model does not use the concept of qualified resident in the base erosion clause, nor does it require the beneficiaries of the payments to be the same person as those mentioned in the ownership clause. The ownership clause mentions all the clauses that confer the status of qualified resident on a taxpayer, except for the ownership and base erosion clause itself. In accordance with the 1996 U.S. Model, in respect of the base erosion test, the beneficiaries of the payments are only required to be residents in one of the contracting states, or a PE situated in one of these states, to determine whether this clause has been complied with.

The 2006 U.S. Model has significantly limited the number of beneficiaries, that are eligible to comply with the base erosion test. The 2006 U.S. Model requires that less than half of the taxpayer's gross income is paid or accrued – directly or indirectly – to persons who are not qualified persons under the following LOB tests: individual,

---

116. Spector 1993, p. 165 and Winandy 1996, p. 21.

governmental bodies, tax-exempted organizations, pension funds and publicly traded companies. The persons who comply with these LOB tests may be residents of either contracting state. Therefore, these persons are taken into account regardless of which contracting state they reside in. In addition, the 2006 U.S. Model does not contain the PE exemption envisaged in the 1996 U.S. Model. Therefore, payments made to a third-country resident and attributable to a PE located in the taxpayer's state of residence are no longer eligible.

The 2016 U.S. Model has expanded the number of 'tainted payees', since the mentioned qualified residents will no longer be eligible insofar as they are connected persons[117] with respect to the person claiming treaty benefits and incurring any of the following situations. First, when they benefit from a STR with respect to the deductible payment. Second, with respect to a payment of interest, when the payee benefits from notional deductions.

In very few cases, tax treaties follow the 1996 U.S. Model.[118] Most of them have worded the base erosion test following the 2006 U.S. Model approach. In the 2006 U.S. Model, the base erosion clause is defined in terms similar to the ownership clause. In order to determine that a company has not eroded its tax base, it is necessary to verify that no more than 50 percent of its gross income was used to make payments which are deductible, and whose beneficiaries are not considered to be qualified residents. Therefore, any payment made to a 'tainted payee' will be taken into account to determine whether the percentage of 50 percent has been exceeded.

On the contrary, the very few treaties which follow the 1996 U.S. Model use this logic. The base erosion clause only requires that no more than 50 percent of the taxpayer's income be used to make payments to beneficiaries that do not reside in either of the contracting states, except where the beneficiary of the payment is a PE located in one of these states. As can be observed, the 1996 U.S. Model is more flexible, since it does not require the recipient of the payments to be a qualified resident. The beneficiaries are only required to reside in one of the contracting states or to be a PE. In this respect, it is important to be warned of the inconsistencies between the 1996 U.S. Model's ownership and base erosion clause, and the treaties that follow it. In the ownership clause, the shareholders are required to be qualified residents. By contrast, the base erosion clause does not require the beneficiaries of the payments to be qualified residents. The beneficiaries are only required to reside in a contracting

---

117. According to Article 3(2)(m) of the 2016 U.S. Model two persons shall be 'connected persons' if one owns, directly or indirectly, at least 50 percent of the beneficial interest in the other (or, in the case of a company, at least 50 percent of the aggregate vote and value of the company's shares) or another person owns, directly or indirectly, at least 50 percent of the beneficial interest (or, in the case of a company, at least 50 percent of the aggregate vote and value of the company's shares) in each person. In any case, a person shall be connected to another if, based on all the relevant facts and circumstances, one has control of the other or both are under the control of the same person or persons. The term is analysed in sections III.A.2.b and IV.B.2.b.3 of this chapter.
118. The only treaties which follow the 1996 U.S. Model are the treaties signed with Italy, the Netherlands and Slovenia.

state.[119] This discrepancy does not arise in the treaties that follow the 2006 and 2016 U.S. Models. In both clauses, the shareholders and the beneficiaries of the payments are required to be 'certain qualified residents'.

II.F.3.c Deductible Expenses

To determine if a company has used more than 50 percent of its gross income to make payments to beneficiaries who are not eligible for the purpose of the base erosion test, the U.S. Models stipulate that only payments that are deductible from the tax base will be considered. Any non-deductible payment made to tainted payees will not be taken into account.

The U.S. Models have not limited the application of this requirement to interest and royalties, despite the fact that treaty shopping structures, and specifically, stepping stone structures, are mainly developed with these types of income.

On the few occasions that a treaty has only expressly referred to these types of income, for example in the 1970 (as amended in 1987) DTC between Belgium and the U.S., the U.S. Senate stated that it was against the limited extension of this clause. In the opinion of the U.S. Senate, if only applied to interest and royalties, the base erosion clause would not be broad enough to achieve its objective. Consequently, at least in the tax treaties concluded by the U.S., the clause is not restricted to these types of income.[120]

This is precisely the conclusion arrived at in the U.S. Models. The base erosion clause comprises all payments made to non-eligible beneficiaries, in the event that the payments are deductible from the paying company's tax base.

To determine whether or not payments are deductible, it is essential to refer to the state of residence's domestic legislation. The tax base of the company receiving the income is calculated in accordance with the state of residence's legislation. Logically, this regulation establishes when it is possible to deduct the expenses billed by residents in third states or by non-qualified residents. Therefore, the source state must rely on the state of residence's legislation to verify the above.[121]

The Technical Explanations of the 1996 (paragraph 304) and 2006 U.S. Models include some clarifications regarding the payments which fall under the scope of the application of the rule. It indicates that the deductions made in the form of amortization or depreciation are not included, as no payment is made in this case. In our opinion, in this respect, the Technical Explanations are based on an error. Except for in the case of a donation, at the time an asset recorded under the company's fixed assets is acquired, a payment is effectively made. Entirely unrelated, is the fact that due to the accounting and tax treatment of this type of asset, its cost is not fully deducted in the year in which

---

119. The clause provided in paragraph 20 of the Commentaries on Article 1 of the OECD Model is similar to that provided in the U.S. Model.
120. Bennett 1991, p. 7. The mentioned reference of the 1970 DTC Belgium-U.S. is no longer included in the 2006 Belgium-U.S. DTC.
121. Therefore, for example, if the interest paid is not deductible in accordance with a domestic rule regarding thin capitalization, it will not be taken into account.

the asset is acquired, but rather is apportioned over various years based on the asset's useful life. Accordingly, in our opinion, based on the wording of this clause, there is no reason to exclude these cases if the beneficiary of the payment is a non-qualified resident.[122]

However, the exclusion of the deductions made for amortization and depreciation purposes may be justified for other reasons. It is reasonable to believe that an entity would perform a transaction consisting in the acquisition of assets recorded under its fixed assets for real business purposes. Consequently, if these transactions are performed for real business reasons, they should not be included among the expenses taken into to account to calculate the percentage provided in the treaty. These, in our opinion, are the grounds underlying the affirmation made in the Technical Explanation.

To prevent these 'legitimate payments' from being affected by the rule, the 2006 and 2016 U.S. Models, and some tax treaties, have laid down a list of transactions on which the rule may not be applied. As can be observed, the logic behind these exclusions is similar to the general assumptions on which the LOB clauses are based.

The 2006 and 2016 U.S. Models exclude payments in the ordinary course of business for services or tangible property. In both cases, the amounts billed for the goods purchased or the services rendered must be at arm's length.[123] The 2016 U.S. Model has added the so-called intragroup transactions to the list of excluded payments because, under this Model, the 50 percent rule of the base erosion test refers both to the company's gross income and the tested group's income.

Lastly, it is worth noting that the tax treaties with Ireland and the U.K. include a new case of an 'excluded tax expense' not provided in any of the previous treaties. As in the previous case, this base erosion clause is made significantly more flexible. Payments for credit transactions to banks which are residents of third states will not be taken into account, as long as the payments are made to a bank's PE situated in one of the contracting states.[124]

Although these treaties are the only ones which provide this exception, this is not really a novelty, as the 1996 U.S. Model excludes payments to PEs located in any of the contracting states. The treaties with Ireland and the U.K. only provide a more restrictive form of the clause provided in the 1996 U.S. Model which only excludes payments to banks' PEs.[125]

The grounds for this exclusion are related to the fact that the PE is liable to tax on worldwide income in the contracting state where it is located. Therefore, the income received by the entity requesting access to the treaty by means of the ownership and

---

122. Van Weeghel 1998, p. 235, footnote 77.
123. Also, paragraph 20 of the Commentaries on Article 1 of the OECD Model.
124. The difference is that payments made to banks residing in third states are not taken into account. If the bank is a resident in Ireland or the U.S., it will also be excluded in the calculation of the percentage, as only deductible payments to entities that do not comply with any of the LOBs provided in the treaty are taken into account. Banks generally access the treaty by means of the activity clause, because, for the purposes of the treaty they are considered to engage in active trade or business. In other cases, they may also access the treaty by means of the stock exchange clause.
125. Paragraph 20 of the Commentaries on Article 1 of the OECD Model also provide for this case.

base erosion clause will be taxed in the contracting state where it is located. However, the above does not prevent the PE from 'redirecting' this income to another state by means of a stepping stone structure. The PE may also erode its tax base in respect of this income.

From the standpoint of the assumptions on which the LOB clauses are based, the treaty benefits are granted to those with a sufficient nexus or a real business purpose for the obtainment of this income from the state of residence. Based on the manner in which these two aspects are specified in the U.S. Models and tax treaties, we do not consider this exclusion to be justified on the basis of the first assumption underlying these clauses. First, the PE does not have a sufficient nexus to any of the contracting states, within the meaning of the LOB clauses. It should be noted that the PE is not a qualified resident. Besides, in these cases the 1996 U.S. Model and the aforementioned treaties are referring to a PE owned by a taxpayer that resides in a state other than the states party to the treaty. The fact that the PE is liable to tax on worldwide income does not alone give rise to a sufficient nexus in respect of the income allocated to it. It should be borne in mind that the aforementioned PE may erode its tax base in respect of the income received.

Furthermore, this exclusion cannot be justified based on the existence of a real business purpose. First, it should be pointed out that this clause does not take this criterion into account, but rather mainly considers whether there is a sufficient nexus. Second, in the case that the grounds provided for this exclusion are the existence of a real business purpose, as in the case of the activity clause, the entity will be required to engage in a trade or business. This exclusion in the 1996 U.S. Model does not establish any requirement in this respect. It is indifferent as to whether or not the PE engages in a trade or business. However, in the treaties with Ireland and the U.K. this requirement is provided for, bearing in mind that the PE is required to engage in banking activity. Therefore, based on the above, we consider that there are only grounds for this exclusion in the DTCs with Ireland and the U.K, since it is related to one of the assumptions on which the LOB rule is based. On the contrary, there are no grounds for this exclusion in the 1996 U.S. Model, because the exclusion is not related to either of these two assumptions. The latter may explain why the PE exclusion was removed from the 2006 and 2016 U.S. Models.

II.F.4 *Final Remarks*

Based on an analysis of this clause, its application is limited to companies in which residents of one of the contracting states have a majority shareholding. In addition, it limits the volume of transactions with non-residents when deductible expenses are generated for the entity. Except on certain occasions (concept of full income, deductible expenses which are taken into account, etc.), the activity that the taxpayer who requests the application of the treaty engages in is not taken into consideration.

Due to the strictness of its requirements, on many occasions it is likely for an entity that engages in a perfectly legitimate activity to be excluded, either because it is mainly owned by non-residents or because its transactions with residents in third states reach a very significant volume in certain taxable years.[126] In fact, the clause may cause the same taxpayer to be included or excluded from the scope of the clause, depending on the taxable year.

If they do not comply with this clause, companies which are not publicly traded have no other option but to try to access the treaty by means of the activity clause or through the request for the application of the clause to the tax authorities (bona fide clause). The fact that the entity will not be considered to be a qualified resident in either of these cases, and the related consequences, should also be taken into account. Furthermore, the position of these entities is not the most favourable as they will be required to individually verify whether each item of income obtained complies with the activity clause, or in the case that they try to access the treaty by means of the bona fide clause, they will be forced to await the decision of the tax authorities, which may be negative.

III NON-QUALIFIED RESIDENTS THAT ARE ENTITLED TO RECEIVE FULL OR PARTIAL TREATY BENEFITS

III.A Activity Clause

III.A.1 Preliminary Remarks

The contents of the clauses analysed in the previous sections are based on the taxpayer's characteristics and not on the nature of the activity in which it engages.[127] In the case of the stock exchange and the ownership and base erosion clauses, the taxpayer is not required to engage in any active trade or business.

The criteria used is mainly the company's quotation on the stock market, the shareholders' residence and the residence of the beneficiaries of payments made by the entity claiming the treaty benefits. Where these criteria are met, the LOB rule assumes that there is a sufficient nexus to one of the contracting states.

Entities in which a majority shareholding is held by residents in third states, or otherwise, whose transactions are mainly with residents in third states, are rarely able to comply with the previous clauses, and in particular, with the ownership and base erosion clause.[128] Consequently, these rules significantly reduce the subjective scope of tax treaties.

As stated by the Commentaries on Article 1 of the OECD Model, when the inclusion of LOB clauses is considered, 'the extent to which bona fide economic activities might be unintentionally disqualified by such provisions' (paragraph 12) should be borne in mind.[129]

---

126. Debatin/Endres 1990, p. 469.
127. An exception is the case of non-profit organizations (*see* section III.C of this chapter).
128. Rivier 1998, p. 306.
129. As a final addition, all the LOB clauses proposed by the OECD Model and its Commentaries include an activity clause that examines whether the entity requesting the application of the treaty engages in active trade or business.

The stock exchange clause and the ownership and base erosion clause do not consider this parameter: the performance of legitimate economic activities. Consequently, it is possible that an entity which engages in a legitimate economic activity may not be entitled to the application of the treaty, where neither of these two clauses are complied with.

The activity clause provides different criteria, in order to prevent taxpayers that carry on a legitimate economic activity from not being able to claim the treaty benefits.[130] In this clause, the nature of the activity engaged in by the taxpayer and the connection between the aforementioned activity and the income obtained in the source state is examined.

As observed in Chapter 2 (section II.B.3), the assumptions on which the LOB clauses rest are the existence of a sufficient nexus to the state of residence and the existence of a real business purpose justifying the obtainment of income from the state of residence.

The activity clause relates to the second assumption.[131] This rule comprises two requirements: the company is required to engage in a substantial active trade or business in the state of residence, and the income obtained in the state of residence is required to have a direct or complementary relation to this trade or business.[132]

It may be asserted that persons who engage in an active trade or business in the state of residence have a sufficient nexus to this state. From this standpoint, the performance of an active trade or business would be sufficient to fulfil the assumptions on which the LOB clauses are based. However, both the U.S. Models, as well as the two forms of the clauses proposed by the OECD, also require that the income obtained at source be related to the trade or business in the state of residence. This second aspect relates the rule to the second assumption on which the LOB clauses are based, i.e. the existence of a real business purpose to obtain the income from the source state. The rule assumes that if there is no such connection between the active trade or business and the income obtained, the treaty should not be applied.

This requirement should be understood from the viewpoint of the assumptions on which these norms are based. The ownership and base erosion clause allows for access to the treaty due to the taxpayer's nexus to the territory. Such a nexus will exist in view of the shareholders' residence and the residence of the beneficiaries of the payments made by this company. By contrast, in the activity clause, since the company's active trade or business is taken into account, the income obtained at source must contribute thereto in some manner, and accordingly, a direct or complementary relationship is required to exist.[133]

---

130. Troup 1993, p. 100.
131. Bates/Berman/Gani/Gutmann/Imamura/Klugman/Rust 2013, p. 396.
132. In this case, the Commentaries on Article 1 of the OECD Model provide an isolated activity clause (paragraph 19.b) and an activity clause similar to that provided in the U.S. Model, which is included in the set of LOB provisions, is provided for in paragraph 20 of the Commentaries on Article 1 of the OECD Model.
133. Kim 1990, p. 998.

Chapter 3: Limitation on Benefits Clauses

In the case of this clause, although a sufficient nexus to the territory can be demonstrated, simply engaging in an active trade or business is not sufficient. It is also essential for there to be a direct or complementary connection which provides grounds for obtaining the income from the state of residence.

In summary, this clause not only requires a connection between the entity and the state of residence, i.e. the performance of an active trade or business, but also a relation between the income obtained at source and the element which attaches the entity to the state of residence, i.e. a direct or complementary connection between the income and the company's active trade or business.

Given the structure of the activity clause, it is easy to understand why compliance therewith does not entitle the taxpayer to fully apply the treaty. This rule does not confer the treaty benefits upon the taxpayer that obtains the income due to the characteristics thereof, but rather due to the nature of the activity in which it is engaged and the connection between this activity and the income obtained.[134]

When the income obtained by an entity satisfies both requirements, this entity will only benefit from the part of the convention that regulates this income. This rule requires verification of compliance with the clause each time income is obtained in the source state. Accordingly, a case may arise where a taxpayer is only entitled to the application of the treaty regarding a portion of the income obtained in the source state.[135] The income not connected with or incidental to the trade or business carried on in the state of residence will not be covered by the treaty and will be taxed in accordance with the source state's laws. In short, the activity clause must be applied item by item.

As can be observed, the position of the taxpayers that are only able to comply with this clause is clearly different from that of taxpayers who comply with a clause by which they are deemed to be a qualified resident.

First, this is due to the fact that the circumstances which determine whether the treaty is to be applied do not necessarily have to be the same each time income is obtained. Without a doubt, this represents an additional cost, since by contrast, the effort required by those who comply with the ownership and base erosion clause is always the same. They are only required to certify that the taxpayers who own the capital stock, and the beneficiaries of their payments, are qualified residents. For this reason, 'it clearly is preferable to qualify for full treaty benefits under the publicly traded company test or the ownership/base erosion test'.[136]

Second, this is due to the terms of this clause in the U.S. Models, the OECD Model and its Commentaries and the treaties being studied. The previous clauses use objective elements which are easy to verify. Despite their strictness on some occasions, at least the taxpayer is certain as to whether or not it has complied with these clauses.[137] By contrast, the activity clause includes a number of inexact legal concepts

---

134. Jacob 1991, p. 16.
135. Berman/Hynes 2000, p. 696.
136. Bates/Berman/Gani/Gutmann/Imamura/Klugman/Rust 2013, p. 396.
137. For example, significant problems do not arise in relation to the verification as to whether an entity is publicly traded on a recognized stock exchange, or as to whether 50 percent of a

which do not provide the taxpayer with sufficient certainty and confidence in regard to its compliance therewith.[138] As pointed out by Goossen, due to the complexity, inexactness and vagueness of the concepts forming part of this clause, on many occasions it would be more worthwhile to try to access the treaty by expressly requesting the source state's tax authorities to authorize its application (bona fide clause).[139]

Furthermore, the activity clause suffers from the same defects as the previous clauses.

The activity clause only takes into account the trade or business conducted by the taxpayer in the state of residence. The branches of the company located in third states are not taken into consideration regardless of their importance. Only the DTC between the Netherlands and the U.S., prior to its amendment in 2004, took the latter into account, but as shall be observed, with few consequences. As in the case of the previous LOB clauses, when a contracting state is a member of an international organization such as the EU, the fact that only the activity in the state of residence is taken into account may be incompatible with EU Law.

Also, based on its wording, all entities engaged in activities which may objectively be considered as legitimate are probably not covered by this clause. If this were the case, the LOB clauses would be limiting the subjective scope of the treaties more than strictly necessary. It should be borne in mind that if the activity clause is not complied with, the taxpayer may only access the treaty by means of authorization from the source state's tax authorities (bona fide clause).[140]

This clause will be analysed below based on the different versions of the U.S. Model and the treaties which follow it. In this regard, it should be mentioned that the activity clause provided in the detailed LOB rule of Action 6 of the BEPS project follows the 2006 U.S. Model.

First, the concept of active trade or business will be analysed, and subsequently, the direct or incidental relation which is required between the income obtained at source and the trade or business in the state of residence will be discussed.

---

company's capital stock pertains to a qualified resident, or as to whether the company has used more than half of its gross income to pay expenses billed by non-residents.

138. As pointed out by Debatin/Endres 1990, p. 465, 'this provision hardly satisfies the requirements of legal preciseness and verifiability'.
139. Goossen 1993, p. 32. From a practical standpoint, this may effectively be the case. However, it should be borne in mind that this activity clause directly confers the treaty benefits upon taxpayers. When the tax authorities are requested to authorize the application of the treaty, the taxpayer obtains the right to apply the treaty by means of administrative authorization and not directly by the treaty itself.
140. Nevertheless, it is important to note that in the DTCs including either a derivative benefits or a headquarters company clause, verification of the compliance therewith will be required prior to resorting to the bona fide clause.

III.A.2 Concepts of Active Trade or Business, Indirect Activity and the Substantiality Requirement

III.A.2.a Concept of Active Trade or Business

The first requirement of this clause is that an entity be engaged in the conduct of an active trade or business in the state of residence. As shall be observed, it is not essential for the entity engaged in the conduct of the trade or business to be the same as the company that obtains the income generated at source.[141]

The U.S. Models have never defined the concept of active trade or business. The activity clause only states in a negative way that certain activities are not considered being an active trade or business. The excluded activities are mainly the business of making or managing investments.

Article 22(3)(b) of the 1996 U.S. Model reads as follows:

> For purposes of this paragraph, the business of making or managing investments will not be considered an active trade or business unless the activity is banking, insurance or securities activity conducted by a bank, insurance company or registered securities dealer.

The wording of this provision in the 2006 U.S. Model is very similar, although an adjustment has been included that makes this requirement appear more lenient. Whereas the 1996 U.S. Model provided that making or managing investments would never qualify (except in the case of a banking, insurance, or securities activity conducted by a bank, insurance company, or registered securities dealer), the exclusion in the 2006 U.S. Model only applies to 'making or managing investments for the resident's own account' (except in the case of banking, insurance, or securities activities carried on by a bank, insurance company, or registered securities dealer).[142] Therefore, when the business of making or managing investments is performed on the account of a third person, this activity is not excluded, although the person conducting the banking, insurance or securities activity is not a bank, insurance company or registered securities dealer.

The 2016 U.S. Model follows the same pattern as the previous Models, although the wording is slightly different:[143]

> For purposes of this Article, the term 'active conduct of a trade or business' shall not include the following activities or any combination thereof:
>
> (i) operating as a holding company;

---

141. Burge/Endres 1990, p. 549.
142. Miller/Stone 2008, p. 4. Some of the tax treaties signed by the U.S. do not mention securities activities carried on by a registered securities dealer. *See,* among others, the treaties with Austria, Cyprus, the Czech Republic, Ireland, Luxembourg, Portugal, the Slovak Republic and Spain. Moreover, the isolated activity clause proposed in the Commentaries on Article 1 of the OECD Model (paragraph 19.b) does not exclude any type of business or trade. The activity clause included in paragraph 20 of the Commentaries on Article 1 of the OECD Model is worded in the same way as in the 2016 U.S. Model.
143. *See* Article 22(3)(a) 2016 U.S. Model.

(ii) providing overall supervision or administration of a group of companies;
(iii) providing group financing (including cash pooling); or
(iv) making or managing investments, unless these activities are carried on by a bank, insurance company or registered securities dealer in the ordinary course of its business as such.

The 2016 U.S. Model seems to have expanded the number of excluded activities. However, as will be outlined below, the new activities, which seem to be affected by the exclusion were not considered either an active trade or business in the previous Models.

In principle, since an active trade or business is not defined in the U.S. Models or in the treaties, and since it is not possible to determine the meaning of this concept from context, it shall have the meaning it has under the law of the state applying the treaty.[144]

According to the Technical Explanations of the 1996 (paragraph 309) and 2006 U.S. Models, the concept of active trade or business is defined in Article 367(a)(3) of the IRC and in the Federal Regulations § 1.367(a)-2T(b)(2) y § 1.367(a)-2T(b)(3). According to these regulations, it will be necessary to determine if the activity is of a business nature based on the circumstances. In general, a trade or business will be considered to be a unified group of activities that constitute or could constitute an independent economic enterprise, which are carried on for profit. Additionally, the appropriate material and personal means to engage in this activity are required.[145]

In our opinion, it makes more sense to define the scope of this concept from the standpoint of the activities which are expressly excluded in the U.S. Models and the treaties analysed even though they may be of a business nature. According to the U.S. Models, the business of making or managing investments is excluded except in the case of banking, insurance, or securities activities carried on by a bank, insurance company, or registered securities dealer.

The generic terms in which the expression 'the business of making or managing investments' is defined, make it difficult to determine its scope. On first consideration, it may be concluded that the rule is excluding those entities whose main activity is precisely the management and making of investments. When these types of activities are merely incidental, it should be understood that they are not excluded. Whether the income obtained from this part of the activity later complies with the requirement that there be a direct or incidental relation between the income obtained at source and the activity in the state of residence is unrelated.

Moreover, based on the wording of the clause, companies engaged in activities which are typical of a bank or an insurance company are included within the scope of

---

144. Rasmussen/Bernhardt 2001, p. 148.
145. As stated by Schinabeck 1996, p. 35, U.S. domestic law is not very useful, or at least does not give rise to a high level of certainty regarding the meaning of this concept. The Internal Revenue Code uses this expression on numerous occasions and not always with the same meaning. Furthermore, the existing tax queries do not establish a clear parameter. The existence of an active trade or business is verified case by case, based on the circumstances, meaning that when the facts are not exactly the same, it is not possible to extrapolate the criteria established in one query to other cases.

Chapter 3: Limitation on Benefits Clauses

'the business of managing and making investments.' An entity included within an enterprise group, whose main activity is to act as intermediary between the group lenders and the group or independent borrowers would be excluded, since this is a bank activity not conducted by a financial institution authorized for this purpose.[146] Within the meaning of the U.S. Models, bank and insurance activity are only trades or businesses, if conducted by authorized financial institutions and insurance companies. Some treaties have clarified this matter, specifying that it only includes authorized entities to the extent they strictly conduct bank and insurance activities.[147] Any other activity would not be covered by this case. In any event, it should be highlighted that in the 2016 U.S. Model the activity of providing group financing (including cash pooling) is expressly excluded.

Second, as opposed to the U.S. Models, some treaties do not exclude the trading of securities by registered security dealers from the concept of 'the business of making or managing investments.'

This exclusion has no consequence whatsoever in respect of transactions performed by these entities on the account of third persons. The taxation of security purchase and sale transactions which these entities are relied on to make are not governed by the treaty entered into by the source state and the state of residence of the securities dealer. The tax treaty applicable to such transactions is that entered into by the source state and the state of residence of the person who has relied on these entities to trade its securities. Consequently, the exclusion does not affect transactions on the account of a third party. On the contrary, transactions performed for one's own account are excluded.

In our opinion, the fact that not all the treaties being studied provide for the case described in the U.S. Models is unreasonable. Technically, a large part of the transactions performed by these entities are on the account of a third party, meaning that their access to or exclusion from the treaty does not directly affect their customers. On the other hand, it makes no sense for the transactions performed for one's own account to be excluded, since, as in the case of the stock exchange clause, these entities are subject to strict controls by the administrative authorities. As both situations are similar, it does not seem reasonable to apply a different regime in this case. Whether these entities perform transactions which are only apparently performed for their own account is an entirely different matter. The objective of these types of actions may be to assure that the treaties entered into by these entities' state of residence are applied rather than the treaties of the customer's state of residence. Even so, in our opinion, there are not sufficient grounds to fully exclude these transactions, since they may be perfectly corrected by means of the beneficial ownership clause.

The Technical Explanations of the 1996 and 2006 U.S. Models state that the expression, 'the business of making or managing investments' also comprises entities that function solely as headquarter companies. These entities centralize certain group

---

146. This is not understood to be the case by Langereis/Van Herksen 1997, pp. 267–268 who refer to the Dutch intragroup financing companies. In our opinion, these entities are excluded unless the taxpayer is formally considered to be a financial entity, which is not the case.
147. Debatin/Endres 1990, p. 465 and Schinabeck 1996, p. 35.

activities, such as audits, purchasing policies, financing, etc. In any event, it should be highlighted that in the 2016 U.S. Model the activity of providing overall supervision or administration of a group of companies is expressly excluded. However, as shall be observed in section III.B of this chapter, some treaties, and also the 2016 U.S. Model, have included a specific clause (headquarters company clause) to allow some of these types of entities to claim treaty benefits.

Lastly, either in view of the application of the concepts of active trade or business provided under domestic law, or in view of their express exclusion in the U.S. Models, holding companies do not comply with this clause.[148] However, as shall be observed below, the U.S. Models do not require the taxpayer obtaining income to be the same as the taxpayer who is engaged in the conduct of an active trade or business. Also included within the scope of the treaty's application are cases of an indirect trade or business that refer to cases where the business activity is carried on by a taxpayer with which the entity obtaining the income is related or connected.[149] Therefore, for example, a holding company which has shareholdings in entities that are engaged in the conduct of an active trade or business (operating companies) could claim the treaty benefits in respect of the income obtained in the source state, as long as this income is connected or incidental to the trade or business conducted by the operating companies in which the holding company owns a shareholding.

III.A.2.b   Indirect Trade or Business

The body of the 1996 U.S. Model does not appear to provide for the case of indirect trade or business. The person that obtains income in the source state was also required to be engaged in the conduct of an active trade or business in the state of residence. Therefore, according to the 1996 U.S. Model, in principle, the income should be obtained by the same person that is engaged in the active conduct of a trade or business.

Before the 2006 U.S. Model was released, certain treaties expressly include some cases in which, under certain circumstances, the income does not have to be obtained by the same person that is engaged in the active conduct of trade or business.[150] In fact, in some cases, as in the tax treaties with Austria and Germany (prior to its amendment in 2006), cases of indirect trade or business are not provided for in the body of the treaty, but rather in the Memorandum of Understanding. The cases of indirect trade or business in the DTC with Germany were provided for in the examples regarding this clause included in the Memorandum.

The 2006 U.S. Model added a new attribution rule whereby, for purposes of the active trade or business clause, a person's activities are deemed to include the activities of persons 'connected' to such person. According to Article 22(3)(c) of the 2006 Model,

---

148. Casero 1996, p. 469.
149. Rasmussen/Bernhardt 2001, p. 149.
150. *See,* among others, the treaties with Austria, France (prior to its amendment in 2009), Germany (prior to its amendment in 2006), Ireland, Luxembourg, the Netherlands (prior to its amendment in 2004) and the U.K. *See* Vega 2006, pp. 171–179.

persons are considered to be connected if: (1) a 50 percent ownership test is satisfied; (2) one person has control of the other; or (3) both are under the control of the same person or persons.[151] This rule clearly makes it easier for the relevant company in a group to satisfy the active trade or business test without 'foot-faulting' by reason of activities being conducted by the 'wrong' member of the group.[152]

The 2016 U.S. Model also contains this rule. However, the term 'connected persons' is no longer defined in the LOB Article. Its definition is now established in Article 3 of the Model along with the rest of definitions that this article, both in the U.S. and the OECD Models, usually contains. The latter is due to the fact that the scope of this term in the 2016 U.S. Model is wider than in the previous Model. Its scope of application goes beyond the LOB rule, now also being applicable to the STRs clause[153] and the concept of construction or project PE.

Finally, it should be highlighted that the U.S. Models do not take into account active trade or business conducted in third states. Therefore, the activity carried out, directly or indirectly, by the entity requesting treaty benefits under this LOB test must take place in the contracting state where it resides.

III.A.2.c   Volume of Activity: The Substantiality Test

The 1996, 2006 and 2016 U.S. Models include a substantiality test.[154] According to this test, the activity directly or indirectly carried on in the state of residence by the entity receiving the income is not only required to be of a business nature, but also to be substantial.

According to the wording of the 1996 U.S. Model, this requirement seems to be applicable in every case. However, the 2006 and 2016 U.S. Models have clarified that the substantiality test only applies when an item of income derives from a related person. As will be seen below, this conclusion is also applicable to the 1996 U.S. Model and the treaties following it.

The substantiality test imposes a quantitative requirement on the trade or business. Therefore, the requirements on the activity carried on in the state of residence are not only qualitative, i.e. they are required to be of a business nature, but also quantitative.

---

151. The wording of the rule is the following: 'For purposes of applying this paragraph, activities conducted by persons connected to a person shall be deemed to be conducted by such person. A person shall be connected to another if one possesses at least 50 percent of the beneficial interest in the other (or, in the case of a company, at least 50 percent of the aggregate vote and value of the company's shares or of the beneficial equity interest in the company) or another person possesses at least 50 percent of the beneficial interest (or, in the case of a company, at least 50 percent of the aggregate vote and value of the company's shares or of the beneficial equity interest in the company) in each person. In any case, a person shall be considered to be connected to another if, based on all the relevant facts and circumstances, one has control of the other or both are under the control of the same person or persons'.
152. Miller/Stone 2008, p. 4.
153. *See* section IV.B.2 of this chapter.
154. This requirement is also provided in the activity clause proposed in the Commentaries on Article 1 of the OECD Model.

In mentioned cases, in order for the trade or business carried on in the state of residence to be taken into consideration, this activity is required to be substantial in relation to the activity in the other state generating the income. The volume of trade or business in the state of residence is established in comparison to the activity generating the income in the source state.[155]

The purpose of this requirement is to prevent taxpayers without either a sufficient nexus to the state of residence, or a real business purpose for obtaining the income generated at source from the state of residence, from being able to access the treaty regime.

If this clause were not to provide this requirement, it would be easy to comply therewith. Imagine the following case. A company residing in the U.S. is owned by non-residents operating in the videogames industry and obtains an enormous profit. In order to obtain the dividends paid by the company residing in the U.S. from France, and thereby, benefit from the tax ceiling provided in the treaty concluded by these two states, the company's shareholders incorporate a company in France whose only activity is the sale of videogames through a tiny store in France. The shares of the company residing in the U.S. would also be transferred to the company residing in France.

In principle, if there were no quantitative requirement on the state of residence's company, the clause would be complied with, as the income obtained in the U.S. is derived from an activity directly related to the activity generating a profit in the U.S.[156] Consequently, the clause requires the trade or business carried on in the state of residence to be substantial in order to assure that the clause is effective in countering treaty shopping structures. On the contrary, it would be sufficient for the company receiving the income to be engaged in minimal trade or business directly related to the trade or business generating the income at source to comply with the activity clause. To prevent this type of situation, the activity carried on in the state of residence must be of a certain volume or significance in relation to the activity generating income in the source state.

Although not included in all of the treaties being studied herein, in practice, it will always be necessary to satisfy this requirement, or at least, when the U.S. is the source state. For example, although the DTC between Germany and the U.S., prior to its amendment in 2006, did not mention this requirement, the Memorandum of Understanding considered compliance therewith to be necessary.[157] Technically, since this requirement is not expressly provided in the treaty, if a formal interpretation were

---

155. Burge/Endres 1990, p. 549.
156. This is the example included in the Technical Explanation of the U.S. Model. However, it should be taken into account that a doubt would arise as to whether the company residing in France is engaged in the conduct of an active trade or business, since, despite the fact that it is engaged in an activity of this type, the majority of its activity would be the holding of shares in the company residing in the U.S. The Technical Explanation does not take this standpoint, meaning that if it were not for the substantiality requirement, the company would comply with this clause.
157. Debatin/Endres 1990, p. 475 criticize the fact that this requirement is introduced by means of the Memorandum, since this is a merely interpretative document which may not add anything not already provided in the text of the treaty.

made in these cases, it is unlikely that that there would be grounds for this requirement. However, in practice, it is likely that requiring a strict application of the treaty text would not be effective, as the U.S. tax authorities would probably directly apply its domestic legislation, under which this requirement is expressly included.[158]

Second, the U.S. Models seem to require the fulfilment of the substantiality test in the cases of both direct and incidental relations between the activity carried on in the state of residence and the income obtained at source. Regardless of whether the income generated at source is connected with or incidental to the activity carried on in the state of residence, the trade or business carried on in the state of residence is always required to be substantial.

However, some of the tax treaties being examined in this study have limited this requirement to cases where there is a direct relation.[159] Consequently, in practice, this requirement may only be made when the income obtained at source is derived in connection to the business or trade carried on in the state of residence. When the income generated is incidental to the activity, it is not necessary to pass 'the substantiality test.'

Furthermore, the substantiality requirement has to be fulfilled only with respect to income derived from related persons. As shall be observed below, the 1996 U.S. Model and some treaties provide an objective rule to facilitate verification of compliance with the substantiality test. Based on the application of this rule, it can be deduced that compliance with this requirement is not necessary when the taxpayer that obtains the income does not directly or indirectly hold shares representing the capital stock and voting power of the entity that pays the income in the source state. When no shareholding is held, it is not necessary to satisfy this requirement, since it will automatically be satisfied.[160] That objective rule allows us to conclude that, under the 1996 U.S. Model, as it occurs in the 2006 and 2016 U.S. Model, the substantiality test only applies to income derived from related persons.

In summary, compliance with the 'substantially test' is only required when there is a direct relation and the company that obtains the income is related to the entity that pays this income in the source state.[161]

Verification of compliance with this requirement is a matter of fact. The volume of activity in the source state is compared to the volume of activity in the state of residence. The U.S. Models and the treaties do not provide any specific criterion. It is simply stated that 'whether a trade or business is substantial for purposes of this paragraph will be determined based on all the facts and circumstances'.

---

158. The branch profit tax law also contains this requirement. *See* International Income Taxation. Code & Regulations. Selected Sections, Commerce Clearing House, Inc., Chicago, 1993, p. 1095.
159. Berman/Hynes 2000, p. 695.
160. Thill/Milhac 1995, p. 9, Gouthière 1995, p. 99 and Muntendam 1996, p. 39.
161. Based on the wording of paragraph 20 of the Commentaries on Article 1 of the OECD Model, the substantiality test only has to be satisfied when the entity paying the income and the recipient thereof are associated in accordance with Article 9 of the OECD Model. Also, paragraph 20 does not seem to exclude this requirement when the income is incidental to the activity.

When the volume of the activity in the state of residence is higher than that of the activity at source, there seem to be no doubts that this requirement has been satisfied. Doubts increase to the same extent as the volume of activity in the source state increases.

To facilitate compliance with this requirement, the 1996 U.S. Model and some treaties laid down a 'safe harbour' or objective rule. The persons that comply with this rule automatically pass the 'substantiality test.'[162] In this regard, it must be highlighted that the 2006 U.S. Model eliminated this safe harbour. However, this objective rule provided in the 1996 U.S. Model may be useful to verify, in some cases, if the substantiality test has been complied with. Nevertheless, in the tax treaties which the 'objective rule' is not provided for, it will not function as a safe harbour rule, although it could be considered as strong evidence that the requirement has been fulfilled.

According to the 1996 U.S. Model, the volume or 'substantiality' of the activities carried on in the source state and in the state of residence is determined by comparing three ratios: (a) the asset values used in the state of residence to engage in the conduct of a trade or business and those used in the source state to generate the income; (b) The gross income obtained in each contracting state; (c) The payroll expense in each in each contracting state. In summary, the substantiality or volume of both entities is determined by comparing the asset values, the gross income obtained by each entity and the payroll expense incurred by each one.[163]

The ratios for the taxable year in which the income is obtained are not used to make this comparison, but rather those for the previous taxable year or for the average of the three preceding taxable years. This rule lets you know whether the rule has been complied with from the first day of the taxable year.

The substantiality test is passed if each ratio individually exceeds more than 7.5 percent and the average of the three ratios is higher than 10 percent. To calculate these percentages, the factors must be prorated in the following cases: First, when the entity receiving the income owns less than 100 percent of the shares representing the capital stock and voting power of the payer company. In this case, the assets, gross income and payroll expense of the entity that pays the income are prorated; Second, when the entity receiving the income indirectly complies with the requirement, whereby it must be engaged in the conduct of a trade or business, the assets, gross income and payroll expense of the company engaged in the conduct of a trade or business in the state of residence are prorated.

---

162. It can be found in the DTCs with Austria (in the Memorandum), Estonia (Article 22(3)(c)), Ireland (Article 23(3)(b)(ii)), Italy (Article 2(3)(e) of the Protocol), Latvia (Article 23(3)(c)), Lithuania (Article 23(3)(c)) and Luxembourg (Article 24(3)(c)). It is not provided in paragraph 20 of the Commentaries on Article 1 of the OECD Model. Following the 2004 amendment of the DTC between Netherlands and the U.S., this rule is not provided for in the text of the treaty but it is provided in the Memorandum (section XXII).
163. Note that these three factors are the same as those used by the fractional apportionment method to distribute the income among the different jurisdictions in which the same company operates. *See* section I.B of Chapter 2.

This system of percentages is rather complicated to apply, but without a doubt, it resolves the uncertainty which may result from the unspecific legal concept used to define this requirement. Despite this fact, a number of objections may be raised.

First, this system of percentages is based on the 'presumption' that the size of the U.S. economy, in the case that the U.S. is the source state, is significantly larger than the economy of any of the EU Member States with which it has entered into a treaty that includes this provision. This is evidenced by the fact that the volume of activity in the EU Member States is only required to represent at least 10 percent of the activity carried on in the U.S. in order to comply with this rule.

It is truly strange, as pointed out by experts in this field, that the same percentages have been established in all DTCs even though the size of the economy of each EU Member State is different.[164] In this respect, the system would have been more consistent if the percentages had been established based on the actual size of each state's economy in relation to the U.S. economy.

Second, it is important to note that except in the treaty entered into with the Netherlands, the three ratios used (assets, gross income and payroll expense) refer exclusively to each state's territory. Therefore, for example, the assets located in third states which may have contributed to the performance of the activity are not taken into consideration.

For the application of these percentages, the DTC between the Netherlands and the U.S. takes into account the trade or business conducted in EU Member States. This regime is only applicable when the entity receiving the income resides in the Netherlands. Therefore, the treaty established a legal fiction whereby the business activity conducted in other states is understood to have been carried out in Dutch territory for calculation purposes.

However, the application of this regime is not automatic. For it to be possible, a comparison must be previously made between the volume of activity conducted in the Netherlands in relation to the volume of activity carried on in the rest of the EU Member States. The ratios taken into account are the same as those previously described, i.e. asset value, gross income and payroll expense. In this preliminary phase, and as evidenced by means of the consideration of these three ratios, the activity conducted in the Netherlands is required to represent 15 percent more than the volume of activity generated in the EU. In this case, it is not necessary for the three ratios to collectively exceed a certain percentage.

As can be observed, in order to be able to calculate the activity conducted in the other EU Member States, the activity conducted in the Netherlands must previously reach a certain volume.[165] In the treaty, this percentage is 15 percent of the total activities in the EU. If the activity in the Netherlands exceeds this amount, it is possible to move on to the next phase, which consists in comparing activity in the EU Member State with activity in the U.S.

In the case where the activity conducted in EU Member States is not taken into account, each of the three ratios is required to exceed 7.5 percent and the average of the

---

164. Morrison/Bennett 1993a, p. 339, footnote 14, Schaffner 1997, p. 168 and Winandy 1996, p. 22.
165. Bennett/Morrison/Daniels/De Hosson 1995, p. 112.

three must exceed 10 percent. These percentages increase significantly when the overall activity conducted within the EU Member States territory is taken into account. The increase in the percentages is logical considering that if the size of the market being compared has increased, the percentages should also be raised. In this case, the activity in the U.S. is not being compared to the activity in the Netherlands, but rather to the activity in the EU. The individual percentages (assets, gross income and personal expense) increase from 7.5 to 50 percent and the average of the three increases from 10 percent to 60 percent.

Taking into consideration the percentage amounts, it may not make much sense to avail of this option. In the majority of cases, if the requirements provided for its application are complied with, it can be assumed that the requirement of the first option, i.e. that only the activity in the Netherlands should be taken into account, has also been satisfied. Logically, if the first option is applicable, it makes no sense to determine if the requirements of the second option have been satisfied, because the result will ultimately be the same. It would be an unnecessary effort without any practical effect.

To be able to take into account the activity in other EU Member States, the activity conducted in the Netherlands must first represent 15 percent of the whole activity carried on in the EU. Additionally, each ratio, i.e. EC assets, gross income and payroll expense, must exceed 50 percent. A closer inspection reveals that 15 percent of 50 percent is exactly 7.5 percent. The latter percentage is that which, at a minimum, each ratio must exceed separately when only the activity in the Netherlands is taken into account. This demonstrates that it may not make much sense to use this option as it implies that the requirements of the previous option have been satisfied.

The same occurs with the overall percentage of 60 percent. Fifteen percent of 60 is equal to 9 percent. It should be noted that this percentage is only slightly less than that required in the case of the first alternative (10 percent). Based on the above, it is evident that in the case of the second option, the volume of business activity which is required in the state of residence, which in this case is the Netherlands, is very similar to the volume required in the first option. Therefore, there will be few cases in which it really compensates to resort to the second alternative, since the new percentages will not free the company from having a volume of assets, income and payroll expenses in the Netherlands which is practically identical to the volume required in the case of the first alternative.[166]

Consequently, the option provided in the Dutch treaty does not make much sense from the standpoint of the 'substantiality test.' However, it may make sense from the standpoint of the last requirement of the activity clause, i.e. that the income obtained at source must be directly or incidentally related to the activity in the state of residence. It is possible that this requirement would not be satisfied if only the activity in the Netherlands were taken into account. On the contrary, this requirement might be satisfied through the inclusion of the activities where the company is engaged in other EU Member States.

---

166. In this respect, among others, *see*, Peters/Holdem/Smith 1995, p. 3 and Berman/Hynes 2000, p. 703.

III.A.3 Relation Between the Income Generated and the Activity Conducted

III.A.3.a Direct Relation ('in Connection with')

According to the activity clause, treaty benefits will extend only to income derived in connection with or incidental to a trade or business conducted in the state of residence.

The 1996 U.S. Model provides a description of circumstances in which income will satisfy the 'in connection with' requirement. Article 22(3)(d) of the 1996 Model reads as follows:

> Income is derived in connection with a trade or business if the activity in the other State generating the income is a line of business that forms a part of or is complementary to the trade or business.

The 2006 U.S. Model eliminated this definition. However, its Technical Explanation provides a similar definition:

> An item of income is derived in connection with a trade or business if the income-producing activity in the State of source is a line of business that 'forms a part of' or is 'complementary' to the trade or business conducted in the State of residence by the income recipient.

The 2016 U.S. Model has substituted the term 'in connection with' for the term 'emanates from'. According to the Preamble to the 2016 U.S. Model, this new term intends to modify the meaning of this requirement:

> The change to the active-trade-or-business test [...] was motivated by a concern that the existing active-trade-or-business test can, in certain circumstances, allow third-country residents to treaty shop through an entity that has an active trade or business in a treaty partner with respect to income, in particular intra-group dividends and interest, that does not in fact have a nexus to the activities in the treaty partner. [The] concern arises from the standard applied to determine whether income is 'derived in connection with' an active trade or business in the residence country [...]. To more directly address this concern, the active-trade-or-business test of the 2016 Model has been changed to require a factual connection between an active trade or business in the residence country and the item of income for which benefits are sought. Specifically, the 2016 Model requires that the treaty-benefitted income 'emanates from, or is incidental to,' a trade or business that is actively conducted by the resident in the residence state.

Since the term is not defined in the Model, the Preamble states that the Technical Explanation accompanying the 2016 U.S. Model will provide guidance on when an item of income, in particular an intra-group dividend or interest payment, is considered to emanate from the active conduct of a trade or business of a resident. This guidance, according to the Preamble, is expected to differ from the 1996 and 2006 Technical Explanations of the meaning of the term 'derived in connection with.'

An example that the U.S. Department of the Treasury is considering including in the Technical Explanation is dividends and interest paid by a commodity-supplying subsidiary that was acquired by a company whose business in the state of residence depends on a reliable source for the commodity supplied by the subsidiary. Under this example, such dividends and interest would be considered to emanate from the active trade or business of the parent company. Another possible example could involve dividends and interest paid by a subsidiary that distributes products that were manufactured by the parent company in its state of residence. According to the Preamble, the mere fact that two companies are in a similar line of business would not be sufficient to establish that dividends or interest paid between them are related to the active conduct of a trade or business. The Preamble to the 2016 U.S. Model also provides the following:

> The Treasury Department invites comments with additional examples for potential inclusion in the technical explanation that would illustrate dividend or interest income that should be considered to emanate from an active trade or business in the residence state. Comments should take into account the extent to which suggested interpretations could facilitate treaty shopping by third-country residents with large global operations, and the extent to which the new derivative benefits and headquarters company tests—including the treatment of a headquarters company as a potential equivalent beneficiary with respect to intra-group dividends and interest income for purposes of the derivative benefits test—provide the more appropriate LOB tests for dividends and interest income and supplant any role for the active-trade-or-business test with respect to such income.

According to the above, the meaning of the term 'emanates from' will remain unclear until the Department of the Treasury releases the Technical Explanation. In any event, it is obvious that with this new term the Treasury intends to limit the application of treaty benefits to dividends and interest through this LOB clause.

Hereafter, the term used by the 1996 and 2006 U.S. Models will be analysed. As mentioned above, the term 'in connection with' is defined in the 1996 U.S. Model and in the Technical Explanation to the 2006 U.S. Model. Some treaties provide the same definition as the 1996/2006 U.S. Models and other treaties do not provide any definition. The situation of the treaties, where this term is not defined, can be overcome by interpreting this term, according to the definition provided for in the U.S. Models.[167]

On first consideration, the aspect which should be analysed is the trade or business carried on by both entities, i.e. the income payer and the recipient thereof. There should be a degree of integration between both activities. The exact degree will depend on whether the activity at source is a line of business that forms a part of the activity in the state of residence or is simply complementary thereto.

In the first case, both entities are required to manufacture the same goods or render similar services.[168] There may be three levels of integration: upstream, downward or parallel. For example, it is of an upstream nature if the entity in the state

---

167. Moreover, in addition to the definition provided in this Model, the DTC between Luxembourg and the U.S. considers that the item of income is derived in connection with a trade or business if such item of income accrues in the ordinary course of such trade or business and the beneficial owner owns, directly or indirectly, less than 5 percent of the shares (or other comparable rights) in the payer of the income's item. *See* Muntendam 1996, p. 39.
168. For the purpose of verifying compliance with this requirement, the Technical Explanation of the Netherlands-U.S. DTC stipulates that it may be useful to refer to the *Standard Industrial Classification*. This is a document published by the U.S. tax authorities which classifies activities by industry. Bennett/Morrison/Daniels/De Hosson 1995, p. 93.

Chapter 3: Limitation on Benefits Clauses

of residence engages in the supply of goods required by the entity in the source state to carry out its manufacturing process. In the case of a downward relation, the entity in the source state distributes and sells the goods manufactured in the state of residence. Finally, in the case of a parallel relation, both entities are engaged in the conduct of the same trade or business.

Moreover, according to the Technical Explanation of the 2006 U.S. Model, for two activities to be considered 'complementary', the activities need not relate to the same types of products or services, but they should be part of the same overall industry and be related in the sense that the success or failure of one activity will tend to result in success or failure for the other. Where more than one trade or business is conducted in the source state and only one of the trades or businesses forms a part of or is complementary to a trade or business conducted in the state of residence, it is necessary to identify the trade or business to which an item of income is attributable. In this regard, royalties will generally be considered to be derived in connection with the trade or business to which the underlying intangible property is attributable. With respect to dividends, this type of income will be deemed to derive first, out of earnings and profits of the treaty-benefited trade or business, and then out of other earnings and profits. Finally, interest income may be allocated under any reasonable method consistently applied. According to the Technical Explanation, a method that conforms to U.S. principles for expense allocation will be considered a reasonable method.

As can be observed, these concepts significantly limit the cases in which a trade or business is connected. It should be taken into account that would it be very difficult to comply with this clause in the event that both entities were to operate in industries that are very different. In these cases, despite the fact that both entities are engaged in the conduct of an active trade or business and, that the income and expenses are generated in the course of this activity, the treaty will not be applied. For example, a company providing tax advisory services will only be entitled to claim the treaty benefits if it renders these services to a company that is engaged in a trade or business in the same industry.

In this respect, it has been proposed that as in the case of the DTC between Luxembourg and the U.S., in order to determine if there is a direct relation, the connection between the income and the activity in the source state should not be examined, but rather the connection between the income and the activity in the state of residence.[169] For there to be a connection, the income generated at source is required to result from the active trade or business carried on by the recipient company in the state of residence. By changing the activity with which the comparison is made, compliance with this requirement is facilitated in cases where the payer and recipient companies operate in different industries.

In summary, the relation should only be required to exist between the income and the active trade or business of the entity that receives this income.[170] Experts in this field have pointed out that this correction of the comparative item should only be made

---
169. Cohen/Pollack/Scherer 1997, p. 66.
170. This is the option provided in paragraph 20 of the Commentaries on Article 1 of the OECD Model. The item of comparison is also the same in the case of an incidental relation.

when the recipient does not directly or indirectly own shares representing the capital stock of the payer entity.[171] This is confirmed by the DTC between Luxembourg and the U.S., as it prohibits the recipient entity from owning shares representing more than 5 percent of the capital stock of the payer entity. This may lead one to conclude that this method should only be used when the substantiality test is not required. As observed in the previous section, it is only necessary to comply with the substantiality clause when related parties are involved.

III.A.3.b Incidental Relation ('Incidental to')

According to the activity clause, treaty benefits will extend only to income derived in connection with or incidental to a trade or business conducted in the state of residence.

The 1996 U.S. Model provides a description of circumstances in which income will satisfy the 'incidental to' requirement. Article 22(3)(d) of the 1996 Model reads as follows:

> Income is incidental to a trade or business if it facilitates the conduct of the trade or business in the other State.

The 2006 U.S. Model eliminated this definition. However, its Technical Explanation provides a similar definition:

> An item of income derived from the State of source is 'incidental to' the trade or business carried on in the State of residence if production of the item facilitates the conduct of the trade or business in the State of residence.

The term remains in the 2016 U.S. Model but, as in the case of the 2006 U.S. Model, it is not defined.

According to the above, income is incidental to a trade or business if it facilitates the conduct of the trade or business in the state of residence. In this regard, the Technical Explanation accompanying the 2006 U.S. Model and some treaties[172] provides an example in which the income is considered to be incidental to the activity: 'An example of incidental income is the temporary investment of working capital of a person in the State of residence in securities issued by persons in the State of source.'

As experts in this field have correctly pointed out, the amount of income which can access the treaty's regime is directly proportional to how broadly the previously mentioned definition of that which is incidental to a trade or business is interpreted.[173] Each time income is received it will be necessary to verify whether it facilitates the conduct of a trade or business in the state of residence.

---

171. Cohen/Pollack/Scherer 1997, p. 66.
172. *See*, among others, the treaties with Germany (example VI, letter A, of the Memorandum of Understanding signed in 1989), Luxembourg (Article 24(3)(d), the Netherlands (section XVIII of the Memorandum of Understanding signed in 1992) and the U.K. (2001 Exchange of Notes).
173. Morrison/Bennett 1993a, p. 338.

Chapter 3: Limitation on Benefits Clauses

III.A.4 Final Remarks

As in the case of the previous clauses, the complexity of the activity clause is significant. As can be observed in the chart included below, many phases are required to determine if the clause is complied with. Verification of compliance must be performed for each item of income. However, for the purposes of facilitating compliance with this clause, to the extent that the income is similar and the circumstances have not changed, entities should be freed from the burden implied to verify compliance in all cases.

On the other hand, the two essential elements of the clause, i.e. the objective characteristics of the trade or business and the relation of the income obtained thereto, have been defined in very restrictive terms. It is likely that many activities which are objectively considered to be legitimate trades or businesses are unable to claim the treaty benefits by means of this clause. Although this clause is applied for each item of income, it directly grants access to the treaty benefits. If the activity clause is not complied with, the taxpayer will only be able to claim the treaty benefits by means of a request to the tax authorities (bona fide clause).

III.A.5 Charts

Following generally operates and an example of a 'substantiality test'.

III.A.5.a Activity Clause

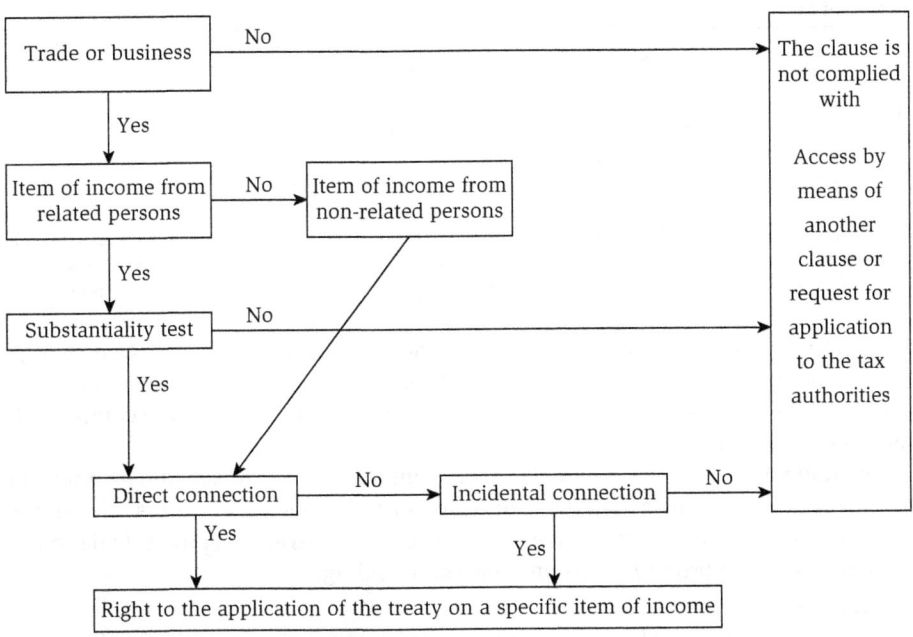

III.A.5.b Example of the Substantiality Test ('Safe Harbour' Rule 1996 U.S. Model)[174]

Company F resides in the U.S. Company F pays dividends to companies A, B, C, D and E, which reside in Spain. Company R, a resident in Spain, is engaged in the conduct of an active trade or business within the meaning of the treaty. This activity is connected to the dividend that company F pays to companies A, B, C, D and E.

The assets of company R are valued at 1 million units of account and those of company F at 6 million units of account. The gross income of R amounts to 10 million and that of F to 40 million. The payroll expense of R amounts to 1 million and that of F to 5 million. Pursuant to the treaty, all the above data refers to the taxable year previous to the year in which the income was obtained.

The voting power and capital stock of company F are distributed in the following manner: 50 percent is owned by company A, and the remainder is equally owned (12.5 percent) by companies B, C, D and E, all of which are residents in Spain.

The voting power and capital stock of company R are distributed in the following manner: 50 percent is owned by company E, and the remainder is equally owned (12.5 percent) by companies A, B, C and D. The following chart provides an outline of the above data:

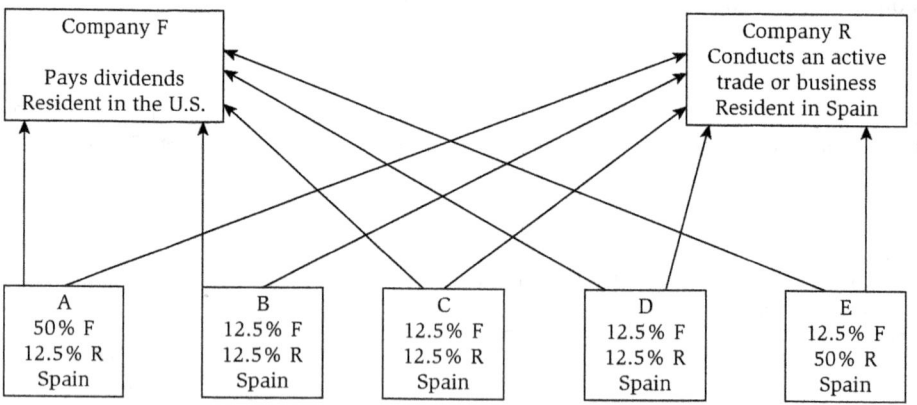

Company F pays dividends to its shareholders, i.e. A, B, C, D, and E. Although these companies are not directly engaged in the conduct of an active trade or business in the state of residence, they do so indirectly, as all of them are related to company R, which is engaged in a business activity.

As none of the companies involved, i.e. company F, which pays the income and company R, which is engaged in the conduct of an active trade or business, are wholly owned by the companies that receive the income, when performing the calculation, it will be necessary to prorate based on their shareholding.

---

174. Example developed based on the example provided in section XV of the Memorandum of the DTC between the Netherlands and the U.S. and the contents in Strauch 1997, pp. 66-67.

Chapter 3: Limitation on Benefits Clauses

The ratios are calculated by first dividing the volume of assets, gross income and payroll expense of the company engaged in the business activity, which is prorated based on the company's shareholding, by the volume of assets, gross income and payroll expense of the company that pays the dividends. The resulting amount is then multiplied by 100.[175] The result of this calculation is shown in the following table:

	R Spain	F U.S.	A Spain	B Spain	C Spain	D Spain	E Spain
Asset value	1 million	6 million	4.2%	16.7%	16.7%	16.7%	66.7%
Gross income	10 million	40 million	6.25%	25%	25%	25%	100%
Payroll expenses	1 million	5 million	5%	20%	20%	20%	80%
Average of these values			5.2%	20.5%	20.5%	20.5%	82.2%

As can be observed, all the companies that obtain dividends from the company residing in the U.S., except for company A, are entitled to claim the treaty benefits. It is necessary to simultaneously fulfil the two requirements as evidenced by this calculation. All the percentages of each ratio (assets, gross income, payroll expenses) are required to exceed 7.5 percent. The average of the three percentages must also exceed 10 percent.

In no case does company A exceed the percentage of 7.5 percent, and accordingly, does not exceed the average of 10 percent. In the other cases, both requirements are satisfied, which implies that the dividends paid by the U.S. company to companies B, C, D and E will be taxed at a maximum rate of 15 percent pursuant to Article 10 of the treaty between Spain and the U.S. Since the shares owned in the U.S. company represent less than 25 percent of its voting power, the reduced tax rate of 10 percent will not be applicable. The dividends obtained by company A will be taxed at the rate established by U.S. domestic law, which is currently 30 percent.

A simpler case based on the same data would be one where the shares representing the capital stock and voting power of the company residing in the U.S. are wholly owned by company R, which is a resident in Spain engaged in the conduct of an active trade or business. The resulting percentages, taking the same data into account, would be 16.6 percent for the assets, 25 percent for gross income and 20 percent for payroll expenses. The average of these three would be 20 percent, meaning that

---

175. Therefore, for example, the proportionate share of company A in the assets of company R is divided by the proportionate share of company A in the assets of F and the resulting amount is multiplied by 100. The same step needs to be performed in the case of the rest of the companies (B, C, D, and E) and the rest of the factors (gross income of both companies and payroll expenses). Accordingly, with respect to company A, the asset value ratio is calculated in the following manner. First, the numerator is the result of determining the percentage of A in the assets of company R based on its shareholding, i.e. 12.5 percent of one million units of account (125,000). The denominator is the result of determining the percentage of A in the assets of company F based on its shareholding, i.e. 50 percent of six million units of account (3,000,000). This amount is multiplied by 100. The rounded result is 4.2 percent.

company R would be entitled to claim the treaty benefits with respect to the dividend payments made by F, since the individual percentages of 7.5 percent and the average percentage of 10 percent are exceeded.

III.B Headquarters Company Clause

This clause is only provided in some of the treaties signed by the U.S. with EU Member States.[176] This clause reads as follows in all the mentioned treaties:

> A person that is a resident of a Contracting State shall also be entitled to all the benefits of this Convention otherwise accorded to residents of a State if that person functions as a headquarters company for a multinational corporate group and that resident satisfies any specified conditions for the obtaining of such benefits other than those of this Article. A person shall be considered a headquarters company for this purpose only if:
>
> a) it provides a substantial portion of the overall supervision and administration of the group, which may include, but cannot be principally, group financing;
> b) the corporate group consists of corporations resident in, and engaged in an active business in, at least five countries, and the business activities carried on in each of the five countries (or five groupings of countries) generate at least 10 percent of the gross income of the group;
> c) the business activities carried on in any one country other than the Contracting State of residence of the headquarters company generate less than 50 percent of the gross income of the group;
> d) no more than 25 percent of its gross income is derived from the other Contracting State;
> e) it has, and exercises, independent discretionary authority to carry out the functions referred to in subparagraph a);
> f) it is subject to the same income taxation rules in its country of residence as persons described in paragraph 4; and
> g) the income derived in the other Contracting State either is derived in connection with, or is incidental to, the active business referred to in subparagraph b).
>
> If the gross income requirements of subparagraphs b), c), or d) of this paragraph are not fulfilled, they will be deemed to be fulfilled if the required ratios are met when averaging the gross income of the preceding four years.

The 1996 and 2006 U.S. Models do not provide anything in this respect. The detailed version of the LOB clauses proposed in Action 6 of the BEPS project does not include the headquarters company clause.[177]

Article 22(5) of the 2016 U.S. Model provides a headquarters company test that is based on analogous tests found in the existing U.S. tax treaties, but with important modifications. One of the main differences is that the new provision does not entitle the

---

176. *See*, among others, the treaties with Austria, Belgium, France (prior to its amendment in 2009), Hungary (2010 treaty, not yet in force), the Netherlands, Poland (2013 treaty, not yet in force) and Spain (2013 Protocol, not yet in force).
177. Nor does paragraph 20 of the Commentaries on Article 1 of the OECD Model.

headquarters company to access all treaty benefits. Entities that comply with the headquarters company test shall be entitled to benefits under the tax treaty only with respect to 'dividends and interest paid by members of its multinational corporate group'. On the contrary, the headquarters company test envisaged in U.S. tax treaties qualifies the company to claim all treaty benefits. Another relevant difference is that the 2016 U.S. Model has included a base erosion test.

This clause, in the treaties where it is provided, authorizes the application of the treaty in respect of those companies which function as the headquarters company of a multinational corporate group. The financial management of these group companies (manufacturing policy, sales policy, personnel policy, etc.) is centralized by means of this company. Imagine, for example, a company residing in the Netherlands responsible for the central administration of a group of companies residing in different states. The company residing in the Netherlands requests the application of the treaty concluded by its state of residence and the U.S.

The Technical Explanations of the 1996 and 2006 U.S. Models do not consider this type of activity to be an active trade or business. Article 22(3)(a)(iii) of the 2016 U.S. Model confirms this interpretation, since the wording of the activity clause expressly provides that the term 'active conduct of a trade or business' does not include the activity of 'providing supervision or administration of a group of companies'. Consequently, these types of entities may not claim the treaty benefits by means of the activity clause.

In order to allow them to claim the treaty benefits, the aforementioned treaties, and now the 2016 U.S. Model, have included this provision.[178] It is essentially a special form of the activity clause, which has multiple specific features, that will be described below.

The clause provided for in the 2016 U.S. Model deviates in important aspects from the rule provided in the mentioned treaties. For this reason, our analysis will focus on the provision laid down in the 2016 U.S. Model, yet some references to the headquarters company clause of the mentioned treaties will be made.

The requirements provided in the 2016 U.S. Model aim to guarantee that only entities that are effectively engaged in the central administration of a multinational corporate group may access the treaty by means of this clause.[179] In this regard, the new provision requires a headquarters company to exercise primary management and control functions –and not just supervision and administration, as in the mentioned treaties- in its residence country with respect to itself and its geographically diverse subsidiaries. Likewise, a base erosion test is added to the clause, which is similar to the one established in the ownership and base erosion clause. As previously mentioned, this additional requirement is not provided in any of the U.S. treaties that contain the

---

178. Amico 1993, p. 1336.
179. Goossen 1993, p. 33.

headquarters company rule. Hence, it is easy to realize that compliance with this clause is quite burdensome in view of its complexity and the number of requirements made.[180]

The 2016 U.S. Model lays down six requirements, which can be divided into four groups.

The first group refers to the activities engaged in by the company responsible for the central administration of a multinational corporate group. The company must exercise primary management and control functions (and not just supervision and administration). These functions must be developed in the contracting state where the company resides, with respect to itself and its geographically diverse subsidiaries. Therefore, those functions cannot be located in any other state.[181]

The second group of requirements is related to the entities managed by the headquarters company and the location of the income obtained by the entities that form part of the multinational corporate group.

The companies forming part of the group are required to reside and engage in the conduct of an active trade or business in at least four states. Subsequently, two requirements with respect to the minimum and maximum amount of income that may be obtained in each of the states in which the group operates are provided. In this respect, the trade or business carried on in each of the four countries (or four groupings of countries) generates at least 10 percent of the group's gross income. However, the income obtained may not exceed 50 percent of the group's gross income in any state, except in the state in which the headquarters company resides.[182] The headquarters company may not obtain more than 25 percent of its gross income in the source state.

The previous calculations are made in respect of the gross income for the taxable year. However, if the limits established by these percentages are not met based on the gross income for the year, this clause allows the calculation to be performed using the average gross income for the four preceding years.[183]

---

180. It is pointed out by Fournier 1994, p. 494 and Schaffner 1997, p. 170, that due to the large number of requirements made it is likely that few companies will be able to access the treaty provisions through the application of this clause.
181. The clause provided in the mentioned U.S.-EU Member States tax treaties only requires that the headquarters company provides 'a substantial portion of the overall supervision and administration of the group, which may include, but cannot be principally, group financing'. No reference is made to the country where those functions must be developed.
182. As pointed out by Morrison/Bennett 1993a, p. 341, the groups 'centre of gravity' should rest on the company responsible for its principal management and administration. If the activity of an entity forming part of the group is significant and represents over 50 percent of the group's overall income, it would be logical for the group's centre of gravity to be established in this company. Therefore, the treaty stipulates that none of the companies, other than the headquarters company, may have income above this amount. If the contrary were to occur, it would only be logical for that company to be responsible for the group's central administration. If this were not the case, it would be understood that the group's structure is not based on strictly business related reasons, but rather other reasons, among which could include treaty shopping.
183. The clause provided in the mentioned U.S.-EU Member States tax treaties establishes similar requirements. There are only two differences. The first is that those treaties require at least five countries instead of four. The second difference is related to the fact this clause applies to all income and not only to dividends and interest, as in the 2016 U.S. Model. The income obtained

Chapter 3: Limitation on Benefits Clauses

Third, the headquarters company must be subject to the same taxation rules in its state of residence as the companies engaged in the conduct of a trade or business. Therefore, the aforementioned company may not be subject to a preferential tax regime in the state in which it resides.[184]

Lastly, the provision provides a base erosion test similar to the one contained in the ownership and base erosion clause. The only difference is the following; Payments that are at arm's length and made in respect of financial obligations to a bank that is not a connected person are not taken into consideration as deductible payments.

As can be observed, this clause requires many circumstances to concur for the treaty to be applicable with respect (only) to dividends and interest paid by members of the headquarters company. In all likelihood, the 2016 U.S. Model has limited the scope of this clause to dividends and interest, since, in comparison to similar provisions provided in prior U.S. tax treaties, the headquarters company is not required to prove that the income obtained at source is connected or incidental to its activity. From this perspective, the new headquarters clause is a crossover between the activity clauses and the ownership and base erosion clause. On the one hand, it takes the base erosion prong from the latter. On the other hand, it takes the fact that the company must develop certain sound activities from the activity test.

Finally, it is very likely that the headquarters company test will appear more often in U.S. tax treaties than it has done in the past, due to it being included in the 2016 U.S. Model.

III.C Derivative Benefits Clause

This clause is a special form of the ownership and base erosion clause. As opposed to the general clause, the derivative benefits clause does not confer the status of qualified resident upon a taxpayer. This form essentially has two special aspects. First, in both parts of the clause, i.e. ownership and base erosion, not only qualified residents are taken into account, but also EU, NAFTA and EEA Member State residents.[185] As was previously shown, these residents were also taken into account in the other clauses (stock exchange clause and activity clause). However, as will be seen below, such geographic restriction has disappeared in the derivative benefits provision proposed both in the 2016 U.S. Model and in Action 6 of the BEPS project.

Specific to this clause is the concept of a 'derivative benefit' or 'alternative relief'.[186] In relation to some types of income –normally, dividends, interest and royalties- the benefits of the convention are conditional upon the fact that the treaty

---

in the source state by the headquarters company is required to be connected or incidental to its activity as the headquarters of the multinational corporate group.
184. The clause provided in the mentioned U.S.-EU Member States tax treaties establishes the same requirement.
185. For the meaning of the concept of EU, NAFTA, and EEA Member State resident, refer to section II.E.3.b of this chapter.
186. The term derivative benefits clause is that used in the DTCs entered into by the U.S. The Commentaries on Article 1 of the OECD Model propose a similar clause called the alternative relief provision (paragraph 19.e).

concluded between the source state and the state of residence of the shareholders in the entity that obtains the income does not establish a less favourable regime. For example:

> Company R obtains a royalty in state F. Company R is controlled by persons residing in state T. The DTC between state R and state F authorizes the source state to levy a tax not exceeding 5 percent of the total amount of the royalty. The DTC between state F and state T confers the exclusive right to tax royalties upon the state of residence, meaning that the source state may not levy any tax whatsoever. As can be observed, the regime of the DTC between the source state and the state of residence of the shareholders (state T) is not 'less favourable' than the DTC between the latter state and the state of residence of the company that obtains income (state R). If the DTC between states F and T authorized a tax of more than 5 percent, this treaty would be 'less favourable.'

The application of the treaty is conditional upon the regime established in the other DTC concluded by the source state and state of residence of the shareholders of the entity claiming the treaty's benefits. This requirement will only be satisfied in the case where the latter treaty provides an equal or more favourable regime. On the contrary, when a less favourable regime is provided, the clause is not complied with.

The problems arising in relation to the fulfilment of this requirement, i.e. whether or not a less favourable regime exists, will be analysed later. It should be pointed out that the regime being compared is that provided in the treaties on taxation in the source state. Since the regime established for each item of income is compared individually, the same taxpayer may not comply with this clause in all cases. This may occur mainly in the case of dividends, interest and royalties, as the treaties normally differ in how these items of income are taxed.

Although it is not provided in the 1996 and 2006 U.S. Models, this clause has been included in many of the treaties being examined in this study.[187] The main reason it is not provided in the 1996 and 2006 U.S. Models is that the U.S. has been opposed to the inclusion of these types of clauses.[188] Such position seems to have changed with the release of the 2016 U.S. Model, since it includes a derivative benefits provision. The same applies to the derivative benefits rule provided in Action 6 of the BEPS project.

On first consideration, it should be borne in mind that this clause rules out the possibility of a treaty shopping structure being developed. Pursuant to the treaty entered into with the source state by the state in which the shareholders reside, if the same or a better tax regime is applied to shareholders at source, the obtaining of income from another state by means of the interposing company does not provide any additional benefit.[189] This circumstance also rules out obtaining the income generated at source from the other state merely for tax purposes.

---

187. *See*, among others, Belgium, Bulgaria, Denmark, Finland, France, Germany, Ireland, Luxembourg, Malta, the Netherlands, Poland (2013 treaty, not yet in force), Spain (2013 Protocol, not yet in force), Sweden and the U.K.
188. Nevertheless, it should be pointed out that it was included for the first time in the 1980 Jamaica-U.S. DTC. A similar provision was also provided in the December 1981 version of the U.S. Model (*see* Bennett 1991, p. 7). Paragraph 20 of the Commentaries on Article 1 of the OECD Model does not include this clause.
189. Rosenbloom 1993, p. 336.

Despite the above, the U.S. put forward a number of arguments to justify not including these clauses. First, the DTCs should not be analysed alone based on the specific regime established for each type. It is possible that the negotiation of the tax regime for a certain item of income may have been able to significantly affect the final rules established for the other items of income provided by the treaty. Accordingly, although the regimes of the tax treaties being compared may be the same in respect of one item of income in particular, the other rules provided in the treaties may differ significantly.[190]

An overall view of the tax treaties explains the reluctance of the U.S. to negotiate the inclusion of these types of clauses. This reluctance also follows from the 2016 U.S. Model, due to the large number of requirements that have been provided in order to be entitled to treaty benefits under this LOB test.

In addition to these reasons, the difficulties involved in the application of this clause are also argued. As shall be observed, in certain cases it may be complex to establish whether the regimes of both treaties are equivalent. Also, it is not clear how to resolve cases where the shareholders reside in more than one state and some of those states have not entered into a treaty with the source state, or in the event that a treaty has been concluded, that a less favourable regime is provided. Finally, the source state's tax authorities could have problems in verifying effective compliance with this clause. The shareholder's state of residence could refuse to respond to a request for information by the source state in this regard, as this is an issue that is not covered by the treaty. It should be noted that the information requested is not for the purposes of the application of the treaty between the source state and the shareholder's state of residence, but rather for a treaty with the state of residence of the entity in which this person has a shareholding.[191]

Along the same lines, the U.S. considered –at least until the release of the 2016 U.S. Model- that these types of clauses might not be well received by a third state (shareholder's state of residence), because such clauses may favour the accumulation of income in an intermediary state through the use of base companies by residents in the third state.[192] However, as pointed out by Bennett, this issue should not be taken into account by the U.S., as it corresponds to this state to adopt measures to preserve the third state's resident tax liability.[193] If this situation were to arise, it would correspond to the latter state to make a decision regarding the adoption of CFC rules. Even so, the reluctance of the U.S. on the basis of this argument may be understandable from the following point of view. The main concern consisted in preventing clauses of this type from affecting future negotiations with third states with which DTCs have also

---

190. It was pointed out by Rosenbloom 1993, pp. 337–338 that this clause safeguards the interests of a state both in the facets of source state as well as state of residence. The residents of this state obtain at least equal benefits in a third state, since the derivative benefits clause requires the DTC with the third state to provide at least an equal regime.
191. Bennett 1991, p. 8. In our opinion, this problem may arise when the exchange of information clause provided in the treaty between the source state and the state of residence is a minor clause.
192. Van Weeghel 1998, p. 238.
193. Bennett 1991, p. 8.

been concluded. Without a doubt, in the hypothetical case that these clauses fostered the previously mentioned phenomenon, this could negatively influence future negotiations with the third state, and could even cause it to unilaterally withdraw from a treaty that had already been concluded.

However, the reasons discussed have not prevented the use of this clause through its inclusion in DTCs entered into by the U.S.[194] This clause has been used in connection with the ownership and base erosion clause. In this respect, this requirement has been added to a modified version of this clause that not only takes qualified residents into account but, also 'equivalent beneficiaries', i.e. EU, NAFTA and EEA Member State residents and, following the 2016 U.S. Model and Action 6 of the BEPS project, any resident in a country with which the source state has signed a tax treaty, provided that a number of conditions are fulfilled.[195] In this manner, this rule is consistent with the assumptions on which the LOB clauses are based, requiring the taxpayer to have a sufficient nexus to the state of residence, and presuming that this is the case when the shareholders are residents in one of the aforementioned states.

Also, it should be borne in mind that the scope of this clause is more limited than it may first appear, since it may only be applied in the case of shareholders residing in one of these states (EU, NAFTA and EEA). In any other case, although the treaty entered into with the shareholder's state of residence does not establish a 'less favourable' regime, these shareholders will not be taken into account. Although this clause is extended to residents in the aforementioned states, because the ownership and base erosion clause must also be complied with, it is very difficult to access the treaty by means of this clause.[196] Even so, it should be taken into consideration that this clause contributes to an increase in the number of taxpayers that may access the treaty.

In any event, this situation has been substantially changed by the adoption of the 2016 U.S. Model and Action 6 of the BEPS project, since geographical restrictions have been ruled out. In all likelihood, the following U.S. tax treaties which include the derivative benefits provisions will only require shareholders from third states to be 'equivalent beneficiaries', i.e. persons who would have been entitled to equivalent or more favourable treaty benefits if they had derived the income in question directly.[197]

The wording of this clause is not exactly the same in the tax treaties in which it is provided. The same happens if the 2016 U.S. Model and the derivative benefits clause of Action 6 of the BEPS project are compared.

A preliminary classification of these clauses would be based on their scope of application. In this case, the treaties which extend the scope of application to all the provisions of the treaty would be differentiated from treaties in which it only applies to certain items of income. However, in practice there is no such difference.

The tax treaties forming part of the first group only provide the requirement that the treaty concluded with the shareholder's state of residence may not be 'less

---

194. In addition to the DTCs entered into with EU Member States, the DTCs entered into between the U.S. and Canada, Mexico and Switzerland included it. Van Weeghel 1998, pp. 237–238.
195. Some treaties also include Switzerland. See the tax treaties between the U.S. and Belgium, Denmark, Finland and Sweden.
196. De Lignie 1995, p. 73.
197. Levine/Miller 2016, p.

Chapter 3: Limitation on Benefits Clauses

favourable' with respect to certain types of income, and particularly dividends, interest, royalties and, in some cases, the branch tax. Effectively there is only one derivative benefit or in OECD terminology, alternative relief clause, with respect to these items of income. As for the other items, the treaty provides an ownership and base erosion clause allowing other taxpayers in addition to qualified residents to be taken into account.

Taking the above into account, the derivative benefits clause only has a limited scope in the treaties being studied. In the DTCs where the wording of this clause is strict, it is applied only on dividends, interest, royalties and, in some cases, the branch tax.

Concerning other income types, the derivative benefits clause only requires that the shareholder be entitled to all the treaty benefits entered into between the source state and the third state. In this regard, U.S. tax treaties, and also the 2016 U.S. Model and Action 6 of the BEPS project, establish an additional requirement. In order to be considered an 'equivalent beneficiary', a resident of a third state needs to be entitled to the benefits of a comprehensive tax treaty between the source state and the third state under an LOB test similar to the ones mentioned in the ownership and base erosion clause, i.e. individuals, governmental bodies, public traded companies (only direct access), tax-exempted organizations and pension funds. As can be seen, not all residents of a third state, which have signed a treaty with the source state, qualify for the derivative benefits clause; insofar as they have to comply with conditions equivalent to the ones established by the ownership and base erosion clause.

If the tax treaty between the source state and the third state does not contain a compressive LOB rule, this requirement will be applied in a fictitious way: It has to be determined whether the owner would have passed the tests of the LOB clause had he been a resident of the same state as the company.[198]

Another classification criterion would take into account the existence of a minimum of 'local ownership'. The derivative benefits clause is included in the ownership and base erosion clause. In the latter clause, a certain percentage of ownership (capital stock and voting rights) is required to be owned by qualified residents in one of the contracting states. The derivative benefits clause makes it possible for EU, NAFTA and EEA Member State residents to be taken into consideration. However, some tax treaties (France and the Netherlands), before they were amended, required that a certain percentage of shares were owned by qualified residents, i.e. a certain volume of 'local ownership' is required.[199] In all other tax treaties, this volume of local ownership is not required. Consequently, this classification criterion would distinguish between cases in which local ownership is required and cases in which it is not.

Finally, the last classification criterion would consist in differentiating between the non-qualified residents that are taken into account. All treaties take EU and NAFTA Member State residents into consideration. The residents in EEA Member States are

---

198. Rust 2015, p. 136.
199. However, and logically, for this clause to be of some advantage, it significantly reduces the percentage of local ownership.

included in all treaties except Ireland, Luxembourg and Spain. Switzerland is a 'qualifying state' in the treaties with Belgium, Denmark and Sweden. However, this classification has lost its significance in the 2016 U.S. Model and Action 6 of the BEPS project since geographical restrictions have been eliminated.

Bearing the above in mind, the specific wording of this clause will be analysed.

The derivative benefits provision requires a percentage of the shares to be held by residents in qualifying countries. In most tax treaties, and also in the 2016 U.S. Model and Action 6 of the BEPS project, to comply with the ownership clause, at least 95 percent of the voting power and capital stock is required to be directly or indirectly owned by residents in qualifying countries. They also require that this percentage of shares be owned by only a maximum of seven persons that are equivalent beneficiaries. If owned by a higher number of persons, this prong of the derivative benefits test would not be complied with based on the literal wording of the rule.

Although the percentage of shares is quite high, this clause allows companies not owned in (some) part by qualified residents to access the clause, i.e. by residents in one of the contracting states that comply with one of the tests by which this status is conferred upon them. This does not mean that the qualified residents are not taken into account in this calculation. The shares of the qualified residents are still taken into consideration, in view of the fact that these taxpayers are considered by default equivalent beneficiaries.

Moreover, the derivative benefits clause does not have significant effects on the base erosion requirement. The only difference lies in the fact that in addition to the qualified residents, equivalent beneficiaries will be taken into account.[200] The applicable percentage is the same one provided in the ownership and base erosion test, i.e. 50 percent.[201]

Finally, it is necessary to analyse the main issue regarding compliance with this clause, i.e. when the treaty of the shareholder's state of residence establishes a 'less favourable' regime.

This requirement is peculiar as it conditions the application of a treaty's regime upon the regime established in another treaty. The regimes established in the two treaties must be compared. The regime of the tax treaties involved is compared with the treaty entered into by the source state and the shareholder's state of residence. The clause is complied with if the regime established in the latter treaty is equal to, or more favourable than the former.[202]

---

200. See the remarks made in section II.F.3.B of this chapter on the base erosion clause.
201. However, the Malta-U.S. DTC establishes 25 percent for the base erosion prong of this clause.
202. Following the 2004 amendment of the DTC between the Netherlands and the U.S., a new element was included for the purposes of this comparison. Besides taking into account the regime of the DTCs, the regime provided for the income affected in the EU directives which may have been approved in this regard are taken into consideration. This case is only applicable if the entity requesting the application of the DTC between the Netherlands and the U.S. resides in the U.S. Accordingly, for example, if a company residing in the EU is wholly owned by a company residing in Luxembourg, although the DTC between Luxembourg and the Netherlands establishes a limit of 15 percent in regard to dividends, and in the DTC between the Netherlands and the U.S., this percentage is 0, the requirement will have been satisfied because the Directive on parent companies and subsidiaries establishes 0 percent taxation at source. A

The object being compared is the tax regime in the source state provided by the treaties. In principle, this comparison process is relatively simple. In regard to interest and royalties, the tax limit provided in each treaty is compared. Where the treaty entered into by the source state and the shareholder's state of residence provides a higher rate, the clause is not complied with.

Regarding dividends, this process is not as simple. Tax treaties generally establish a different regime based on the type of shareholding (direct investment or portfolio investment). The duality of the regimes makes it difficult to identify the elements which should be compared. For example:

> In accordance with the DTC between the U.S. and state R, dividends can only be taxed at source at a rate of 15 percent. In the case of a direct investment (shareholding of more than 25 percent), the tax rate is reduced to 5 percent. An individual residing in state T holds shares representing 20 percent of the capital stock of a company residing in state R. This company owns 50 percent of the shares representing the capital stock of a company residing in the U.S. The DTC between the U.S. and state T establishes the same regime in regard to dividends as that established in the DTC between the U.S. and state R.

Based on these facts, there are three possible alternatives. In the first, the elements which would be compared are the treaty applied to individuals (U.S.-T DTC) and the treaty provided for companies residing in state R (U.S.-R DTC). In this case, the clause would not be complied with. The shareholding directly owned by the individual would only enable him to apply the general tax rate provided in the DTC between the U.S. and T (15 percent). By contrast, the company residing in state R would receive better treatment, because it would be entitled to apply the reduced tax rate provided in the DTC between the U.S. and R (5 percent).

In the second alternative, the tax regime applicable to the company residing in state R in accordance with the DTC between the U.S. and R, and that to which the company would be subject if it resided in T (U.S.-T DTC) would be compared. In this case, the clause would be complied with. In both cases, the regime is the same (5 percent for holding a substantial amount of shares).

Lastly, the tax to which the individual would be subject in the source state if it resided in state R would have to be analysed. As in the previous case, the terms of the

---

similar provision has been included in the following treaties between the U.S. and EU Member States: Belgium, Bulgaria, Denmark, Finland, France, Germany, Poland, Sweden and Spain. Using the example of the France-U.S. DTC, this rule reads as follows:

> with respect to dividends, interest, or royalties arising in France and beneficially owned by a company that is a resident of the U.S., a company that is a resident of a member state of the European Union shall be treated as satisfying the requirements of subparagraph (f)(i)(bb) for purposes of determining whether such United States resident is entitled to benefits under this paragraph if a payment of dividends, interest, or royalties arising in France and paid directly to such resident of a member state of the European Union would have been exempt from tax pursuant to any directive of the European Union, notwithstanding that the income tax convention between France and that other member state of the European Union would provide for a higher rate of tax with respect to such payment than the rate of tax applicable to such United States company under Article 10 (Dividends), 11 (Interest), or 12 (Royalties) of this Convention.

clause would be met. The individual would be subject to the same tax in both states (15 percent) since a reduced tax rate is not applicable to the directly owned shares.

The treaties that include a derivative benefits clause have not generally provided a way to resolve this problem. The first alternative has been rejected by experts in this field as the elements being compared are not similar, and because this option is the most restrictive.[203] To determine whether two situations receive different treatment, the elements being compared must be similar.[204] In the first case, two situations that are not similar are being compared, i.e. the regime of the company residing in R and that of the individual residing in T. Consequently, in view of the dissimilarity of the situations compared, the first alternative has been ruled out.[205]

The second and third options do compare similar situations. The DTC between Luxembourg and the U.S. has expressly stated how the comparison is to be made, and has chosen the third alternative.[206] This solution is consistent with the purpose of the LOB clauses. These rules aim to prevent the application of the treaties to interposed companies, whose purpose is to access the DTCs regime entered into by a state. One of the basic criteria on which these rules are based, consists in examining the shareholder's place of residence.[207] In this respect, it is logical that the derivative benefits clauses compare the regime that the shareholder is subject to rather than the regime to which the entity that holds a shareholding is subject. The treaty benefits are granted precisely because the shareholder does not obtain any benefit from interposing the company. In this case, the possibility of developing a treaty shopping structure is ruled out. However, it should be borne in mind that this issue is not resolved in all the treaties that provide this clause.[208]

However, it is important to point out that some U.S. treaties signed or amended following the amendment of the tax treaty with the Netherlands in 2004, contain the following provision that addresses the issue from a different approach:[209]

> For the purposes of applying paragraph 3 of Article 10 (Dividends) in order to determine whether a person, owning shares, directly or indirectly, in the company claiming the benefits of this Convention, is an equivalent beneficiary, such person shall be deemed to hold the same voting power in the company paying the dividend as the company claiming the benefits holds in such company.

---

203. Winandy 1996, p. 23.
204. García Prats 1998, p. 94.
205. Winandy 1996, p. 23 and Bennett/Morrison/Daniels/De Hosson 1995, p. 121.
206. Based on the Memorandum of Understanding of the DTC between the Netherlands and the U.S., it could be deduced that the second option should be followed. However, this reference is made in relation to the criteria for the application of the bona fide clause, and not with respect to the derivative benefits clause. As shall be observed (section V.B), one of the criteria based on which to decide if the tax authorities should grant the benefits of the treaty is similar to the contents of this clause. Bennett/Morrison/Daniels/De Hosson 1995, pp. 121-122.
207. As pointed out by Winandy 1996, p. 23, LOB clauses effectively lift the legal entity's corporate veil. Therefore, the shareholder and not the entity should be compared.
208. This third alternative was adopted in the treaty with Luxembourg. In this treaty, the issue is resolved through an agreement regarding the interpretation of the treaty (exchange of notes dated 3 April 1996) and not in the body of the treaty.
209. *See*, among others, the treaties with Germany, the Netherlands and the U.K.

Chapter 3: Limitation on Benefits Clauses

As can be observed, this rule does not coincide with any of the cases discussed. In this case, it is presumed that the qualifying shareholder has the same shareholding in the company that pays the dividend as the company that receives it. Without a doubt, this interpretation facilitates the fulfilment of this requirement of the derivative benefits clause. A similar rule is not provided in the 2016 U.S. Model nor in the LOB rule proposed in Action 6 of the BEPS project.

In any case, if the clause is complied with, it is important not to lose sight of the fact that the treaty is applied to companies and not to the shareholders.

Finally, we will briefly refer to some of the latest developments of the derivative benefits clause provided for in the 2016 U.S. Model.

According to Article 22(7)(e)(i)(A) of the 2016 U.S. Model, the following individuals shall not be considered equivalent beneficiaries:

> an individual who is (1) liable to tax in his or her state of residence with respect to foreign source income or gains only on a remittance or similar basis, or (2) whose tax is determined in that Contracting State on a fixed-fee, 'forfait' or similar basis, shall not be considered an equivalent beneficiary;

This requirement seems to deviate from the rationale of LOB clauses, as it takes into account the actual liability of the taxpayer in the state of residence in order to decide if treaty benefits should be applicable. This provision seems to be influenced by the BEPS project, as the provision is intended to mitigate instances of double non-taxation whereby a taxpayer uses provisions in the tax treaty, combined with special tax regimes, to pay no or very low tax in either treaty country.

Moreover, the 2016 U.S. Model has increased the number of types of income where the treaties benefits have to be compared in order to determine if an equivalent (or better) regime is provided. In addition to dividends, interest and royalties, the following items of income have been included: business profits, capital gains and 'other income'.

The 2016 U.S. Model has also addressed other issues. Under all derivative benefits provisions in existing U.S. tax treaties, in order to qualify as an equivalent beneficiary with respect to dividends, interest or royalties, a third-country resident must be entitled to a tax treaty rate with respect to the particular category of income that is, less than or equal to, the rate applicable under the tax treaty under which benefits are being claimed. Persons that fail to satisfy this rate comparison test, even by a narrow margin, are not entitled to treaty benefits, and therefore generally subject to the domestic law, withholding tax on source payments of dividends, interest and royalties. The 2016 U.S. Model has removed this so-called cliff effect,[210] by entitling a resident of the treaty partner to the highest rate of withholding to which its third-country resident owners would be entitled. This measure is not established in the LOB rule (Article 22), but in the dividends, interest and royalties Articles.

Another cliff effect solved by the 2016 U.S. Model is where; under existing treaties that include a derivative benefits test, subsidiaries of private companies are unable to qualify for benefits with respect to dividends under the derivative benefits test because,

---

210. Bates/Berman/Gani/Gutmann/Imamura/Klugman/Rust 2013, p. 401.

individual shareholders are only entitled to a 15 percent rate on dividends, and therefore the cliff effect would preclude any reduction in dividend withholding. In order to overcome this problem, the 2016 U.S. Model allows certain companies relying on derivative benefits to qualify for the 5 percent rate of withholding on dividends even if the company's shareholders are individuals who would not be entitled to that rate. To achieve the latter, the new provision allows individual shareholders to be treated as companies for purposes of the rate comparison test with respect to dividends, provided that the company seeking to qualify under derivative benefits has sufficient substance in its resident country to indicate that the individual shareholders are not simply routing income through a corporate entity in order to benefit from the lower company rate.

Moreover, the 2016 U.S. Model allows certain categories of qualified persons in the source state to be treated as equivalent beneficiaries, provided that such persons do not, in the aggregate, own more than 25 percent of the tested company. This is a relevant modification, as persons residing in the source state do not qualify for the ownership and base erosion clause. However, the rule does not clarify what happens when that percentage is exceeded. It is our understanding that in such a situation the first 25 percent will continue to be considered as being held by equivalent beneficiaries, but not the rest. Therefore, the first 25 percent will continue to qualify for the purpose of this LOB test.

Finally, the ownership prong of the derivative benefits clause has been drafted in line with the equivalent prong of the ownership and base erosion clause. Thus, equivalent beneficiaries will not be eligible if they are connected persons with respect to the person claiming treaty benefits and incur in any of the following situations; First, if they benefit from a STR with respect to the deductible payment.[211] Second, regarding an interest payment, if the payee benefits from notional deductions.

IV EXCLUSION PROVISIONS

IV.A Permanent Establishment Clause

In Chapter 1, the possibilities offered by the figure of a PE in international tax planning were analysed. The international taxation of the PE may give rise to situations where double and even triple taxation occur, but it may also trigger cases of non-taxation. The latter can be achieved by appropriately combining the differences that exist between the tax treaties and the state's domestic law.

PEs are used in treaty shopping structures in the case of a 'direct strategy' or direct conduit model. Taxation in the intermediary company's state is eliminated by attributing the income obtained in the source state to a PE located in a low-tax territory. Additionally, the income attributed to the PE must not be taxed in the intermediary state.

---

211. *See* section IV.B.2.b of this chapter.

The purpose of this clause is precisely to deny the application of the treaty when the above described situation arises. As is demonstrated, this clause is provided to deny the application of the treaty. Therefore, this rule assumes that the taxpayer is entitled to claim the treaty benefits in accordance with one of the previously discussed LOB clauses.

On first consideration, denying the application of the treaty in these cases could give rise to an element which would not be consistent with the assumptions on which the LOB clauses are based. If a taxpayer complies with one of these clauses, it is 'presumed' that he or she has a sufficient nexus to the state of residence or a real business purpose to obtain the income from this state. In principle, these clauses are not based on the assumption that the income obtained at source will be subject to a certain level of taxation in the source state or any other place.

However, this is precisely the assumption on which the PE clause is based. According to this provision, when income is attributed to a PE situated in a third state, the treaty will only be applied if the overall income is subject to a certain level of taxation. If this were the case, this rule would include an element that is not in line with the assumptions underlying the LOB clauses. However, as evidenced by the specific analysis of the treaties that include this clause, this problem has been conveniently corrected to assure that such a discrepancy does not arise. This clause is generally not applied if the income attributed to the PE is obtained in relation to an active trade or business developed by the PE itself.

A detailed analysis of these corrections will be performed later. However, it is important to highlight that these corrections are in line with the original purpose of the LOB clauses. The treaty will be applied despite the fact that the income was shifted to a PE located in a low-tax territory, as long as there is a real business purpose for doing so, such as the engagement by this PE in the conduct of an active business or trade. In this case, the application of the treaty is justified, despite the fact that the effective taxation is very low. Consequently, the existence of a PE clause does not distort the assumptions on which LOB clauses are based; because the elements required for this clause lead back to the assumptions on which the LOB tests are based for the purposes of applying this treaty, i.e. the existence of a real business purpose.

This clause is not provided in the 1996 and 2016 U.S. Models. However, some references to this type of conduct are found in the Commentaries on the OECD Model. In particular, the commentaries on Article 24 (paragraph 71) state the following:

> If the Contracting State of which the enterprise is a resident exempts from tax the profits of the permanent establishment located in the other Contracting State, there is a danger that the enterprise will transfer assets such as shares, bonds or patents to permanent establishments in States that offer very favourable tax treatment, and in certain circumstances the resulting income may not be taxed in any of the three States. To prevent such practices, which may be regarded as abusive, a provision can be included in the convention between the State of which the enterprise is a resident and the third State (the State of source) stating that an enterprise can claim the benefits of the convention only if the income obtained by the permanent establishment situated in the other State is taxed normally in the State of the permanent establishment.

The tax treaties entered into by the U.S. with a large number of EU Member States[212] include a provision similar to that proposed by the OECD in the Commentaries on its model treaty. Moreover, it should be highlighted that the BEPS project contains a provision in this regard. A template of this provision was first included in Action 6.[213] However, the final wording of the PE rule has been slightly modified in 2016, due to the release of the Multilateral Convention to Implement Tax Treaty Related Measures to Prevent BEPS (hereinafter, 2016 BEPS Multilateral Instrument).[214] Article 10 of the 2016 BEPS Multilateral Instrument provides a provision similar to the one contained in U.S. tax treaties. Finally, the 2016 U.S. Model has introduced a PE rule in its Article 1(8), which differs in some aspects, from the one provided for in previous U.S. tax treaties and the 2016 BEPS Multilateral Instrument.

Hereinafter, the PE rule provided for in U.S. tax treaties will be analysed in light of the 2016 BEPS Multilateral Instrument and the 2016 U.S. Model.

The reason this clause is only provided in certain U.S. tax treaties lies in the fact that the viability of this structure depends, to a large extent, on the tax treatment of the income attributed to the PE by the state of residence (intermediary state). It is necessary that the state of residence uses the exemption method. Therefore, for example, in the DTC between Austria and the U.S., this provision is only formally applied when the entity resides in Austria.[215] Besides, from a material standpoint, this structure cannot be developed when the entity resides in the U.S., as this state does not use the exemption method to eliminate the international double taxation that the entity, to which the PE belongs, may be subject.[216] For this reason, although in certain treaties the PE clause affects both contracting states, in practice it will only have effect when the entity resides in a state other than the U.S. In the 2016 BEPS Multilateral Instrument and the 2016 U.S. Model, the provision applies to both contracting states.

In fact, in view of the wording of the tax treaties with Bulgaria, Belgium, Denmark Ireland, Luxembourg and Sweden, and Article 10 of the 2016 BEPS Multilateral Instrument, the PE clause is only applied if the income is exempt from tax in the state of residence, or in other words, it has not been effectively taxed.[217] If this income is even minimally taxed in the state of residence, technically the clause will not be applicable. Imagine a case in which 99 percent of the income is exempt from tax.

This wording does not contribute to the primary objective of the clause, i.e. that all income be subject to a certain level of taxation. Given its wording in the mentioned treaties and the 2016 BEPS Multilateral Instrument, the application of the clause can

---

212. *See*, among others, the treaties with Austria (Article 16(4)), Belgium (Article 21(6)), Bulgaria (Article 21(5)), Denmark (Article 22(6)), France (Article 30(5)), Finland (Article 16(5)), Germany (Article 28(5), Hungary (Article 22(6) of the 2010 treaty, not yet in force), Ireland (Article 23(7)), Luxembourg (Article 24(5)), Malta (Article 22(5)), the Netherlands (Articles 12(8) and 13(6)), Poland (Article 22(6) of the 2013 treaty, not yet in force), Spain (Article 17(6) of the 2013 Protocol, not yet in force) and Sweden (Article 17(5)).
213. OECD 2015a, pp. 75–78.
214. The Multilateral Instrument is one of the outcomes of the OECD/G20 BEPS project.
215. The same also occurs in the tax treaties with Belgium, Bulgaria, Denmark, Finland, Ireland and Sweden.
216. Keijzer/Larking 1993, p. 2 and Schinabeck 1996, p. 37.
217. Cohen/Pollack/Scherer 1997, p. 71 and Berman/Hynes 2000, p. 707.

easily be avoided without complying with the assumption on which the clause is based. Consequently, we consider the clause in the rest of the treaties to be worded more correctly, as all income is not required to be exempt from tax in the state of residence for the clause to be applied. It is of paramount importance to examine the tax that the income is subject to in the state of residence and in the PE state in order to determine if the income is subject to 'normal taxation'.

The main problem relating to this type of clause consists in determining when the income attributed to the PE has been 'taxed normally'. U.S. tax treaties provide an objective rule to eliminate the uncertainty that the previous concept may cause. Accordingly, the consequences of the clause will be applied when the tax that the income is subject to in the state of residence and in the state where the PE is located, is a certain percentage less than the tax to which it would have been subject in the state of residence if the income had not been attributed to the PE. The 2016 BEPS Multilateral Instrument follows the same pattern.

The DTCs with Ireland and Luxembourg establish a percentage of 50 percent. In the other U.S. treaties and the 2016 BEPS Multilateral Instrument a percentage of 60 percent has been established.[218] For example, in the case of the DTC between France and the U.S., the provision will be applied when combined tax that is actually paid in the state of residence and in the state where the PE is located is less than 60 percent of the tax that would have been paid in the state of residence if the item of income has not been attributed to the PE.

The 2016 U.S. Model establishes a different pattern, and the rule applies in any of the following two situations. The first situation is similar to the provision provided in previous U.S. tax treaties and the 2016 BEPS Multilateral Instrument, as it looks into the actual taxation of the income attributed to the PE. In this regard, the rule applies if the profits attributed to the PE are subject to a combined aggregate effective tax that 'is less than the lesser of (i) 15 percent or (ii) 60 percent of the general statutory rate' of corporate income tax applicable in the state of residence. As can be seen, this rule deviates slightly from the U.S. tax treaties' PE rule, because it takes two percentages as a benchmark instead of only one. This minor deviation has its explanation in other new provisions introduced in the 2016 U.S. Model such as the STRs and subsequent changes in law provisions.[219]

The second situation completely deviates from previous U.S. tax treaties and the 2016 BEPS Multilateral Instrument. In this regard, the PE rule would apply if the country where the PE is located does not have a comprehensive tax treaty in force with the source state, unless the income attributed to the PE is included in the tax base of the state of residence of the entity who owns the PE. In our view, it does not make any sense to deny treaty benefits in this case. The fact that the mentioned circumstances do not concur – existence of a tax treaty or inclusion of the income in the state of residence's tax base –, does not, by itself, lead to low or non-taxation of the PE. From

---

218. The 2016 U.S. Model establishes a different pattern, since the rule will only apply if aggregate effective tax is actually paid.
219. See section IV.B.2 of this chapter.

our perspective, this mayor deviation lacks a solid legal base, which might explain why the 2016 BEPS Multilateral Instrument has ruled out its inclusion.

Moreover, based on the wording of this clause in most U.S. tax treaties[220] and the 2016 BEPS Multilateral Instrument, the item that is compared is the effective tax that the income would have been subject to in the state of residence if it had not been allocated to the PE. Logically, it will be necessary to determine the effective tax rate that would have been applicable to the company in the case that the income had not been attributed to the PE.

On the contrary, in the U.S. tax treaties with Austria, Ireland and the Netherlands, and also in the PE rule provided in the 2016 U.S. Model, this does not seem to be the item of comparison.[221] In these cases, the item to be compared is the general corporate income tax rate in force in the state of residence. In these cases, the percentage of 60 or 50 percent, as appropriate, should not be applied on the effective tax rate that the company is subject to, but rather on the general rate provided by the corresponding state's legislation. Performing the calculation in this manner effectively increases the tax levied on the income attributed to the PE as the effective tax rates are usually less than the rates established by law. For example:

> A company residing in the Netherlands obtains royalties in the U.S., which are attributed to a PE located in the Dutch Antilles. As a consequence of this territory's tax regime, these royalties are not taxed. Additionally, this income benefits from the exemption method under Dutch law. If the royalties had not been attributed to the PE, they would have been taxed in the Netherlands at the company's effective average rate, which is imagined to be 20 percent. The general tax rate in the Netherlands is 35 percent (fictitious). If the effective tax rate is taken into consideration, the income must be taxed at a rate exceeding 12 percent. If the general tax rate is taken into account, the income is required to be taxed at a rate exceeding 21 percent. In any case, in this example the clause is applicable because no tax has been levied on the income.

Once the requirements of the clause are satisfied, it is necessary to analyse the consequences of its application. In this respect, it is possible to differentiate between two types of treaties based on the clause's scope of application.

The first type includes the DTCs with France, Germany, Hungary, Ireland, Luxembourg, Malta, Poland and Spain. The 2016 U.S. Model and 2016 BEPS Multilateral Instrument follow this pattern. The clause is general because all income obtained in the source state is affected. Regardless of the nature of the income attributed to the PE, it will be necessary to verify whether the taxation thresholds provided in the treaty are exceeded. If this is not the case, the source state recovers the right to tax this income without the limits provided in the treaty. However, in the mentioned U.S. tax treaties, the treaty benefits are partially maintained, despite the application of the clause, in regard to dividends, interest and royalties. The tax levied

---

220. U.S. tax treaties with Bulgaria, Belgium, Denmark, Finland, France, Germany, Hungary, Luxembourg, Malta, Poland, Spain and Sweden.
221. Despite the clarity with which the DTC between Austria and the U.S. is worded, Schuch/Toifl 1998, p. 29, it seems to sustain that the calculation should be made as it is in the DTCs with France and Luxembourg.

on this income in the source state may not exceed 15 percent of the gross amount thereof. Although this tax ceiling is higher than that provided for this income by the treaty, it is significantly lower, for example, than the limit established under U.S. domestic law (30 percent).[222] This exception is not provided for in the 2016 U.S. Model and 2016 BEPS Multilateral Instrument. In our view, this new approach is reasonable, bearing in mind that there are no grounds for giving better treatment to the mentioned types of income.

The permanent establishment clause has a partial scope of application in the U.S. tax treaties with Austria, Belgium, Bulgaria, Denmark, Finland, the Netherlands and Sweden, and only affects interest, royalties and insurance premiums (only in the tax treaties with Finland and Sweden). In this case, tax treaties establish a 15 percent tax ceiling in the event that the clause is applicable, as in the aforementioned case. However, in the DTC between Austria and the U.S., if the PE clause is applicable to the interest and royalties obtained in the U.S., this state is entitled to tax the income in accordance with its domestic legislation without being constrained by the treaty limits. The same occurs in the tax treaties with Finland and Sweden concerning insurance premiums. In the other treaties, the tax may not be higher than the tax ceiling of 15 percent of the gross income.

Finally, U.S. tax treaties provide three exceptions to the application of this clause. The 2016 U.S. Model and the 2016 BEPS Multilateral Instrument also contain some exceptions, which will be briefly analysed after the study of the rules provided for in the U.S. tax treaties.

The first exception, i.e. the conduct of an active trade or business by the PE, is provided in almost all U.S. tax treaties –and in the 2016 BEPS Multilateral Instrument-.[223] The inclusion of this exception makes the PE rule consistent with the assumptions underlying LOB clauses. The treaty is still applied despite the low level of taxation, as there is a real business purpose that justifies attributing income to the PE. Furthermore, it is important not to lose sight of the fact that the entity that the PE belongs to is entitled to the application of the treaty as it complies with one of the LOB tests. Consequently, both the PE and the entity that it belongs to, comply with one of the assumptions on which the LOB clauses are based.

This exception is established in terms similar to the activity clause.[224] The income obtained in the source state is required to be connected or incidental to the active trade or business conducted by the PE.[225] As in the case of the activity clause, merely making or managing investments will not be considered to be an active trade or business. The problems relating to the application of this exception are to be resolved the same way

---

222. In the above example, if the treaty were fully applied, the royalties obtained in the U.S. by a Dutch company would not be taxed in the U.S. Since the assumptions of the PE clause are complied with, the maximum tax levied will be equal to 15 percent of the company's gross income. In accordance with U.S. law, if this special limit were not to exist, the tax levied on this income would be equal to 30 percent of the company's gross income.
223. In the Finland-U.S. DTC and the Sweden-U.S. DTC, this exception is not applicable to insurance premiums. The Malta-U.S. DTC does not contain this exception.
224. Walsh 1997, p. 329.
225. Cunningham 1997, pp. 551–552.

as in the activity clause. Therefore, the corresponding section of this chapter should be referred to in this regard. However, it is important to highlight that the treaties do not formally include the 'substantiality test'. Therefore, it may be considered that this test is not required in these cases.[226]

Notwithstanding the above, it should be remembered that, the fact that this exception is established in terms similar to the activity clause does not mean that the entity to which this PE belongs should necessarily access the treaty by means of this clause. This aspect is independent from the applicability of this exception. The entity that the PE belongs to would only need to comply with one of the clauses provided in the treaty, among which could be the activity clause itself. However, this is unlikely.[227] As discussed when analysing the activity clause, it is applied by individually examining the income obtained by the company in the state of residence. Only if the income obtained in the source state is connected or incidental to the active trade or business conducted in the state of residence will the entity be entitled to the application of the treaty. When the trade or business is carried on by a PE located in a third state, it would not be taken into account for the purpose of compliance with the activity clause, because only the business activities carried on in the state of residence will be considered. In this case, the trade or business is not carried out in this state.

As previously discussed, only in the treaty with the Netherlands, before its amendment in 2004, could the activity clause be applied in respect of the income attributable to the PE, because this treaty allows business activities carried on in other EU Member States to be taken into account. Consequently, if the PE is located in one of the EU Member States, it could be taken into consideration. In any case, although the possibility provided in the DTC between the Netherlands and the U.S., before its amendment in 2004, may appear to be of interest, in practice, this is not the case, since it would significantly increase the percentages that must be complied with to pass 'the substantiality test.'

The second exception is specific to royalties.[228] According to this exception, the PE rule will not apply when royalties are received as compensation for the use of, or the right to use, intangible property produced or developed by the PE itself. It is important to consider that the treaties only state that intangible property must have been produced or developed by the PE, which does not imply that the intangible was necessarily developed in the state where the PE is located. In view of the wording of this clause, this exception should be admissible, for example, when the intangible property has been developed in a third state, but the financing required for this purpose has been supplied by the PE.[229]

The third exception is only provided in the tax treaty with Austria. The treaty will still be applicable when the income affected by this clause is subject to tax in any of the

---

226. Keijzer/Larking 1993, pp. 3-4 and Strauch 1997, p. 101.
227. Keijzer/Larking 1993, p. 3.
228. In regard to royalties, the DTCs with Austria, Belgium, Bulgaria, Denmark, Finland, the Netherlands and Sweden do not make express reference to the activity clause. They only contain the mentioned second exception. This exception is not provided in the following treaties: the Ireland-U.S. DTC, the Luxembourg-U.S. DTC and the Malta-U.S. DTC.
229. Keijzer/Larking 1993, p. 3.

contracting states, in accordance with a CFC rule.[230] This clause in the DTC between Austria and the U.S. is only provided for cases where the U.S. taxes income in accordance with this regime. The reason for the above is that the clause is only applied when the company to which the PE belongs resides in Austria, and as pointed out by Strauch, when this treaty was concluded, there were no CFC rules in Austria.[231]

Otherwise, this exception is in line with the purpose of this clause, i.e. that the income is subject to a reasonable level of taxation. This is achieved when the income is taxed in accordance with CFC rules, although the income is effectively taxed in a state other than that in which the PE is located. As opposed to the first exception, this one does not include any of the assumptions on which the LOB clauses are based.

Moreover, the 2016 BEPS Multilateral Instrument contains the first exception provided in almost all U.S. tax treaties, i.e. the conduct of an active trade or business by the PE. However, this exception is not established in the 2016 U.S. Model. In fact, the 2016 U.S. Model does not establish any exception to the PE rule.

However, the 2016 U.S. Model contains an 'escape clause' similar to the LOB bona fide clause (*see* section V of this chapter). This 'escape clause' is also provided in the 2016 BEPS Multilateral Instrument.

The 'escape clause' allows the taxpayer to request, from the source state tax authorities, treaty benefits regarding a specific item of income that have been denied under the PE rule. According to this clause, the tax authorities may grant the requested benefit if it is determined that such granting of benefits 'is justified in light of the reasons such resident did not satisfy the requirements of this paragraph (such as the existence of losses)'. The following is also established:

> The competent authority of the Contracting State to which the request has been made shall consult with the competent authority of the other Contracting State before either granting or denying a request made under this paragraph by a resident of that other Contracting State.

In our view, the 'escape clause' is expressed in very ambiguous terms. In this regard, it seems awkward that not a single criterion has been established in order to determine which reasons should lead to the treaty benefits being granted and which ones should not, depending on the requirements of the PE rule that were not satisfied. It is our understanding, that it would have been more advisable to apply the same criteria here as that established in the bona fide clause, i.e. if the establishment, acquisition or maintenance of the resident and the conduct of its operations did not have as one of its principal purposes the obtaining of benefits under the treaty. In this case, the taxpayer should give evidence of sound business reasons that justify the attribution of the income to a PE situated in a third jurisdiction.

---

230. Schuch/Toifl 1998, p. 29.
231. Strauch 1997, pp. 102–103.

IV.B Exclusion Clause

IV.B.1 OECD and U.S. Approach to Tax Treaty Measures Against Preferential Tax Regimes

Among the methods proposed by the OECD in the Commentaries on Article 1 of the OECD Model is the exclusion approach.[232] Its purpose consists in totally or partially excluding from the application of the treaty certain entities and tax regimes suitable for the channelling of treaty shopping structures from the state of residence.

The purpose of treaty shopping structures consists in reducing taxation at source on certain income by means of tax treaties. This is achieved either because it confers the exclusive right to tax income upon the state of residence or because it limits taxation of the income in the source state. When developing this tax planning structure, not only is it necessary to choose the treaty entered into by the source state, which reduces taxation in this state the most. It is also essential that the legislation in the state of residence allows the income that is the object of the treaty shopping structure to be 'channelled' to the state where the original owner thereof resides at the least tax cost possible. For this purpose, two circumstances must coincide: the income must not be taxed, or it must only be minimally taxed in the intermediary company's state of residence; and the income must not be subject to taxation when transferred to a third state.

The last two phases of the structure depend, to a large extent, on the existence of a tax regime in the intermediary state which allows for this structure. The objective of this method consists in expressly excluding entities that enjoy a tax regime that allows for the above from the treaty benefits. In this respect, there is a fundamental difference between this clause and the previously mentioned LOB clauses. As a result of compliance with the latter clauses, the right to apply the tax treaty is granted. As a result of compliance with the exclusion clause, taxpayers are prevented from accessing the tax treaty.

Exclusion may be full or partial. The first solution, as stated by the OECD, is the most extreme, as it excludes the affected taxpayers from the convention's scope of application. The second alternative is more flexible. It would only deprive the affected entities from the exemption or reduction of taxation in the source state provided in the treaty. The clause proposed by the Commentaries on Article 1 of the OECD Model, since the 1992 version,[233] is expressed in the following terms:

---

232. *See* paragraphs 21.1–21.3 and 21.5 of the Commentaries on Article 1 of the 2003–2014 OECD Model. Prior to the 2016 U.S. Model, the U.S. Models did not include this approach. However, as shall be seen later, some tax treaties entered into by the U.S. have used it. The 2016 U.S. Model has introduced the special tax regime clause (STR clause) which, to a certain extent, could be considered as an exclusion clause.
233. *See* paragraphs 15–16 of the Commentaries on Article 1 of the 1992–2003 OECD Model. In the 2003–2014 OECD Model, this clause is provided in paragraph 21 of the Commentaries on Article 1.

> No provision of the Convention conferring an exemption from, or reduction of, tax shall apply to income received or paid by a company as defined under section ... of the ... Act, or under any similar provision enacted by ... after the signature of the Convention.

The consequences of this provision can be even more limited, restricting exclusion to a specific category of income, which normally includes dividends, interest and royalties. Regardless of the types of income affected in the case of partial exclusion, the taxpayers are still protected under Article 24 of the OECD Model (non-discrimination) and may request commencement of a mutual agreement procedure (Article 25 OECD Model). Furthermore, the contracting states will continue to be entitled to exchange information with respect to these taxpayers (Article 26 OECD Model).[234] If the exclusion is partial, the affected taxpayers continue to be within the subjective scope of the treaty, although they are unable to enjoy the provisions affected by the exclusion clause. By contrast, when the exclusion is total, the taxpayers comprised by the clause are not included in the subjective scope of the treaty.

Exclusion provisions are clear and their application is simple when tax treaties precisely identify the regimes and/or entities which are not eligible for tax treaty benefits. To a large extent, the terms of the exclusion method facilitate its application. In order to know whether or not the method is applicable, it will simply be necessary to determine the recipient of the income in the case that the clause refers to certain taxpayers, or which tax regime it is subject to in the case that the clause refers to a specific regime. The relative simplicity of the clause contrasts with the excessive complexity of the rest of the LOB tests.

However, the need for the excluded cases to be defined with precision may be contrary to the effectiveness of this rule, given that the rule will only be applicable in the expressly provided cases, albeit not in other cases which are similar. Thus enabling states to avoid exclusion clauses where such application shall affect entities or regimes established under its domestic law. The referred states will only be required to enact a new rule establishing a tax regime for a series of entities which attain the same purpose, despite the fact that the new rule is not defined in terms similar to those applicable to the entities affected by the exclusion clause.

The latter peril explains why the exclusion clause provided in the Commentaries expounds that the clause will be applicable to the mentioned entities or regimes and 'any similar provision enacted [...] after the signature of the Convention'. However, this second part of the provision holds a clear disadvantage, i.e. its application could be complex. Thus, it is likely for conflicts to arise where what is discussed is the fact that there are arguments on whether or not the clause is applicable to entities or regimes regulated under a later rule to which the treaty refers. International practice proves such a situation has in fact occurred.[235]

---

234. As in the case of the LOB clauses provided in the 1996, 2006 and 2016 U.S. Models. *See* Doernberg/Van Raad 1997, p. 174.
235. Wurm 1992, p. 663. A good example of this is the exclusion clause provided in the DTC Luxembourg-Spain which affects Luxembourg holding companies, within the meaning of the Act of 31 July 1929 and the Decree (arrêt, grand-ducal) of 17 December 1938. The Spanish tax authorities have tried to extend this exclusion clause to the Société de Participation Financière

This exclusion is difficult to resolve by means of renegotiating the treaty for the purpose of including those new entities and regimes that may be suitable for use in treaty shopping tax planning structures within the scope of the exclusion clause.[236] The treaty negotiation process is complex enough to prevent the renegotiation of the treaty paired to the legislation of the state that created these privileged tax regimes. This is not only due to the slowness of the states' procedures for the ratification and entry into force of the treaties, but also due to the difficulties that the negotiating parties may have in reaching an agreement on which new entities and regimes should be excluded.[237] Logically, the state that has established a new regime will resist agreeing upon its exclusion.[238]

In this regard, in 1998 the OECD published the report, Harmful Tax Competition: An Emerging Global Issue.[239] (1998 Report, OECD, 1998). This report laid the foundations for the OECD's work in the area of harmful tax practices and created the Forum on Harmful Tax Practices to carry out this work. It was published in response to a request by governments to develop measures to counter harmful tax practices with respect to geographically mobile activities. The 1998 OECD report laid down a series of factors to determine whether a preferential regime is potentially harmful.

By reason of the 1998 OECD report, in the 2003 version of the OECD Model, Commentaries on Article 1 were substantially modified to include a series of 'sample clauses' whose objective were the exclusion of treaty benefits to entities benefiting from preferential tax regimes.[240] It is our understanding that these modifications are just a development of the exclusion clause envisaged in the Commentaries on Article 1 prior to the 2003 version of the OECD Model. In this regard, the Commentaries presented three types of provisions: those which are aimed at entities benefiting from

---

(SOPARFI) and to certain Luxembourg collective investment entities on the basis of this open clause provided in the treaty. See Raventós 1994a and 1995b and Vega 2003, pp. 305–311.
236. Schwarz 1994, p. 69.
237. Another means by which to channel the inclusion of these new regimes is through an agreement between the competent authorities. However, the treaty must have previously allowed it. The changes to the exclusion method in the Commentaries on the 2003–2014 OECD Model do provide for this case. An example of this case can be found in the Luxembourg-U.S. DTC. As in the case of the DTC Luxembourg-Spain, Article 24(9) of the tax treaty excludes Luxembourg holding companies, within the meaning of the Act (loi) of 31 July 1929 and the Decree (arr^t, grand-ducal) of 17 December 1938, or any subsequent revision thereof, or such other companies that enjoy a similar special fiscal treatment by virtue of the laws of Luxembourg. In an exchange of notes dated 3 April 1996, the mentioned countries agreed to also exclude investment companies within the meaning of the Act dated 30 March 1988. However, although the inclusion of new cases is included by this means, there is still an underlying problem, i.e. that the states are required to come to an agreement and logically the state which has established the regime will oppose.
238. In this respect, the negotiation process relating to the Ireland-U.S. DTC was significant. The Irish negotiators convinced the U.S. to give up in its intention to exclude entities enjoying the regime of 'International Financial Services Centre'. Crowdus 1997, p. 559 and Haccius 1995, pp. 1057–1058.
239. See OECD 1998.
240. Martín Jiménez 2004a, p. 21.

Chapter 3: Limitation on Benefits Clauses

preferential tax regimes, those which are aimed at particular types of income and those which are aimed at preferential regimes introduced after the signature of the convention.[241]

The main problem of the mentioned provisions, as stated in the Commentaries, is the difficulty of including a general clause in tax treaties, which defines the criteria to be met by a regime in order to be categorized as a preferential tax regime. The situation described explains why tax treaties signed after 2003 seldom include general clauses defining preferential tax treaty regimes, such as the ones set forth in the Commentaries. The only clauses that have still been used are those which precisely identify the entities or regimes that are within its scope, in spite of the fact that in some cases the treaty adds the possibility of extending the clause to similar regimes enacted upon the convention's signature. In all likelihood, general clauses of preferential tax regimes have not been developed at treaty level due to the challenges presented both by the definition of the clause and by its application in practice. In addition, these clauses lead to conflicts between the contracting states, because its application by the source state does not require the consent of the resident state.

The OECD's work on preferential and harmful tax regimes has continued since the 1998 Report. The BEPS project is the latest stage of this work, its Action 5 deals expressly with this topic.[242] However, the final document of this Action does not provide any proposals to modify the OECD Model in order to include a general clause whose objective is the exclusion of treaty benefits for taxpayers who benefit from preferential tax regimes. Neither were such proposals provided for in Action 6 of the BEPS project, apart from a reference included at the very end of the final document to the STRs clause provided in the 2015 U.S. Draft.[243] Nonetheless, it should be mentioned that one of the objectives of Action 6 is to clarify 'that tax treaties are not intended to be used to generate double non-taxation'. This clarification is provided through a reformulation of the title and preamble to the OECD Model.[244] This objective appears in other actions of the BEPS project creating a strong double non-taxation language.[245] Finally, it should also be noted that the Multilateral Convention to Implement Tax Treaty Related Measures to Prevent BEPS, published by the OECD on 24 November 2016, does not provide any exclusion clause.

As it has been mentioned in previous sections, the 2016 U.S. Model has introduced the so-called STR clause. As discussed in the next section, the main purpose of this provision is to deny treaty benefits at the source when the corresponding income enjoys a preferential tax regime in the resident state, i.e. income is not subject to tax or is subject to very low tax in the resident state. This provision contained in the 2016 U.S. Model can be considered as an attempt by the U.S. to introduce a general clause against preferential tax regimes, which does not require identifying them in advance in the tax

---

241. *See* paragraphs 21.1–21.3 and 21.5 of the Commentaries on Article 1 of the 2003–2014 OECD Model.
242. OECD 2015c.
243. OECD 2015a, pp. 96–98.
244. OECD 2015a, pp. 91–93.
245. Brauner 2014, p. 28.

treaty in order to have legal effect.[246] The Treasury justifies this clause on some of the objectives of the BEPS project noting that tax treaties should eliminate double taxation without creating opportunities for non-taxation or reduced taxation through tax evasion or avoidance. For this purpose, the final wording of the STR clause provides a set of criteria which try to be as objective as possible, but, as it will be seen in the next section, are really difficult to apply in practice and can, at the same time, create a controversy with the other contracting state, as the provision does not require any prior agreement between the parties to the treaty. The STR clause will be analysed in the following section, as together with its primary effects, i.e. to deny certain treaty benefits at the source when the corresponding income enjoys a preferential tax regime in the resident state, it impinges in the LOB rule provided for in Article 22 of the 2016 U.S. Model.

Moreover, when defining the exclusion clause, the states should be especially careful, because, on the contrary, there is a risk that the entities which enjoy a privileged tax regime 'for legitimate reasons', both from an economic standpoint and the standpoint of tax justice principles, might be affected.[247] The example used by the OECD is the favourable tax treatment that non-profit organizations usually receive.[248]

In view of the difficulties involved in defining the entities and regimes affected, the effectiveness of this clause in countering the abusive use of the treaties is very limited. In the case that the objective is to exclusively target situations suitable for treaty shopping structures, only those that objectively enjoy a tax treatment which enables this type of conduct to be developed should be included, but not cases which may accidentally serve for this purpose even though it may not be their sole objective.

In this respect, it is important to point out that the exclusion method is not in line with the assumptions on which the LOB clauses are based. These clauses allow access to the treaty when the taxpayer has a sufficient nexus to the state of residence or a real business purpose to obtain the income generated at source. When the exclusion clause is applied, the taxpayer loses the right to apply the treaty even though it has applied with one of these assumptions. As opposed to the case of the PE clause, the exclusion clause does not include any exception which allows for this clause to be traced back to the principles underlying the LOB clauses. In the cases in which this clause has been included, the affected taxpayers will not even be able to access the treaty by means of the bona fide clause.[249]

Bearing the above in mind, it is understandable that an author has pointed out that clauses such as the one proposed by the OECD are not true anti-treaty shopping clauses.[250] It has also been claimed that this rule does not directly attack treaty

---

246. *See* Preamble 2016 U.S. Model, p. 2: 'However, the new provisions also reflect the United States' preference for addressing BEPS concerns through changes to objective rules that apply on a prospective basis, rather than introducing subjective standards that could call into question agreed treaty benefits or applying wholly new concepts to prior years'.
247. Picciotto 1992, p. 161.
248. OECD 1986, paragraph 27.
249. This is based on the wording of Articles 24(10) and 17(6) of the DTCs with Luxembourg and Portugal, respectively.
250. Cavestany 1993, p. 100.

shopping but rather it does so 'in passing'.[251] There is no doubt that this is the case, as although the entity or regime is suitable for this purpose it does not mean that a structure will effectively be developed. Furthermore, from the standpoint of the assumptions on which the LOB clauses are based, the presence of this entity in the state of residence may be fully justified, i.e. the taxpayer could have a sufficient nexus to the state of residence or a real business purpose to obtain the income from this state.

Therefore, the exclusion clause is not a limitation on benefits clause. It is used for other purposes although this does not mean that it might not also affect treaty shopping structures. In this respect, this method can be included within the harmful tax measures taken by the OECD and the EU since 1998. The purpose of these measures is to eliminate cases in which competition is distorted. Based on the criteria used by these international organizations, characteristic of regimes under which competition is distorted is that they give rise to zero or very reduced taxation, among other factors. In essence, the 1977 and 1981 U.S. Models were based on the idea that access to the treaty should only be allowed if the entity obtaining the income was subject to a reasonable level of taxation. The exclusion clause is simply another method for countering regimes under which harmful tax competition arises.

This is exactly the direction taken by the changes included in the Commentaries on Article 1 of the OECD Model in 2003. These changes developed this method by including one of the criteria established in the OECD report on harmful tax competition to determine which regimes should be excluded from the application of the treaty.[252] However, as already mentioned, the truth is that tax treaties signed after 2003 seldom include general clauses defining preferential tax treaty regimes, such as the ones provided in the Commentaries. The only clauses that have still been used are those which precisely identify the entities or regimes that are within its scope, in spite of the fact that in some cases the treaty adds the possibility of extending the clause to similar regimes enacted upon the convention's signature.

Moreover, it is important not to lose sight of the fact that the establishment of a preferential tax regime by a state may be justified for other reasons that may be perfectly legitimate. The exclusion of these regimes from the subjective scope of the treaties may limit the objectives that these regimes attempt to achieve.

In this regard, the exclusion clause has been used in some tax treaties to prevent the treaty from being applied to taxpayers established in certain low-tax areas. It is

---

251. Wurm 1992, p. 663, states that 'the exclusion of those companies from treaty benefits is not really an attack against treaty shopping, but only generates the avoidance of treaty shopping as a by-product'.
252. Although with respect to measures adopted by the EU in this regard, this direction is also taken by means of the Code of Conduct in the 1999 DTC between Portugal and the Netherlands. The DTC states that the right to the application of the treaty provided for taxation in the source state will not be conferred upon 'residents of a Contracting State which benefit from tax measures which are harmful within the meaning of the EC Code of Conduct for business taxation, as agreed by the Ecofin-meeting of December 1, 1997'. 'However, [tax measures] shall not be considered harmful if they are accepted and to the extent they are authorised by the European Community as an appropriate support for the economic development of a particular area and do not undermine the integrity and coherence of the Community legal order, including the internal market and common policies'. This is the case of Madeira. See Van den Ende/Smit 2001, p. 101 and Herédia 2002, pp. 471–472.

common knowledge that there is a proliferation of low-tax regimes in EU states, which use tax relief techniques to foster investment and economic activity in the affected territory. In some cases, these regimes have been authorized by EU institutions, as they consist in state aid compatible with Articles 107 and 108 of the Treaty on the Functioning of the EU. Among these include the Madeira area in Portugal and the regime of the special area of the Canary Islands in Spain (ZEC entities). Characteristic of all these regimes is that the tax benefits are not granted subjectively, but rather for the performance of certain activities, and that they are limited in time. It appears reasonable that they have been authorized to foster the development of the affected areas and once such development takes place, the regime should disappear.

In spite of their low taxation, these regimes should not be affected by the exclusion clauses so that they are allowed to achieve their objectives. However, it is important not to lose sight of the fact that the contracting states may not be in agreement with respect to the 'good faith' of the regime established. In fact, even though the regime of Madeira has been authorized by EU institutions, this did not prevent the tax treaty between Portugal and the U.S. from expressly excluding it.[253] The arguments based on which the EU authorities have authorized this regime as state aid appears not to have convinced the U.S., and accordingly, this state has forced this area to be excluded in the treaty with Portugal.

From the standpoint of the tax treaties entered into by EU Member States, there is also evidence of these states' opposition to this regime. For example, although Spain has not forced the Madeira area from being excluded from its treaty with Portugal, a look-through clause was introduced in the tax treaty. Despite the fact that this clause is general in nature, it surreptitiously aims to limit the application of the treaty where entities residing in Portugal enjoy the Madeira area regime.

In summary, it can be concluded that the exclusion clause is not in line with the assumptions on which the LOB clauses are based. This method only aims to exclude certain entities and regimes that give rise to situations of low or non-taxation.[254] Although the exclusion of these entities and regimes may affect the performance of treaty shopping structures, it is not their main objective. The clause attempts to exclude taxpayers that enjoy a certain regime under which they are not subject to 'normal tax' in the state of residence. The fact that the excluded taxpayers have an effective nexus to the state of residence or a real business purpose to receive the income from this state is irrelevant for the purposes of this clause. The cases that will be excluded by this method depend, essentially, on the stance taken by the states when negotiating the treaties. In this regard, the latest development of this approach is the STR clause provided for in the 2016 U.S. Model.

---

253. Yan 1995, p. 23, states that the DTC with the U.S. is the first treaty entered into by Portugal in which this area has been excluded. As pointed out earlier, in the Irish treaty, there is no such exclusion, notwithstanding the fact that the rest of the LOB clauses are fully applicable. The Spain-U.S. DTC does not exclude ZEC entities. However, it should be borne in mind that this treaty was entered into prior to the commencement of this regime. It would not be unimaginable for a future renegotiation of this treaty to give rise to their exclusion. Logically, the Spanish tax authorities would be opposed to a clause of this nature.
254. Sanz Gadea 2001, p. 86.

Chapter 3: Limitation on Benefits Clauses

IV.B.2 *The Special Tax Regime Clause in the 2016 U.S. Model*

IV.B.2.a Preliminary Remarks

The STR clause established in the 2016 U.S. Model is a completely new provision, which cannot be found in the U.S. tax treaty network. A similar provision to the STR clause of the 2016 U.S. Model is not provided for in the OECD Model, nor in the BEPS project; apart from a reference to the STR clause provided in the 2015 U.S. Draft,[255] found in the final document of Action 6 of the BEPS project. However, the STR clause provided for in the 2016 U.S. Model contains substantial differences in comparison to the one provided in the 2015 U.S. Draft. The Treasury Department introduced relevant modifications in the clause due to comments received on the 2015 U.S. Draft. Additionally, it should be emphasized that the Multilateral Convention to Implement Tax Treaty Related Measures to Prevent BEPS published by the OECD on 24 November 2016, does not contain a provision similar to the STR clause included in the 2016 U.S. Model.

The main purpose of the STR clause is to deny treaty benefits at the source when the corresponding income enjoys a preferential tax regime in the resident state. Without prejudice to further details, Article 3(1)(l) of the 2016 U.S. Model considers a special tax regime as any regime that results in an effective tax rate, which is less than the lesser of either 15 percent or 60 percent of the general statutory corporate tax rate in the source country.

However, the STR clause does not affect all types of income covered by the Model, just interest, royalties and certain guarantee fees (the ones which fall under Article 21 of the Model). The consequences of the STR clause are set out in Articles 11 (interest), 12 (royalties) and 21 (guarantee fees) of the 2016 U.S. Model. These Articles allow the source state to tax the mentioned types of income in accordance with domestic law, when such income benefits from a special tax regime in the resident state. Article 3 (1)(m), which defines when two persons shall be 'connected persons', supplements the definition of 'special tax regime' provided for in Article 3(1)(l), since the STR clause only affects 'connected persons' payments (i.e. related-party payments) of interest, royalties and guarantee fees (Article 21).

Together with these primary effects, as it has been already highlighted, the STR clause also has some collateral effects, as it impinges in the LOB rule provided for in Article 22 of the U.S. Model. The LOB rule establishes several base erosion tests. These tests, as discussed in previous sections, require that less than a certain percentage of the person's gross income be paid, directly or indirectly, to certain 'tainted payees'. The 2016 U.S. Model has added persons benefitting from a special tax regime to the list of 'tainted payees'.

As it was mentioned in the previous section, the STR clause contained in the 2016 U.S. Model can be considered as an attempt by the U.S. to introduce a general clause against preferential tax regimes, which does not require identifying them in advance in

---

255. OECD 2015a, pp. 96–98.

the tax treaty in order to have legal effect.[256] The Treasury justifies this clause on some of the objectives of the BEPS project noting that tax treaties should eliminate double taxation without creating opportunities for non-taxation or reduced taxation through tax evasion or avoidance. For this purpose, the STR clause provides a set of criteria which try to be as objective as possible, but, as it will be seen in the next section, are really difficult to apply in practice and can, at the same time, create a controversy with the other contracting state, as the provision does not require any prior agreement between the parties to the treaty.

Without a doubt, the attempt to establish an objective standard for detecting STRs is laudable, especially as it is not an easy task. In fact, the final clause has been significantly modified in comparison to the one contained in the 2015 U.S. Draft, in order to be as specific as possible. This contributes to strengthening legal certainty, as a very generic STR clause will have the risk of causing asymmetries when applying the treaty, especially given that its application does not require previous consensus between the authorities of the contracting states.

Notwithstanding the foregoing positive aspects, the STR clause provided for in the 2016 U.S. Model calls for some concerns to be highlighted.

First, it is surprisingly out of character for the U.S. to include this provision in its treaty model; as the Treasury, does not usually drop provisions into a U.S. Model before they have appeared in an actual treaty.[257] So far, the U.S, as with many other states, has only used the exclusion approach in tax treaties by listing the regimes which were not eligible for treaty benefits in the tax treaty.

However, this general assertion may have one exception. The 2004 Protocol to the U.S.-Barbados tax treaty introduced a provision to deny treaty benefits with respect to dividends, interest and royalties to persons entitled to a STR. According to Article 22(6)(b) of the U.S.-Barbados treaty, a 'special tax regime is any legislation or administrative practice that provides for an effective tax rate substantially lower than the generally applicable tax rate for companies or individuals, as appropriate'.[258] Even though the treaty provides for a general definition of the term 'special tax regime', it has only been applied in practice to the specific regimes agreed by the contracting states. An exchange of notes signed simultaneously to the Protocol lists five Barbados tax laws as within the scope of the STR definition –it does not mention any U.S. tax regimes.[259]

---

256. *See* Preamble 2016 U.S. Model, p. 2: 'However, the new provisions also reflect the U.S.' preference for addressing BEPS concerns through changes to objective rules that apply on a prospective basis, rather than introducing subjective standards that could call into question agreed treaty benefits or applying wholly new concepts to prior years'.
257. As Harrington has pointed out, 'the departure from tradition in this case is presumably because Treasury is signalling a desired change in its tax treaty policy, rather than formalizing a change in treaty policy as would normally be the case'. *See* Harrington 2015, p. 2.
258. The STR clause in the U.S.-Barbados treaty also has effects on the application of the LOB rule provided in the treaty. In this regard, in the base erosion prong of the ownership/base erosion test, payments made to residents entitled to a special tax regime do not qualify in order to comply with this test.
259. The listed regimes are the following: '(1) the Exempt Insurance Act, Cap. 308; (2) the International Financial Services Act, 2002; (3) the International Business Companies Act, Cap. 77; (4) the Societies with Restricted Liability Act, Cap. 318B; or (5) the Insurance (Miscellaneous Provisions) Act, 1998'.

It also states that a STR will be considered as 'any such legislation or administrative practice enacted or adopted after the signing of this Protocol pursuant to which the income of a person is entitled to the same or substantially similar tax benefits to those granted under the [five listed regimes]'.

It is apparent that there is no clear precedent in the U.S. tax treaty network containing a provision against preferential tax regimes with a general wording.

Second, the inclusion of the STR clause in the U.S. Model raises another question, i.e. if this measure will wind up being a so-called must-have-as-is provision, in the same way as other provisions of the U.S. Model have, such as, the U.S. branch tax rules, the Foreign Investment in Real Property Tax Act of 1980 FIRPTA and the LOB rules. Although only time will answer this question, it remains unlikely that this will happen, given the complexity and lack of clarity of some aspects of the STR clause, which will be addressed in the next section. This is evidenced by the Treasury's own doubts concerning this clause, insofar as it had to be significantly modified in comparison to the one envisaged in the 2015 U.S. Draft.

In our view, the option chosen by the U.S. Model does not seem the most appropriate means to achieve the objectives pursued. On the one hand, it is self-evident that if a jurisdiction has a large amount of preferential tax regimes that lead to low or non- taxation, the solution for this problem is not the STR clause. In this case, the U.S., and most probably any other state, would typically not enter into a tax treaty with such jurisdiction.[260] If this situation were to materialize upon the signature of the convention –the appearance of a bundle of preferential tax regimes-, the way to respond would almost certainly be to terminate the treaty. However, this last resort will not always be necessary, if the treaty includes another new provision contained in the 2016 U.S. Model, i.e. the subsequent changes to legal provisions set forth in Article 28. The purpose of this provision is to remove some benefits from the treaty when one of the contracting states' statutory-rate of company tax falls below a certain percentage or provides an exemption from taxation to resident companies regarding substantially all foreign source income (including interest and royalties).

On the other hand, the approach taken by the U.S. to this problem could have been different. It is clear from the Preamble to the 2016 U.S. Model that the Treasury's main concern is not that treaty benefits apply to income benefitting from a preferential tax regime in the resident state; it is the fact that those payments may be eroding the U.S. tax base, as, in most cases the income involved will imply a deductible payment for the payer. The Preamble states the following:

> It is inappropriate for tax treaties to reduce U.S. statutory withholding rates on deductible U.S. source payments when the related income is subject to no or very little tax. The current ability of foreign-parented companies to engage in these types of transactions creates strong incentives to erode the U.S. tax base and gives foreign-parented companies an advantage over U.S.-parented companies, which cannot use these regimes to avoid paying tax on their U.S. income.

---

260. In fact, Action 6 of the BEPS project proposes to include in the Commentaries to Article 1 of the OECD Model some policy considerations that, in general, countries should consider before deciding to enter into a tax treaty with another country.

If this is truly so, it would have been easier, from a policy point of view, to move the issue to domestic law instead of bringing the problem to treaty level. In order to do this, it will be sufficient to reject the deduction of those expenses. In other words, a U.S. domestic rule will deny the deduction of expenses when the corresponding income is earned by a non-resident who benefits from a preferential tax regime, without questioning the application of the treaty benefits. From the U.S. point of view, this measure will have an equivalent effect, whilst avoiding creating a treaty issue. This approach is not incompatible with the approach taken by the U.S., and also the OECD Commentaries and other states, before releasing the 2016 U.S. Model, i.e. listing which entities or regimes were excluded from the application of treaty benefits in the treaty.

IV.B.2.b   Legal Framework of the Clause

IV.B.2.b.1   Introduction

Article 3(1)(l) of the 2016 U.S. Model establishes formal and substantive requirements for classifying another state's tax regime as a STR. The application of the clause by one contracting state, the source state, does not require prior approval from the other contracting state, the resident state.

The STR clause does not include all types of income covered by tax treaties. The rule only applies to interest, royalties and certain guarantee fees (Article 21). Additionally, the 2016 U.S. Model establishes that only transactions where connected persons are involved will fall within the scope of the STR clause. Therefore, arrangements between independent persons are set aside, even though a preferential tax regime is applicable to the person who earns the income. The term 'connected persons' is defined in Article 3 (1) (m).

The primary effects of the STR clause are established in the Articles of the Model where the mentioned types of income are set out, i.e. Articles 11(2)(c), 12(2)(a) and 21(2)(a). Interest, royalties and guarantee fees affected by the clause will be taxed by the source state in accordance with domestic law without applying tax treaty benefits. Thus, the 2016 U.S. Model provides in Articles 11(2)(c), 12(2)(a) and 21(2)(a) that:

> [Interest, royalties, or guarantee fees] arising in a Contracting State and beneficially owned by a resident of the other Contracting State that is a connected person with respect to the payor of [such interest, royalties, or guarantee fees], may be taxed in the first-mentioned Contracting State in accordance with domestic law if such resident benefits from a special tax regime with respect to such [income] in its Contracting State of residence.

However, the clause has certain collateral effects, which take place in the context of the application of the LOB rule provided in Article 22 of the 2016 U.S. Model. Hence, the STR clause, when applicable, excludes certain treaty benefits at source and also threatens compliance with some of the tests provided for in the LOB rule. As is well-known, the LOB rule strengthens the requirements that persons, mainly entities, must comply with in order to be eligible for treaty benefits.

Chapter 3: Limitation on Benefits Clauses

In the following sections the legal framework of the STR clause as provided for in the 2016 U.S. Model will be analysed. Nonetheless, some references will be made to the 2015 U.S. Draft.

IV.B.2.b.2 Types of Income Covered

The STR clause embraces interest, royalties and certain guarantee fees (Article 21). The application of the terms interest and royalties does not raise any more issues than usual, as they have been defined in both the U.S. and in the OECD Models from the beginning. However, the latter does not occur with the term guarantee fees, which is not defined in the 2016 U.S. Model. In fact, this term is rarely found in the world tax treaty network.[261] The few occasions in which that term expressly appears in the tax treaties, it is included with the objective of classifying this income under the interest article (Article 11). That occurs in the Protocols of the Indonesia-Norway (1998) and the Panama-Netherlands (2010) tax treaties.

The term seems to refer to the fee charged by a person to guarantee that an investor in a loan will receive all scheduled principal and interest payments until the loan is repaid. This interpretation is based on the 2006 U.S. Model and some U.S. Technical Explanations when they provide examples on what types of income should be qualified as 'Other Income', both under the U.S. Model and the OECD Model.[262]

As mentioned above, the STR clause only applies to guarantee fees when Article 21 is applicable. Thus, this clause will not apply where the guarantor is engaged in the business of providing such guarantees. In this case, the income should be qualified under the business profits article: Article 7 of the U.S. and OECD Models. Guarantee fees should not be treated as interest under the U.S. and the OECD Models given that they are not compensation for the use of money, notwithstanding that the guaranteed transaction could be a loan.[263]

In summary, guarantee fees refer to the income obtained by the guarantor of a loan transaction. This income will only be affected by the STR clause when it qualifies under Article 21 of the U.S. and the OECD Models. For the latter it is necessary that the guarantor is not frequently involved in these types of transactions. Therefore, the STR

---

261. Furthermore, after searching this term in the IBFD Tax Platform tax treaty database the result is that the term guarantee fees is only established in three of the 12,246 treaties contained in that database. They are the following: Indonesia-Norway (2010), U.S.-Japan (2003) and Panama-The Netherlands (2010).
262. The 2006 U.S. Model Technical Explanation states: 'Further, in most cases guarantee fees paid within an intercompany group would be covered by Article 21, unless the guarantor were engaged in the business of providing such guarantees to unrelated parties'. The same reference may be found in the following U.S. Tax Treaties Technical Explanations: Japan (2003 Protocol), Belgium (2006), Bulgaria (2007), Iceland (2007), France (2009 Protocol) and Hungary (2010).
263. M. Helminen 2016, section 5.1.2.3.4. Moreover, the U.S. Tax Court in a decision dated 17 February 2010 (*Container Corporation v. Commissioner of Internal Revenue* case) ruled that guarantee fees could not be qualified as interest under the U.S. Tax Code source rules. This decision was affirmed by the U.S. Court of Appeals for the Fifth Circuit. See Felgarden/Aaronson, 2010.

clause will not primarily affect banks, given that they are generally involved in these transactions. This conclusion applies even where a situation of reduced or non-taxation takes place.

The fact that the STR clause only applies to guarantee fees when they qualify under Article 21 of the U.S. and OECD Models may explain why this type of income has been provided for. The rule seems to proceed on the assumption that when this transaction is carried out by a taxpayer not generally involved in this type of transaction it is because it may have the intention of eroding the tax base of the person or entity whose transactions are guaranteed. In any case, it should be remembered that the STR clause only kicks in when a transaction takes place between connected persons.

IV.B.2.b.3 Subjective Scope: Connected Persons

The STR clause only applies to particular payments of interest, royalties or guarantee fees from a 'connected person' to a resident of a treaty country that benefits from a STR. Article 3(1)(m) of the 2016 U.S. Model defines the term 'connected persons' as follows:

> m) two persons shall be 'connected persons' if one owns, directly or indirectly, at least 50 percent of the beneficial interest in the other (or, in the case of a company, at least 50 percent of the aggregate vote and value of the company's shares) or another person owns, directly or indirectly, at least 50 percent of the beneficial interest (or, in the case of a company, at least 50 percent of the aggregate vote and value of the company's shares) in each person. In any case, a person shall be connected to another if, based on all the relevant facts and circumstances, one has control of the other or both are under the control of the same person or persons.

This term is not entirely new to the 2016 U.S. Model, as it had already been included in the 2006 U.S. Model. However, in the 2006 U.S. Model that concept was only applicable within the context of the LOB rule. In this regard, and for the purpose of applying the activity business test, the LOB rule allowed activities conducted by persons connected to the person claiming the treaty benefits to be taken into account.

The 2016 U.S. Model provides a definition of 'connected persons' identical to the one provided for in the 2006 U.S. Model. However, this definition is now established in Article 3 of the Model amongst the general definitions usually contained in this article, both in the U.S. and the OECD Model. The latter is due to the fact that the scope of this term in the 2016 U.S. Model is wider than in the previous Model. Its scope of application goes beyond the LOB rule, now also being applicable to the STR clause and the construction PE concept. In order to calculate the 12-month period, the Model allows for the accumulation of the time spent by connected persons.

The 'connected persons' term is similar to the concept of associated enterprises provided in Article 9 of the U.S. and the OECD Models. That is because the wording of both provisions is very similar. In both cases, the main driver is that one party is under the control of the other party or that both are subject to the control of a third party.

According to Article 3(1)(m) of the 2016 U.S. Model, a person shall be connected to another if, based on all the relevant facts and circumstances, one has control of the other or both are under the control of the same person or persons. The Model specifies this general rule establishing that the latter control occurs, in any event, when one person owns, directly or indirectly, at least 50 percent of the beneficial interest in the other or another person owns, directly or indirectly, at least 50 percent of the beneficial interest. When companies are involved, these thresholds are referred to as the aggregate vote and value of the company's shares.

IV.B.2.b.4   Characteristics of the Special Tax Regime

IV.B.2.b.4.a   Procedural Aspects

Applying the consequences of the STR provision requires that one of the contracting states tax regimes has previously qualified as a 'special tax regime'. This qualification corresponds to the source state. Therefore, this competence does not lie with the tax authorities of the state where the person who benefits from the special regime resides.

The 2016 U.S. Model provides, that before identifying any tax regime as a 'special tax regime', the contracting state that intends to classify the other party's regime as such, must first allow the other party to the treaty a hearing. In this regard, Article 3(1)(l)(v) establishes the following:

> v) after consultation with the first-mentioned Contracting State, has been identified by the other Contracting State through diplomatic channels to the first mentioned Contracting State as satisfying clauses (i) through (iv) of this subparagraph.

During this consultation period, the country invoking the STR clause has to submit evidence that the requirements provided in the Model are satisfied. Even though this procedural requirement is mandatory (previous consultation), the Model does not require mutual agreement.[264] Therefore, one of the contracting states may apply the consequences of the clause even when the other contracting state opposes.

The effects of a regime qualifying as a 'special tax regime' are not immediate. In this regard, the 2016 U.S. Model establishes that they will not begin until thirty days after the date on which the other contracting state issues a written public notification identifying the regime as satisfying the requirements of the clause. The last paragraph of Article 3(l) (l) reads as follows:

> No statute, regulation or administrative practice shall be treated as a special tax regime until 30 days after the date when the other Contracting State issues a written public notification identifying the regime as satisfying clauses (i) through (v) of this subparagraph;

This clarification is highly relevant, because it prevents the retroactive application of the STR clause. The latter implies that this provision will not be applicable to income received before it has legal effect.[265] Therefore, income obtained

---

264. Tobin 2016, p. 2.
265. *See* Christians/Ezenagu 2016, p. 1054.

before that moment will not lose treaty benefits, even though the person benefits in the state of residence from a regime qualified *a posteriori* as a 'special tax regime'.

The qualification as a 'special tax regime' made by one state with the opposition of the other state could lead to a complex situation, at least from a political point of view. In fact, this outcome could lead to the state, whose regime has qualified under this provision, deciding to terminate the tax treaty.

IV.B.2.b.4.b Substantive Aspects

IV.B.2.b.4.b.1 Preliminary Remarks

The qualification of a tax regime as a 'special tax regime' requires verifying a large number of circumstances. In practice, this analysis could be complex to carry out. This is due, among other reasons, to the fact that it implies the assessment of statutes, regulations and administrative practices of a contracting state that, obviously, is not the one who invokes the clause.[266]

The identification of the STR could be difficult when it derives from a so-called administrative practice. In this regard, little information is provided about the meaning of this term, as the 2016 U.S. Model does not define it. The only reference to its meaning can be found in the 2015 U.S. Draft, where the advance draft of the Technical Explanation to the STR clause states, 'For purposes of this definition, an administrative practice includes a ruling practice'. There is no mention of audit practice, although it seems reasonable to conclude that an audit practice could also be qualified as an administrative practice.[267] However, it can be extremely challenging to prove its existence, as audit procedures and outcomes are rarely published.

Likewise, it could be controversial to determine how many cases (rulings, audits, etc.) have to concur in order to assert the existence of an administrative practice. Moreover, the cost of probing the latter could sometimes be inefficient, in the event that the STR affects a limited number of taxpayers. Moreover, it should be recalled that the characterization of a regime as an STR will only have prospective effects. That implies that all the efforts to identify the statute, regulation or administrative practice will be worthless in respect of income obtained before the regime is officially acknowledged as a STR.

Under the wording of Article 3(1)(l) of the 2016 U.S. Model, a tax regime would be considered a STR if it meets four conditions. The most relevant are the first and third conditions. The second and forth conditions are actually grounds for exclusion from the consequences of the clause. The first and third conditions are analysed in section IV.B.2.b.4.b.2. The regimes and entities excluded from the application of the STR clause will be discussed in section IV.B.2.b.4.b.3.

---

266. According to the first paragraph of Article 3 (1) (l), the term 'special tax regime' means 'any statute, regulation or administrative practice in a Contracting State with respect to a tax described in Article 2 (Taxes Covered) that meets all of the following conditions [...]'.
267. Harrington 2015, p. 4.

IV.B.2.b.4.b.2 Features of the STR

A tax regime will be categorized as a STR, when it leads to a situation of low or non-taxation. According to the 2016 U.S. Model, the above situation occurs when the regime is expected to result in an effective tax rate which is less than the lesser of either 15 percent or 60 percent of the statutory corporate tax rate. In this regard, it should be highlighted that the 60 percent rule should be applied to the general statutory rate of the source state and not to that of the resident state. This interpretation is based on the wording of the STR clause, which is somewhat confusing,[268] and the Preamble to the 2016 U.S. Model, which states the following:

> The 2016 Model provides an exception for preferential regimes that are generally expected to result in a rate of taxation which is at least 15, or 60 percent of the general statutory rate of company tax in the source country, whichever is lower. In order to provide additional clarity, the 2016 Model provides language that would be included in an instrument reflecting an agreed interpretation between the two treaty countries. Such instrument would provide that the rate of taxation generally would be calculated based on the income tax principles of the country that has implemented the regime in question.

As can be seen, the reference rate will usually be a 15 percent rate, unless the general statutory corporate tax rate in the source country is below 25 percent. This is due to the fact that 60 percent of 25 is 15. Moreover, as it has been pointed out by some authors,[269] the 15 percent rate does not appear to call for a minimum rate. The 15 percent rate would be the ceiling at which a rate would be considered a preferential tax rate. Therefore, any rate higher than 15 percent applied by the state of residence would not be considered preferential, even if the general rate in the source state is much higher.

In addition to this requirement, the regime must accomplish any of the following three features. They all refer to the legal framework of the special regime, which could be a preferential rate, a permanent reduction in the tax base or a combination of both.[270]

---

268. Article 3 (1) (l) (iii) reads as follows:

> [The special tax regime] iii) is generally expected to result in a rate of taxation1 that is less than the lesser of either:
>
> A) 15 percent; or
> B) 60 percent of the general statutory rate of company tax applicable in the other Contracting State;

269. Christians/Ezenagu 2016, p. 1054.
270. The 2015 U.S. Draft, with regard to interest, also included as a special tax regime any rule, whether or not generally available, that provides notional deductions with respect to equity. In the final version 'Notional Interest Deductions' (NID) with respect to equity are no longer treated as special tax regimes. Instead, Article 11 (Interest) includes a new rule that would allow a treaty partner to tax interest arising in that country in accordance with domestic law if the interest is beneficially owned by a related person that benefits from a notional interest deduction.

The first feature is a regime with a preferential taxation rate of the income covered by the clause (interest, royalties and guarantee fees, or a combination thereof) compared to the one applicable to income from sales of goods. For example, if a country imposes a rate of 25 percent on a certain type of interest when the general rate on income from the sale of goods is 30 percent, the rate would be preferential. A drop in the general rate to 25 would reverse the proposition.[271]

The wording of the second feature is similar to the latter, although here the special regime consists of a permanent reduction in the tax base without a comparable reduction for income from sales of goods or services. However, in this case the permanent reduction has to be a result of either of the four following circumstances: an exclusion from gross receipts; a deduction without regard to any corresponding payment or obligation to make a payment; a deduction for dividends paid or accrued; or taxation that is inconsistent with the principles of business profits and associated enterprises established in Articles 7 and 9 of the Model. For example, a royalty regime would be preferential if it allowed the use of a non-arm's length transfer pricing method to calculate a reduced base relative to what an arm's length method would produce.[272]

The third feature is drafted as a combination of the two features already described, therefore the low or non-taxation may be due to a preferential tax rate or a permanent reduction in the tax base that complies with one of the mentioned circumstances. However, in this case, in order for the regime to be considered preferential, the relevant aspect is that it applies due to the fact that the entity is an off-shore company. Therefore, the company is not engaged in the active conduct of a trade or business in the contracting state where it resides, being all or substantially all of its income foreign source income. It can be seen here that the relevant aspect is if the company is an off-shore company, and not the fact that the preferential treatment is different to that applied to income from sales of goods or services.

The STR provision requires the assessment of the described features and circumstances; this is extremely burdensome, especially as they require profound knowledge of the contracting state's domestic law. Additionally, in many cases, the verification of these features and circumstances could not be accomplished just by analysing the legal framework of the STR. It may also be necessary to evaluate all facts and circumstances of a particular taxpayer, in order to determine if the requirements established by the STR clause concur. From this perspective, the effectiveness of the STR provision could be very limited, taking into account the prospective effects of the decision of the contracting state categorizing a certain regime as a STR.

IV.B.2.b.4.b.3   Excluded Entities and Regimes

Sections (ii) and (iv) of Article 3(1)(l) of the 2016 U.S. Model exclude the application of the STR provision to certain so-called patent-box regimes and entities, despite complying with the above-mentioned requirements.

---

271. Christians/Ezenagu 2016, p. 1052.
272. Christians/Ezenagu 2016, p. 1053.

Chapter 3: Limitation on Benefits Clauses

It is well known that the so-called patent-box regimes are preferential tax regimes on royalties and other payments received from patents and intellectual property. These regimes have been analysed in Action 5 of the BEPS project to determine which requirements should be fulfilled in order to avoid being categorized as a harmful tax regime. In this regard, the key element for Action 5 is the nexus approach: royalties should only benefit from a preferential tax treatment to the extent that the taxpayer itself incurred the research and development expenditures that contributed to that intangible.[273] Therefore, in the context of Action 5, it is irrelevant where research and development activities took place, as long as the taxpayer itself incurred the mentioned expenditures.

Section 'ii' is the U.S. Model's answer to 'patent box' regimes. However, the approach taken by the 2016 U.S. Model is different from the OECD approach, since the consequences of the STR provision will only be inapplicable when the benefits of the preferential tax regime are linked to the fact that research and development activities have taken place in the resident state. Article 3(1)(l)(ii) reads as follows:

> ii) in the case of any preferential rate of taxation or permanent reduction in the tax base for royalties, does not condition such benefits on the extent of research and development activities that take place in the Contracting State;

In all likelihood, this location-based approach will not be accepted by other countries when negotiating a treaty with the U.S., unless the OECD approach to patent-box regimes is provided for. This is because a great number of countries have modified their patent-box regimes to bring them into line with OECD recommendations.[274]

Moreover, section 'iv' excludes income obtained by pension funds, charitable entities and certain collective investment vehicles from the STR provision.

The exclusion of pension funds and charitable entities is reasonable. In fact, the 2016 U.S. Model also clarifies that these entities are residents of a contracting state 'notwithstanding that all or part of its income or gains may be exempt from tax under domestic law'. Likewise, these entities are considered qualified residents according to the LOB rule provided in Article 22 of the 2016 U.S. Model, as long as they comply with certain requirements.

The STR clause also excludes collective investment vehicles that: are marketed primarily to retail investors, are widely held, hold real property (immovable property), have a diversified portfolio of securities, or a combination thereof, and are subject to investor-protection regulation in the contracting state in which they are set-up. The exception applies when these regimes achieve a single level of taxation, that is, income is not taxed at an entity level; rather, it is allocated among the shareholders, who report and pay tax on their share of the entity's income on their individual income tax returns. Therefore, at this point, the key factor is that income obtained by these entities is taxed either, at an entity level or at a shareholder level. The provision allows for the deferral

---

273. OECD 2015c, p. 31.
274. *See* Gil García 2016, p. 62.

of allocating income to the entity's shareholders, but with a one year deferral limit. No further guidance is given on how that time limit should be counted.

Finally, the STR clause provided in the 2015 Draft established that the contracting states could agree to exclude 'from the definition of special tax regime any legislation, regulation or administrative practice'. A similar provision cannot be found in the final version of the STR clause. Theoretically, the latter does not impede reaching that agreement between the contracting states under the consultation procedure provided for in the Mutual Agreement provision of tax treaties. However, as the competent authorities are bound by the tax treaty, they cannot come to a conclusion that overrides the text of the treaty. Therefore, this mutual agreement will not be suitable to exclude regimes which clearly comply with the definition of 'special tax regime'. In this regard, it is advisable to include in the STR clause the possibility of excluding certain regimes through mutual agreement by the contracting states.

IV.B.2.b.5   Effects of the Clause

IV.B.2.b.5.a   Primary Effects

The primary consequences of the STR clause are regulated in each of the articles of the 2016 U.S. Model on the types of income covered by this provision.[275] When the STR clause kicks in, interest, royalties and guarantee fees (Article 21) will be taxed by the source state according to its domestic law without applying the limits of the treaty.

The 2016 U.S. Model does not give any guidance regarding the possibility of crediting the tax paid to the source state in the resident state when the source state applies the STR provision. At least in theoretical terms, the taxpayer should be allowed to credit the tax levied at source, given that the effects of the STR clause do not fall within the scope of treaty and domestic measures to relieve double taxation. Additionally, this is not a case where a tax was erroneously paid to the source state, since the source state's taxing rights limits provided in the tax treaty were not applicable due to the application of the STR clause.

It is true, however, that in most cases the amount of the tax credit applicable in the state of residence will be scarce, because as a general rule, tax treaties and domestic law only provide for an 'ordinary credit'. The fact that a preferential tax regime is applicable in the resident state implies that the tax due in this state (if any) will normally be lower than that of the tax collected by the source state. However, the latter depends on other factors such as the approach followed by the state of residence to calculate the foreign tax credit (overall-limitation, per-country limitation, etc.).

Nevertheless, the application of the tax credit, with the limitations derived from the legal form of the ordinary credit method, could encounter some reluctance from the state of residence. That reluctance might occur when the state of residence disagrees with the categorization of one of its regimes as a 'special tax regime' by the source state. This is not a trivial issue, as mentioned in a previous Section, the application of the STR

---

275. See Articles 11(2)(c), 12(2)(a) and 21(2)(a) of the 2016 U.S. Model.

Chapter 3: Limitation on Benefits Clauses

rule by the source state does not require the state of residence's consent. Therefore, it is possible that the source state applies the STR provision with opposition or rejection from the other party to the treaty. If that were the case, it is possible that the resident state refuses to give a credit with respect to the amount of tax raised in the source state in excess of the limits provided for in the tax treaty.

The aforementioned situation could lead to a problematic outcome, unless it is solved by the contracting states through the mutual agreement procedure. In fact, one of the developments of the 2016 U.S. Model is the inclusion of a provision on mandatory binding arbitration to resolve disputes between tax treaty partners.

Moreover, the 2016 U.S. Model makes no comment on the possibility for taxpayers to challenge the classification of a tax regime as a 'special tax regime'. From our point of view, any challenge in that regard should take place in the context of an audit procedure, where the benefits of the tax treaty have been denied based on the previous categorization of a state of residence tax regime as a 'special tax regime'. The administrative or judicial court where the action was brought should have the authority to decide whether the conditions relating to the existence of a 'special tax regime' are met. However, it is our understanding that there are at least two situations in which the court should confirm the decision made by the tax authorities of the state which invoked the provision.

The first situation arises, when the state of residence, during the consultation procedure provided in Article 3(1)(l)(v) of the 2016 U.S. Model, accepts the proposition of the source state to classify one of its regimes as a 'special tax regime'. The latter could be considered as a 'subsequent agreement between the parties regarding the interpretation of the treaty or the application of its provisions' and, therefore, according Article 31(3)(a) of the VCLT, it should be taken into account by the court for the interpretation of the tax treaty. The second situation arises when the case has been submitted to arbitration in the context of the application of the mutual agreement provision.

IV.B.2.b.5.b   Collateral effects: LOB Rule

The STR clause has other effects, which essentially take place, as explained in previous sections, in the framework of the application of the LOB rule provided for in Article 22 of the 2016 U.S. Model. The LOB rule sets several base erosion tests, where certain deductible payments may prevent the fulfilment of the requirements of the rule in order to be eligible for treaty benefits. The base erosion test ensures that the source state only has to grant treaty benefits if a substantial part of the income is attributable to qualified residents of the other contracting state. According to the rule, treaty benefits are denied if more than 50 percent of the gross income is passed on to third-country residents in the form of deductible payments that erode the tax base of the other contracting state.

The base erosion tests are set forth in the following parts of the LOB rule: subsidiaries of publicly traded companies (Article 22(2)(d)(ii)), ownership and base erosion test (Article 22(2)(f)(ii)), derivative benefits clause (Article 22(4)) and headquarters companies clause (Article 22(5)). The 2016 U.S. Model has added to the base erosion test, payments to residents who benefit from a STR. Therefore, these payments, although they are made to persons who are qualified residents under the LOB rule, will not be eligible in order to verify the fulfilment of the base erosion test.[276]

The inclusion of the STR clause in the LOB rule somewhat distorts the original rationale of that rule. In accordance with legal doctrine and the Technical Explanations of the 1996 and 2006 U.S. Models, the objective of the LOB rule was that tax treaty benefits should only be applied either, where the taxpayer has obtained income from the state of residence for a real business purpose or, that the taxpayer has a sufficient nexus to the state of residence.[277] The LOB rule, prior to the 2016 U.S. Model, made no assumptions regarding the actual taxation of income in the resident state. In fact, although this criterion may have shown-up in the LOB rule at times, it was not decisive for the application of the treaty, as long as one of the two previously mentioned conditions were met.

With the insertion of the STR clause in the base erosion test of the 2016 U.S. Model LOB rule, the original rationale of the LOB rule is partially distorted as, to a certain extent, it considers the taxpayer's effective liability in the state of residence in order to decide if treaty benefits should be applicable. It is somewhat striking that this new rationale is taken into account in some of the LOB rule tests (the ones that incorporate the base erosion test) but not other tests. In this regard, no justification is given, as the 2015 Draft did not contain an advance draft of the Technical Explanation to the LOB rule. Nor is any explanation given in this respect in the Preamble to the 2016 U.S. Model.

Moreover, the STR provision should be applicable in the context of the LOB rule in the same manner. The latter means that only interests, royalties and guarantee fees (Article 21) will be affected by the provision. It is important to point this out, since the wording of the LOB rule only refers to payments made to persons who benefit from a STR, with no distinction whatsoever on the nature of the payment. This interpretation is based on the wording of the definition of 'special tax regime' provided in Article 3(1)(l) of the 2016 U.S. Model, where only the three mentioned types of income are referred to. Therefore, the only payments affected by the inclusion of the STR clause in the LOB rule will be interest, royalties and guarantee fees that are within the scope of Article 21 (Other Income) of the 2016 U.S. Model.

Additionally, all the substantial and procedural requirements of the STR provision described in previous sections are applicable to the LOB rule. Hence, the consequences of the provision will only be applicable to income and payments made after the decision of one of the contracting states declaring the regime as a 'special tax regime' which produces its effects. As provided for at the very end of Article 3(1)(1) of the 2016 U.S. Model:

---

276. Julien/Koch/Szudoczky 2017, p. 20.
277. *See* ALI 1992, p. 150, Doernberg/Van Raad 1997, p. 171 and Rust 2015, p. 130.

Chapter 3: Limitation on Benefits Clauses

[no] statute, regulation or administrative practice shall be treated as a special tax regime until 30 days after the date when the other contracting state issues a written public notification identifying the regime as satisfying clauses (i) through (v) of this subparagraph.[278]

Finally, the STR provision could also have some effect on the bona fide clause of the LOB rule. These aspects will be analysed in the next section (*see* section V.C.), where the bona fide clause is studied.

V BONA FIDE CLAUSE

V.A General Wording

The LOB clauses analysed in the previous sections allow direct access to the treaty benefits. As long as an exclusion clause is not applicable, compliance with any of these clauses will cause the income obtained in the source state to automatically receive the treaty benefits.

When none of these clauses are complied with, the taxpayer is not entitled to the application of the provisions affected thereby. It is not strange for this to occur as these clauses have been worded in very restrictive terms. To prevent cases in which taxpayers acting in good faith are not entitled to the treaty benefits, the 1996, 2006 and 2016 U.S. Models stipulate that the tax authorities may grant the treaty benefits under certain circumstances.[279] The same occurs in the LOB rule provided for in Action 6 of the BEPS project.[280]

---

278. This procedural requirement is also applicable to the base erosion prong of the derivative benefits clause, since the only requirement removed by Article 22 (4) (b) (iii) of the 2016 U.S. Model is the one provided for in Article 3 (l) (v). The Model establishes that before identifying a tax regime as a 'special tax regime', the contracting state that intends that categorization must hear the other party to the treaty. A consultation is required with that state, after which the first contracting state has to notify the other state through diplomatic channels that the regime satisfies all the conditions established in the STR definition. Article 22 (4) (b) (iii) reads as follows:

> b) less than 50 percent of the company's gross income, and less than 50 percent of the tested group's gross income, is paid or accrued, directly or indirectly, in the form of payments that are deductible for purposes of the taxes covered by this Convention in the company's Contracting State of residence [...] (iii) to persons that are equivalent beneficiaries that are connected persons with respect to the company described in this paragraph and that benefit from a special tax regime with respect to the deductible payment, provided that if the relevant comprehensive convention for the avoidance of double taxation does not contain a definition of a special tax regime analogous to the definition in subparagraph (l) of paragraph 1 of Article 3 (General Definitions), the principles of the definition provided in this Convention shall apply, *but without regard to the requirement in clause (v) of that definition;*

279. The Commentaries on Article 1 of the 2003–2014 OECD Model also provide this case. Like in the rest of the clauses, an isolated general bona fide clause is provided (paragraph 19.a) in addition to bona fide clause included in the group of clauses, similar to Article 22 of the 1996, 2006 and 2016 U.S. Models, provided in paragraph 20 of the Commentaries on Article 1 of the 2003–2014 OECD Model.
280. OECD 2015a, pp. 43–46. The simplified LOB provision of the 2016 BEPS Multilateral Instrument also contains in its Article 7(12) a bona fide clause.

Characteristic of this form of access is that the treaty is applied in accordance with an administrative decision. In fact, if any of the clauses are complied with, the taxpayer directly claims the treaty benefits. When it is necessary to resort to this form of access, the application of the treaty depends on an administrative decision.[281]

The 1996 U.S. Model did not stipulate in which cases the tax authorities should grant the application of the treaty. However, based on the Technical Explanation of the 1996 U.S. Model (paragraph 325), the treaty benefits were granted when the establishment, acquisition or maintenance of the person seeking benefits under the Convention, or the conduct of such person's operations did not have the obtaining of benefits under the tax treaty as one of its principal purposes.[282] Article 22(4) of the 2006 U.S. Model contains a proposition similar to the Technical Explanation of the 1996 U.S. Model, insofar as the tax authorities of a contracting state 'may, nevertheless, grant the benefits of [the] Convention, or benefits with respect to a specific item of income, if it determines that the establishment, acquisition or maintenance of such person and the conduct of its operations did not have as one of its principal purposes the obtaining of benefits under [the] Convention'. The detailed version of the bona fide provision of the LOB rule set forth in Action 6 of the BEPS project is similar to the bona fide provision of the 2006 U.S. Model.[283]

The 2016 U.S. Model also contains the bona fide clause, although it adds, at least from a formal point of view, a new requirement: taxpayers who claim access to treaty benefits via this route must also demonstrate a 'substantial non-tax nexus to the contracting state of residence'. Article 22(6) of the 2016 U.S. Model reads as follows:

> If a resident of a Contracting State is neither a qualified person pursuant to the provisions of paragraph 2 of this Article, nor entitled to benefits under paragraph 3, 4 or 5 of this Article, the competent authority of the other Contracting State may, nevertheless, grant the benefits of this Convention, or benefits with respect to a specific item of income, taking into account the object and purpose of this Convention, but only if such resident demonstrates to the satisfaction of such competent authority a substantial non-tax nexus to its Contracting State of residence and that neither its establishment, acquisition or maintenance, nor the conduct of its operations had as one of its principal purposes the obtaining of benefits under this Convention. The competent authority of the Contracting State to which the request has been made shall consult with the competent authority of the other Contracting State before either granting or denying a request made under this paragraph by a resident of that other Contracting State.

Despite the fact that this may be deduced from the clause's wording, this is not purely an attempt to determine the intention of the taxpayer as some authors have suggested.[284] On the contrary, it is important to determine whether or not there is such an intention by objectively analysing the circumstances under which the taxpayer requests the application of the treaty. If this form of access to the treaty were expressed

---

281. Raventós 1994b, p. 10.
282. The terms of the bona fide clause provided in the new paragraph 20 of the Commentaries on Article 1 of the 2003–2014 OECD Model are the same.
283. The same occurs with the bona fide clause provided for in the simplified LOB provision of the 2016 BEPS Multilateral Instrument.
284. Morrison/Bennett 1993a, p. 333.

in subjective terms, it would be difficult for it to be applied, as in most cases the competent authorities do not have the means to effectively verify whether or not such an intention exists. Logically, it is unlikely for a taxpayer to 'confess' that this was in fact its intention. For this means to make sense, verification should be made on the basis of objective facts.[285]

The bona fide clause places the burden of proof on the taxpayer. When a taxpayer resorts to this means of access, the burden of proof rests on the taxpayer requesting the treaty's application. The taxpayer is required to prove that the main purpose of its presence in the state of residence is not to enjoy the treaty benefits.[286]

The factor that is considered when deciding whether treaty benefits shall be conferred in the treaties being studied, is the same as that provided in the U.S. Models and Action 6 of the BEPS project. The tax authorities will authorize the application of the treaty if the taxpayer proves that one of the principal purposes of its presence and the conduct of its operations from the state of residence is not to access the treaty benefits.

Generally, tax treaties have not developed the bona fide clause through the establishment of criteria which serve to determine if this purpose exists. This lack of criteria has led to a large amount of criticism by experts in this field. The fact that specific criteria are not established gives rise to a high level of uncertainty regarding compliance therewith. The lack of criteria also effectively implies that the tax authorities are left with a large margin of discretion to decide on the application of the treaty.[287] In fact, the terms used to refer to this clause by some authors (grace clause, discretionary clause, etc.) may lead one to believe that this is a case in which the tax authorities may discretionally exercise this competence and its decision is not subject to administrative review.[288]

Despite the fact that specific criteria have not been provided to determine when 'such a purpose' exists, it cannot be asserted that the bona fide clause establishes a case of true discretionary administrative competence. In this regard, it must be emphasized that this is not the approach taken by U.S. authorities. According to section 3.05(2)(b) of the Revenue Procedure 2015-40 (Procedures for Requesting Competent Authority Assistance under Tax Treaties), published by the IRS on 12 August 2015, 'a decision by the U.S. competent authority not to grant discretionary benefits is final and not subject to administrative review'. However, U.S. courts have not accepted this approach and have ruled that IRS decisions on the application of the bona fide clause may be subject to judicial review.[289] Therefore, according to the bona fide clause, tax authorities are

---

285. ALI 1992, pp. 178–179. According to the Commentaries on the bona fide clause (discretionary relief) provided for in the detailed LOB rule of Action 6 of the BEPS project 'It is not necessary to find conclusive proof of intent, but the competent authority must be able to conclude, after an objective analysis of the relevant facts and circumstances, that none of the principal purposes for the establishment, acquisition or maintenance of the person and the conduct of its operations was to obtain benefits under the Convention'. OECD 2015a, p. 44.
286. Carrión 2016, p. 250.
287. Vogel/Shannon/Doernberg/Van Raad 1989, Article 16, p. 112.
288. Peters/Holdem/Smith 1995, p. 4, Van Herksen 1996, p. 24 and Strauch 1997, p. 103.
289. *See* Sparagna 2015 and Gleicher/Gard 2016.

required to approve the taxpayer's request if it has proven that one of the main purposes for its presence in the state of residence is not to claim the treaty benefits.[290]

However, it is undeniable that by having expressed this rule in such generic terms, this clause may be leaving a door open to arbitrary actions by the tax authorities when making a determination.[291] This situation should be corrected by requiring the tax authorities to provide sufficient reasons, in each case, for its consideration that there are circumstances leading to the understanding that the assumptions on which the rules are based are not complied with.

In some cases, the bona fide clause is developed in the Memorandum or in the Technical Explanation by the U.S. tax authorities. In the case of this clause, certain factors are taken into account to determine when the taxpayer is not present in the state of residence merely for tax purposes. Most of the criteria laid down has been taken from the U.S. branch tax law and proposals by the American Law Institute.[292] In the following section, these will be analysed in depth.

The bona fide clause is always of a subsidiary nature. Taxpayers may only resort to this means of access, if either none of the previous LOB tests have been complied with, or if a case of exclusion is applicable.[293] The U.S. Models and the states which are a party to the tax treaties have expressed their concern that the bona fide clause should be prevented from becoming a means of access to the treaties which is more flexible than compliance with the other LOB tests.[294] Definitively, they aim to prevent taxpayers from requesting the application of the treaty by this means without having first verified whether any of the clauses has effectively been complied with. For example, according to section 3.05(2)(a) of the IRS Revenue Procedure 2015-40, '[...] the U.S. competent authority will not accept a discretionary LOB request if the applicant as a part of its request does not represent that, and explain why, it does not qualify for the requested benefits under the relevant LOB provisions'.[295]

---

290. Rust 2015, p. 139.
291. Bennett/Morrison/Daniels/De Hosson 1995, p. 53.
292. Vogel/Shannon/Doernberg/Van Raad 1989, Article 16, p. 83. The Commentaries on the bona fide clause (discretionary relief) provided for in the detailed LOB rule of Action 6 of the BEPS project establish the following criteria: 'Whilst it is impossible to provide a detailed list of all the facts and circumstances that would be relevant to the determination referred to in paragraph 5, examples of such facts and circumstances include the history, structure, ownership and operations of the resident that makes the request, whether that resident is a long standing entity that was recently acquired by non-residents for non-tax reasons, whether the resident carries on substantial business activities, whether the resident's income for which the benefits are requested is subject to double taxation and whether the establishment or use of the resident gives rise to non-taxation or reduced taxation of the income'. OECD 2015a, p. 46.
293. Van Herksen 1996, p. 27. However, it should be borne in mind that the taxpayers affected by the exclusion method used in the tax treaties with Luxembourg and Portugal may not even access the benefits of the treaty through this means.
294. Peters/Holden/Smith 1995, p. 5.
295. Bates/Berman/Gani/Gutmann/Imamura/Klugman/Rust 2013, p. 402, disagree with this view: 'This seems unnecessary; the company should be permitted to seek benefits under the discretionary provision while nonetheless maintaining that one or more other LOB tests might be satisfied'.

In our opinion, the bona fide clause does not have the characteristics required for it to become a simpler means of access.[296] In accordance with this clause, the taxpayer is required to prove that one of the principal purposes for its presence in the state of residence is not to claim the application of the treaty. Without a doubt, this requirement does not facilitate access to the treaty, unless the criteria used by the tax authorities to decide on the requests are 'more flexible' than those used by the rest of the LOB tests. However, even in the case where tax authorities do not exercise this competence in a strict manner, it is important not to lose sight of the fact that there is a significant disadvantage related to the bona fide clause. As opposed to the other LOB clauses which directly grant the treaty benefits, in this case the right to the application of the treaty depends on the tax authorities' decision. If a favourable decision is not handed down, the taxpayer will not be entitled to the treaty benefits. For example, under U.S. regulations, taxpayers may not claim treaty benefits while a 'bona fide clause request' is pending.[297] Finally, it should also be taken into account that some countries (e.g. the U.S.),[298] charge a fee to taxpayers that request treaty benefits through the bona fee clause. These fees do not apply when the rest of LOB tests are applicable.

Moreover, the tax authorities to which the request should be made depends on the treaty benefit being claimed in each case. LOB clauses mainly affect the exemptions and reductions in non-resident tax in the source state and the measures to eliminate double taxation in the state of residence. Depending on the benefit being requested, the request should be made to either the tax authorities of the source state or the state of residence.[299]

The treaties mainly affect taxation at source, and accordingly, the request for the application of the bona fide clause will normally be made to the tax authorities of the state, which in each case, acts as the source state. The material effects of the treaties on the taxation in the state of residence may be scant, taking into account that the domestic legal orders usually provide measures to eliminate international double taxation. In any case, since the request can be made in both the state of residence and the source state, a certain degree of coordination is essential to prevent contradictory decisions.

For this purpose, some tax treaties, for example, the ones signed by U.S. with Austria, Ireland and the Netherlands, stipulate that the tax authorities with knowledge of the request should previously inform the competent authorities of the other contracting state of their decision to reject it. Such a measure should be required in all treaties to prevent contradictory decisions. The latter explains why this procedural requirement has been introduced in the 2016 U.S. Model, where the tax authorities of both contracting states must consult each other before either granting or denying a request made under the bona fide clause. Under the detailed version of the bona fide clause provided for in Action 6 of the BEPS project the competent authority of one

---

296. Peters/Holden/Smith 1995, p. 5.
297. IRS 2016, p. 11.
298. *See* section V.C. of this chapter.
299. OECD 2015a, p. 45.

contracting state is only required to consult the competent authority of the other contracting state before rejecting the request. It is our understanding, that this procedural requirement should always take place, in order to develop uniform criteria in both states.[300]

The obligation to consult the other state may also serve for other purposes. First, it allows for uniform criteria to be used by the tax authorities of both states, both when the state acts as the source state and as the state of residence. Additionally, this channel may aid those acting as the tax authorities of the state of residence in each case, to control to a certain extent the way this competence is exercised by the source state. The denial of the benefits at source may have repercussions on tax revenue in the state of residence, particularly if measures are unilaterally established to eliminate double taxation. Therefore, it is understandable that the state of residence will have an interest in the manner in which this competence is exercised in the source state. This control also benefits the taxpayer, since it consists in an additional means (indirect) of protection against the arbitrary exercise of this competence. This consultation process does not, however, require that the competent authority to which the request has been presented, to obtain the agreement of the competent authority that is consulted.[301]

Below, the criteria provided in some Technical Explanations, Memorandums and under U.S. law to facilitate the application of the bona fide clause will be analysed. Subsequently the procedural matters concerning this clause will be analysed.

V.B Criteria for the Competent Authority Determination

The criteria that should govern the tax authorities' decision is whether the main purpose for the taxpayer's presence in the state of residence is to obtain the application of the treaty. Although this rule is not generally provided in the U.S. Models, some treaties, and particularly, the 1992 tax treaty between the Netherlands and the U.S., include a number of criteria based on which to determine whether or not this rule is complied with. Logically, the objective of these criteria is to determine whether or not the taxpayer has effectively demonstrated that it did not acquire the status of resident for the main purpose of obtaining the reduction in taxation at source provided in the treaty, or the measures for eliminating double taxation in the state of residence.

Most of the criteria provided in the 1992 DTC between the Netherlands and the U.S. and in other treaties has been taken from the U.S. domestic branch tax law. Therefore, in our opinion, the use of these criteria in the treaties which do not stipulate anything in this respect is permissible. As previously mentioned, if a taxpayer is deemed to be a qualified resident for purposes of the branch tax law, it is unlikely that

---

300. The bona fide clause provided for in the simplified LOB provision of the 2016 BEPS Multilateral Instrument establishes this consultation process in both cases: 'Before either granting or denying a request made under this paragraph by a resident of a Contracting Jurisdiction, the competent authority of the other Contracting Jurisdiction to which the request has been made shall consult with the competent authority of the first-mentioned Contracting Jurisdiction'.
301. OECD 2015a, p. 45.

the U.S. tax authorities will deny the request for the application of a treaty.[302] It should also be taken into account that in the tax treaties where criteria has been provided, it has been included in the Memorandum of Understanding. In principle, the Memorandum does not introduce new aspects in the treaty, but rather provides an interpretation of the treaty agreed upon by the contracting states.

The criteria will be analysed based on those listed in the 1992 Memorandum of the tax treaty between the Netherlands and the U.S. (sections XIX, XX y XXI).[303] It should be noted that these criteria generally have the same value, and that compliance therewith does not automatically lead to the approval of the request. The tax authorities will assess whether the benefits should be granted based on all the circumstances involved, and may refer to other criteria, as long as they adapt to the general rule established by each treaty.[304] These criteria are as follows:

(a) The date of the corporation's incorporation in relation to the date that the tax treaty entered into force

Based on these criteria, the fact that an entity was incorporated prior to the date that the convention entered into force is an indication that it has not been incorporated in the state of residence solely to benefit from the treaty's application. However, this factor alone does not resolve the matter being judged in this case. It cannot be overlooked that the company may have been incorporated in this state prior to this date mainly, to access the DTCs entered into by this state. Moreover, if the company was incorporated prior to the entry into force of the treaty, there is even more reason to believe that this was the company's intention. Once a treaty with LOB provisions has entered into force, the company will have fewer reasons to use this state for the development of treaty shopping structures. For example, it makes less sense to use the Netherlands to develop structures of this type following the entry into force of the 1992 tax treaty with the U.S., bearing in mind that to a large extent, the LOB clauses provided in this treaty make the application of such a structure more difficult. By contrast, under the previous treaty, it was sufficient to be a resident within the meaning of the treaty in order to be able to benefit from the treaty's legal framework. For this reason, the complete opposite may occur, i.e. there were more reasons to use a certain state in treaty shopping structures prior to the new treaty entering into force. However, these criteria would be valid in the case where no treaty had been concluded prior to the new treaty entering into force.

(b) The continuity of the historical business and ownership of the corporation

If a company maintains both aspects at the date on which the treaty enters into force, the existence of an avoidance purpose may be ruled out. By contrast, changes in both of these aspects will be valued negatively, as long as there is no real business purpose

---

302. Bennett/Morrison/Daniels/De Hosson 1995, p. 62.
303. Following the 2004 amendment of the DTC between the Netherlands and the U.S., the references in this regard can be found in sections XXIV and XXVIII of the Memorandum of Understanding.
304. Van Herksen 1996, pp. 25-26 and Schaffner 1997, p. 169.

for such a change. This factor aims primarily to expose the practice of purchasing shell companies or holding companies for the purpose of reducing the overall tax liability and obtaining specific treaty benefits.[305]

(c) The extent to which the corporation is claiming special tax benefits in its country of residence

If the entity is subject to the general tax regime provided in a certain state, the possibilities that the establishment's principal purpose is to develop treaty shopping structure would be reduced. On the contrary, the enjoyment of a special tax regime in the state of residence will be valued negatively. The Commentaries on the detailed bona fide clause of Action 6 of the BEPS project also refer to this criterion:

> Similarly, where a foreign company is engaged in a mobile business such as financing, or where the domestic law of a Contracting State provides a special tax treatment for certain activities conducted in special zones or offshore (e.g. licensing intangibles) those factors will not be evidence of a non-tax business reason for locating in that State. In such cases, additional favourable business factors must be present to establish a substantial relationship to that State.[306]

Van Herksen proposes the use of these criteria to examine the existing treaty benefits entered into by the source state and the state of residence of the persons controlling the company. In this manner, the effective tax on the income obtained at source can be determined rather than merely whether these persons are subject to a preferential tax regime in the state of residence.[307]

(d) The business reasons for the corporation residing in its state of residence

In this case, the taxpayer is required to explain the reasons why it choose to conduct its business or trade in its state of residence. The taxpayer must justify the reasons that the chosen state has more favourable conditions than others for engaging in the activity considered to be the company's corporate purpose. These reasons will make sense insofar as the elements on which this decision has been justified are not also found in other states.[308]

(e) The contracting states' membership in certain international organizations

In view of the contracting states' membership in certain international organizations (EU, NAFTA, etc.), these contracting states might be in breach of international obligations as a result of the LOB provisions. In this respect, for example, the ownership clause may be contrary to the EU freedom of establishment principle, as it limits the application of the treaty to those companies in which a shareholding is held by taxpayers residing in one of the contracting states. As asserted by experts in this

---

305. Van Herksen 1996, p. 25.
306. OECD 2015a, p. 44.
307. Van Herksen 1996, p. 26.
308. Van Herksen 1996, p. 25.

field, this form of access may be an appropriate means for resolving the possible incompatibilities and breaches that may arise.[309]

With respect to the EU, the Memorandum (section XI)[310] of the DTC between the Netherlands and the U.S. states that a request for the application of the treaty should be approved if the breach was a result of a change in the company's capital stock structure as a result of a business restructuring process (merger, spin-off) performed in accordance with EU law.

(f) The extent to which the corporation would be entitled to treaty benefits is comparable to those afforded by this Convention, if it had been incorporated in the country where the majority of its shareholders reside

This criterion is worded in terms similar to the derivative benefits clause. The fact that the source state and the state of residence of the majority of the shareholders of the company receiving the income has concluded a treaty which, provides a similar or more favourable regime, is an indication that the exclusive purpose for incorporating the entity in this state is not to access the network of treaties, and in particular, to the treaty entered into with the source state.

However, the fact that this situation has arisen does not automatically imply that the source state's tax authorities will recognize the right to the application of the treaty. For this recognition to be made, there must be additional elements evidencing that a treaty shopping structure will not be developed.

If this is not the case, the application of the treaty due to compliance with this requirement, would cause the inclusion of the derivative benefits clause to be absurd. As previously discussed, in all cases a certain percentage of the shares representing the capital stock of the company receiving the income is required to be owned by either qualified residents or residents of EU, NAFTA or EEA Member States. Additionally, compliance with the base erosion clause is required. Accordingly, if the treaty benefits were automatically applied in these cases, access by exceptional means (bona fide clause) would be simpler than access by normal means.

(g) The extent to which the corporation's business activity in the other state is dependent on the capital, assets or personnel of the corporation in its state of residence

As pointed out by Van Herksen, this requirement aims to prevent companies engaged in the conduct of a trade or business of scant importance, from being entitled to access the treaty. Notable examples of these are certain financing and holding companies whose trade or business in the state of residence is scant, since their function is limited to either accessing the capital market in order to make loaned capital available to associated companies or the holding of shares.[311]

---

309. Martín Jiménez 1995, pp. 85–86.
310. Section XXVIII.d) following the treaty's amendment in 2004.
311. Van Herksen 1996, p. 26.

(h) The degree or margin to which the LOB clauses are not complied with

A criterion established by the U.S. tax authorities in the 1992 Technical Explanation of the tax treaty between the Netherlands and the U.S. is the degree to which a taxpayer does comply with a limitation on benefits clause. Bearing in mind the strict terms in which the LOB clauses are defined, it is possible that some taxpayers may not satisfy all the requirements of a clause included in the treaty. However, the margin of the shareholding percentage not covered, the volume of income allocated to payments of a deductible nature, etc. may be very reduced. Despite the fact that the terms of the clause are not met, the company may nearly comply with them (the narrow margin factor). In the opinion of the U.S. tax authorities, this factor should be taken into account when deciding whether the right to apply the treaty will be conferred upon a taxpayer. Obviously, this alone is not a determinant factor, but on the basis of this and other facts, the treaty benefits might be granted.[312] In fact, the U.S. tax authorities have required that the requests presented by the taxpayers disclose the fact that incompliance with a certain clause is by a narrow margin.[313]

Finally, although not provided anywhere, another criterion that might be taken into account by the taxpayers and the tax authorities is the following. The substantial aspects of the LOB clauses provided in the analysed treaties have been shown to be the same. However, there are certain differences which may, in some cases, broaden the scope of the treaty's application. For example, only some treaties contain derivative benefits and headquarters company clauses, or take the activities carried on in other states for the purpose of meeting the 'substantiality' requirement made in the activity clause.

These differences are a result of having negotiated the treaty at a later date. Since other states had already entered into a significant number of treaties with LOB clauses, the negotiating parties were able to reference these to broaden and improve the existing clauses.[314] Despite the fact that the newer aspects are not provided in certain treaties, the affected taxpayers may justify access by this means, alleging that if the contents of the clauses involved were the same as in other treaties, they would have complied with the clause. Obviously, transferring the aforementioned clauses to other treaties will not give rise to the same consequences, as they do not automatically imply the application of the treaty. However, we consider a request for the application of the treaty with this form of access to be perfectly legitimate. Although the aforementioned clauses are not expressly provided in the treaty involved, they are in line with the assumptions on which the LOB clauses are based. Consequently, they should be assessed favourably for the purposes of the approval of the taxpayer's request.

Although the aforementioned criteria are not definitive, they may contribute to facilitating the work required of the taxpayer and the tax authorities. With respect to the taxpayer, it will make him aware of the manner in which he must justify that the principal purpose of his presence in the state of residence is not to claim the treaty

---

312. Van Herksen 1996, p. 27.
313. Peters/Holden/Smith 1995, p. 5.
314. Brouwer 1997, p. 1105.

benefits. With respect to the competent authorities, it will provide them with some criteria on the basis of which to determine if the taxpayer is present in the state for the stated objective. In any case, the fulfilment of one of these requirements does not automatically imply that the tax authorities' decision will be favourable. However, if these requirements are met, the tax authorities will be required to provide sufficient grounds for their decision in the case that the application of the treaty is denied, since the assumption underlying the rule would not be complied with.

Only in one case does it appear that the tax authorities are always required to approve the request for the application of the treaty.[315] This case is provided in section XX of the 1992 Memorandum of the tax treaty between the Netherlands and the U.S.[316] Based on the wording of this section, it seems that the competent authorities are required to approve an entity's request for the application of the treaty if it: (a) holds stocks and securities, the income from which is not predominantly from sources in the other state; (b) has widely dispersed ownership; and (c) employs, in its state of residence, a substantial number of staff actively engaged in trades of stocks and securities owned by the company.

Finally, it should be pointed out that under U.S. regulations, treaty benefits will not be granted under the bona fide clause in the following cases.[317]

First, when the applicant or any of its affiliates is subject to a STR in its country of residence with respect to the class of income for which benefits are sought. An example of such a regime is a notional interest deduction for equity in the country of residence. Moreover, as it will be discussed at the end of the next section, it is debatable whether U.S. authorities can introduce, through the bona fide clause, the requirements of the STR clause provided for in the 2016 U.S. Model.

Second, when no tax or minimal tax would be imposed on the item of income in both the applicant's country of residence and source country, taking into account both domestic law and the treaty provision ('double non-taxation'). The example provided by the Revenue Procedure 2015-40 is a hybrid instrument that is exempt from withholding and, generated a deduction in the source country and it is exempt from tax in the applicant's country of residence.

Third, treaty benefits will be dismissed when the applicant bases its request solely on the fact that it is a direct or indirect subsidiary of a publicly traded company resident in a third country, and the treaty withholding rate, provided by the tax treaty between the U.S. and the applicant's country of residence, is not lower than that provided by the tax treaty between the U.S. and the parent company or any intermediate owner's country of residence. The Commentaries on the detailed bona fide clause of Action 6 of the BEPS project establish a similar criterion. According to the Commentaries, in the case of a resident subsidiary company with a parent company in a third state, the fact that the relevant withholding rate provided in the tax treaty is not lower than the corresponding withholding rate in the tax treaty between the source

---

315. Spector 1993, p. 174.
316. Corresponds to section XXVIII (b) following the amendment in 2004.
317. *See* Revenue Procedure 2015-40, section 3.05(2)(e).

state and the third state would be a relevant factor, but that fact would not, in itself, be sufficient to establish that the conditions for granting the discretionary relief are met.[318]

V.C Procedural Aspects

The treaties have not regulated the procedure in accordance with which the taxpayer's bona fide clause requests should be processed. Only some treaties (and now also the 2016 U.S. Model and Action 6 of the BEPS project), have laid down a step which should be carried out prior to handing down a decision regarding treaty application requests. As previously discussed, the competent authority of the contracting state with knowledge of the procedure is required to consult the tax authorities of the other state whether the request is granted or denied.[319]

Notwithstanding the aforementioned step, the procedure for the application of the bona fide clause will be regulated under the law of each state. In this respect, when regulating this procedure, the states may take some of the aspects provided under the U.S. branch tax law, the treaties Technical Explanations are taken into account and the Revenue Procedure 2015-40 published by the IRS on 12 August 2015 that establishes general requirements for taxpayers requesting the IRS tax treaty benefits based on the bona fide clause (discretionary LOB clause).

First, the requests should be submitted to the 'competent authority'. Tax treaties define the competent authority in each case. For example, in the DTC between Spain and the U.S., the competent authority is the Secretary of the Treasury or his delegate. In the case of Spain, it is the Minister of Economy and Finance or his authorized representative. The applicant should demonstrate that it does not qualify for treaty benefits under the rest of the LOB clauses and that the establishment, acquisition or maintenance of the resident and the conduct of its operations did not have as one of its principal purposes the obtaining of benefits under the tax treaty. In this regard, domestic law could establish the obligation to include certain information and documentation in the request as does the Revenue Procedure 2015-40.[320]

Second, the references provided in the Technical Explanations of the 1996 and 2006 U.S. Models with respect to the effective date of the decision authorizing access to the treaty should be borne in mind. This decision will be effective commencing on the date on which the treaty enters into force. However, if the entity's establishment in the state of residence or the transaction to which the request refers, takes place later than the aforementioned date, the decision will be effective commencing on the date of establishment or the performance of the transaction. As can be observed, the Technical Explanations allow the decision to be applied retroactively. The Commentaries on the

---

318. OECD 2015a, p. 44.
319. In practice, as pointed out by Brouwer 1997, p. 1103, the U.S. and the Netherlands are processing the corresponding request. From 1994 to 1996 the U.S. authorities received twenty-five requests. The benefits were requested from this state as it was acting as the source state in these cases. During this period, the Dutch authorities only received three requests.
320. *See* section 3(3) of the Appendix to Revenue Procedure 2015-40.

bona fide clause of Action 6 of the BEPS project also establish that any benefits granted by the competent authority may be allowed retroactively.[321]

Back-dating the date on which the decision becomes effective would improve the position of the taxpayers using this means of access. The fact that the competent authorities have not made a decision, or that the request was not made prior to the date on which the income was received, will not prevent the taxpayer from finally claiming access to the treaty's benefits. For example, according to the Revenue Procedure 2015-40, the request must indicate the date on which the applicant requests that the determination made by the competent authority becomes effective. In any case, the request should not be excessively delayed due to the existence of statutory limitation periods for tax refund requests that have been overpaid as a result of the treaty was not being applied.

With respect to the validity period of the authorization, under the branch tax regime it will extend from the year in which the decision was made by the authorities, notwithstanding the fact that it may be retroactive, and the two following years.[322] The validity of the decision is conditional upon the fact that the circumstances have not changed from when the request is presented. If there has been a change, the taxpayer is required to notify the authorities within ninety days, so that it can decide whether the treaty is still applicable.

Moreover, according to Revenue Procedure 2015-40, an applicant that receives a favourable discretionary LOB determination must file a triennial statement to keep that determination in force. The statement must declare that (i) there has not been a material change with respect to any relevant facts as established in the discretionary LOB request, (ii) there has not been a material change in law relevant to the benefits being sought, and (iii) the applicant is not claiming any benefits different from those granted. The failure to file a triennial statement on time will result in a termination of the grant of discretionary benefits from the due date of the triennial statement.

Likewise, under Revenue Procedure 2015-40, the applicant that obtains a favourable determination with respect to a bona fide clause request must notify the IRS within ninety days after becoming aware of any material change in fact or law with respect to such request. Unless the IRS indicates otherwise, a grant of discretionary LOB benefits will terminate upon the occurrence of a material change in law or fact. After the notification of a material change, the IRS will either advise the applicant that the original determination is still in effect or will instruct the applicant to seek a supplemental determination. If a supplemental determination is required, no benefits will be allowed until the IRS has issued a supplemental determination. If a supplemental determination is issued, benefits may be granted retroactively.[323]

The laws of the contracting states may take the previously discussed issues into account to regulate the corresponding procedure.

---

321. OECD 2015a, p. 46.
322. Bennett/Morrison/Daniels/De Hosson 1995, pp. 62–63.
323. O'Connor 2016.

Moreover, it should be pointed out that the Revenue Procedure 2015-40 contains several references to the term STR. These references, to a certain extent, are related to the STRs clause provided in the 2016 U.S. Model which was analysed in section IV.B.2 of this chapter.

First, the procedure outlines various circumstances when the IRS will not exercise its discretion to grant treaty benefits. One of these circumstances is where: 'the applicant or any of its affiliates is subject to a STR in its country of residence with respect to the class of income for which benefits are sought. An example of such a regime for interest income is one that allows a notional interest deduction with respect to equity in the resident country'.

Second, a reference appears in the items of information which the applicant must submit to the IRS: 'A statement whether the applicant received any tax rulings or tax concessions issued to the applicant by the country in which it is organized, and a statement of whether the applicant otherwise benefits from a STR in that country, and a description of those benefits'.

Finally, as pointed out above, it is established that a taxpayer that obtains a favourable determination under the discretionary LOB request, must notify the IRS within ninety days after becoming aware of any material change in fact or law with respect to such request. Rev. Proc. 2015-40 establishes that a material change in law occurs with 'the enactment of a special tax regime that materially affects the applicant's tax liability'.

These references to the term 'special tax regime' raise several doubts, which we just want to mention very briefly. Since this term is not defined in U.S. legislation, the concept of 'special tax regime' should be interpreted according to the definition provided in the 2016 U.S. Model. In this regard, only interest, royalties and guarantee fees (Article 21) will be affected and, at the same time, all the substantial and procedural requirements of the STR clause should be applicable. If this interpretation is correct, the IRS could not invoke the existence of a 'special tax regime' with respect to income accrued before issuing the official determination provided in Article 3(1)(l) of the 2016 U.S. Model. Moreover, it is questionable if U.S. authorities may invoke the STR provision to deny treaty benefits under the bona fide clause in treaties that do not contain that provision. As it has already been pointed out, the LOB rule rationale, at least in U.S. tax treaties that follow the 1996 and 2006 U.S. Models, is based on the existence of a sufficient nexus to the resident state, with the actual level of taxation effectively applied by that state not being decisive.

VI THE COLLECTION OF TAXES FROM NON-RESIDENTS: THE APPLICATION OF TAX TREATIES WITH LOB CLAUSES

VI.A General Aspects

The LOB clauses influence taxation of income in the source state in addition to the application of measures to eliminate double taxation in the state of residence. The main problems relating to these clauses arise in respect of taxation of income in the source

Chapter 3: Limitation on Benefits Clauses

state. Accordingly, only the problems relating to the application of the treaty in the source state will be analysed in this section.

The assessment and collection of the taxes on non-residents is a fundamental issue of any tax system. Providing a rule that provides the non-resident taxpayer's liability to tax on the income obtained in a state is not sufficient. Additionally, measures are required to assure that these taxes are effectively collected.[324]

In most states, the assessment and collection of taxes on non-residents is conditional upon the tax system established. In this respect, two types of taxpayers are differentiated. On the one hand, there are taxpayers that maintain stable and lasting relations with the state territory. These are fundamentally the taxpayers that obtain income through a PE located in the source state. On the other hand, there are non-resident taxpayers that obtain income sporadically or whose nexus to a state's economy and territory is weak.[325]

As a general rule, tax on non-residents, which maintain a lasting and stable nexus to the economy of a state, is structured and managed in the same manner as resident taxpayers. The tax on non-residents that do not have such a nexus is progressively levied on each item of income received by the non-resident without allowing this taxpayer to subjectively lower the tax by the means of a group of tax credits that residents enjoy.

With respect to the assessment and collection of taxes on non-residents without a PE, control over the effective compliance of the tax payment has traditionally been a concern for legislators due to the evident limitations on coercive collection powers by the tax authorities in view of the taxpayer's lack of a personal nexus to the territory. Due to these limitations, non-resident tax laws have provided various specific guarantees tending to assure effective compliance or to facilitate the tax authorities' collection pretences. Among these guarantees is the withholding mechanism.

In this respect, this mechanism has been applied by the withholding tax technique. As stated by Calderón, this is a technique whereby the payer, depositary or manager of the assets and rights of the non-resident (withholding agent) applies a specific withholding tax rate on the gross income paid or obtained, which is the same as the tax owed by the taxpayer.[326] This technique frees the taxpayer from the obligation of filing a tax return.

The final amount of tax withheld will be in accordance with the provisions of domestic law. In this respect, it is necessary to analyse the effect of tax treaties on this tax, when applicable. Tax treaties mainly have an influence on the taxation of non-residents without a PE, due to the existence of 'taxation limits' contained in the treaties.[327]

Fundamentally, there are two systems used to apply the treaty's limits. First, the payer withholds the amount required in accordance with its legal order and without

---

324. González Poveda 1993, p. 451.
325. González Poveda 1993, p. 451.
326. Calderón 1999, pp. 226–227.
327. It should be noted that the OECD Model does not regulate how the states should apply the DTCs. Therefore, in principle, the states should regulate this matter under its laws (principle of procedural autonomy). *See* Williams 1998, pp. 165–166.

239

taking the treaty into account. In these cases, when the tax borne by the taxpayer is higher than that authorized by the treaty, the taxpayer should request a refund of the corresponding amount from the tax authorities in the source state. Second, the payer of the income withholds the amount required taking into account the taxation limits provided in the applicable treaty. Logically, if the treaty confers the exclusive right to tax income on the state of residence, the payer should not withhold any amount.

Currently, the general tendency, on an international level, is to use the second system.[328] The corresponding amount will be withheld in accordance with domestic law but also bearing in mind the treaty limits. As pointed out by Calderón, there are grounds for this tendency because this mechanism provides for the expeditious requirements of international traffic and leads to less financial and management losses for the taxpayer and the tax authorities. Likewise, it should be borne in mind that occasionally the refund system can be slow and complex and the application deadlines can be very brief, in addition to the fact that some countries do not pay interest during the time that the excess income is withheld. Therefore, it seems to be more consistent with the treaties objective to apply a reduced tax system at source for general cases in which tax power distribution rules are established with tax rate limits in a contracting state.[329]

The aforementioned system is the most favourable for the taxpayers affected, and also that which most allows for the achievement of the tax treaties' purposes.[330] However, for this practice to be effective, either the legislation in the source state or the tax treaty itself is required to define the withholding agent's scope of liability when withholding tax and having taken into account the treaty limits.

The withholding agent is the person most interested in the correct application of the treaty.[331] In most legal orders, the obligation imposed on the withholding agent is distinct and independent from that required of the taxpayer. The withholding agent is liable for his own debts and not for a third person's debt. If the treaty is directly applied at the time the tax is withheld, and the tax authorities subsequently consider that the treaty was not applicable, or that it should have been applied in a different manner, the amount not paid will be claimed from the withholding agent. It is also likely that the tax authorities are only able to take actions against the withholding agent in order to collect the tax due, particularly in cases where the non-resident has no assets within the territory of the source state assuring the collection of the tax.[332]

Bearing the above in mind, in practice, the mechanism whereby the treaty is directly applied by the withholding agent is only used if under the law, there is some mechanism which frees the withholding agent from the consequences relating to the incorrect application of the treaty, as long as there has been a certain level of diligence. On the contrary, the withholding agent would be forced to interpret the treaty in the manner least adverse to his own interests, regardless of whether or not the amount

---

328. Bates/Berman/Gani/Gutmann/Imamura/Klugman/Rust 2013, p. 397.
329. Calderón 1997b, pp. 68–69.
330. Williams 1998, p. 191.
331. O'Donnell/Marcovici/Michaels 2000, p. 4.
332. Doernberg 1999, p. 139.

Chapter 3: Limitation on Benefits Clauses

withheld was in accordance with the treaty. In practice, this would lead the withholding agent to withhold tax in accordance with the state's domestic law, in order to avoid any type of tax charge.[333]

When a treaty is applicable, it is first necessary to verify whether the taxpayer that obtains the income is within the subjective scope of the treaty. As is common knowledge, in most treaties, the taxpayer is only required to be liable to tax on worldwide income in accordance with one of the criteria included in Article 4 of the OECD Model. If the taxpayer that obtains the income meets this requirement, in principle, the treaty is applicable and the withholding agent should take the treaty limits into account when withholding tax. To guarantee that the withholding agent withholds the correct amount in accordance with the provisions of the treaty, there must be some case of exemption from liability under law, in order for the withholding agent to avoid any type of liability derived from the incorrect application of the treaty.

In this respect, the taxpayer that obtains the income will normally request that the withholding agent applies the treaty. The taxpayer has to certify to the withholding agent, in some way, that he is entitled to the application of the treaty. The mechanism normally used is a residence certificate issued by the state in which the taxpayer resides. This does not mean that compliance with the treaty can be evidenced in another manner. However, in cases where the taxpayer's entitlement to the application of the treaty is demonstrated through the method recognized under the law of the source state or by the treaty, it is most desirable for the withholding agent to be freed from all liability if the tax authorities subsequently determine that the treaty was not applicable or was applicable in a different manner.

Only in this manner is it possible to guarantee that the withholding agents do not adopt the position least adverse to their interests, which is precisely to withhold tax without taking the tax treaty into account.[334] The source state's law or the treaty involved should resolve the manner in which a non-resident is to demonstrate compliance with the treaty to the withholding agent. One form of doing so is by presenting a valid residence certificate. This does not prevent the use of any other method to evidence compliance with the treaty. However, in this case, when a method which has not been expressly provided is used, the withholding agent could suffer the corresponding consequences in the event that the treaty was subsequently deemed to be inapplicable.

The direct application of the treaty by the withholding agent is significantly more complicated in the case of treaties that include LOB clauses similar to those that have been studied. Verification of their compliance by the withholding agent may be very burdensome and on certain occasions, impossible. To prevent the application of the convention from being resolved in practice by the mechanism of withholding and subsequently obtaining a refund of the excess tax collected, it is necessary for the contracting states, or at least the source state's legislation to provide methods whereby the withholding agent is certain that the limitation on benefit clauses have been

---

333. García Prats 1999, p. 387 and Shay 1993, pp. 344–345.
334. Williams 1998, p. 180.

complied with, or at least, to prevent the consequences where the treaty is applied and the aforementioned clauses have not actually been complied with.

In this respect, it appears that this matter is addressed in the provisions of treaties that have a Memorandum of Understanding. Specifically, section X of the 1992 Memorandum of the tax treaty between the Netherlands and the U.S. provides that the appropriate procedures will be followed in order to facilitate the application of the treaty.[335] As shall be observed in the following section, this provision was effectively developed in this treaty. However, the mechanisms adopted are not similar to those used in the past by Switzerland when applying its domestic laws relating to treaty shopping.

The technique adopted by Switzerland was the following. When Switzerland acts as the state of residence, it will verify whether its domestic anti-abuse laws are applicable. If they are verified to be applicable, it will calculate the non-resident tax that the source state failed to collect in accordance with the application of the treaty. The tax authorities of Switzerland will be responsible for collecting the amounts not paid and will subsequently transfer these amounts to the source state.[336] This technique is a good example not only of assistance between tax authorities in verifying the application of the DTCs, but also in the collection of tax revenues, whose development on an international level has been less frequent until 2003, when Article 27 (Assistance in the Collection of Taxes) was added to the OECD Model.[337]

However, this technique has not been used in the treaties being studied, mainly because the U.S. does not consider it appropriate for the state of residence to be responsible for verifying whether the rules that mainly protect taxation at source have been complied with.[338] In principle, in the treaties being studied, the task of verifying whether the exemptions or reductions provided by the treaty should be applied is the responsibility of the withholding agents and the source state's tax authorities. Unrelated is whether verification mechanisms have been developed by the contracting states to facilitate the application of the treaty by the source state's withholding agent and subsequent verification by the source state's tax authorities. Even so, in our opinion, there is no reason to reject this collection assistance technique unilaterally used by Switzerland, as it does not directly affect the decision regarding whether the treaty is applicable. Moreover, it contributes to freeing the withholding agent from liability, since a mechanism has been put into place which in most cases, prevents him

---

335. Turro 1992, p. 1473.
336. Cohen/Pollack/Scherer 1997, p. 54 and Reinarz 1996, p. 116. From the standpoint of collection, this regime did not favour Switzerland when it acted as the state of residence, since an increase in taxation at source due to the fact that the tax treaty is not applied will almost always give rise to a loss of tax revenue by the state of residence, particularly if the method used to eliminate double taxation is the credit method, even the ordinary form thereof.
337. Grau 2003.
338. Cohen/Pollack/Scherer 1997, p. 55. The U.S.' mistrust has the following explanation. The application of the treaty in the source state not only benefits the taxpayer, but also the state of residence. The reduction in taxation at source implies less loss of tax revenue by the state of residence as a result of the application of methods to eliminate double taxation, particularly if the credit method is used. The U.S. presumes that if the application of the LOB clauses is left in the hands of the state of residence, this state 'will tend to' interpret these clauses more flexibly, bearing in mind that application of the treaty at source is in its favour.

Chapter 3: Limitation on Benefits Clauses

from being the only person to whom the tax authorities of the source state may effectively turn to collect the tax payable.[339]

Bearing the above in mind, the non-resident taxation system in the U.S. and the techniques developed under its legislation and in the treaty with the Netherlands for the application of treaties with LOB clauses, will be analysed. The latter tax treaty will be focused on as it is the treaty in which these clauses are most developed.

VI.B Non-resident Taxation in the U.S. and the Application of LOB Clauses in the Tax Treaty Between the U.S. and the Netherlands

U.S. legislation on non-resident taxation provides two systems for the assessment and collection of tax on non-residents based on the strength of their nexus to the territory. The definition and assessment of non-resident tax distinguishes between taxpayers that obtain income effectively connected with the conduct of a trade or business in the U.S. and other taxpayers.[340] The first system is similar to the taxation of taxpayers with a PE. In this section, only the taxation of persons who obtain income in the U.S. without a PE will be dealt with.[341]

Generally, income obtained by non-residents without a PE is subject to a tax of 30 percent of gross income.[342] This tax is collected by means of the 'withholding tax technique'. As previously discussed, this is a technique whereby the payer, depositary or manager of the assets and rights of the non-resident (withholding agent) applies a specific withholding tax rate on the gross income paid or obtained, which is the same as the tax owed by the taxpayers.[343] This technique frees the taxpayer from the obligation of filing a tax return.[344]

If a tax treaty is applicable, the withholding agent is authorized to withhold tax in accordance with the treaty limits under U.S. law. However, the withholding agent is required to apply the treaty with due caution because in the case that he does not withhold tax or withholds less than the correct amount, the U.S. tax authorities will claim the corresponding tax in addition to applying the corresponding penalties.[345]

To assure that the withholding agent applies the limits laid down in the tax treaty, under U.S. law a system of exemption from liability is implemented in cases where the recipient of the income makes certain documents available to the withholding agent.[346] When the recipient provides the aforementioned documents prior to the payment of the income, the withholding agent will not be deemed liable in the event that the U.S. tax authorities subsequently verify that the treaty was not applicable, unless he has actual knowledge or reason to know that the recipient was not entitled to the treaty

---

339. Cole/Crocker 1998, pp. 274–275.
340. Lesser 1996, p. 38.
341. *See* IRS 2017, p. 2.
342. McDaniel/Ault 1998, p. 50.
343. Heggy 2000, p. 549.
344. McDaniel/Ault 1998, p. 81.
345. O'Donnell/Marcovici/Michaels 2000, p. 4 and IRS 2017, p. 3.
346. Doernberg 1999, p. 148 and IRS 2017, p. 9.

benefits.[347] This rule only requires certain diligence when verifying the validity of the aforementioned documentation and a consideration as to whether there is a lack of data to conclude if the recipient does not have the right to the application of the treaty.[348]

The withholding agent should first verify whether the recipient has provided the form approved by the U.S. tax authorities for the application of the treaty benefits by non-residents. This form is the W-8BEN-E (Certificate of Status of Beneficial Owner for United States Tax Withholding and Reporting (Entities). This form should be filled out by the entity that receives the income.[349] On the W-8BEN-E form, the recipient declares under the penalties of perjury that the data provided on the form is true.[350] Based on U.S. law and the form itself, the taxpayer may be fined with the penalties of perjury if the information declared is later proven to be false. The taxpayer declares four things; that he is the beneficial owner of the income obtained, that he is not a resident in the U.S., that the income obtained is not connected to any trade or business in the U.S. and that the treaty benefits are applicable to him.

The peculiarity of the system used by the U.S. is that it is not based on a document issued by the tax authorities certifying that the taxpayer is a resident for the purposes of the application of the treaty. As observed in the previous section, entitlement to the treaty benefits is usually evidenced by a certificate of residence. In the U.S. system, only a unilateral statement by the recipient, under the penalties of perjury, declaring that the treaty is applicable is required.[351]

---

347. Cole/Crocker 1998, p. 272 and Heggy 2000, p. 549.
348. It was pointed out by Shay 1993, p. 341, that the obligations and charges for which the withholding agent is liable, should vary based on whether or not the recipient of the income is related to him. These criteria can be used to verify if the knowledge or reason to know rule is complied with, taking into account that in the majority of cases, a withholding agent that is related to the recipient may be in a position to know whether the treaty is applicable. It should be pointed out that in those cases where the payer and the recipient are related, the recipient should also complete Form W-8BEN which will be discussed later, or Form 8883, when the income received in the U.S. is over the amount of USD 500,000. See IRS 2017, p. 10.
349. Non-resident individuals must file Form W-8BEN (Certificate of Foreign Status of Beneficial Owner for United States Tax Withholding and Reporting (Individuals).
350. This form stipulates 'Under the penalties of perjury, I declare that I have examined the information of this form and to the best of my knowledge and belief it is true, correct, and complete'. Form W-8BEN (individuals) establishes the same requirement.
351. This system has been partially corrected by requiring that a Tax Identification Number (TIN) assigned by the U.S. authorities is included on this form. For individuals, the form used is the W-7 (Individual Taxpayer Identification Number, ITIN). This form is to be accompanied by the documents evidencing that the taxpayer is not a resident in the U.S. There is no obligation to supply a certificate of residence issued by the state in which the taxpayer resides. The form only refers to certain documents which may evidence residence in a third state (passport, identity card issued by a state or national government authority, driver's licence, school records, etc.). As in the case of the Form W-8BEN-E, the person is required to declare under penalties of perjury. For entities, a TIN can be applied for using form SS-4 (Employer Identification Number, EIN). No additional documentation certifying the entity's non-residence is required. The entity is only required to indicate the state in which the company was incorporated. As in the case of Form W-8BEN-E, the information is also declared to be true under oath.
    The only case in which a certificate of residence is required is when there is no obligation to obtain a TIN. This is the case in respect of certain income derived from marketable securities (see IRS 2017, p. 11). However, in the case of individuals the residence certificate may be substituted by an official document issued by the corresponding state, which includes the

The recipient must submit the form prior to the payment of the income by the withholding agent. On the contrary, the payer would withhold 30 percent. If this is the case, the resident should request the difference from the tax authorities in the form of a refund. It is not necessary to submit a form each time income is paid, as long as the document has not expired. Generally, a separate Form W-8BEN-E must be given to each withholding agent. The withholding agent will apply the treaty limits in the event that Form W-8BEN-E has been correctly completed and has not expired. Generally, this form will remain valid for a period starting on the date the form is signed and ending on the last day of the third succeeding calendar year.[352]

If the withholding agent meets the above requirements it can withhold tax in accordance with the treaty and will be freed from any subsequent liability relating to the non-resident tax, unless he has knowledge or reason to know that the recipient does not have the right to the application of the treaty.

In principle, this system is also applied when the tax treaty contains LOB clauses. Another item declared by the taxpayer on the Form W-8BEN-E, also under penalties of perjury, is that it complies with one of the LOB clauses of the treaty whose application is being requested.[353] As in the previous cases, compliance is only declared in a unilateral form, and the non-resident is not required to prove to the withholding, using the appropriate means, that the LOB clauses has been complied with.

Without a doubt, based on the manner in which the system is structured, its effectiveness rests on the 'good faith' of the recipient. In our opinion, the penalty with which the non-resident may be fined is not a threat to those who request the application of the treaty without meeting the requirements thereof.[354]

In addition to the previous procedure, the U.S. legislation provides a special procedure. Frequently marketable securities are deposited in certain financial institutions. These entities manage a large number of investor's securities that do not directly obtain the income generated. The entity which manages these securities is

---

individual's name, address and a photograph. In the case of entities, the residence certificate may be substituted by an official document issued by the corresponding state, which includes the name of the entity and the address of its principal office in the treaty country. As of 1 January 2003, there is another case in which there is no obligation to obtain a TIN (unexpected payment). *See* IRS 2017, p. 40.

352. Therefore, for example, if the entity signs the form on 30 September 2014, it will be valid until 31 December 2014. The recipient is obligated to inform the withholding agent of any change in circumstances which modifies the form within thirty days, and is required to complete a new form. When the recipient is obligated to include its ITIN or EIN, the form will be valid until there is a change in circumstances. *See* IRS 2016, pp. 3-4.

353. In fact, in the last update of this form (April 2016), new checkboxes have been added to Part III (Claim of Tax Treaty Benefits) for each of the main tests that can be met to satisfy an LOB provision. A taxpayer is required to check the relevant box associated with the LOB test it meets with respect to the treaty benefits associated with this form, or to check a box that it has obtained a favourable discretionary determination (bona fide clause) from the U.S. competent authority that it qualifies for the treaty benefits associated with this form.

354. On the contrary, when the reverse situation occurs, i.e. the residents in the U.S. obtain income in states with which the U.S. has entered into DTCs, U.S. legislation does provide for the issuance of a residence certificate by means of Form 6166. In this regard, see the instructions for Form 8802 (Application for United States Residency Certification) which can be found on the IRS web page: http://www.irs.gov/.

responsible for the obtainment of income. In these cases, the non-resident tax levied can be very burdensome, as these entities operate on the account of many investors and it is likely that each investor's state of residence differs.

To facilitate the assessment and collection of the non-resident tax, the U.S. legislation provides for a figure called the 'qualified intermediary'. These are financial institutions that are residents or non-residents, which manage the securities of third persons and are recognized as such by the U.S. tax authorities.[355] These entities are responsible for furnishing the withholding agents with the information required to withhold the correct amount. Among other aspects, they notify the payer of the treaties which are applicable and which taxation limit should be taken into account when withholding tax. Logically, this information should be gathered from the customers that are the owners of the income that these entities manage. Of most relevance is that the withholding agent, which withholds tax based on information certified by the aforementioned intermediaries, is freed from any subsequent liability, unless he has knowledge and reason to know that the taxpayer involved is not entitled to the application of the treaty.

With respect to the treaties with LOB clauses, these intermediaries must also gather the information required to evidence compliance therewith. However, as in the case of Form W-8BEN-E, it appears that a declaration assuring compliance from the customer is sufficient. Despite this fact, under U.S. legislation there appears to be an obligation to perform a more in-depth investigation to assure that the treaties are complied with. However, it should be borne in mind that this obligation does not fall on the withholding agent, but rather on the 'qualified intermediary', which is responsible for providing the withholding agent the information required for the application of the tax rate that applies.

Despite the apparent ease in claiming the treaty benefits under U.S. law even when the treaties contain LOB clauses, the 1992 tax treaty between the Netherlands and the U.S. developed a special procedure. This procedure was developed mainly due to the concern by the Dutch tax authorities that the residents in the Netherlands might not obtain the application of the treaty by the U.S. withholding agents. In this respect, it is evident that there is a certain distrust of the U.S. system, since it does not perfectly define the scope of the knowledge and reason to know rule.[356]

The Dutch tax authorities have developed a procedure (Form IB 93 USA) certifying compliance with the LOB provisions by the taxpayers residing in the Netherlands.[357] The residents in the Netherlands should request the Dutch tax authorities to certify compliance with these clauses. For this purpose, the taxpayers are required to indicate which clause they comply with and to furnish the documentation

---

355. See O'Donnell/Marcovici/Michaels 2000, pp. 5–9, Lagares 2001 and IRS 2017, p. 13.
356. In this regard, see Van Herksen 1996, p. 28. Moreover, it should be highlighted that according to section 3.05(2)(a) of the Revenue Procedure 2015-40, the IRS will not issue a determination regarding whether an applicant satisfies an objective LOB test.
357. This form and the instructions on how to fill it out can be found in Bennett/Morrison/Daniels /De Hosson 1995, appendix to Article 26, pp. 3–44. Brouwer 1997, pp. 1104–1105 includes some information with respect to the requests decided upon by the Dutch tax authorities between 1994 and 1996.

Chapter 3: Limitation on Benefits Clauses

required to prove compliance therewith.[358] If the Dutch authorities hand down a decision in the taxpayer's favour, they will issue a certificate on which they declare that the taxpayer complies with a certain limitation on benefits clause.

This certificate's temporary period of validity is not very long as it only extends to the year in which the certificate was obtained. Furthermore, validity is conditional upon the fact that the circumstances have not changed since the request was made. Since the period of validity is very short, the taxpayer is required to request a new certificate each year, despite the fact that the circumstances have not varied.[359]

The Dutch tax authorities issue four copies of this certificate. One copy is sent to the U.S. tax authorities, and logically another is held by the Dutch tax authorities. The other copies are given to the taxpayer. The purpose of supplying the taxpayer with two copies is that one is given to the withholding agent in order to demonstrate compliance with the LOB clauses.

The U.S. tax authorities have accepted the validity of these certificates for the purpose of having the treaty taken into account by the withholding agent at the time tax is withheld.[360] The taxpayer residing in the Netherlands must submit the certificate IB 93 USA together with the forms required under domestic law to the withholding agent.[361] This certificate frees the withholding agent from any liability, unless, in spite of these documents, he has knowledge or reason to know that the LOB clauses are not complied with. However, the U.S. tax authorities reserve the right to subsequently verify whether the cited clauses are complied with.[362] Notwithstanding the above, as has been observed, this certificate enables the taxpayer to obtain the application of the treaty directly from the withholding agent.

In our opinion, the system established in the 1992 tax treaty between the Netherlands and the U.S. is a good method to guarantee that LOB clauses are effectively complied with, and also to facilitate the application of the treaties in the source state. Similar mechanisms have not been developed in other treaties. This situation gives rise to a number of questions.

First, there is no indication as to whether the procedure provided in the DTC between the Netherlands and the U.S. excludes the procedure provided under U.S. domestic law. As has been evidenced, in practice, this system does not require any verification of effective compliance with the LOB rule prior to withholding tax. The entire form rests on the good faith of the recipient and the warning of possible criminal penalties applicable to those who do not act in such a manner. If this procedure were not excluded, it seems that it would be unnecessary to request the certificate IB 93 USA

---

358. The instructions to Form IB 93 USA include a number of indications regarding the documentation that should accompany the request.
359. Spector 1993, p. 161.
360. The U.S. tax authorities state their position in resolution 94-85 published in no. 1994-35 of the Internal Revenue Bulletin.
361. At the time of this declaration the 1984 withholding rules were still in force. The previous system is similar to that discussed here. The withholding agent could base the amount withheld on a certificate similar to form W-8BEN, namely Form 1001. Form 1001 was only required for interest and royalties. With respect to dividends, it was sufficient to demonstrate that the taxpayer's domicile was located in the state with which the U.S. had entered into the treaty.
362. Peters/Holdem/Smith 1995, pp. 3–4.

from the Dutch tax authorities because the U.S. system allows for easy obtainment of the treaty benefits. On the other hand, if it is excluded, residents in countries with which a similar procedure has not been established may effectively access the treaty more easily. However, there is no indication that the general U.S. procedure cannot also be applied in the case of the treaty between the Netherlands and the U.S.[363]

In our opinion, if the LOB clauses have been included in the treaty, these should effectively be applied. This requires some type of verification when the source state, through the withholding agent, applies the treaty benefits. To assure that this duty does not fall on the withholding agent, particularly since it would be difficult for him to perform such verifications alone, an appropriate method is the one developed by the Dutch tax authorities in the treaty entered into with the U.S.

VI.C Conclusions

In practice, at least under U.S. domestic law, compliance with the LOB clauses is not verified when the treaty is applied directly by the withholding agent.[364] As previously observed, the taxpayer only has the obligation to furnish certain documentation to the withholding agent. This documentation does not prove compliance with the LOB clauses, since it only includes a declaration by the taxpayer in which it asserts that the clauses have been complied with. If there is any such verification, it will subsequently be performed by the tax authorities.[365]

The above situation may lead us to reconsider the meaning of these clauses, since the fact that there is no verification at the time tax is withheld and, that the withholding agent is the person who actually applies the treaty seems to indicate that they have only been included so that the U.S. tax authorities may deny the treaty's application in the hypothetical case that verification is subsequently made.[366] In this respect, effectively when tax is withheld there is no reversal of the burden of proof characterizing these clauses.

---

363. Bennett/Morrison/Daniels/De Hosson 1995, p. 131, points out that this procedure is optional.
364. The Technical Explanation of the Spain-U.S. tax treaty confirms the above and states the following: 'Article 17 is not intended to impose any additional burden on the withholding agents of the Contracting States, and withholding agents will not be required to verify the accuracy of a person's claim to treaty benefits. In applying Article 17, the normal burden of proof rules apply. In claiming U.S. benefits, a resident of Spain would follow the normal U.S. procedures, in effect at the time, for claiming reduced rates of tax or exemption under a U.S. tax treaty. The Internal Revenue Service, of course, retains the right to consider, on audit, whether any particular grant of benefits was appropriate'. The Spanish tax authorities do not verify compliance with the limitation on benefits clauses provided in Spanish tax treaties, and in particular, those provided in the tax treaty with the U.S., and generally bases proof of the entitlement to apply the treaty solely on the fact that a residence certificate has been furnished. *See* Vega 2003, pp. 334–341.
365. Bennett/Andersen 1998, p. 730.
366. It should be noted that the burden of proving compliance with the LOB clause generating the right to apply the treaty falls on the taxpayer. Therefore, when the tax authorities verify the taxpayer's situation, it is required to demonstrate compliance with one of these clauses. When this is not the case, the tax authorities deny the benefits of the treaty since the taxpayer has not proved that the requirements entitling them to apply the treaty have been met. It is important to bear in mind that in these cases the denial of the benefits of the treaty is not based on the

Chapter 3: Limitation on Benefits Clauses

The U.S. tax authorities appear to have promoted their inclusion to facilitate the denial of the treaty in a procedure whereby verification is made later. The treaty benefits will be denied to those who do not comply with the clauses. In this manner, the tax authorities are freed from the difficult task of applying GAARs, since the application of the treaty is denied based solely on the fact that the limitation on benefit clauses are not complied with. Accordingly, the tax authorities will deny the application of the treaty to the taxpayers that do prove compliance with one the LOB clauses in the verification procedure.

However, when the U.S. tax authorities subsequently verifies that the LOB clauses were not complied with, it will be difficult to collect the tax payable in cases where the non-resident has no asset in the territory. The possibility of taking action against the withholding agent is forbidden under its own law if it is based on the documentation referred to above and the fact that the withholding agent did not have actual knowledge or reason to know that the treaty was not applicable. In these cases, only international assistance methods for the collection of tax revenues would allow the U.S. to collect the tax amounts owed.

Bearing this in mind, the words of Loengard take on a new meaning. He stated in 1993 that if LOB clauses are not giving rise to considerable obstacles to the application of the treaties benefits, it is because, in practice, they are not being applied.[367] Due to the procedure for the assessment and collection of non-resident tax followed under the U.S. legal order, the assertion made by this author is not unwise, in the case that only the time at which the withholding agent applies the treaty is taken into account. Only in cases where there is subsequent verification by the U.S. tax authorities will the LOB clauses effectively be applied. Obviously, this will occur in the minority of cases taking into account the limited means of all tax authorities.[368]

---

application of a general anti-avoidance rule, which as previously discussed, presumes that in principle, the taxpayer has the right to apply the treaty. In the treaties without LOB clauses, in the event that the tax authorities wish to deny the application of the convention by applying the general anti-avoidance rule, the tax authorities are required to prove that the assumptions on which this general rule is based are met.

On the other hand, if the relation between the non-resident and withholding agent is considered, the taxpayer only has the obligation to furnish certain information for the withholding agent to apply the treaty. In this case, the taxpayer is not obligated to prove that the LOB clauses have been complied with, but rather must simply declare on Form W-8BEN-E, that it complies with these clauses. With respect to the relation between the tax authorities and the withholding agent, when the latter applies a treaty, it has the obligation to demonstrate certain diligence, which consists in having applied the treaty on the basis of documentation furnished by the taxpayer, and this documentation is precisely that established by U.S. legislation.

367. Loengard 1993, p. 282.
368. In this regard, Gouthière 2010, p. 182, states the following: 'This very detailed [LOB rule] is certainly helpful for the tax authorities in their efforts to combat tax avoidance and evasion schemes. However, as a practical matter, it is very seldom that tax inspectors in the field take it into consideration when auditing companies, at least in France (in the author's experience, he has never seen or heard a case of it)'.

CHAPTER 4
Limitation on Benefits Clauses and European Union Law

I PRELIMINARY REMARKS

Since the conclusion of the DTC between Germany and the U.S. (1989) experts in this field have questioned the possible incompatibility of the LOB clauses with EU law.

In the Ruding report (1992), it was concluded that these rules might be incompatible with EU principles and rules, and particularly with the principle of non-discrimination and its particular manifestations on the fundamental freedoms provided under the European treaties (freedom of establishment and to provide services and the freedom of capital and payments).[1] In addition, a member of the European Parliament submitted a written question to the Commission regarding whether the LOB clauses provided in the DTC between Germany and the U.S. were incompatible with EU law. This question was never answered.[2]

The European Commission has referred to the possible incompatibility of these clauses with EU law in several documents[3] prior to the Anti-Tax Avoidance Package being launched by the Commission in January 2016.[4] The latter explains why the European Commission, in the Anti-Tax Avoidance Package,[5] has decided not to follow

---

1. Ruding Report 1992, pp. 30–31.
2. Written Question 2046/90, made in July 1990 by Gijs De Vries (*see* Winandy 1996, p. 26). However, there is a written question indirectly referring to this matter which the Commission replied to in the Answer to Written Question 2047/90 presented 5 September 1990 by the same parliament. The answer can be found in the Official Journal C-195, pp. 1–2. Also *see* Vega 2003, p. 345, footnote 1.039.
3. *See*, among others, the following documents: EU 2001a, p. 362, EU 2001b, EU 2003, p. 11 and EU 2005, points 19 and 29, EU 2016a, p. 6 and EU 2016b, pp. 29 and 49.
4. Dourado 2016, p. 440.
5. The Anti-Tax Avoidance Package is part of the Commission's agenda for fairer, simpler and more effective corporate taxation in the EU. The Chapeau Communication outlines the political, economic and international context of the Anti-Tax Avoidance Package and gives an overview of

one of the proposals of Action 6 of the BEPS project in order to adopt measures against treaty shopping strategies, i.e. to include a detailed LOB rule similar to the one provided for in the U.S. Model and the U.S. tax treaties. The Commission considers that LOB clauses 'limit the benefits of tax treaties to entities owned by residents of only one Member State, and therefore can be seen as detrimental to the Single Market by discouraging cross border investment. These rules can be problematic for the Capital Markets Union'.[6] As outlined in further sections, the European Commission recommends Member States to follow Action 6 BEPS's proposal of including a general anti-abuse rule based on a PPT rule in tax treaties.[7] However, the Commission has introduced some modifications in the wording of the BEPS' PPT rule in order to align it with the case law of the ECJ with regards to the abuse of law.

Moreover, the ECJ has not yet decided on any case in which the possible incompatibility between the LOB clauses in the tax treaties between the U.S. and the EU Member States and EU law is argued. However, as shall also be observed below, the possible incompatibility of these rules can be sustained based on the reasoning used by the ECJ in other cases.[8]

It is important to highlight that despite the fact that the ECJ has not yet expressly ruled on this matter, it is possible that the ECJ may be required to make a judgment on future proceedings for failure to fulfil obligations under EU law brought by the European Commission (Article 258 of the TFEU, ex Article 226 of the EC Treaty).[9] In fact, the European Commission announced, in a Communication released in 2003,[10] that in 2004 it was to present an initiative on the different and complex problems relating to bilateral and multilateral double taxation treaties in the internal market in order to provide an analysis and legal interpretation of the ECJ's decisions. If the LOB clauses are considered incompatible with EU law, it would not be at all surprising if the Commission were to bring an action before the ECJ in accordance with Article 258 of the TFEU (enforcement procedure). This is because in another part of the aforementioned 2003 Communication (p. 7), the Commission states that one of the reasons preventing a higher degree of uniformity with respect to corporate income tax is the reluctance on the part of some Member States to coordinate their tax systems. The Communication advises that in view of this situation, the Commission will continue to insist on the unequivocal respect of EU law in taxation and it will design its policy for launching appropriate infringement procedures in a more targeted and proactive way.

---

the different elements (*see* EU 2016a). The Anti-Tax Avoidance Package is composed of the following initiatives: a proposal for an Anti-Tax Avoidance Directive; a Recommendation on Tax Treaty issues (EU 2016c); a proposal for a Directive implementing the G20/OECD Country by Country Reporting (CbCR); a Communication on an External Strategy; and a Staff Working Document, which provides further analysis and supports these initiatives (2016c). The Anti-Tax Avoidance Directive (ATAD) was adopted by the Council on 20 June 2016: Directive 2016/1164 laying down rules against tax avoidance practices that directly affect the functioning of the internal market.

6. EU 2016a, p. 6. *See also* EU 2016c, pp. 29 and 49.
7. *See* section II.A, Chapter 2.
8. Osterweil 2009, p. 248.
9. Lyal 2015, p. 9.
10. EU 2003, p. 11.

Chapter 4: Limitation on Benefits Clauses and European Union Law

The assertions made by the Commission in the 2003 Communication should not be overlooked. To date, the majority of cases relating to direct taxes on which the ECJ has ruled, have their origin in preliminary rulings (Article 267 TFEU, ex Article 234 EC Treaty) and not in an infringement procedure initiated by the Commission (Article 258 TFEU). If the Commission were to undertake a strategy in which, all cases where the Member State's corporate income tax was suspected to be incompatible with EU freedom, were brought before the ECJ, there is no doubt that these could include the DTCs, and particularly, the DTCs with limitations on benefits clauses. In this respect, although this matter will be discussed in depth later, it should be taken into account that a number of rulings on transport cases, and specifically, bilateral air transport agreements between several Member States and the U.S., which were handed down on 5 November 2002, arose out of the enforcement procedure commenced by the Commission in accordance with Article 258 of the TFEU.[11] These rulings are relevant, *inter alia*, because the ECJ found that a clause provided in the aforementioned treaties, the contents of which are very similar to those of the LOB clauses, was contrary to EU law.

However, so far the Commission has not formally initiated the action announced in 2003, at least not in respect of tax treaties. This trend may change in the current context of the BEPS project and the Anti-Tax Avoidance Package. These changes are occurring, for example on 19 November 2015, the European Commission requested that the Netherlands amended the LOB provision provided in the existing Dutch-Japanese tax treaty, which came into force on 1 January 2012. This LOB provision is similar to the one contained in the U.S. Model and Action 6 of the BEPS project, although it only affects certain tax treaty benefits, i.e. dividends, interest, royalties, capital gains and 'other income'.[12] According to the press release, the Commission bases the incompatibly of the LOB rule, among others, on the ECJ's *Open Skies* rulings.[13] The Dutch government had two months to respond to the Commission. That timeline elapsed in January 2016 and to date, the Dutch government has published no official response, nor has the Commission issued any public update with respect to any further steps it has taken.[14] It will take some time for the matter to be finally resolved and see if the Commission refers the Netherlands to the ECJ.

---

11. The ECJ judgments referred to are those dated 5 November 2002, C-466/98 to C-469/98, C-471/98, C-472/98, C-475/98 and C-476/98). Experts commonly refer to these judgments as the *Open Skies* rulings. See Craig 2003, p. 63.
12. Hofland/Pötgens 2011, p. 215.
13. The wording of the Commission's press release is as follows: 'The Commission believes that, on the basis of previous cases such as C-55/00 Gottardo and C-466/98 Open Skies, a Member State concluding a treaty with a third country cannot agree better treatment for companies held by shareholders resident in its own territory, than for comparable companies held by shareholders who are resident elsewhere in the EU/EEA. Similarly, it cannot agree better conditions for companies traded on its own stock exchange than for companies traded on stock exchanges elsewhere in the EU/EEA. However, under the current terms of the LOB clause, some entities are excluded from the benefits of the tax treaty. This means that they suffer higher withholding taxes on dividends, interest and royalties received from Japan than similar companies with Dutch shareholders or whose shares are listed and traded on "recognized stock exchanges", which include certain EU and even third-country stock exchanges [...]'.
14. Duffy/Fahy/Galvin 2016.

In any case, the fact is that there has not yet been any express ruling by the ECJ finding that the LOB clauses contained in the treaties entered into by EU Member States with the U.S. are incompatible with EU law.

II COMPETENCE OF EU MEMBER STATES TO CONCLUDE DTCs with Third States

Before analysing if LOB clauses infringe EU law, a competence issue first needs to be addressed. Based on the actual development of EU law, it is essential to determine whether the competence for concluding tax treaties between Member States, and between Member States and third states corresponds to the EU Member States themselves or to the EU Institutions. If the competence were to correspond to the EU Institutions, there would be no need to analyse the material contents of these clauses.

As pointed out by experts in this field, EU Institutions are only vested with the powers conferred upon them, and accordingly, may only exercise the competence conferred upon them in the treaties.[15] In the case that competence is conferred upon the EU, the EU Member States will inevitably be disinvested of the corresponding powers within the same area. However, a state is only disinvested of competence when this competence is effectively exercised by the EU. The correlative disinvestment of the state's competence is not a result of the EU merely being vested with powers for legal purposes, but rather a result of the effective exercise of this EU competence by EU Institutions.[16]

The Treaty of the Functioning of the European Union (TFEU) does not expressly confer any competence upon the EU Institutions in relation to direct taxation. Only Article 115 of the TFEU (ex Article 94 of the EC Treaty) provides that 'The Council shall, acting unanimously [...], issue directives for the approximation of such laws, regulations or administrative provisions of the Member States as directly affect the establishment or functioning of the common market'. Only a few Directives have been approved on the basis of this provision.

In the fields regulated by these Directives, the related competence was conferred upon the EU. A doubt arises as to whether such competence also has external effects. Based on the ruling by the ECJ on 31 December 1970, *AETR*, C-22/70, and the Opinion 1/94, of 15 November 1994, it appears that the Member States, whether acting individually or collectively, lose their right to assume obligations with third states only in so far as common rules, which could be affected by these obligations, are provided (*in foro interno, in foro externo* principle).[17] With respect to the Parent-Subsidiary

---

15. Mangas/Liñán 1996, pp. 305–306.
16. Mangas/Liñán 1996, p. 312.
17. Mangas/Liñán 1996, p. 317.

Directive, most experts consider that it does not imply that external powers have been exclusively conferred to EU Institutions.[18] This Directive would only affect the treaties concluded between Member States.[19]

With respect to treaties concluded with third states, the Member States would continue to have the competence to negotiate the tax to be levied on dividends from significant shareholdings, both in the source state and the state of residence, in tax treaties or any other international instrument. In any case, although it could be sustained that external competence had been transferred to EU institutions, it is important not to lose sight of the fact that the Member States would only be disinvested thereof in the event that these powers were to be effectively exercised by the EU Institutions, and to date, this has not occurred.

In this same respect, it should be taken into account that the EU, through the Commission, has stated its intention to extend its competence externally in relation to some matters which have been harmonized. Noteworthy is that Article 17(2) of the Directive 2003/48/EC, on taxation of savings income in the form of interest payments, states that 'Member States shall apply these provisions from 1 January 2005 provided that: (i) the Swiss Confederation, the Principality of Liechtenstein, the Republic of San Marino, the Principality of Monaco and the Principality of Andorra apply, from that same date, measures equivalent to those contained in this Directive, in accordance with agreements entered into by them with the European Community, following unanimous decisions of the Council'.[20]

Furthermore, Article 293 of the EC Treaty did not confer such powers upon the EU either. This article stated that Member States shall, so far as is necessary, enter into negotiations securing, for the benefit of their nationals: '[...] the abolition of double taxation within the Community'. Based on this article, the Member States have both internal and external competence over direct taxation.[21] The fact that this article has not been reproduced in the TFEU does not affect the proposition.

However, although internal and external competence corresponds to Member States, this does not mean that these powers do not have to be exercised in accordance with EU law. As pointed out by the ECJ on numerous occasions, 'although direct

---

18. *See* Hinnekens 1994, p. 157, Malherbe/Delattre 1996, pp. 13-14, Avery Jones 1998, p. 102, Calderón 2002, p. 17, footnote 73. Terra/Wattel 2001, pp. 111-112, Hamaekers 1990, pp. 358-359 and Jeffery 1999, p. 154, consider the external competence with respect to the aspects covered by the Directive to correspond to the EU.
19. Van Unnik/Boudesteijn 1993, p. 107 and Calderón 2002, p. 20.
20. Terra/Wattel 2012, p. 158 and Kemmeren 2012, p. 167.
21. Avery Jones 1998, pp. 95-97 and Calderón 2002, pp. 13-14 In this respect, the ECJ Judgment of 21 September 1999, *Saint-Gobain*, C-307/97, paragraph 56, states that 'in this regard, it must be observed first of all that, in the absence of unifying or harmonising measures adopted in the Community, in particular under the second indent of [Article 293 of the EC Treaty], the Member States remain competent to determine the criteria for taxation of income and wealth with a view to eliminating double taxation by means, *inter alia*, of international agreements. In this context, the Member States are at liberty, in the framework of bilateral agreements concluded in order to prevent double taxation, to determine the connecting factors for the purposes of allocating powers of taxation as between themselves'. This article has not been reproduced in the TFEU. However, the general provisions of Article 4(3) of the TEU prescribe that the Member States shall facilitate the achievement of the Union's tasks and refrain from any measure which could jeopardize the attainment of the Union's objectives.

taxation is a matter for the Member States, they must nevertheless exercise their taxation powers consistently with Community law.'[22] This obligation to exercise these competences in accordance with EU Law is derived not only from the principle of primacy of EU law, but also the EU loyalty or sincere cooperation principles provided in Article 4(3) of the Treaty on European Union (TEU) (ex Article 10 of the EC Treaty).[23] According to this article, 'The Member States shall take any appropriate measure, general or particular, to ensure fulfilment of the obligations arising out of the Treaties or resulting from the acts of the Union institutions. The Member States shall facilitate the achievement of the Union's tasks and refrain from any measure which could jeopardize the attainment of the Union's objectives'. Consequently, the states are required to respect the obligations arising from EU law when entering into tax treaties with other Member States and with third states.[24]

However, according to Article 351 of the TFEU (ex Article 307 of the EC Treaty), these obligations need to be qualified in the event that a treaty was concluded with third states prior to the treaty entering into force on 1 January 1958, or with respect to acceding states, before the date of their accession. In regard to the treaties analysed in Chapter 3, the special rule provided in Article 351 of the TFEU affects the tax treaties entered into by Finland and Greece with the U.S. In the case of Greece, the treaty was concluded in 1950, and this state acceded to the European Community in 1974. Finland acceded to the European Community in 1994 and the treaty with the U.S. was concluded in 1989. The same applies to the tax treaties entered into by the thirteen states, which were taken into the EU in later years, insofar as those tax treaties were concluded before accessing the EU.

According to Article 351 of the TFEU, the rights and obligations arising from those agreements shall not be affected by the provisions of this Treaty. This article establishes a special rule in order to protect the rights of third states and the obligations assumed by EU Member States with respect to these non-European states.[25]

The existence of certain previous agreements entered into by Member States may represent an obstacle to the objectives provided in the Treaties establishing the EU. To prevent the above, Article 351 of the TFEU is not limited to laying down the principle that such agreements should be observed. In the second paragraph, it also establishes that 'the Member State or States concerned shall take all appropriate steps to eliminate the incompatibilities established', and advises that 'Member States shall, where necessary, assist each other to this end and shall, where appropriate, adopt a common attitude.'[26]

This provision lays down an obligation governing the conduct of the Member States which specifically requires these states to use valid means under international law to resolve possible conflicts. Since this is an obligation governing conduct rather than an obligation to achieve a given result, the states will only be in breach of the

---

22. Paragraph 58 of the *Saint-Gobain* judgment.
23. Kemmeren 1998, p. 17 and Terra/Wattel 2012, p. 147.
24. Calvo 1998, p. 54.
25. Kemmeren 1998, p. 18 and Díez-Hochleitner 1998, p. 170.
26. Díez-Hochleitner 1998, p. 186.

obligations arising under EU law if they do not adopt any initiative to resolve the incompatibility.[27] Noteworthy among the appropriate steps offered under international law to resolve the conflict, is the negotiation with a third state with a view to amending or denouncing the agreement by the Member State.[28] In the event that this were a matter of EU competence, the replacement thereof with an agreement entered into with the EU or accession to this agreement would also be possible.

In conclusion, it should be taken into account that the subordination of the treaties entered into by Member States with third states differs depending on whether or not the treaties were concluded prior to the date on which the EU obligations became applicable. This will be of relevance where the LOB clauses contained in the treaties being studied are concluded to be incompatible with EU law.

III COMPATIBILITY OF LOB CLAUSES WITH EU LAW

The compatibility between the LOBs and EU law should be analysed in light of the principles and rules provided in the Treaty on European Union and the Treaty on the Functioning of the European Union (TFEU). In particular, it is important to elucidate whether these provisions are contrary to the principle of non-discrimination on the grounds of nationality, provided in Article 18 of the TFEU (ex Article 12 of the EC Treaty), and its specific manifestations on the EU freedom of establishment and the freedom of capital and to provide services.

However, in principle only those clauses with specific manifestations of the EU principle of non-discrimination will be compared. As stated by the ECJ in its ruling dated 13 April 2000, *Baars*, C-251/98, 'as to Article [12 of the EC Treaty], it follows from the case-law of the Court of Justice that that article, which lays down a general prohibition of all discrimination on grounds of nationality, applies independently only to situations governed by Community law for which the Treaty lays down no specific non-discrimination rules' (paragraph 23).

The examination of these clauses will be divided into two different sections. In the first section, the clauses contained in the tax treaties entered into by EU Member States with the U.S. will be analysed. In the second section, the clauses contained in the tax treaties concluded between EU Member States will be addressed. For illustrative purposes, reference will be made to the tax treaties entered into by Spain with different EU states. This division of the clauses is justified since the consequences of the possible incompatibility thereof differ depending on whether they are applicable on an EU or non-Member State level.

---

27. Díez-Hochleitner 1998, p. 189.
28. Díez-Hochleitner 1998, p. 190.

III.A Treaties with Third States

III.A.1 Individualized Analysis of LOB Clauses

This study may be performed following two different approaches. The first approach consists in individually analysing each clause in the light of EU law (stock exchange clause, property and base erosion clause, activity clause and the bona fide clause). The second approach consists in comparing the system for accessing the benefits of a treaty in accordance with these clauses and EU law. As shall be observed, the two methods do not contradict one another. This study will commence with the first method.

Beforehand, it should be taken into account that the taxpayers affected by the LOB clauses are mainly entities. As previously discussed, the status of qualified resident is directly conferred upon individuals residing in one of the contracting states and, accordingly, the full benefits of the treaty are applicable to them. Consequently, the study of the compatibility of these clauses with EU law requires the verification as to which legal entities are beneficiaries of the EU freedom of establishment and to provide services and the freedom of movement of capital.

First, with respect to the stock exchange provision, it should be borne in mind that this clause requires the shares of a company residing in a contracting state to be listed on a stock exchange recognized by the tax treaty or by the competent authorities of the states that concluded the treaty. Generally, only stock exchanges located in one of the contracting states are recognized. Consequently, for example, a company residing in Spain whose shares are listed on the Amsterdam stock exchange would not comply with the stock exchange clause in the DTC between Spain and the U.S. Therefore, this clause limits the stock markets on which the shares of a company that wishes to claim access to the benefits of the treaty with the U.S. may be publicly traded.

In this respect, from an EU standpoint, a company residing in an EU Member State may not be publicly traded on just any stock exchange located in EU Member States if it wishes to access the treaty by means of this clause. Pursuant to this clause, generally the shares may only be publicly traded on stock exchanges located in the state in which the company is a resident. However, some treaties do expand the list of 'recognized stock exchanges' by including precisely those stock exchanges situated in other EU Member States.[29] However, this list is not expanded in all tax treaties and when expanded, it does not always include all the stock exchanges located in EU Member States.

This limit may be an obstacle to the free movement of capital regulated in Articles 63–66 of the TFEU (ex Articles 56–60 of the EC Treaty). Section III.B of the nomenclature of capital movements referred to in Article 1 of Directive 88/361 includes *inter alia*, the issue and placing of securities on a capital market. In respect of precisely this purpose, Directive 2001/34/EC of the European Parliament and of the Council of 28 May 2001 on the admission of securities to official stock exchange listing and on information to be published on those securities, aims to assure that any company

---

29. *See* section II.E.2.C, Chapter 3.

residing in a Member State may be quoted on the secondary markets located in Member States. As the tax treaties being studied limit the secondary markets on which shares can be listed, the stock exchange clause may be creating an obstacle to the free movement of capital. This clause prevents companies whose shares are listed on a stock exchange, other than those provided in the treaty, from obtaining the status of qualified resident by means of this clause.[30] In this respect, the stock exchange clause forces companies to be quoted on one of the recognized stock exchanges, which are normally those located in the state of residence, because on the contrary, they may not claim the benefits of the treaty. Moreover, the indirect publicly traded test is also of little help. If the shareholding is lower than what is established in the LOB clauses, the test will not be met. In addition, the shareholders need to be resident in one of the contracting states.[31]

Second, it is necessary to analyse the consequences of the property and base erosion clause on EU freedoms.

It can be observed that the first part of the clause, i.e. the ownership requirement, limits the application of the tax treaty to entities which are majority-owned by persons that reside in the same state as the company. If the company is more than 50 percent owned by taxpayers that do not reside in either of the contracting states, the ownership requirement will not be met and the company will be unable to access the treaty by means of this clause. Therefore, for example, a company residing in Spain, the majority of whose shares are owned by individuals residing in France will not comply with this clause for the purposes of the DTC between Spain and the U.S. Additionally, it should be borne in mind that the shareholders are also required to be qualified residents. As discussed earlier, this status is only conferred upon individuals, public bodies and entities that comply with the stock exchange clause, and depending on the treaty concluded, also those taxpayers that comply with the ownership and base erosion clause.

As all experts in this field have pointed out, this requirement can be an obstacle to the freedom of establishment regulated in Articles 49–55 of the TFEU (ex Articles 43–48 of the EC Treaty).[32] In particular, it could be a hindrance to the freedom of secondary establishment. The freedom of secondary establishment comprises the incorporation by an individual or legal entity operating a principal establishment within the territory of a Member State of a branch or subsidiary in another Member State.[33] The ownership clause hinders the incorporation of subsidiaries in other Member States, because, in the event that taxpayers residing in third states have a shareholding therein, these companies will be unable to claim the benefits of the tax treaties containing this clause, entered into by the state in which the company was established. A company incorporated by individuals or legal entities in another EU Member State will not be able to access the benefits of the treaty entered into by the

---

30. Calejo 2011, p. 90.
31. Calejo 2011, p. 90.
32. *See,* among others, Becker/Thömmes 1991, pp. 173–174, Eilers/Watkins 1993, p. 19, Vanistendael 1994, p. 306, Hinnekens 1995, pp. 228–229, Doyle 1995, p. 16, Martín Jiménez 1995, pp. 81–82, García Prats 2002, p. 183 and Calejo 2011, p. 90.
33. Abellán/Vilà 1998, p. 265.

state of residence as the majority of shares in the company are owned by residents in third states. From this standpoint, the ownership clause gives rise to a restriction on the freedom of establishment by the host state, i.e. the state in which the subsidiary is established. This restriction arises due to the fact that entities that are majority-owned by residents in states that are not a party to a DTC concluded between the host state and the U.S. are denied the benefits thereof.[34] Problems arise with respect to EU law if the shareholders are beneficiaries of the freedom of establishment provided in the TFEU. The ownership clause provides for treatment which differs based on the shareholders' residence.[35]

The ECJ judgment of 25 July 1991, *Factortame*, C-221/89, expressly states that criteria similar to that used by the ownership clause are contrary to the freedom of establishment. This judgment ruled on one of the requirements made by the U.K. to register vessels. For registration purposes, the owners of the vessel were required to be U.K. citizens or, in the case that the owner was a company, it was required to have been incorporated in the U.K.. Additionally, at least 75 percent of the company's capital stock was required to be owned by U.K. citizens. The ECJ considered this requirement to be contrary to the freedom of establishment. As can be evidenced, the requirement made under U.K. legislation is similar to that provided in the ownership clause.[36]

Moreover, in the *Open Skies* judgments, the ECJ ruled that a clause contained in a number of treaties concluded between EU Member States and the U.S. concerning air services was contrary to the freedom of establishment. These treaties allowed any contracting state to revoke, suspend or limit traffic rights to entities of another state when these entities were not owned by citizens of the contracting state. Therefore, for example, the ECJ's judgment on the C-466/98 case ruled that by concluding and applying an Air Services Agreement signed on 23 July 1977 with the U.S. which allows a non-member country to revoke, suspend or limit traffic rights in cases where air carriers designated by the U.K. are not owned by it or its nationals, the U.K. has failed to fulfil its obligations under Article 43 of the EC Treaty/Article 49 of the TFEU.

As pointed out by experts in this field, the ECJ's judgments on the *Open Skies* cases confirm that the LOB clauses, included in the tax treaties of various EU Member States that exclude from the treaty benefits those entities in the contracting state that

---

34. Vanistendael 2000, p. 53.
35. *See also* Article 55 TFEU (ex Article 294 EC Treaty) and Doyle 1995, pp. 16–17.
36. The purpose of the requirement under U.K. legislation was to prevent a phenomenon similar to treaty shopping. This requirement aimed to prevent citizens from other Member States, and fundamentally Spanish nationals, from registering vessels under the British flag in order to access the fishing quotas assigned to the U.K. by the European institutions (quota hopping). Nevertheless, it should be taken into account that the ECJ ruled that the stipulation of a condition for the purpose of assuring that the vessel has a real economic link to the state in which it was registered is not contrary to European law, as long as this link refers only to the relation between the vessels' fishing operations and the populations dependent on fisheries and related industries. Also, *see* the ECJ judgment dated 14 December 1989, on the *Jaderow*, C-216/87 case in addition to the judgment on the *Agegate Ltd*, C-3/97 case. As can be observed, this criterion does not refer to the ownership of the capital stock of the company to which the vessel belongs, but rather to the business activity the company is engaged in. Strictly speaking, this criterion refers to the company's business activity and the state in which it is incorporated. This matter referred to in the activity clause will be examined later.

Chapter 4: Limitation on Benefits Clauses and European Union Law

are controlled by more than a certain percentage of citizens from another Member State, might be in breach of Article 49 of the TFEU.[37]

The aforementioned conclusions are not prejudiced by the ECJ ruling of 12 December 2006, C-374/04, *ACT Group Litigation*. In this ruling, the ECJ considered that Articles 43 and 56 of the EC Treaty (Articles 49 and 63 of the TFEU) 'do not preclude a situation in which a Member State does not extend the entitlement to a tax credit provided for in a [tax treaty] concluded with another Member State for companies resident in the second State which receive dividends from a company resident in the first State to companies resident in a third Member State with which it has concluded a [tax treaty] which does not provide for such an entitlement for companies resident in that third State'. This ruling was made on the basis of most-favoured-nation treatment and not, as in the *Open Skies* rulings, on the basis of the freedom of establishment.

In the *ACT Group Litigation* cases, as well as in the *D* case,[38] the ECJ rejected the theory that the TFEU requires the granting of most-favoured-nation treatment.[39] However, the *Open Skies* rulings did not involve a claim regarding most-favoured-nation treatment. In the *Open Skies* judgments, the ECJ ruled that a company was being treated differently based on its shareholders place of residence.[40] In this regard, as experts in this field have already mentioned, the total absence of reference to the *Open Skies* judgments and the comparison with the most-favoured-nation treatment 'make it impossible to draw any conclusions from the [ACT Group Litigation case] as to the compatibility of LOB clauses with EU law'.[41] In fact, as referred above in section I of this chapter, the European Commission bases, the infringement procedure issued in 2015 against the Netherlands with respect to the LOB provision included in its tax treaty with Japan, on the ECJ's *Open Skies* rulings.

The second part of this clause, i.e. the base erosion requirement, may also negatively affect EU freedoms. The base erosion test effectively limits transactions between a taxpayer and persons residing in third states, which give rise to an expense deductible from its tax base. Generally, when the transactions with residents in third states give rise to deductible expenses amounting to over 50 percent of the entity's gross income, this requirement is not satisfied.

Therefore, it could also be concluded that the base erosion test restricts the freedom of establishment. As a result of the application of the tax treaty with the U.S., the consequences of performing a high number of transactions which give rise to a deductible expense in the state of residence, may dissuade taxpayers from establishing an entity in that state.

From the standpoint of the freedom to provide services, the same conclusion may be reached. The ECJ found that restrictive rules leading to greater difficulties in applying a tax deduction, when services are provided within the territory of another Member State rather than when they are provided within domestic territory, are in

---

37. Clark 2003, p. 25 and Martín Jiménez/Calderón 2003, p. 1217.
38. *See* the ECJ judgment of 5 July 2005, *D. v. Inspecteur van de Belastingdienst*, C-376/03.
39. Holfland/Pötgens 2011, p. 218.
40. Holfland/Pötgens 2011, p. 218.
41. Calejo 2011, p. 87. *See also* Plansky/Schneeweiss 2007, p. 493, De Broe 2008, pp. 1052–1057 and Kemmeren 2012, p. 172.

breach of the freedom to provide services.[42] In these cases, it is clear that the tax rule is a disincentive to those requesting a service, taking into account that they will avoid obtaining services from taxpayers residing in other states.[43] When the service is provided by a non-resident, the tax rule worsens the conditions under which the related expenses may be deducted. As pointed out by experts in this field, the ECJ's judgment in this regard is similar to the rule provided in Article 24(4) of the OECD Model.[44]

The effects of the base erosion clause are similar. Obviously, in these cases the clause does not affect the deductibility of an expense from the tax base. However, the provision of a service by a resident in a third state will affect the application of a treaty. To the extent that there are an increased number of transactions with taxpayers who are not qualified residents, it is likely that the maximum limit for compliance with this clause is exceeded. As in those cases analysed by the ECJ, this consequence will make the services provided less attractive to taxpayers that do not reside in the same state as the service provider.

Finally, the base erosion test could represent a mechanism that infringes the free movement of capital, 'since it discourages companies from freely operating, establishing limits to the natural flow of capital and dissuades companies from obtaining financing abroad'.[45]

The effects of the ownership and base erosion clause are only partially corrected in treaties that provide an expanded version of this clause.[46] The said treaties, take into account the shares owned by EU residents and the transactions therewith in the ownership and base erosion requirements. However, this expanded version does not resolve the problems that arise in relation to this clause for the reasons provided below.

First, not all residents of EU Member States are included, but rather only those who comply with the requirements of this clause.[47] Second, in some cases, it is essential that a part of these requirements is met by qualified residents in the entity's state of residence. The DTC between France and the U.S., before its amendment in 2009, required at least 30 percent of the shares representing the company's capital stock and voting power to be owned by qualified residents in France. The same requirement was contained in the DTC between the Netherlands and the U.S. before its amendment in 2004.[48]

---

42. *See* the ECJ judgment of 28 October 1999, *Vestergaard*, C-55/98.
43. With respect to the freedom to provide services, *see* the ECJ judgment of 28 April 1998, *Safir*, C-118/96.
44. *See* Martín Jiménez/Calderón 2000, p. 163 and Van Raad 1986, p. 173.
45. Martins 2016, p. 282.
46. Besides the persons residing in either of the contracting states, these types of clauses usually take residents in EU Member States into account. In some cases, the application of this special form of the base and ownership clause is conditional upon the fact that DTC of the 'EU shareholder or beneficiary's' state of residence does not establish a less favourable regime (derivative benefits clause).
47. As discussed in the previous chapter, the concept of EU Member State resident does not cover all persons who are residents in an EU Member State for tax purposes.
48. Kemmeren 1998, p. 141 and footnote 94.

Third, this expanded version of the clause does not always refer to all the income covered by the treaty. Generally, in the case of dividends, interest and royalties, compliance with the derivative or equivalent benefits clause is also required.[49] Pursuant to this clause, the related provisions of the clause only apply if, the treaty concluded between the source state and the state of residence of the taxpayer holding shares in the entity receiving the income, does not establish a less favourable tax regime. This clause is not complied with when the tax regime at source, of the treaty applicable to the shareholder, is more burdensome. Consequently, if a treaty contains a derivative benefits clause, the problems relating to the ownership and base erosion clause are not completely resolved, particularly in the case that requirements for the application of the treaty are not met due to the inclusion of this clause. Therefore, although this clause resolves some cases, it does not always do so.[50]

The third clause that should be compared with EU law is the activity clause. This clause requires that a trade or business be conducted in the state of residence, which is connected or incidental to the income obtained in the source state. Therefore, for example, if the whole of the trade or business of a company incorporated in the U.K. were conducted in Denmark, the activity clause provided in the DTC between the U.K. and the U.S. would not be complied with as the business activity is not conducted in the state of residence.

In relation to the activity clause, the scope of the EU freedom of establishment in respect of legal entities should be determined, bearing in mind that this clause has two aspects. The first aspect refers to the type of activity, and the second refers to the location of the activity conducted by the entity. The activity clause requires the activity to be of a business nature and to be conducted in the state of residence.

First, the requirement relating to where the entity's trade or business must be located will be addressed. Article 54 of the TFEU establishes when a company has a right to the freedom of establishment.[51] As evidenced, this rule provides flexible criteria. A company's right to the freedom of establishment will be protected under EU law as long as the company has been incorporated in accordance with the law of a Member State and has any of the following within the EU: its registered office, central administration or principal place of business.

In accordance with the above, two observations can be made. First, in principle, the company is not required to have been incorporated in the same state in which any of the three aforementioned elements are located. Accordingly, although a company is not engaged in the conduct of any activity in the EU, if it is incorporated in accordance with U.K. law, and its registered office is located in the U.K., it would be protected by the freedom of establishment. Second, pursuant to Article 54 of the TFEU, none of the

---

49. *See* section III.C, Chapter 3.
50. Malherbe/Delattre 1996, p. 20, Martín Jiménez 1995, p. 86 and Martins 2016, p. 288.
51. Article 48 TFEU states that 'Companies or firms formed in accordance with the law of a Member State and having their registered office, central administration or principal place of business within the Union shall, for the purposes of this Chapter, be treated in the same way as natural persons who are nationals of Member States. "Companies or firms" means companies or firms constituted under civil or commercial law, including cooperative societies, and other legal persons governed by public or private law, save for those which are non-profit-making'.

three aforementioned criteria are required to be met in the state in which the company was incorporated. Even though the company was incorporated in accordance with Dutch law, it is possible for its central administration to be located in Denmark.

As can be observed, only the latter two criteria, central administration and principal place of business represent a nexus of a factual nature to the EU territory.[52] The registered office, which is also stipulated in the TFEU, is not a nexus of this nature, but rather of a formal nature. However, based on various elements, it follows that the intention of EU law is not to grant protection to those companies with only a formal nexus to EU territory, as in the case of the registered office criteria.

In this respect, the General Programme of 1961 concerning the freedom of establishment stipulates that the activities of a company which only has a registered office within the Community must show a real and continuous link with the economy of one of the Member States. If this is not the case, it will not be considered to have been established for the purpose of enjoying protection under European law.[53]

Nevertheless, it is important not to lose sight of the fact that after having finalized the transitory period, it is questionable whether the aforementioned General Programme is still in force. In fact, having ended the transitory period for which these Programmes were drawn up, Articles 49 and the subsequent articles of the TFEU have a direct and unconditional effect, meaning that there are no grounds for any additional requirement not provided in Article 54 of the TFEU.[54] Along the same lines as the General Programme, the rejection of merely formal links can be observed in the regulations of EU secondary legislation in force relating to the freedom of establishment and the freedom to provide services, which can be said to embody a clear tendency of EU Law, namely the materializing tendency or principle.[55] The Council Regulation 2137/85/EEC of 25 July 1985 on the European Economic Interest Grouping stipulates that the central administration of the entities included in one of these groupings must be located in one of the Member States. In any case, it should be noted that it is not necessary for the entity to be incorporated in the same state as that where its central administration is located.

The terms of the Directives 2009/65/EC of the European Parliament and of the Council of 13 July 2009 on the coordination of laws, regulations and administrative provisions relating to undertakings for collective investment in transferable securities (UCITS), and 95/26/EC of 29 June 1995, amending several Directives in the fields of credit institutions and life insurance, are more restrictive. Both Directives require the entity's head office and central place of management to be located in the same legal order as the registered office for the purposes of the application of the Directive. An

---

52. Van Thiel 1989, p. 978, states that the Treaty has placed these different points of connection on the same level: the formal concept of registered office, the operating concept of central administration and the economic concept of principal place of business.
53. *See* paragraph 75 of the ECJ ruling of 5 November 2002, *Überseering*, C-208/00.
54. Garcimartín 2001, p. 94. However, it should be taken into account that the ECJ judgment mentioned in the previous footnote does not confirm that it is in force either. The judgment only refers to this Programme to indicate that the case being resolved is not the same as the case upon which a judgment was handed down.
55. Sancho 2001, p. 208.

Chapter 4: Limitation on Benefits Clauses and European Union Law

effective nexus of another type is not considered to be sufficient. This tendency appears to be partially confirmed in the Council Regulation 2157/2001, of October 2001, on the Statute for a European company (SE). Article 7 of the regulation establishes that the registered office of an SE shall be located within the EU, in the same Member State as its head office.[56] The regulation also provides a number of measures to guarantee that they are in the same state.[57] The Council Regulation 1435/2003 of 22 July 2003 on the Statute for a European Cooperative Society (SCE) regulates these matters in similar terms (*see* Article 6 of this Regulation).

This same tendency could be observed in the Proposal for a Directive of the Council on a common system of taxation applicable to interest and royalty payments made between associated companies of different Member States, which was presented by the Commission on 6 March 1998. As is common knowledge, this Proposal for a Directive gave rise to the approval of Council Directive 2003/49/EC of 3 June 2003 on a common system of taxation applicable to interest and royalty payments made between associated companies of different Member States, although modifications were made.

The 1998 Proposal for a Directive provided that it would be applied to companies residing in European Member States as in the case of the Parent-Subsidiary Directive. However, the Proposal for a Directive added a requirement not provided in the Parent-Subsidiary Directive. According to Article 3 of the Proposal, 'a company of a Member State' means [...] any company formed in accordance with the law of a Member State and having its registered office, central administration or principal place of business within the Community and whose activities present an effective and continuous link with the economy of that Member State'. The Proposal did not require the registered office, central administration or principal place of business to be established in the same state. However, it did include a requirement of a factual nature, in the regard that the company was required to maintain an effective and continuous link to the economy of the state in which the company was incorporated. This requirement was not made in the Directive that was finally approved in June 2003. Article 3 of the Directive only requires that the company take on one of the forms listed in the Annex.

From the aforementioned group of provisions, it may follow that the European legislator's intention was to include elements of a factual nature to allow companies to access the EU freedoms. In some cases, these links are only required to be materialized in one of the Member States, and in others, a link is required in the same state in which the company was incorporated.

Some ECJ judgments include this tendency of secondary EU Law. First, this tendency prevails in the judgments already mentioned, i.e. *Jaderow*, *Agegate* and

---

56. Nevertheless, it should be pointed out that Article 69(a) of the Regulation provides that 'five years at the latest after the entry into force of this Regulation, the Commission shall forward, to the Council and the European Parliament, a report on the application of the Regulation and proposals for amendments, where appropriate. The report shall, in particular, analyze the appropriateness of: (a) allowing the location of an SE's head office and registered office in different Member States'.
57. Garcimartín 2002, pp. 15–16.

Factortame. From these judgments, it follows that the states may include requirements to assure that the company has an effective economic nexus to the state in which the entity was incorporated. However, these judgments may not be the most appropriate on which to base a general rule of interpretation of Article 54 of the TFEU, since they refer to a very specific matter, i.e. the use of fishing quotas assigned to Member States.[58]

The judgments of 10 July 1986, on the *Segers*, C-79/85 case, of 9 March 1999, on the *Centros*, C-212/97 case and of 5 November 2002, on the *Überseering* case, provide a general interpretation of the contents of Article 54 of the TFEU. These judgments have no effect on any aspect regulated by secondary EU law as in the case of the judgments mentioned in the previous paragraph. They refer to companies incorporated in accordance with the law of a European Member State which carry on the whole of their trade or business or whose effective head office is located in another Member State. In paragraph 16 of the *Segers* judgment, the ECJ found that Article 54 of the TFEU 'requires only that the companies be formed in accordance with the law of a Member State and have their registered office, central administration or principal place of business within the Community. Provided that those requirements are satisfied, the fact that the company conducts its business through an agency, branch or subsidiary solely in another state is immaterial' (paragraph 16). Equally, in the *Centros* judgment, it was ruled that 'it is immaterial that the company was formed in the first Member State only for the purpose of establishing itself in the second, where its main, or indeed entire, business is to be conducted' (paragraph 17).

On the basis of these judgments two conclusions can be reached. In order to be protected under EU law, the companies are required to maintain a nexus of a factual nature with one of the EU Member States. This requirement is based on the concept of establishment.[59] However, this nexus is not generally required to be in the state in which the company was incorporated. It is sufficient that the nexus of a factual nature is located in any of the EU Members States, it is not necessary that it is located in the same EU Member State where the company was incorporated.

In summary, on the basis of the above judgments, two different rules are laid down in EU law, depending on whether certain elements are being harmonized or the ECJ's interpretation of Article 54 of the TFEU is being referred to. The Directives harmonizing the regime of financial institutions and insurance companies require the head office and place of management to be located in the state in which the company was incorporated. On the contrary, based on ECJ case law, links of a factual and legal nature to the same state are not required, regardless of the specific form thereof. Despite this inconsistency, it cannot be concluded that these Directives are contrary to Article 54 of the TFEU since special cases are taken into consideration. These Directives have been drawn up for companies which are special due to the fact that they operate

---

58. Paragraph 40 of the *Factortame* judgment states that 'a Member State may lay down conditions designed to ensure that the vessel has a real economic link with that State if that link concerns only the relations between that vessel's fishing operations and the populations dependent on fisheries and related industries'.
59. Martín Jiménez/Calderón 2000, p. 91.

in very regulated industries of the economy (financial institutions and insurance companies) in which this option may be justified due to the state control of these entities. However, this does not mean that a general regulatory model can be based on this special rule.

Despite the above, as pointed out by one author, the requirement provided in the 1998 Proposal for a Directive on interests and royalties may be concluded to be contrary to Article 48 of the EC Treaty (now Article 54 of the TFEU) based precisely on the interpretation made thereof by the ECJ in the *Segers* and *Centros* judgments.[60] In fact, the Proposal required the company 'to maintain an effective and continuous link to the economy of the state in which the company was incorporated'. Based on the *Centros* judgment, the taxpayer's right to the protection of the EC freedom of establishment is not conditional upon the above requirement. In this respect, the requirement provided by the Proposal for a Directive could lead to this freedom being restricted, as it effectively forces companies to establish a factual nexus to the state in which they are incorporated. In principle, according to the ECJ, a nexus can be established to any European state and does not necessarily have to be to the state in which the company was incorporated. Furthermore, the Proposal for a Directive did not regulate aspects relating to highly regulated industries of the economy as in the case of the Directives on financial institutions and insurance companies, in which this special rule could be completely justified. For the above reasons, it is perfectly understandable that the Directive finally approved in June 2003 eliminated this requirement.

Based on the above, some conclusions should be made in regard to this matter. In industries that are not expressly regulated by EU institutions, it may be concluded that a company's elements of a factual nature are not required to be located in the state in which the company was incorporated. However, for such an entity to be protected under EU law, these nexuses should be materialized in an EU Member State.

With respect to the activity clause provided in the tax treaties concluded between the U.S. and EU Member States, as previously discussed, it requires a company's trade or business to be located in the state in which the entity resides, or in other words, this clause only takes the business activity conducted in the state of residence into account. This requirement might be contrary to the freedom of establishment in the terms discussed above. Furthermore, it is important not to lose sight of the fact that this clause only takes into account the activity carried on in the state of residence. Any other trade or business conducted in an EU state would not be taken into consideration. In this respect, the fact that the activity clause only takes into account the trade or business conducted in the state of residence, ignoring any other activity conducted in an EU state, may also be contrary to the freedom of establishment.

This clause would effectively force an enterprise to incorporate a company in all the EU Member States in which it operates, and not only in the state in which it resides, in order for the treaty benefits concluded with the U.S. to be applicable to all the income

---

60. Weber 2000, p. 20.

obtained in the U.S.[61] In this respect, the activity clause might be contrary to EU law even in the event that this legal order were to impose the obligation to be engaged in the conduct of a business or trade in the state in which the company was incorporated. It should be noted that the freedom of establishment does not prevent, but rather fosters secondary establishments in other EU states through the formation of branches. These other activities, which are protected under EU law, would not be taken into account by the activity clause, as this clause only takes the activity conducted in the state of residence into consideration.

In conclusion, the activity clause may be contrary to EU law since it obligates entities to carry on a business activity in the state of residence. It may also be incompatible with EU law since it does not take the activity conducted by a certain company in other EU Member States into account. However, the DTC between the Netherlands and the U.S., prior to its amendment in 2004, partially corrected this aspect, as it also took the activity carried on in other EU Member States into account. Despite this fact, if this DTC is carefully analysed, it becomes clear that the requirements which must be met for the activities in other states to be taken into consideration are so strict that only in very specific cases does it make sense to resort to this 'expanded activity clause.'

The second aspect that should be compared with EU law refers to the type of activity conducted by the company that obtains the income. The activity clause will only be complied with if the company is engaged in the conduct of an active trade or business. In accordance with Article 22 of the U.S. Models and the LOB rule of Action 6 of the BEPS project, the management or making of investment is not considered to be a trade or business, except in the case of activities conducted by a financial institution, insurance company or security dealer, authorized for this purpose.

Regardless of the place in which the company carries on its operations, it can be concluded that Article 54 of the TFEU requires an economic activity to be conducted. The concept of economic activity is neither generally defined in the TFEU nor secondary EU legislation. However, in regard to Value Added Tax (VAT) a definition can be found in Article 9(1) of the Council Directive 2006/112/EC of 28 November 2006 on the common system of value added tax.[62]

---

61. Therefore, for example, in the case of a company residing in Spain with four branches in EU Member States, for the purposes of the Spain-U.S. DTC, only the activity that the company conducts in Spain would be taken into account. The only form in which the branches could claim the benefits of the treaty would be to incorporate a company in each state where the branches are located. Obviously, in these cases, the applicable tax treaty would not be the Spain-U.S. DTC, but rather the treaty concluded between U.S. and the states in which the branches turned into subsidiaries were located. If the conclusions reached by the ECJ in the judgment on the *Saint-Gobain*, C-307/97 case dated 21 September 1999 were applied to this case, the incompatibility of a clause worded in this manner and EU law could be sustained.
62. '"Taxable person" shall mean any person who, independently, carries out in any place any economic activity, whatever the purpose or results of that activity. Any activity of producers, traders or persons supplying services, including mining and agricultural activities and activities of the professions, shall be regarded as "economic activity". The exploitation of tangible or intangible property for the purposes of obtaining income therefrom on a continuing basis shall, in particular, be regarded as an economic activity'.

In the U.S. Models and the LOB rule of Action 6 of the BEPS project, activities conducted by financial institutions, insurance companies and securities dealers are considered to be within the scope of excluded activities ('business of making or managing investments'), unless conducted by authorized entities. Some tax treaties concluded between EU states and the U.S. do not provide for the case of securities dealers. Although these entities have received the corresponding authorization to operate, they may not access the convention by means of this clause. Within the EU, not only has the regime of credit institutions and insurance companies been harmonized, but also the regime of security dealers. The Directive 93/22/EEC of 10 May 1993 on investment services in the securities field was drawn up for this purpose.[63] In this respect, since this is an industry highly regulated by the authorities, meaning that the development of treaty shopping structures can be ruled out, this activity should have been provided for in all the tax treaties. As this is not the case, the activity clause may give rise to a restriction on the conduct of this activity, because it will not be possible for entities carrying on such activities to claim the benefits of the tax treaty by means of this clause.

Furthermore, the concept of business activity used in the tax treaties concluded with the U.S. might exclude holding companies. There may be grounds for this exclusion based on the ECJ's interpretation of economic activity in the Directive on VAT.[64] In this respect, the ECJ's rulings in this regard, which are summarized in the judgment on the *Cibo*, C-16/00 case of 27 September 2001, may be of significance.[65] The ECJ differentiates between two types of holding companies. On the one hand, there are companies which participate directly in the management of the entities in which it owns shares through the provision of certain services, and on the other hand, there are companies whose sole function is to hold and purchase shares. From an EU standpoint, it seems reasonable for the activity clause included in the tax treaties entered into with the U.S. to exclude this second type of holding company. However, the first type of holding company is not considered to be engaged in the conduct of an active trade or business for the purposes of the activity clause included in the U.S. Models, and in addition, to our understanding, it would not be considered to be a business activity in accordance with Action 6 of the BEPS project either.

As can be observed, the terms in which the concept of an active business or trade are defined in the tax treaty are very restrictive from an EU standpoint. Holding companies that directly participate in the management of the companies in which they

---

63. The contents of this Directive are now in the Directive 2004/39/EC of the European Parliament and of the Council of 21 April 2004 on markets in financial instruments amending Council Directives 85/611/EEC and 93/6/EEC and Directive 2000/12/EC of the European Parliament and of the Council and repealing Council Directive 93/22/EEC.
64. Kemmeren 1998, pp. 34-35.
65. Almudí/Serrano 2002, pp. 39-45. De Broe 2008, pp. 1.046, considers that there is not a lot of authority to base this interpretation of the term 'economic activity' on the VAT Directive. This author suggests another approach for the interpretation of Articles 49-54 of the TFEU. However, De Broe recognizes that his approach leads to the same result.

own shares may not access the benefits of the DTC by means of the activity clause. From the standpoint of EU law, this exclusion would not be justified, bearing in mind that for all purposes, these companies carry on an economic activity.[66] Moreover, as asserted by experts in this field, the activity clause may be an obstacle to the incorporation of companies regulated by the European Company Regulation, as one of its main purposes is to allow for the incorporation of holding companies which directly participate in the management of the companies in which shares are owned.[67]

Lastly, in light of EU law, it is necessary to examine the requirement that income obtained in the source state be connected to or incidental to the trade or business conducted in the state of residence in accordance with the activity clause. Based on a very restrictive interpretation of this clause, taxpayers could be deprived of the treaty protection in a large number of cases. This would occur if, the relation between the trade or business and the income were required to be connected to the activity carried on by the entity that pays the income in the source state. If the requirement were interpreted in this manner, the activity clause would only be complied with in the event that the same activities were conducted by both the payer and the recipient company. Therefore, this should not be the item of comparison. It should simply be verified that the income generated at source was obtained in the course of the trade or business conducted by the entity in the state of residence. Under these terms, this criterion is made more flexible for the purpose of reducing the possible restrictive consequences thereof.

Based on the above, in principle, it can be concluded that the activity clause is compatible with EU law. The requirement that the entity receiving the income must perform an active trade or business, is in accordance with the regulations on the freedom of establishment in primary and secondary EU legislation. However, based on the fact that the activity carried on in other EU states is not taken into account and that certain activities are excluded (entities providing investment services and active holding companies), the activity clause could be considered to be contrary to EU law.

Additionally, it is important not to lose sight of the fact that although this clause may be considered to be compatible, the position of the person that accesses the DTC's benefits by means of a clause that confers the status of qualified resident upon taxpayers is very different from that of a person that accesses these benefits by means of the activity clause. It should be noted that in the case of these taxpayers, tax treaty benefits are only granted in respect of income that complies with the activity clause and not in respect of the total income obtained, as in the case of taxpayers that comply with the ownership and base erosion clause. As previously discussed, the latter clause implies that the companies that are majority-owned by residents in EU Member States other than the state of residence will have no other option but to try to access the treaty

---

66. Martín Jiménez 1995, p. 83.
67. Becker/Thömmes 1991, p. 175.

by means of the activity clause, which places them in a less favourable position than that of those taxpayers that may access the treaty by means of the ownership and base erosion clause.[68]

Lastly, the bona fide clause should be analysed. Taxpayers that do not comply with any of the aforementioned clauses may request authorization of the application of the DTC from the corresponding authorities. The competent authorities should grant the tax treaty benefits when the taxpayer proves that one of the main objectives of the incorporation, acquisition and maintenance of the person in the state of residence and the performance of its operations from this state is not to enjoy the treaty benefits.

As pointed out by experts in this field, the bona fide clause may resolve some of the problems arising in relation to the compatibility of the aforementioned clauses with EU law.[69] Among the criteria provided in some of the Memorandums of the tax treaties being studied to specify how the bona fide clause should be applied, the fact that the state with which the DTC has been concluded is a member of the EU has been taken into consideration. By means of this clause, the competent authorities may take into account that the denial of the treaty benefits based on the application of the previously mentioned clauses may affect taxpayers protected under the right to the freedoms of the TFEU and secondary EU legislation. Therefore, for example, the Memorandum of the DTC between the Netherlands and the U.S. provides that cases in which a company entitled to the application of the DTC loses this right following a change in the ownership of its shares, will be taken into account in the event that the new owners of these shares is a resident in a EU Member State. The Memorandum also provides for cases in which the company expands its activities to other EU Member States.

Without a doubt, if the competent authorities take into account the position of taxpayers protected under EU law, it is possible that through the granting of benefits by means of this clause, the cases in which a conflict arises between the LOB clauses and EU law will be significantly reduced.[70] However, doubts regarding whether this will actually be the case in practice are justified. In the majority of cases, the U.S. will act as the source state, and the competent authorities deciding on this matter will be the

---

68. If the ECJ's reasoning in other cases were applied to this case, it could be asserted that this situation would be contrary to EU law. See ECJ judgments dated 13 July 1993, *Commerzbank*, C-330/91 and 15 May 1997, *Futura Participations*, C-250/95 y Caamaño/Calderón 1999.
69. Martín Jiménez 1995, p. 83, Hinnekens 1995, p. 228, Debelva/Scornos/Van den Berghen/Van Braband 2015, p. 142 and Martins 2016, p. 288.
70. For illustrative purposes, the competent authorities could allow companies to be listed on secondary markets in the EU Member States other than those recognized in the DTC. With respect to the ownership and base erosion clause, it could analyze whether the company's shareholders are persons protected by the freedom of establishment and whether the transactions are performed with persons protected by the aforementioned right to the freedom of establishment in addition to the freedom to provide services. With respect to the activity clause, it could take into account the trade or business conducted by entities that provide investment services in accordance with EU law, in addition those holding companies that directly participate in the management of the entities in which they own shares. Furthermore, they should take into account the activity conducted by a taxpayer in other EU Member States.

U.S. tax authorities.[71] The fact that a state which is not a member of the EU will use a legal order (EU law) not applicable thereto as a parameter may be paradoxical.[72]

In any case, if this parameter provided in some tax treaties to make a decision were effectively applied, access to the treaty by companies residing in EU Member States would be possible. However, even if this occurred, it cannot be concluded that the bona fide clause resolves all the problems relating to the incompatibility of the previously mentioned clauses with EU law.

The position of taxpayers claiming the benefits of a DTC by means of the bona fide clause as compared to those accessing the treaty by means of the previously analysed clauses is very different. First, it should be taken into account that the form of access utilized by these taxpayers is more burdensome. They are required to make the corresponding request to the competent authorities. The treaty will only be applicable in the event that the authorities decide in their favour. It is possible that this decision is handed down subsequent to the time at which the income is paid. If this is the case, these taxpayers will first be subject to the source state's tax regime and will be unable to apply the limits laid down in the DTC. Therefore, in the event that the source state tax authorities subsequently decide to apply the bona fide clause, these taxpayers would be obligated to request a refund of the amount exceeding the tax allowed by the treaty. In this respect, and particularly when the source state does not pay interest on the amount withheld when the corresponding amount is refunded, the affected taxpayer will be in a worse position than that of taxpayers to which the limits established in the tax treaty are applied at the time when the payer of the income withholds tax. Consequently, the access conditions are less advantageous.

Notwithstanding the above, the ECJ's judgments on the *Biehl*, C-175/88 case of 8 May 1990 and the *Schumacker*, C-279/93 case of 14 February 1995 should also be taken into account. From the ECJ's decisions, it follows that a procedure by which taxpayers may request the competent authorities to reconsider the discriminatory consequences of a certain regime does not justify a rule contrary to the freedoms regulated by the TFEU/EC Treaty.[73] According to the ECJ, it is not admissible for tax authorities to individually resolve cases where a generally established rule gives rise to discriminatory consequences if so requested by the taxpayer.[74] Finally, as it will be analysed in next section, the bona fide clause does not meet the ECJ's standards on anti-avoidance rules, as treaty benefits will be rejected when bona fide business purposes concur with the purpose of obtaining treaty benefits. Hence, the bona fide

---

71. It makes no sense for the opposite to occur, i.e. for the companies residing in the U.S. to request access to an EU Member State as a source state, by means of this clause. It should be noted that in these cases, these companies will not be protected under EU law. The only companies that will be considered to be U.S. residents in accordance with U.S. law will be the companies incorporated under U.S. law, since this is the only criterion used by this state's tax legislation to subject a company to tax in the U.S. on worldwide income. As previously observed, the companies protected by Article 54 of the TFEU are those incorporated in accordance with the law of an EU Member State.
72. Craig 2003, p. 71.
73. *See* paragraphs 56 and 57 of the *Schumacker* judgment.
74. Kemmeren 1998, p. 37 and Craig 2003, p. 73.

clause does not match EU law, which focuses on 'catching only the wholly artificial arrangements, as laid down in settled ECJ case law'.[75]

As observed, the bona fide clause does not resolve the problems relating to the LOB clauses from the standpoint of EU law. However, its importance should not be overlooked, as even though it does not resolve the matter of incompatibility, this clause will allow the taxpayer to achieve its objective, i.e. that the treaty be applied.

Based on an individualized analysis, it was possible to conclude that all of the LOB clauses do not provide coverage and, accordingly, treaty access to all taxpayers protected under EU law. Despite the fact that the bona fide clause may serve as an alternative means for the purposes of the application of the tax treaty, it does not formally resolve the problem of incompatibility, as this means of access is more burdensome than the others. The fact that, *a priori*, these rules are contrary to EU law does not mean that it is not possible to justify their existence from the standpoint of EU law.

Therefore, in the following section, an analysis regarding whether the system of access to the DTCs provided in these clauses may be encompassed under one of the legitimate grounds provided in the TFEU/EC Treaty and sustained by the ECJ. The analysis of this matter will lead to a study of these clauses from an overall standpoint rather than the individualized perspective detailed above.

III.A.2　*Legitimate Grounds for LOB Clauses: EU Law and Anti-avoidance Rules*

Once it has been demonstrated that the LOB clauses provided in the tax treaties concluded between the EU Member States and the U.S. may be contrary to EU freedoms, an analysis should be performed regarding whether there are legitimate grounds for these clauses, making it possible to conclude that these rules are compatible with EU law despite their discriminatory or restrictive effects.

In its different rulings, the ECJ has not only analysed whether a taxation measure was discriminatory or whether it gave rise to a restrictive effect on an EU freedom. The ECJ has also defined situations which should be safeguarded by a measure in accordance with a principle or, disapproved due to their discriminatory or restrictive effects.[76]

Most legitimate grounds on which the ECJ has ruled appear in the pleadings made by states to sustain the validity of domestic laws considered to be discriminatory or giving rise to a restrictive effect. In each case, the ECJ has established whether the legitimate grounds provided by the states were admissible. With respect to the field of taxation, it should be pointed out that the Court has only accepted the legitimate grounds argued by the states involved on very few occasions (reduction in tax revenue,

---

75. Martins 2016, p. 289.
76. García Prats 1998, p. 159.

counterbalancing advantages, the effectiveness of fiscal supervision, the balance and the reciprocity of the treaties, the need to ensure the coherence of the tax system, risk of tax evasion, etc.).[77]

In this study, each of the legitimate grounds on which the ECJ has ruled will not be studied. The LOB clauses will only be analysed in light of the grounds based on the risk of tax evasion. The ECJ has accepted this risk as legitimate grounds for domestic measures restricting fundamental freedoms, although in practice it is difficult to find cases in which these grounds have been pleaded.[78] In any case, we consider it appropriate to examine the LOB clauses from the standpoint of these grounds, bearing in mind that given the content of these types of rules, they are considered to be anti-avoidance rules.[79]

The LOB clauses were included in the DTCs analysed in order to counter treaty shopping. These rules aim to grant the benefits of a tax treaty only when the affected taxpayer has a sufficient nexus to the state of residence, or a real business purpose to obtain the income generated in the source state from this state. In this respect, these rules aim to prevent 'artificial structures' from receiving the protection of a tax treaty.

EU law does not prohibit EU Member States from adopting the measures required to deny the application of certain regimes in cases of tax evasion or avoidance. As is common knowledge, all of the states' legal orders provide mechanisms to counter tax avoidance.[80] Moreover, EU law protects the application of these measures in the rules adopted for the harmonization of direct taxation. Therefore, for example, Article 15(1)(a) of the Merger Directive provides that 'a Member State may refuse to apply or withdraw the benefit of all or any part of the provisions [of the Directive] where it appears that one of the operations [covered by the Directive] has as its principal objective or as one of its principal objectives tax evasion or tax avoidance.'[81] More recently, the EU has introduced a new common minimum anti-abuse rule in the Parent-Subsidiary Directive[82] and the Anti-Tax Avoidance Directive passed in 2016 that contains a general anti-abuse rule to counteract aggressive tax planning when other rules do not apply.[83]

The ECJ has also found that it is possible to use rules of this type against the abusive use of EU law. The ECJ's judgment on the *Dionisios*, C-373/97 case of 23 March 2001, indicates that 'Community law cannot be relied on for abusive or fraudulent ends [...]; although national courts may, therefore, take account – on the basis of objective evidence – of abuse on the part of the person concerned in order, where appropriate, to deny him the benefit of the provisions of Community law on which he seeks to rely, they must nevertheless assess such conduct in light of the objectives pursued by those provisions' (paragraphs 33–34).

---

77. See García Prats 1998, pp. 159–206, Van Thiel 2002, p. 531, Martín Jiménez/Calderón 2003 and paragraphs 50–51 ECJ judgment on *X e Y II*, C-436/00 case of 21 November 2002.
78. Martín Jiménez/Calderón 2003, p. 1230.
79. Martín Jiménez/Calderón 2003, p. 1240.
80. De Kleer 1996, p. 144.
81. Palao 2003.
82. Weber 2016 and Martín Jiménez/Calderón 2017.
83. Navarro/Parada/Schwarz 2016, pp. 123–125.

Chapter 4: Limitation on Benefits Clauses and European Union Law

Although EU law allows for the use of measures with these characteristics, i.e. rules against cases of tax avoidance, these are dependent on compliance with a number of requirements where the measures give rise to restrictive effects on EU freedoms.[84] The limits on the contents and use of these rules can be deduced fundamentally from the following ECJ judgments: 17 July 1997, *Leur-Bloem*, C-28/95; 16 July 1998, *ICI*, C-264/96; 9 March 1999, *Centros*, C-212/97; 21 November 2002, *X e Y II*, C-436/00; 12 December 2002, *Lankhorst*, C-324/00; 12 September 2006, *Cadbury Schweppes*, C-196/04; and 13 March 2008, *Thin Cap GLO*, C-524/04.[85] In this respect, it is important to point out that in all of these judgments, except the *Leur-Bloem* judgment, the ECJ has ruled on this matter by directly comparing these types of rules to EU freedoms, and particularly the freedom of establishment regulated in the EC Treaty/TFEU. On the contrary, in the case of the *Leur-Bloem* judgment, the ECJ ruled under the framework of the Merger Directive. As discussed in the previous paragraph, this Directive authorizes EU Member States not to apply this Directive when the main objective of the operation is tax evasion or tax avoidance. In our opinion, and although the necessary clarifications must be made, it can be concluded that the criteria used by the ECJ to judge anti-avoidance rules are similar in both cases.[86]

In this respect, it can be asserted that the ruling in the case of the *Leur-Bloem* judgment is nothing more than the application, to this specific case, of the criteria used by the ECJ in the rest of its judgments when considering whether measures, that may hinder or make the exercise of the rights to the fundamental freedoms regulated in the European treaties less attractive, are justified.[87] In fact, the ECJ has repeatedly stated that for these measures to be admissible they must be applied in a non-discriminatory manner, they must pursue a legitimate purpose and they must be appropriate and proportional to the achievement of the objective pursued.[88]

Accordingly, the ECJ's judgments can be summarized in the following manner. The ECJ allows for the application of anti-avoidance and anti-abuse rules giving rise to restrictive effects on EU freedoms only when formulated in such a manner they exclusively affect 'wholly artificial arrangements'. A wholly artificial arrangement is defined in the *Cadbury Schweppes* ruling as a 'structure that does not reflect an economic reality, with a view to escape the tax normally due on the profits generated by activities carried out on national territory'.[89] In this regard, the artificiality of the transaction is based on the absence of a business purpose that justifies the structure used, making it clear that the sole purpose of it is to avoid the tax that would normally

---

84. As pointed out by García Prats 2002, p. 204, EU law does not contain anti-avoidance rules, but rather establishes parameters for their admissibility.
85. Martín Jiménez 2012.
86. Therefore, for example, Martín Jiménez 1999a, p. 584, has stated in his comments regarding the *ICI* judgment that although it is 'not cited', here the ECJ is using the same argument as that used in the *Leur-Bloem* case in relation to the anti-abuse clause stipulated in the Directive on Mergers.
87. Martín Jiménez/Calderón 2003, pp. 1240 and 1265–1267.
88. García Prats 1998, p. 167.
89. Martins 2016, p. 277.

be payable.[90] The demonstration of a supportive business purpose is a sufficient element to exclude the existence of a wholly artificial arrangement.[91]

Taking the above into account, the ECJ does not allow for anti-avoidance rules of a general scope which may indiscriminately affect operations of good faith and artificial operations. As can be observed, the main factor analysed by the ECJ when verifying whether a domestic rule is admissible is not factual (the facts of the specific operation being judged), but rather legal and regulatory, i.e. its legal formulation, and particularly, the objective scope, the type of operations affected and the determinant factor for the anti-avoidance and anti-abuse rule to affect one type of operation or another.[92]

As these are the terms of the ECJ's ruling, it seems that these grounds may only be admissible when the domestic rule allowing for the denial of a certain tax regime, in the case where there is an abusive situation, is applied following an analysis of each case and an overall examination of the operation affected, in order to verify whether or not a wholly artificial arrangement exists. In our opinion, it is very unlikely that the state's specific anti-avoidance or anti-abuse rules are sufficient to comply with the requirements established by the ECJ when they give rise to restrictive effects on EU freedoms. In principle, from the standpoint of their legal and regulatory formulation, only GAARs comply with these requirements. In fact, the conditions of these rules are not those of a general measure in the sense stated by the ECJ (it does not exclude both cases of good faith and artificial operations) and these rules are applied on a case by case basis, following an overall examination of the operations affected.[93]

It is important to bear in mind that, the fact that a large majority of the specific anti-avoidance and anti-abuse rules would not be in line with EU law based on the ECJ's rulings, means that the states are divested of their power to counter international tax avoidance.[94] The fact that the states may resort to the use of GAARs does not completely resolve the above problem, bearing in mind the complexities involved in their application and their ineffectiveness from a practical standpoint to counter generalized cases of unlawful avoidance.

In any case, notwithstanding the criticism against the ECJ's rulings in this regard, the LOB clauses contained in the tax treaties between EU Member States and the U.S. should be examined to determine whether they are in accordance with these rulings. As can be expected, the response is negative.

In fact, the LOB clauses have been worded precisely in terms which are not accepted by the ECJ. As can be observed, the contents of the LOB clauses are based on the 'presumption' that all entities could be conducting avoidance schemes. This is due to the fact that these clauses only apply to legal entities, i.e. only legal entities are required to comply with the LOB clauses to access the treaty's regime, as treaty shopping structures are normally developed by means of legal entities. Individuals may claim the benefits of a treaty merely due to the fact that they are considered to be

---

90. Martins 2016, p. 289.
91. Martins 2016, p. 289.
92. Martín Jiménez/Calderón 2003, pp. 1228–1229.
93. García Prats 2002, p. 202 and Palao 2003.
94. Almudí 2003.

residents in one of the contracting states. Consequently, in the case of the access system provided by means of these clauses, each entity's establishment in the state of residence is not examined to determine whether the entity was incorporated there exclusively for tax purposes, and in particular, to claim the benefits of the DTCs concluded by that state.[95]

Regardless of whether or not a company has an avoidance purpose, it must previously comply with these clauses in order to be entitled to the application of the treaty.[96] Moreover, when none of the clauses established in the treaty are complied with, the taxpayer is required to prove that his principal objective is not tax avoidance by means of the general good faith clause. It would be difficult for such a situation to be in accordance with the criteria resulting from the ECJ's rulings, and particularly the *Leur-Bloem* judgment, since pursuant thereto, the tax authorities have the burden of proving in each case whether an entity is acting fraudulently, to be able to deny the entity's access to a certain tax regime. In the LOB clauses, and mainly in the event that the use of the bona fide clause is required, in each case the taxpayer has the burden of proving that it is not acting fraudulently for the purpose of being entitled to the application of the treaty.

In summary, it can be concluded that the LOB clauses provided in the tax treaties that have been analysed in this book, are not in line with the ECJ's rulings on legitimate grounds based on the risk of tax evasion. Despite the fact that the objective pursued by these clauses might be in accordance with EU law, as they aim to ensure that entities, without a sufficient nexus to the state of residence or a real business purpose to obtain the income generated in the source state from this state, enjoy the protection of the DTCs, the wording thereof gives rise to restrictive effects on EU freedoms.

In fact, at least in the case of the normal form of access, entities established in an EU Member State that are exercising EU freedoms, i.e. companies publicly traded on secondary markets (freedom of capital and payments), companies that are majority-owned by residents in other EU states (freedom of establishment), those performing transactions with non-resident EU members that give rise to deductible expenses (freedom to provide services and the right of establishment), and those that mainly conduct activities in states other the state in which they reside (freedom of establishment) will not be entitled to a treaty's regime. These effects are clearly disproportionate as they 'presume' that there is abusive conduct in these cases, which may not be true, especially if the companies are effectively exercising EU freedoms. It should be noted that EU law does not protect companies without a nexus of a factual nature to EU territory, nor does it consider the company to have a real business purpose when its corporate purpose is solely the purchase and holding of shares.

The excluded entities may only access the treaties by means of the general good faith clause. Although the competent authorities may value the 'EU factor' for the

---

95. García Prats 2002, pp. 183, 199 and 220, stated that the LOB clauses are not in accordance with EU law as they are worded like a 'general anti-abuse clause which prevents the analysis of the consideration of the situations affected case by case, thus preventing non-abusive situations from avoiding the consequences thereof, and thereby undermining the requirements of the principle of reciprocity'.
96. Caamaño/Calderón/Martín Jiménez 2000, p. 425.

purpose of deciding favourably on the request, this clause does not resolve the problem relating to the fact that these taxpayers are in a less advantageous position than other taxpayers. Consequently, based on the above and given the contents of the LOB clauses, they are not compatible with EU law when the taxpayers affected effectively exercise their rights to the freedoms that this legal order recognizes. Moreover, the existence of such clauses cannot be justified in accordance with the criteria established by the ECJ.

In order for the LOB clauses to be consistent with EU law, they should have been established in such a manner that they would provide coverage to the cases protected under EU law. In this respect, they should authorize companies publicly traded on any EU secondary market to claim the treaty benefits, and take into account the shares and transactions affecting the taxpayers protected under EU law for the purposes of the ownership and base erosion clause. Furthermore, the activity clause should neither exclude companies that are authorized to provide investment services, nor holding companies that participate directly in the management of the companies in which they own shares. In line with the parameters of the ECJ judgments, this would not exclude denying the application of the treaty where EU freedoms were evidenced to be exercised in an abusive manner. It should be noted that in this case, the rule would not deny a certain regime without individually analysing whether a company is involved in a wholly artificial arrangement.

In any event, as it was highlighted in section I of this chapter, in the 2016 Anti-Tax Avoidance Package, the European Commission does not recommend EU Member States to include LOB clauses in tax treaties which they might conclude among themselves or with third countries. Instead, the Commission's Recommendation of 28 January 2016 on the implementation of measures against tax treaty abuse advises Member States to follow Action 6 BEPS's proposal of including in tax treaties a general anti-abuse rule based on a PPT rule.[97] In this regard, the Recommendation introduces some modifications in the wording of the BEPS' PPT rule in order to align it with the case law of the ECJ as regards the abuse of law. The GAAR contained in the Recommendation reads as follows:

> Notwithstanding the other provisions of this Convention, a benefit under this Convention shall not be granted in respect of an item of income or capital if it is reasonable to conclude, having regard to all relevant facts and circumstances, that obtaining that benefit was one of the principal purposes of any arrangement or transaction that resulted directly or indirectly in that benefit, unless it is established that *it reflects a genuine economic activity* or that granting that benefit in these circumstances would be in accordance with the object and purpose of the relevant provisions of this Convention.

Moreover, once the restrictive effects of the LOB clauses in the tax treaties analysed has been evidenced, in addition to the inexistence of legitimate grounds for such effects, it is important to determine the consequences of such incompatibility. Paraphrasing the words of Vanistendael, although it may be simple to assert the

---

97. EU 2016b.

Chapter 4: Limitation on Benefits Clauses and European Union Law

incompatibility of the LOB clauses provided in the DTCs concluded with the U.S., determining the manner in which this issue may be resolved and the consequences thereof is more significant.[98] These matters are addressed in the following section.

III.B Treaties Between EU Member States

This section refers exclusively to the tax treaties concluded between EU Member States. For illustrative purposes, only the treaties containing rules against treaty shopping entered into by Spain and EU Member States are referred to. These are the tax treaties that Spain has concluded with Belgium, Croatia, Estonia, Ireland, Latvia, Lithuania, Portugal and Slovenia.[99] These treaties follow the first method or approach against treaty shopping provided in the Commentaries on Article 1 of the 2003-2014 OECD Model (paragraph 13). In particular, they establish a look-through provision that is very similar to the ownership clause provided in the second method or approach provided in the Commentaries on Article 1 of the 2003–2014 OECD Model, although in these tax treaties the look-through clause only affects certain income (dividends, interest, royalties and capital gains). The company receiving this income, loses the right to the application of the DTC if it is over 50 percent owned or controlled directly or through one or more companies who are not residents of a contracting state. However, if a company is engaged in substantive business operations in the contracting state where it is a resident, other than the simple management of securities or other assets, it will not be excluded from the application of a DTC.

In view of the contents of this clause, it is to our understanding that the same arguments that served to explain the incompatibility of the LOB clauses provided in the DTCs entered into with the U.S., also apply in this case, and accordingly, the same conclusion can be reached. The ownership clause excludes all entities in which shares are owned by taxpayers that exercise the right to the EU freedom of secondary establishment. The fact that the application of the DTC is not denied where a company is engaged in the conduct of a business or trade may resolve the problem of incompatibility. However, the same problems arise as in the case of the activity clause provided in the DTCs analysed. Only the business activity conducted in the state of residence is taken into account. Furthermore, based on the definition of the concept of activity, it appears that holding companies that participate in the management of the companies in which it owns shares will also be excluded. If the tax treaties were not applied in these cases, as in case of the clauses discussed in the previous section, these clauses would be contrary to EU law in the event that taxpayers protected under this legal order are affected.[100]

The same conclusion may not be reached in respect of the exclusion clause provided in the DTC between Spain and Luxembourg, which was also provided in the majority of DTCs entered into by Luxembourg with EU Member States. Under the Law

---

98. Vanistendael 1994, p. 306, states that 'it may be easy to say that a treaty provision is in conflict with community law, it is more difficult to decide what to do about it'.
99. See Vega 2016 and De Broe 2008, pp. 1.039–1.043.
100. Caamaño/Calderón/Martín Jiménez 2000, pp. 425–426 and De Broe 2008, pp. 1.058–1.059.

of 1929, the Luxembourg holding companies are excluded from the scope of the convention's application. This exclusion may be justified from the standpoint of EU law, since no trade or business is conducted in the respect expressed by the ECJ in regard to VAT. This conclusion may also be supported by the fact that this regime was included within the measures that meet the requirements of the EU Code of Conduct to consider a tax regime to be harmful. Although the Code is not a regulatory instrument, it is an important reference point for these purposes.[101]

Although the exclusion method is not included in the system used by the LOB clauses to determine whether access to the regime of the treaties entered into with the U.S. will be granted, its use gives rise to a problem which should be discussed briefly.

As was previously pointed out, this method is used to exclude certain tax regimes created by EU Member States which have been authorized by the Commission despite the fact that they are considered to provide state aid within the meaning of Articles 107 and 108 of the TFEU. The intention of these regimes is to foster the development of certain EU territories by means of creating a favourable tax regime that serves to attract investments in this territory. Obviously, the establishment of a regime with such characteristics is not the only means by which to foster the development of these territories, but is the means used in practice and authorized by the Commission.

The objectives which are meant to be achieved through the creation of these low-tax areas can be seriously affected by the establishment of rules which exclude the application of other taxation rules in the event that transactions are performed with entities in these territories. One example of such a rule might be the exclusion clause. The entities established in these territories will not enjoy the protection of the treaty. Particularly when provided in treaties concluded between Member States, these exclusions might be considered as contrary to EU law. The reasons for such incompatibility would not exclusively be those discussed in the case of the LOB clauses. In this case, it would be important to value the extent to which the other EU Member States are obligated by the fact that the Commission has authorized this regime.[102] If the other states are effectively obligated, these states should aid this regime in achieving the desired effects by being obligated to not include an exclusion clause in the treaties concluded with the states in which the affected territory is located.

The ECJ has made no judgment in this respect. However, it is important to note that it is possible to assume that the other states are obligated to not adopt measures which prevent the achievement of the objectives of the regimes authorized by the Commission. Despite the fact that this may be the case, two doubts arise in this respect. In principle, if the measure adopted to foster the development of the affected areas were, for example, the granting of a subsidy, the above problem would not arise.

---

101. *See* Brekelmans 2003.
102. This idea has been noted by Raventós 1995, pp. 71–72 and Vanistendael 2001, p. 159. Rädler/Lausterer/Blumenberg 1997, p. 93, state that the adoption of measures by the EU Member States against these regimes authorized by the Commission, is contrary to the principle of Community loyalty (ex Article 10 EC Treaty, now principle of sincere cooperation under Article 4(3) of the TEU). However, the author that has analyzed this matter in detail, referring particularly to the Madeira area regime is De Sampayo 1997.

Second, if it could effectively be sustained that the rest of the states have an 'obligation not to act', this situation would not be in line with the measures undertaken in the EU through the approval of the Code of Conduct. Moreover, as previously discussed in another section of this study,[103] the inconsistency of the EU's measures in this regard can be criticized, as, for example, on the one hand, in the past it authorized the Portuguese regime of the Madeira area, and on the other hand, it qualified it as a 'harmful tax measure' in application of the Code of Conduct.[104] In this respect, it seems reasonable to require a higher degree of consistency in the EU policy on tax matters.

IV CONSEQUENCES OF THE INCOMPATIBILITY OF THE LOB CLAUSES WITH EU LAW

IV.A Tax Treaties with Third States: The EU Member State's Liability for Damages in the Case of a Breach of EU Law

As in the previous section, the consequences of the incompatibility of the LOB clauses will be analysed by separating the tax treaties concluded with third states and mainly with the U.S., from the tax treaties concluded between EU Member States. As shall be observed, in both cases, the consequences are very different from a material standpoint. There is a very simple explanation for this difference. In the first group of cases, one of the contracting states is not a member of the EU and, accordingly, does not fall under the scope of the application of EU law.

This study will commence with the first case, i.e. tax treaties concluded between EU Member States and the U.S. Beforehand, it is necessary to make a number of clarifications, which to a certain extent, will condition the scope of the consequences of the possible incompatibility between the clauses included in these treaties and EU law.

First, it should be taken into account that the LOB clauses established in the tax treaties being studied, were included at the request of a contracting state which is not a member of the EU, i.e. the U.S.[105] The EU Member States were obligated to include these clauses in the tax treaties entered into with the U.S. In many cases, the renegotiation of the already existing treaties was mainly a result of the U.S.' intention to include these clauses therein. It is unlikely that the conclusion of the treaties would have been possible if the EU Member States had refused to accept their inclusion. Therefore, it can be concluded that it was not the EU Member States that promoted the

---

103. *See* section I.C, Chapter 3.
104. An example in which there is a certain degree of consistency is in the Portugal-Netherlands DTC (1999). In the body of this treaty, it is stated that the following residents shall not be entitled to the application of the benefits provided by the DTC for taxation at source: residents of a contracting state which benefit from tax measures which are harmful within the meaning of the EU Code of Conduct for business taxation. However, tax measures shall not be considered harmful if they are accepted and to the extent they are authorized by the European Community as an appropriate support for the economic development of a particular area. *See* Van Den Ende/Smit 2001, p. 101.
105. Van Unnik/Boudesteijn 1993, p. 113.

inclusion of these clauses. In fact if these provisions had not been accepted, it is likely that the corresponding tax treaties would not have been concluded. This would have given rise to a more burdensome situation, i.e. the lack of a treaty.

Moreover, in the hypothetical case that it were possible to enter into a tax treaty that did not include the LOB clauses, in the case that the EU Members States were to allege that they could not accept the inclusion of the clauses as a result of their obligations as EU Member States, the problem would still not have been resolved in practice. As once stated by Philip Morrison (former head of the U.S. tax negotiation delegation of the DTC between Ireland and the U.S.), the fact that the ECJ were to rule that the EU Member States could not accept the inclusion of the LOB clauses would not represent an obstacle for the U.S. Congress to unilaterally adopt similar rules.[106] Therefore, it can be asserted that if these clauses were not included in the DTCs entered into by the EU countries the problem of incompatibility with EU law would be formally resolved, but the core problem would still exist, i.e. the treaties might not be applied, since under U.S. legislation similar unilateral rules would have been adopted.[107]

Therefore, the reasons that have led EU Member States to accept these rules are perfectly understandable. First, if they had not established a bilateral rule such as the tax treaties, a unilateral rule would have been adopted by the U.S. Second, through the inclusion of these rules in the treaties, the EU Member States have been able to force these rules to be adapted to the assumptions on which EU law is based in the negotiation process. Although the system for accessing the treaty established by these LOB clauses has not been fully adapted to EU law, the result achieved is much more in accordance with EU law than expected, for example, in the U.S. Model. Moreover, by means of the bona fide clause, a large number of the taxpayers protected under EU law that do not comply with any of the previous clauses may still access the treaty. Although this clause does not resolve the problem of the LOBs' incompatibility with EU law, at least it allows the taxpayers to claim treaty benefits.

Lastly, with respect to the above clarifications, it is important to point out that the degree to which the different tax treaties, concluded with the U.S. have been brought into line with the assumptions on which EU law is based, differ. In this respect, a contributing factor is that the treaties have been concluded at different times. It can be evidenced that the extent to which the 'EU phenomenon' is taken into account in the text of the more recent treaties is greater than in the case of older treaties. The experience acquired from previous treaties, and particularly following the conclusion of the DTC between the Netherlands and the U.S. (1992) has essentially contributed to this fact. However, it is important to bear in mind that each state's 'negotiating power' may have also motivated this phenomenon.

Taking into consideration the above clarifications, the consequences of the possible breach of EU law should be analysed. This analysis will be based on the following case, which is the one that normally occurs. Imagine a company residing in

---

106. Winandy 1996, p. 27.
107. Van Unnik/Boudesteijn 1993, p. 114.

Chapter 4: Limitation on Benefits Clauses and European Union Law

an EU Member State that obtains income in the U.S. In this case, the source state (U.S.) is a state that is not a member of the EU. The state of residence in which the company is located is an EU Member State.

The company residing in the U.S. will request the application of the DTC in respect of the income obtained in the U.S. In the case that none of the LOB clauses are complied with, the company must request that the treaty be applied to the U.S. competent authorities (bona fide clause). Among the reasons that may be alleged is the fact that the entity is protected under its right to one of the EU freedoms. Therefore, for example, a company residing in Spain, the majority of whose shares are owned by residents in France could allege that in accordance with the EU treaties, the shareholders exercise their right to the freedom of secondary establishment. Problems will arise in the case that the third state acting as the source state denies the application of the treaty despite the fact that the affected taxpayer is acting under the protection of EU law.

Also, from the state of residence's standpoint, by means of the application of the treaty, the state which acts as such will authorize the application of the measures provided in the treaty to eliminate double taxation when one of the LOB clauses is complied with. If none of the clauses are complied with, the taxpayer may request the application of the treaty by means of the bona fide clause, alleging, among other reasons, that it is protected under EU law. The problems relating to EU law will also arise when the aforementioned measures are denied even though the taxpayer is effectively protected under EU law.

In the first case, where the entity has a relationship with the source state, it would be difficult to find a solution as a third state cannot be required to apply the treaty in view of its obligations under EU law.[108] This conclusion is based on the ECJ's judgment on the *Saint-Gobain* case. This judgment refers to a PE located in an EU country which requested the application of the measures to prevent double taxation provided in the tax treaty concluded with a third state. The matter addressed was whether the PE could claim the application of the measures provided for taxation in the source state. The court's judgment was negative. Although EU freedoms have a direct effect, this effect is not extended to non-Member States.[109] Furthermore, as shall be observed below, in accordance with the ECJ's rulings on state liability for breach of EU law in its judgment on the *Francovich*, C-9/90 case of 19 November 1991, the third state cannot be required to repair the damages caused by the failure to apply the tax treaty at source. Only Member States can be held liable for damages in the event of a breach of EU law.[110]

However, the issue is clearly different where the entity requests the application of the treaty in its state of residence, as long as this state is a member of the EU. In principle, even though the context of this judgment is different, if the ECJ's

---

108. As stated by Calderón 2002, p. 21, EU law does not give rise to legal effects for states which are not members of the EU.
109. As pointed out by Martín Jiménez/Calderón 2002, p. 114, it would be different if in these cases it could be concluded that on the basis of the principle of EU loyalty these states are obligated to attempt to guarantee compliance with EU law when negotiating or renegotiating their DTCs with third states. This issue will be addressed later.
110. Alonso 1997, p. 20.

considerations in the *Saint-Gobain* ruling are applied to this case, the state of residence will be obligated to apply the measures to eliminate double taxation provided in the tax treaty. In this respect, as long as the taxpayer involved is protected by the EU freedoms, the state will be thus obligated, even though none of the convention's clauses are complied with and the application of the convention was not authorized by means of the bona fide clause. If the state of residence were to deny the application of the measures to eliminate double taxation established in the convention, it would be restricting the scope of EU freedoms.

However, the problem is not resolved simply by means of applying the measures to eliminate double taxation provided in the tax treaty. In principle, the state of residence will only be obligated to apply these measures insofar as the treaty allows. Therefore, for example, if the tax treaty with the U.S. provides an ordinary credit method to eliminate double taxation on royalties, and the treaty authorizes the source state to levy a maximum tax of 5 percent of the gross amount thereof, the state of residence will only be obligated to allow for a tax credit of this amount, and not for all of the tax levied at source. It is likely that the tax levied in the source state will be higher in the event that the limits provided in the DTC are not applied at source. Furthermore, if the treaty establishes that the exemption method will be applied to eliminate double taxation, the state of residence will only be required to allow for this exemption, but it would not be held liable for the higher tax to which the taxpayer is subject in the source state as a result of not applying the treaty.

In essence, the issue that needs to be addressed is whether the EU Member State acting as the state of residence is obligated to place the taxpayer in the position in which it would have been if the treaty had been applied. Imagine the following case. The DTC with the U.S. authorizes the source state to levy a maximum tax of 5 percent on dividends. If there is no applicable DTC, the tax levied amounts to 30 percent under U.S. legislation. Correspondingly, the state of residence should eliminate the double taxation by means of the exemption method. Although the state of residence were to apply the DTC, the taxpayer's position would not be the same based on a comparison of the position of a taxpayer that has obtained the protection of the DTC at source and a taxpayer that has not had the same luck. In this case, the tax levied on the income of the latter would be six times the tax levied on the former. The former is subject to a tax rate of 5 percent and the latter to a tax rate of 30 percent, which is the tax established under U.S. legislation. The question is whether the state of residence would be obligated to refund the difference.

As pointed out earlier, this question gives rise to the problem of the EU states' liability for damages where a breach of EU law occurs.

First, it should be noted that the fact that there has been a breach, from an institutional standpoint, could result in the Commission commencing infringement proceedings in accordance with Article 258 of the TFEU (ex Article 226 of the EC Treaty).[111] As a last resort, the commencement of such proceedings may give rise to a finding against the state by the ECJ. However, this judgment will not affect the validity

---

111. Article 259 of the TFEU (ex Article 227 of the EC Treaty) also provides that any Member State which considers that another EU Member State has failed to fulfil an obligation under the EU

of the agreement or be binding on the third state from an international law standpoint. Furthermore, in accordance with Article 260 of the TFEU (ex Article 228 of the EC Treaty), the EU Member State will be obligated to adopt the required measures to comply with the judgment, and for this purpose, should use all the means within its reach under international law to withdraw from the agreement. Its withdrawal from the treaty in the terms permitted under international law will ultimately be the solution.[112]

This does not appear to be the solution to the problem. Private persons do not have legal capacity to initiate infringement proceedings. Even if they had such legal capacity, their situation would remain unchanged since a finding against the state, does not, per se, grant the right to the repair of damages, i.e. for the private person to be placed in the same position as it would have been in if the treaty had been applied. Moreover, as a result of this verdict, the affected EU Member State will be under the obligation to adopt all measures required to withdraw from the agreement, which in our opinion, would lead to greater harm, if we place ourselves in the position of the taxpayers that are entitled to the application of the DTC.[113]

Faced with this problem, the only possible solution consists in determining whether the states of residence that are EU Member States will be held liable to pay the damage caused in cases of breach. In this respect, the conditions which must be met for an infringement of EU law to give rise to a Member State's liability should be examined.[114] It is important to bear in mind that mere infringement does not automatically (give rise to) the liability of the state in breach.[115]

The enforceability of liability to pay for damages is not conditional upon a previous judgment by the ECJ for breach.[116] It is sufficient for such an infringement to have occurred and for the conditions required under ECJ case law to have been met. These conditions are as follows E Bas: The infringed EU rule must confer rights upon an individual (being indifferent as to whether or not he enjoys the direct effect thereof); the infringement, due to an action or failure to act by any of the state bodies should be a sufficiently serious breach; and there must be a direct causal link between the infringement of the obligation imputed to the state and the damage suffered by the victims.

The first controversial matter consists in determining whether EU law confers a right upon the affected taxpayers in this particular case. In principle, the reduction of tax at source is a result of the conclusion of the treaty. In the case that the treaty had not been entered into, the taxpayer would not be entitled to any reduction in the source

---

treaties may bring the matter before the Court of Justice. It would be unlikely for this to occur in this case, bearing in mind that almost all EU Member States are potentially in breach.
112. Díez-Hochleitner 1998, p. 147. The above would only be applicable to the DTCs signed after the entry in force of the TFEU/EC Treaty or the accession of the corresponding state. The TFEU establishes a special regime for previous treaties, which is that provided in Article 351 (ex Article 307 of the EC Treaty). This rule only obligates the EU Member State involved to adopt 'all appropriate steps to eliminate the incompatibilities established'.
113. Hinnekens 1995, p. 228 and Doyle 1995, p. 20.
114. See Díez-Hochleitner/Martínez 2001, p. 321, Barav 1996 and Alonso 1997.
115. Alonso 1997, pp. 71–72.
116. Díez-Hochleitner/Martínez 2001, p. 321.

state. The same case occurs when a treaty is concluded between two EU Member States. The reduction of non-resident tax is made in accordance with the treaty and does not stem from EU law.

The only rights granted under EU law correspond to the rights to exercise EU freedoms. The EU Member States are obligated to respect these rights, and accordingly, are prohibited from adopting measures which hinder the exercise thereof. As previously discussed, the LOB clauses create an obstacle to these freedoms whenever these clauses do not allow certain taxpayers, protected under EU law, to claim the benefits of the treaty. Moreover, in most cases, the excluded taxpayers are precisely those that effectively exercise these freedoms. From this standpoint, the existence of a right could be evidenced. When there is a rule, which in this case would be a rule contained in the treaty, that provides for discriminatory treatment based on whether or not the taxpayers exercise EU freedoms, the corresponding states must compensate the affected taxpayers since they are in breach of the obligation to not create obstacles to the exercise of EU freedoms, and consequently the right to be treated in the same manner as though it were a national of that state. It should be noted that the taxpayers that normally comply with the LOB clauses are those that do not exercise EU freedoms, such as companies publicly traded on a secondary market located in the state in which they reside or companies wholly owned by individuals residing in the same state.

Arguments justifying the conferral of a right on individuals can also be found in the *Saint-Gobain* judgment. As a consequence of this judgment, the state of residence is obligated to apply the measures to eliminate double taxation included in the treaty concluded with a third state to PEs located within the state's territory. These measures are not provided under EU law, but rather under a treaty. The obligation to also apply them to PEs is a consequence of the obligation to not adopt measures that restrict the establishment in this state by taxpayers exercising EU freedoms. However, in the case described above, solely applying the measures to avoid double taxation does not resolve the problem created by the measure that is contrary to EU law. It is also necessary to compensate the damages suffered in the source state. In this respect, the conferral of a right upon a taxpayer could be sustained, although it should be recognized that this may be difficult to evidence.

If the fact that a right has been conferred upon an individual is recognized, we consider that there will be no problems relating to the acceptance of the fact that there is a causal link between the infringement and the harm. The harm is a result of the fact that the treaty was not applied in the source state, precisely because the access criteria laid down in the LOB clauses are contrary to EU law.[117]

---

117. Alonso 1997, p. 102. However, Terra/Wattel 2012, p. 163, consider that the causal link between the alleged damages and the tax treaty negotiation result seems very doubtful. In this regard, 'if the EU Member State concerned had not agreed to the LOB clause insisted upon by the third State, no tax treaty, or at least no reduction of source taxation would have been concluded at all. Insisting on a third State waiver of LOB clauses would have jeopardized the very treaty negotiation result'.

Finally, most doubts arise in regard to the nature of the infringement, i.e. whether there is a sufficiently serious breach. The infringement will be of this nature if a Member State obviously and seriously violates the limits imposed at its own discretion when applying EU law.

The ECJ has identified two cases in which the violation of EU law should be considered to be a sufficiently serious breach. First, as established in the judgment on the *Braserie du pêcheur*, C-46/93 and C-48/93 cases of 5 March 1996, a breach of EU law will clearly be sufficiently serious if it has persisted despite a judgment finding the infringement in question to be established, or a preliminary ruling or settled case law of the Court on the matter from which it is clear that the conduct in question constituted an infringement. Second, in the judgment on the *Dillenkofer*, C-178/94 case of 8 October 1996, the ECJ ruled that non-transposition of a directive within the prescribed time limit of itself amounted to a sufficiently serious breach.

Besides these two judgments, in the case of the *Braserie du pêcheur* judgment, the ECJ established the following criteria to determine, in a specific case, whether the violation imputed to a Member State can be considered to be a 'sufficiently serious breach': the clarity and precision of the rule breached, the measure of discretion left by that rule to the national or Community authorities, whether the infringement and the damage caused was intentional or involuntary, whether any error of law was excusable or inexcusable, the fact that the position taken by a Community institution may have contributed towards the omission, and the adoption or retention of national measures or practices contrary to Community Law.

As pointed out by experts in this field, if these criteria are taken into account, it would be difficult to conclude that there is a sufficiently serious breach in the case of the LOB clauses.[118] This case cannot be brought within either of the two ECJ judgments which assert the existence of a sufficiently serious breach. This is not a case in which the application of a Directive is not appropriate nor has the ECJ ruled that these clauses are incompatible. Moreover, so far the Commission has never referred an infringement proceeding in this regard to the ECJ, despite the fact that experts assert the incompatibility of the LOB clauses, and the Ruding report itself and other documents from the Commission warn that these rules may be contrary to EU law.[119] However, this does not mean that an infringement procedure may be referred to the ECJ in the near future, especially due to the procedure initiated against the Netherlands on 19 November 2015 concerning the LOB provision contained in the Dutch-Japanese DTC. However, it should be highlighted that this treaty, is not a treaty signed with the U.S.

Furthermore, it cannot be concluded that the infringed freedoms establish clear and precise obligations in this regard. EU law does not require Member States to correct the discriminatory actions of third parties. In the past there were already effects similar to those caused by the LOB clauses. The treaties entered into by EU Member States prior to the treaties being studied were affected by the unilateral rules established by the U.S.

---

118. *See* Terra/Wattel 2001, p. 114 and Prechal 1998, p. 15.
119. *See* section I, Chapter 4.

Besides, even though it could be asserted that EU law establishes clear and precise obligations in this regard, this criterion would need to be valued in light of the other criteria established by the ECJ. As previously discussed, it must also be taken into account whether the infringement or harm caused was intentional or involuntary. In this case, the Member States cannot be considered to have committed this breach intentionally. As previously mentioned, the EU Member States were obligated to accept these clauses because on the contrary either the treaty would not have been concluded or the U.S. would have adopted these rules unilaterally.

One of the principles of the EU liability for breach system established by the ECJ, is the principle of sincere cooperation in Article 4(3) of the TEU (principle of Community loyalty, ex Article 10 of the EC Treaty). In this case, this principle cannot be considered to have been violated due to the fact that the LOB clauses are contrary to EU law. On the contrary, it can be concluded that the EU Member States have complied with this duty as long as they have negotiated to ensure that the 'EU phenomenon' was taken into account insofar as possible in the limitation on benefits clause at the time the treaty was concluded.

From this standpoint, the Member States cannot be understood to be in breach of Article 4(3) of the TEU, which states that Member States shall 'refrain from any measure which could jeopardize the attainment of the Union's objectives'. The measures being analysed were not first adopted by the Member States, meaning that this part of the rule would not be applicable. The Member State also fulfilled the duty imposed by the first paragraph of Article 4(3), which establish that 'Member States shall take any appropriate measure, general or particular, to ensure fulfilment of the obligations arising out of the Treaties or resulting from acts of the institutions of the Union'. The duty of loyalty to the EU was complied with, considering that the EU Member States have tried to correct the effects that are contrary to EU law arising as a result of the unilateral and bilateral policy of the U.S., through the adoption of limitation on benefit clauses, the terms of which assure compliance with the EU freedoms insofar as possible.[120] Although the rules finally included in the treaties are not compatible with EU law in all cases, they cannot be considered to be in breach of the principle of sincere cooperation stipulated in Article 4(3) of the TEU.[121]

The ECJ's findings in the judgments handed down in the *Open Skies* cases cannot put forward this conclusion. In these cases, the ECJ considered that a rule similar to the ownership clause, but contained in a treaty relating to air transport could not be justified, and ruled that the other state party to the treaty, which was the U.S., had forced the inclusion of this rule. The ECJ considered a breach of EU law to exist even

---

120. See Calderón 2002, p. 21, footnote 88 and Martín Jiménez/Calderón (2002), p. 114. In this regard, Terra/Wattel 2012, p. 163, state the following: 'This means that there is a justification for – reluctantly – consenting to the LOB provision, and that the Member State's tax treaty negotiation result is proportional in relation to the mandatory requirement of public interest that comprehensive tax treaties are concluded by EU Member States with, e.g. the US and Japan which mutually reduce restrictive source taxation. Such treaties are manifestly more important for the internal market than avoiding possible but rather remote unequal treatment of EU nonresidents at the cost of not having a tax treaty or no reduction of source taxation at all'. *See also* De Broe 2008, pp. 1.037–1.039 and Calejo 2012, pp. 94–95.
121. Van Unnik/Boudesteijn 1993, pp. 114–115 and Hinnekens 1995, p. 229.

though the EU Member State did everything possible to assure that this clause was in line with EU law. In our opinion, which is the same as that of the ECJ, this argument does not justify the restrictive effects of the LOB clauses provided in the DTCs that have been analysed.[122] However, from the standpoint of the criteria used to analyse whether the state should be held liable for breach of EU law, in a case such as that described, we consider that the condition, of the existence of a sufficiently serious breach, is not met.

IV.B Tax Treaties Between EU Member States

In the event that the two contracting states are EU Member States, the same problems do not arise as in the aforementioned cases. Both states are subject to compliance with the obligations stipulated under EU law.

In this case, both the state acting as the source state and that which acts as the state of residence are required to share in paying the damage caused to a taxpayer that was denied access to a treaty and protected under EU law. As opposed to the case discussed in the previous section, the fact that the tax treaty is not applied in the source state should be directly resolved without the need to resort to the system of liability for the breach of EU law. Therefore, the source state must apply the limits provided in the treaty for the taxation of non-residents.[123]

IV.C Possible Solutions for the Incompatibility of Tax Treaties with Third States

The conclusions reached in relation to the tax treaties concluded with the U.S. are clearly discouraging. The LOB clauses can deprive certain taxpayers protected under EU law from the protection of a tax treaty. With respect to the application of methods to eliminate double taxation in the state of residence, it could be admissible for EU law to impose the application thereof. However, this would not resolve all the problems arising in relation to the fact that the tax treaty is not applied in the source state. In view of the substantive criteria used to determine if states should be held liable to pay damages for the breach of EU law, there is no obligation to compensate the affected taxpayer in the event that a DTC is not applied in the source state.

Given this situation, the issue can only be resolved through '*lege ferenda* proposals'. As asserted by experts in this field, actions by the Institutions of the EU are required to resolve this problem.[124] It could also be useful for the EU Member States to take a common position in this regard. It has been evidenced that the separate negotiation of tax treaties with the U.S. has not been sufficient to resolve this problem.

---

122. *See* Clark 2003, pp. 25–26 and particularly paragraphs 130–139 and 144 of the ECJ judgment on case C-471/98 of 5 November 2002.
123. The above is based on the ECJ's *Saint-Gobain* judgment. As pointed out by Martín Jiménez/Calderón (2002), p. 110, the ruling in case of the *Saint-Gobain* judgment may also have effects on the source state in the event that it is an EU Member State. This means that the source state (EU) is obligated to apply the DTC of the state (EU) in which the PE is located.
124. Eilers/Watkins 1993, p. 20 and Van Unnik/Boudesteijn 1993, p. 115.

The LOB clauses and even the expanded versions thereof included in the treaties analysed (and also the 2016 U.S. Model and the LOB rule of Action 6 of the BEPS project), do not comprise all 'EU cases'. Furthermore, from both formal and material standpoints, the bona fide clause does not resolve this issue either.

In view of the above, 'EU action' seems to be the only option which might resolve this issue. The need for such action is increasingly more imperative, especially considering that in the Commentaries on Article 1 of the 2003 OECD Model (paragraph 20) and the BEPS project, the OECD has adopted the same policy as the U.S., in view of the fact that the Commentaries and the BEPS project propose a group of LOB clauses similar to those provided in the U.S. Models. However, it should be noted that the Commentaries recognize that these clauses could suffer from adaptations and changes based on the states entering into the treaty. In addition, Action 6 of the BEPS project only requires adopting a minimum standard to address treaty abuse. The LOB rule proposed in Action 6 of the BEPS Model does not form part of the minimum standard described in this Action, as it does not require LOB clauses to be included in any event. As it has been pointed in previous sections, the European Commission, in the context of the 2016 Anti-Avoidance Tax Package, does not recommend that EU Member States include, in their tax treaties, an LOB rule similar to the one proposed in Action 6 of the BEPS project.

In view of this state of affairs, the EU action should attempt to fully include the requirements of EU law in these clauses. A different position, i.e. opposition to the existence of these clauses within the system by which DTCs are accessed, does not seem to be a possibility, bearing in mind that as a result of 2003-2014 OECD Model and the BEPS project, these purely American clauses have received the support of an international organization such as the OECD, of which all EU Member States are members. Moreover, the EU itself belongs to this organization.

There are various proposals regarding what the 'EU action' should comprise. The first proposal would consist in the conclusion of a multilateral convention between EU Member States. This would mean that the negotiation of tax treaties with third states would in some manner, correspond to EU Institutions.[125] Second, there is a proposal consisting in the existence of an EU Model Tax Convention. These proposals have been made by both experts in this field[126] and the European Commission.[127]

A third proposal solution in this regard would be a tax treaty sponsored by the Commission that would affect U.S.-EU relations.[128] Such a treaty between the U.S. and the EU Member States would have the merit of eliminating discrepancies in the tax

---

125. In relation to how a multilateral convention should be drawn up, see Lang 1998. It is important to note that in 1968, following the recommendations of the 1962 Neumark report, the Commission presented a proposal for a Community multilateral treaty to eliminate international double taxation between Member States. This proposal was not adopted due to the opposition of the majority of Member States, which were unwilling to give up such a relevant portion of their tax sovereignty when the Community was still in such an early stage of construction. See Calderón 2002, p. 42.
126. See Becker/Thömmes 1991, p. 176, Hinnekens 1995, p. 230 and Pistone 2002, pp. 268-270.
127. EU 2003, p. 12.
128. Mason 2005, pp. 130-131 and Calejo 2012, p. 95.

treaties between Member States and the U.S. In this regard, the LOB provision of this treaty will only affect those resident in third states.

Although the impact of each would differ, these initiatives would have a significant impact on the exclusive competence of the EU Member States to enter into conventions for the avoidance of double taxation.[129] In regard to the third proposal, it must be highlighted that it would be very difficult to achieve consensus in regard to a tax treaty meeting the demands of all Member States and a non-Member State, such as the U.S.[130]

In view of this situation, and as has occurred in other cases, it would be unlikely for the EU Member States to give up this competence, bearing in mind that in principle, the fact that the LOB clauses may be contrary to EU law, does not give rise to any liability to pay damages to the affected taxpayers as the previously discussed conditions are not met. Therefore, for example, only an ECJ judgment ruling that the LOB clauses were in breach of the obligations stipulated under the EU treaty would force the states to renounce their competence. It should be borne in mind that in the case where a ruling against an EU Member State were handed down by the ECJ, it would facilitate the fulfilment of the 'sufficiently serious breach' condition. In this respect, only if such a judgment were handed down would it be possible for a phenomenon similar to that resulting from the ECJ judgments on the *Open Skies* cases to occur. In fact, the Transport Council agreed, on 5 June 2003, on a package of measures that passes the responsibility for conducting key air transport negotiations to the Commission. In particular, the package gave the Commission a mandate to begin negotiations for a new transatlantic air transport agreement with the U.S.[131]

In this regard, it is possible that the infringement proceedings initiated by the European Commission against the Netherlands in 2015, in reference to the LOB clauses contained in the tax treaty with Japan, may have that intention. However, it is surprising that the European Commission has initiated an infringement proceeding with respect to a tax treaty signed with Japan and not with the U.S., as almost all tax treaties concluded by EU Member States with the U.S. contain LOB clauses.[132] The same does not occur with tax treaties entered into by EU Member States with Japan.

In any event, the three mentioned 'EU actions' should form the subjective scope of the DTCs in accordance with the requirements of EU law.[133] In this respect, although competence to negotiate with third states was not conferred upon EU institutions, the

---

129. Furthermore, we consider both initiatives to be perfectly justifiable from the standpoint of the principle of subsidiarity established in Article 5 of the TEU (ex Article 5 of the EC Treaty). As is common knowledge, this principle conditions the exercise of the EU institutions competences. In the areas which the EU does not have exclusive powers, the EU institutions may act 'only if and in so far as the objectives of the proposed action cannot be sufficiently achieved by the Member States, either at central level or at regional and local level, but can rather, by reason of the scale or effects of the proposed action, be better achieved at Union level'. In the case described above, it has been evidenced that the EU Member States have not individually been able to resolve the EU's problems relating to the limitation on benefits clauses. Therefore, an 'EU action' might be justified.
130. Calejo 2012, p. 95.
131. De Ceulaer 2003, p. 501.
132. *See* section I, Chapter 3.
133. Avery Jones 1998, p. 103.

mere fact that the states would be able to negotiate on the basis of an EU Model Tax Convention might be of significance in terms of adapting the regime of the LOB clauses to the assumptions on which EU law is based. However, the truth is that the European Commission ruled out this possibility: in the Anti-Avoidance Tax Package it recommends the EU Member States to not include the LOB rule proposed in Action 6 of the BEPS project.

Moreover, the EU Member States should also allege that measures to avoid harmful tax regimes have been adopted within the EU under the application of the Code of Conduct, the state aid system and the Anti-Avoidance Tax Package. Although these measures do not refer to the assumptions on which the LOB clauses are based, they may have a significant influence on the use of EU Member States as intermediary states. As observed, for the treaty shopping structures to be developed, it is necessary for the intermediary state to provide a suitable tax regime for the elimination or significant reduction of taxation in the intermediary state. The existence of these EU actions would make it difficult to use an EU Member State to channel treaty shopping strategies. Therefore, in the case that LOB clauses were established, the above would be a convincing argument to force the LOB clauses to be adapted to EU law.

V FINAL REMARKS

The competence to conclude tax treaties still corresponds to EU Member States. This competence should be exercised respecting the requirements of EU Law. The LOB clauses, as worded, negatively affect EU freedoms. The fact that there is a bona fide clause does not formally resolve the incompatibility problem, although it does allow for the application of the treaty. There are no legitimate grounds for these clauses under EU law. However, despite their incompatibility no significant consequences arise, as long as the conditions stipulated for the state in breach to be held liable to pay the damages caused are not fulfilled. In view of this state of affairs, an 'EU action' comprising the conclusion of a multilateral treaty, the existence of an EU Model Tax Convention or a sole tax treaty between EU Member States and the U.S., could aid in assuring that these clauses do not prevent taxpayers protected by the right to exercise EU freedoms from accessing a treaty.

Bibliography

Arthur Andersen 1997, *Holding, Royalty and Finance Companies in the Netherlands*, AA, 1997.
Abellán/Vilà 1998, *Lecciones de Derecho Comunitario Europeo*, Ariel, Barcelona, 1998.
ALI 1992, *International Aspects of United States Income Taxation II*, Philadelphia, 1992.
Almudí 2001, 'Transparencia fiscal internacional y convenios de doble imposición', *QF*, n° 21, 2001.
Almudí 2003, 'Las libertades fundamentales comunitarias impiden la aplicación del Régimen de transparencia Fiscal Internacional incluso cuando la entidad participada es residente en terceros estados', *QF*, n° 19, 2003.
Almudí/Serrano 2001, 'La residencia fiscal de las personas físicas en los convenios de doble imposición y en la normativa española', *RCT*, n° 221/222, 2001.
Almudí/Serrano 2002, 'La tributación por el IVA de las Sociedades *holding*', *QF*, n° 2, 2002.
Alonso García 1997, *La responsabilidad de los Estados miembros por infracción del Derecho Comunitario*, Civitas-Fundación Universidad Empresa, Madrid, 1997.
Amico 1989, 'United States: Tax Treaty Project Raises Treaty Shopping Question', *ET*, n° 7, 1989.
Amico 1993, 'Planning Under Article 26 of the 1992 U.S.-Netherlands Tax Treaty', *TNI*, n° 2, 1993.
Arespacochaga 1998, *Planificación fiscal internacional*, Marcial Pons, Madrid, 1998.
Arespacochaga 2000, *El trust, la fiducia y figuras afines*, Marcial Pons, Madrid, 2000.
Armelin 2016, 'Treaty Abuse and Beneficial Ownership: Latest OECD Developments': *Preventing Treaty Abuse*, Linde, Wien, 2016.
Arnold 2004, 'Tax Treaties and Tax Avoidance: The 2003 Revisions to the Commentary to the OECD Model', *BIT*, n° 6, 2004.
Atchabahian 1975, 'El Grupo Andino y su enfoque de la doble imposición internacional', *HPE*, n° 32, 1975.
Avery Jones 1989, 'The Treatment of Trust under the OECD Model Convention', *ET*, n° 12, 1989.
Avery Jones 1998, 'Flows of Capital Between the EU and Third Countries and the Consequences of Disharmony in European International Tax Law', *EC Tax Review*, n° 2, 1998.
Avi-Yonah/Benshalom 2010, 'Formulary Apportionment: Myths and Prospects', *Public Law Working Papers No. 221*, University of Michigan, 2010.

Bibliography

Baena 1994, *La obligación real de contribuir en el Impuesto sobre la Renta de las Personas Físicas*, Aranzadi, Pamplona, 1994.

Báez 2016, 'La cláusula del propósito principal (Principal Purpose Test). Un análisis crítico de la acción 6 del Proyecto BEPS', *RCT*, n° 404, 2016.

Báez 2017, 'GAARs and Treaties: From the Guiding Principle to the Principal Purpose Test – What Have We Gained from BEPS Action 6?', *Intertax*, n° 6/7, 2017.

Baker 1994, *Double Taxation Conventions and International Tax Law*, Sweet & Maxwell, London, 1994.

Barav 1996, 'State Liability in Damages for Breach of Community Law in the National Courts', *Yearbook of European Law*, vol. 16, 1996.

Bates/Berman/Gani/Gutmann/Imamura/Klugman/Rust 2013, 'Limitation on Benefits Articles in Income Tax Treaties: The Current State of Play', *Intertax*, n° 6/7, 2013.

Becker 1988, 'Germany (Federal Republic): Treaty Shopping/Treaty Override', *ET*, n° 12, 1988.

Becker/Wurm 1988, *Treaty Shopping: An Emerging Tax Issue and Its Presents Status in Various Countries*, Kluwer Law and Taxation Publishers, Deventer, 1988.

Becker/Wurm 1988, 'Double-Taxation Conventions and the Conflict Between International Agreements and Subsequent Domestic Laws', *Intertax*, n° 8/9, 1988.

Becker/Thömmes 1991, 'Treaty Shopping and EC Law: Critical Notes to Act. 28 of the New German-U.S. Double Taxation Convention', *ET*, n° 6, 1991.

Bennett 1991, 'The U.S.-Netherlands Tax Treaty Negotiations: A U.S. Perspective', *BIT*, n° 1, 1991.

Bennett/De Hosson/Morrison 1993, *The 1992 United States Netherlands Tax Convention*, Kluwer Law and Taxation Publishers, Deventer, 1993.

Bennett/Morrison/Daniels/De Hosson 1995, *Commentary to the US-Netherlands Income Tax Convention*, Kluwer, The Hague, 1995.

Bennett 1998, 'The New U.S.-Switzerland Income Tax Treaty: Highlights of U.S. Taxation of Swiss Residents', *RDADF*, n° 3/4, 1998.

Bennett/Andersen 1998, 'Practical Issues in the Application of Double Tax Conventions', *CDFI*, vol. LXXXIIIb, Kluwer Law International, The Hague, 1998.

Berman/Hynes 2000, 'Limitation on Benefits Clauses in U.S. Income Tax Treaties', *TMIJ*, n° 12, 2000.

Betten 1992, 'Report on Rulings Practice', *ET*, n° 10, 1992.

Betten 1993, 'News on Ruling Practice', *ET*, n° 5, 1993.

Betten 1998, *Income Tax Aspects of Emigration and Immigration of Individuals*, IBFD, Amsterdam, 1998.

Bierlaagh 2000, 'The CARICOM Income Tax Agreement for the Avoidance of (Double) Taxation', *BIT*, n° 3, 2000.

Blanco-Morales 1997, *La transferencia internacional de sede social*, Aranzadi, Pamplona, 1997.

Blázquez Lidoy 1999, *El régimen de los grupos de sociedades en la Ley 43/1995*, Centro de Estudios Financieros, Madrid, 1999.

Blumenberg 1994, 'Recent Developments in German International Taxation', *Tax International Tax Journal*, n° 3, 1994.

Bogaerts 2002, 'Corporate Tax Reform Influences Luxembourg's International Competitiveness as Holding Company Location', *ET*, n° 9, 2002.

Boidman 1989, 'Canadian Approach to Treaty Shopping', *Intertax*, n° 8/9, 1989.

Borrás 1991, 'Problemática general que suscita la aplicación del convenio': *Estudios sobre el convenio entre España y Estados Unidos para evitar la doble imposición*, GF, Madrid, 1991.

Brauner 2014, 'BEPS: An Interim Evaluation', *World Tax Journal*, vol. 3, n° 1, 2014.

Bravo 2016, 'Limitation on Benefits: Qualified Persons': *Preventing Treaty Abuse*, Linde, Wien, 2016.

Brekelmans 2003, 'Luxembourg to Amend Holding Company Regime', *TNI*, n° 9, 2003.

Brignoli 2013, 'Treaty Shopping and International Tax Planning': *Limits to Tax Planning*, Linde, Vienna, 2013.

Briones 1993, 'Consecuencias fiscales en España de la planificación fiscal de las inversiones españolas en el extranjero', *PSF*, n° 41, 1993.

Brouwer 1997, 'Netherlands-U.S. Tax Treaty in Practice', *TNI*, n° 14, 1997.

Buhler 1968, *Principios de Derecho Internacional Tributario*, Editorial de Derecho Financiero, Madrid, 1968.

Burge/Endres 1990, 'Treaty Shopping: The New German-US Treaty Raises More Questions than It Answers', *Intertax*, n° 11, 1990.

Burke 1983, 'Report on Proposed United States Model Income Tax Treaty', *Harward International Tax Review*, n° 2, 1983.

Caamaño/Calderón 1999, 'Accounting, the permanent establishment and EC Law: The Futura Participactions case', *EC Tax Review*, n° 1, 1999.

Caamaño/Calderón/Martín 2000, *Jurisprudencia del Tribunal de Justicia de las Comunidades Europeas (1996–1999)*, La Ley, Madrid, 2000.

Calderón 1997a, *La doble imposición internacional y los métodos para su eliminación*, McGraw-Hill, Madrid, 1997.

Calderón 1997b, *La doble imposición internacional en los convenios de doble Imposición y en la Unión Europea*, Aranzadi, Pamplona, 1997.

Calderón 1999, *Comentarios a la Ley del Impuesto sobre la Renta de No Residentes*, Civitas, Madrid, 1999.

Calderón 2002, 'Algunas consideraciones en torno a la interrelación entre los convenios de doble imposición y el derecho comunitario europeo: ¿Hacia la 'comunitarización' de los CDIs', *Documentos del IEF*, n° 4, 2002.

Calejo 2011, 'Limitation on Benefits Clauses and EU Law', *ET*, vol. 51, n° 2/3, 2011.

Calvo Salinero 1998, 'Convenios bilaterales y discriminación fiscal en la Unión Europea', *QF*, n° 16, 1998.

Carrión 2016, 'Limitation on Benefits: Derivative Benefits and Discretionary Relief': *Preventing Treaty Abuse*, Linde, Wien, 2016.

Casero 1996, 'Spain: New Holding Company Regime for Outbound Investments', *Intertax*, n° 12, 1996.

Cavestany 1992, 'El artículo 17 del convenio entre España y los Estados Unidos para evitar la doble imposición', *Carta Tributaria*, n° 152, 1992.

Cavestany 1993, 'El *treaty shopping* en el modelo de convenio de la OECD de 1992', *Impuestos*, 1993-II.

Christians/Ezenagu 2016, 'Kill-Switches in the U.S. Model Tax Treaty', *Brooklyn Journal of International Law*, vol. 41.

Clark 2003, 'The Limitation on Benefits Clause Under an Open Sky', *ET*, n° 1, 2003.

Cohen/Pollack/Scherer 1997, 'Analysis of the New U.S.-Switzerland Income Tax Treaty', *TMIJ*, n° 2, 1997.

Cole/Crocker 1998, 'Highlights of the New US Withholding Tax System for Income Paid to Foreign Investors in the United States', *RDADF*, n° 3/4, 1998.

Collado/Delgado 2001, 'Pasado, presente y futuro del régimen de los precios de transferencia en España': *Fiscalidad Internacional*, Centro de Estudios Financieros, Madrid, 2001.

Combarros 1984, 'La interpretación económica como criterio de interpretación jurídica', *REDF*, n° 44, 1984.

Craig 2003, 'Open Your Eyes: What the "Open Skies" Cases Could Mean for the US Tax Treaties with the EU Member States', *BIT*, n° 2, 2003.

Crowdus 1997, 'Highlights of New Income Tax Treaty Between United States and Ireland', *TMIJ*, n° 11, 1997.

Cunningham 1997, 'Article 23 of the Proposed United States-Ireland Tax Treaty', *BIT*, n° 12, 1997.

Chica/Johnson 1993, 'The New U.S.-Netherlands Tax Treaty: Understanding the International Tax Planning Implications', *TNI*, june, 1993.

Dahlberg 1997, 'New Tax Treaty Between Sweden and the US Raises Questions about Treaty-Shopping', *Intertax*, n° 8/9, 1997.

Debatin/Endres 1990, *Das neue Doppelbesteuerungsabkommen USA/ Bundesrepublik Deutschland*, Beck'sche Verlagsbuchhandlung, Munich, 1990.

Debelva/Scornos/Van den Berghen/Van Braband 2015, 'LOB Clauses and EU-Law Compatibility: A Debate Revived by BEPS?', *EC Tax Review*, n° 3, 2015.

De Broe 2008, *International Tax Planning and Prevention of Abuse*, IBFD, Amsterdam, 2008.

De Broe/Luts 2015, 'BEPS Action 6: Tax Treaty Abuse', *Intertax*, n° 2, 2015.

DeCarlo/Granwell/Van Weeghel 1993, 'An Overview of the Limitation on Benefits Article of the New Netherlands-U.S. Income Tax Convention', *TMIJ*, n° 6, 1993.

De Castro 1972, *El negocio fiduciario*, Reus, Madrid, 1972.

De Ceulaer 2003, 'Community Most-Favoured-Nation Treatment: One Step Closer to the Multilateralization of Income Tax Treaties in the European Union', *BIT*, n° 10, 2003.

Delattre 1995, 'France-United States New Tax Treaty', *BIT*, n° 2, 1995.

De Kleer 1996, 'Towards a European Anti-Abuse Doctrine in Direct Taxation?', *Intertax*, n° 4, 1996.

Del Arco 1977a, *Doble imposición internacional y Derecho tributario español*, Escuela Financiera de Hacienda Pública, Madrid, 1977.

Del Arco 1977b, 'Comentarios al informe del profesor Viñuales sobre el Régimen Fiscal de las Empresas operando en varios países', *HPE*, n° 46, 1977.

De Lignie 1995, 'Limitation on Benefits: Recently Signed US Treaties Compared to the 1992 US-Netherlands Treaty', *BIT*, n° 2, 1995.

Bibliography

De Sampayo 1997, *Regional Policy and Direct Taxation Policy: A Case of EC Operational [Des] Co-ordination?*, IBFD International Tax Academy, Amsterdam, 1997.
Díez-Hochleitner 1998, *La posición del Derecho Internacional en el Ordenamiento comunitario*, McGraw-Hill, Madrid, 1998.
Díez-Hochleitner/Martínez 2001, *Derecho de la Unión Europea: textos y comentarios*, McGraw-Hill, Madrid, 2001.
Díez-Picazo 1979, *La representación en el Derecho privado*, Civitas, Madrid, 1979.
Doernberg/Van Raad 1992, 'The Forthcoming U.S. Model Income Tax Treaty and the Saving Clause', *TNI*, vol. 5, n° 15, 1992.
Doernberg/Van Raad 1997, *The 1996 United States Model Income Tax Convention*, Kluwer Law International, The Hague, 1997.
Doernberg 1999, *International Taxation*, West Publishing Company, St. Paul, 1999.
Dourado 2016, 'The EU Anti Tax Avoidance Package: Moving Ahead of BEPS?', *Intertax*, n° 6/7, 2016.
Dourado/Kofler/Reimer/Rust 2015, 'Article 3. General Definitions': *Klaus Vogel on Double Tax Conventions*, Kluwer Law International, Alphen aan den Rijn, 2015.
Douvier/Bouzoraa 2001, 'France: Court of Appeals Confirms Incompatibility of CFC Rules with Tax Treaties. Decision of the Court of Appeals of Paris of 30 January 2001', *ET*, n° 5, 2001.
Doyle 1995, 'Is Article 26 of the Netherlands-United States Tax Treaty Compatible with EC Law?', *ET*, n° 1, 1995.
Duffy/Fahy/Galvin 2016, 'The Recent Intrusion of the European Commission into Double Tax Treaties', in http://www.matheson.com/news-and-insights/article/the-recent-intrusion-of-the-european-commission-into-double-tax-treaties (accessed 19 April 2017).
Du Toit 1999, *Beneficial Ownership of Royalties in Bilateral Tax Treaties*, IBFD, Amsterdam, 1999.
Easson 2000, 'Do We Still Need Tax Treaties?', *BIT*, n° 12, 2000.
Easson 2004, *Tax Incentives for Foreign Direct Investment*, Kluwer Law International, The Hague, 2004.
Ebenroth/Daiber 1990, 'Dual-Resident Companies under German Law', *ET*, n° 7, 1990.
Edwardes-Ker 1994, *Tax Treaty Interpretation*, In-Depth Publishing, London, 1994.
Eilers/Watkins 1993, 'Article 28 of the German-U.S. Double Taxation Treaty of 1989: An Appropriate Solution to the Treaty Shopping Problem', *TPI*, n° 9, 1993.
Ellis/Falke 1992, 'Limitation-on-Benefits Article from the Dutch Perspective', *TNI*, n° 27, 1992.
Ellis 1999, 'Are Measures to Curb Harmful Tax Competition Necessary?', *ET*, n° 3, 1999.
Eynatten/De Haen/Hostyn 2003, 'The Concept of Beneficial Ownership under Belgian Tax Law: Legal Interpretation is Maintained', *Intertax*, n° 12, 2003.
EU 2001a, Commission staff report on Company Taxation in the Internal Market, SEC (2001) 1681 final, 23 October 2001.
EU 2001b, Communication from the Commission to the Council, the European Parliament and the European Economic and Social Committee: Towards an Internal Market without tax obstacles A strategy for providing companies with a

consolidated corporate tax base for their EU-wide activities, COM(2001)582 final of 23 October 2001.

EU 2003, Communication from the Commission to the Council, the European Parliament and the European Economic and Social Committee: An Internal Market without company tax obstacles achievements, ongoing initiatives and remaining challenges, COM(2003)726 final of 24 November 2003.

EU 2005, EC Law and Tax Treaties, TAXUD E1/FR DOC (05) 2306 (working document of the European Commission presented in June 2005).

EU 2007, Communication from the Commission to the Council, the European Parliament and the European Economic and Social Committee: The application of anti-abuse measures in the area of direct taxation – within the EU and in relation to third countries, COM(2007)785 final of 10 December 2007.

EU 2016a, Communication from the Commission to the European Parliament and the Council: Anti-Tax Avoidance Package: Next steps towards delivering effective taxation and greater tax transparency in the EU, COM(2016) 23 final of 28 January 2016.

EU 2016b, Commission recommendation of 28 January 2016 on the implementation of measures against tax treaty abuse, C(2016) 271 final.

EU 2016c, Commission Staff Working Document Accompanying the Document COM(2016) 23 final, SWD(2016) 6 final of 28 January 2016.

Felgarden/Aaronson 2010, 'U.S. Tax Court Holds That Guarantee Fee Is Sourced to Location of Guarantor', *International Tax Journal*, vol. 36, n° 3, 2010.

Fock 2000, 'Sitztheorie im deutschen internationalen Steuerrecht nach der *Centros*-Entscheidung', *Recht der Internationales Wirtschaft*, n° 1, 2000.

Forns 1960, *La doble imposición internacional*, Cámara Oficial de Comercio de Madrid, Madrid, 1960.

Fournier 1994, 'U.S.-France Treaty Tightens Limitation of Benefits, Adds Pensions Provisions', *TJIT*, n° 11, 1994.

Freitas 2012, 'United States: US Policy to Counter Treaty Shopping – From Aiken Industries to the Anti-Conduit Regulations: A Critical View of the Current Double-Step Approach from the Perspective of Treaty Objectives and Purposes', *BIT*, n° 6, 2012.

Frommel 1988, 'EEC Companies and Migration: A Set-Back for Europe', *Intertax*, n° 12, 1988.

Frommel 1989, 'The Real Seat Doctrine and Dual-Resident Companies under German Law: Another View', *ET*, n° 10, 1989, pp. 267 a 274.

Füger/Rieger 1998, 'Ende des Mythos der Monaco-Entscheidung', *IStR*, n° 12, 1998.

Gallo/Casertano 1995, 'The Clause Anti-Abuse in the Italian Double Tax Treaties and their Compatibility with the EC Law', *Intertax*, n° 12, 1995.

García Prats 1996, *El establecimiento permanente*, Tecnos, Madrid, 1996.

García Prats 1998, *Imposición directa, no discriminación y derecho comunitario*, Tecnos, Madrid, 1998.

García Prats 1999, *Comentarios a la Ley del Impuesto sobre la Renta de No Residentes*, Civitas, Madrid, 1999.

García Prats 2000, 'La propuesta de directiva de imposición sobre el ahorro: algunos apuntes', *CT*, n° 96, 2000.
García Prats 2001, 'Limits on the Abuse of Low-Tax Regimes by Multinational Businesses: Current Measures and Emerging Trends', *CDFI*, vol. LXXXVIb, Kluwer Law International, The Hague, 2001.
García Prats 2002, 'Las medidas tributarias anti-abuso y el Derecho comunitario': *Las medidas anti-abuso en la normativa interna española y en los convenios para evitar la doble imposición internacional y su compatibilidad con el Derecho comunitario*, IEF, Madrid, 2002.
García Prats 2015, 'Los límites a la planificación fiscal agresiva y al abuso de las normas tributarias', *Revista Técnica Tributaria*, n° 110, 2015.
Garcimartín 1999, 'La *Sitztheorie* es incompatible con el Tratado CE (Algunas cuestiones del Derecho internacional de sociedades iluminadas por la Sentencia TJCE de 9 de marzo de 1999)', *Revista de Derecho Mercantil*, n° 232, 1999.
Garcimartín 2001, 'La sentencia Centros: el *status quaestionis* un año después', *NUE*, n° 195, 2001.
Garcimartín 2002, 'El reglamento de la sociedad europea: una primera lectura', *Gaceta Jurídica de la Unión Europea y de la Competencia*, n° 217, 2002.
General Explanation of the Tax Reform Act of 1986, Prentice Hall, Inc., Englewood Cliffs, 1987.
Gil García 2016, 'El patent box en la era post-BEPS: ¿futuro perfecto o incierto?': *IV Encuentro de Derecho Financiero y Tributario (3.ª parte)*, Instituto de Estudios Fiscales, Madrid, 2016.
Gleicher/Gard 2016, 'Rev. Proc. 201540: The Next Chapter in Competent Authority', *TMIJ*, vol. 45, n° 2, 2016.
Gliksberg 1999, 'Taxation of Non-profit Organizations', *CDFI*, vol. LXXXIVa, Kluwer Law International, The Hague, 1999.
Godfrey 1983, *Handbook on Tax-Exempt Organizations*, Prentice Hall, Inc., New Jersey, 1983.
González Poveda 1993, *Tributación de no residentes*, La Ley, Madrid, 1993.
Goossen 1993, 'Limiting Treaty Benefits', *The International Tax Journal*, n° 1, 1993.
Gouthière 1995, 'France: New Tax Treaty with the United States', *ET*, n° 3, 1995.
Gouthière 2010, 'Significant Amendments to the France–United States Tax Treaty', *ET*, n° 5, 2010.
Goyette 1999, *Countering Tax Treaty Abuses: A Canadian Perspective on and International Issue*, Canadian Tax Foundation, Toronto, 1999.
Grady 1983, 'Income Tax Treaty Shopping: An Overview of Prevention Techniques', *Northwestern Journal of International Law & Business*, n° 5, 1983.
Grau Ruiz 2003, *Mutual Assistance for the Recovery of Tax Claims*, Kluwer Law International, The Hague, 2003.
Grundy 1984, *The World of International Tax Planning*, Cambridge University Press, Cambridge, 1984.
Hamen 2001, 'Changes in Netherlands Ruling Policy Released', *TPIR*, n° 5, 2001.
Hamaekers 1990, 'Corporate Tax Policy and Competence of the European Community: An EC Tax Convention with Non-Member States', *ET*, n° 12, 1990.

Hamaekers 1999, 'Precios de transferencia: Historia, evolución y perspectivas', *REET*, n° 3, 1999.

Haccius 1995, *Ireland in International Tax Planning*, IBFD, Amsterdam, 1995.

Harrington 2015, 'U.S. Model Treaty Update And BEPS: Is the United States Catching Up or Wandering Off?', *TMIJ*, n° 11, 2015.

Heggy 2000, 'Withholding Tax on Payments to Foreign Payees: A (Cargo) Pocket Guide to the New Regulations', *TMIJ*, n° 10, 2000.

Helminen 2016, *Article 11: Interest – Global Tax Treaty Commentaries*, IBFD Tax Platform, 2016.

Herédia 2002, 'The Case of the Madeira: Portugal v Netherlands', *Intertax*, n° 11, 2002.

Hernández 2015, *El concepto de beneficiario efectivo en los convenios tributarios sobre la renta y sobre el patrimonio*, Universidad Pontificia Comillas, Madrid, 2015.

Hinnekens 1989, 'The Application of Anti-treaty Shopping Provisions to Belgian Co-ordination Centers', *Intertax*, n° 8/9, 1989.

Hinnekens 1994, 'Compatibility of Bilateral Tax Treaties with European Community Law. The Rules', *EC Tax Review*, n° 4, 1994.

Hinnekens 1995, 'Compatibility of Bilateral Tax Treaties with European Community Law – Applications of the Rules', *EC Tax Review*, n° 4, 1995.

Hinnekens 1996, 'Tax Treaty Shopping and Anti-tax Treaty Shopping Measures', *Skatteret*, n° 14, 1996.

Hinnekens 1999, 'Uncertainties in the Interpretation of the General Anti-Avoidance Statue', *ET*, n° 9, 1999.

Hinojosa Martínez 1997, *La regulación de los movimientos internacionales de capitales desde una perspectiva europea*, McGraw-Hill, Madrid, 1997.

Hofland/Pötgens 2011, 'The LOB Provision in the New Japan–Netherlands Tax Treaty', *ET*, n° 5, 2011.

Hübner 1988, 'Abuse of Double Tax Conventions', *ET*, n° 7, 1988.

IBFD 1981, 'Further Attacks on Treaty Shopping', *ET*, n° 5/6, 1981.

IBFD, *International Tax Glossary*, IBFD, Amsterdam, 1996.

IFA 1988, *International Tax Treatment of Common Law Trusts*, Kluwer Law and Taxation Publisher, 1988.

IFA 1995, *How Domestic Anti-Avoidance Rules Affect Double taxation Conventions*, Kluwer Law International, The Hague, 1995.

IFA 2000, *The OECD Model Convention – 1998 and Beyond; The Concept of Beneficial Wwnership in Tax Treaties*, Kluwer Law International, The Hague, 2000.

IFA 2001, *Abusive Application of International Tax Agreements*, Kluwer Law International, The Hague, 2001.

Infanti 2001, 'Curtailing Tax Treaty Overrides: A Call to Action', *University of Pittsburgh Law Review*, n° 62, 2001.

Institute for Fiscal Studies, *Tax Avoidance: A Report by the Tax Law Review Committee*, IFS, London, 1997.

International Income Taxation. Code, & Regulations. Selected Sections, Commerce Clearing House, Inc., Chicago, 1993.

Irawan 2016, 'Historical Development of the OECD's Work on Treaty Abuse': *Preventing Treaty Abuse*, Linde, Wien, 2016.

IRS 2016, *Instructions for Form W-8BEN-E* (https://www.irs.gov/).
IRS 2017, *Publication 515 (2017). Withholding of Tax on Nonresident Aliens and Foreign Entities* (https://www.irs.gov/).
Isenbergh 1996, *International Taxation*, vol. III, Little, Brown and Company, Boston, 1996.
Ismer/Riemer 2015, 'Article 4. Resident': *Klaus Vogel on Double Tax Conventions*, Kluwer Law International, Alphen aan den Rijn, 2015.
Jacob 1991, *Handbook on the 1989 Double Taxation Convention Between the Federal Republic of Germany and the United States of America*, IBFD, Amsterdam, 1991.
Jeffery 1999, *The Impact of State Sovereignty on Global Trade and International Taxation*, Kluwer Law International, London, 1999.
Jiang 2015, 'Treaty Shopping and Limitation on Benefits Articles in the Context of the OECD Base Erosion and Profit Shifting Project', *BIT*, n° 3, 2015.
Jiménez-Valladolid 2017, 'La posición de los Estados Unidos en relación con el Plan de Acción BEPS': *El Plan de Acción sobre Erosión de Bases Imponibles y Traslado de Beneficios: G-20, OCDE y Unión Europea*, Aranzadi, Cizur Menor, 2017.
Julien/Koch/Szudoczky 2017, 'What Has Changed in the Limitation on Benefits Clause of the 2016 US Model?: Technical Modifications, Policy Considerations and Comparisons with Base Erosion and Profit Shifting Action 6', *Intertax*, n° 1, 2017.
Jung 2011, 'Trends and Developments in Swiss Anti-Treaty Shopping Legislation and Treaty Shopping Case Law', *ET*, n° 6, 2011.
Kaplan 1982, 'The Shoppable Treaty: Should It Become Extinct?', *TMIJ*, n° 6, 1982.
Kaplan 1986, 'Reasons, Old and New, for the Erosion of United States Tax Treaties', *BTR*, n° 4, 1986.
Kaplan 1993, 'Treaty Shopping under the New US-Netherlands Treaty', *BIT*, n° 47, 1993.
Keijzer/Larking 1993, 'Netherlands/U.S. Protocol to Counter Tax Haven Structures', *ITR*, n° 12, 1993.
Kemmeren 1998, 'EC Law: Specific Observations' – *The Compatibility of Anti-Abuse Provisions in Tax Treaties with EC Law*, Kluwer Law International, London, 1998.
Kemmeren 2012, 'Double Tax Conventions on Income and Capital and the EU: Past, Present and Future', *EC Tax Review*, n° 3, 2012.
Kerekes 2016, 'Limitation on Benefits Clauses – Function, Purpose and History', *Preventing Treaty Abuse*, Linde, Wien, 2016.
Killius 1996, 'Access to Tax Treaty Benefits: Procedural Aspects. Germany', *TMIF*, n° 3, 1996.
Kim 1990, 'The U.S.-West German Income Tax Treaty: Can Article 28's Limitation on Benefits Serve As a Model for the Treasury's Anti-Treaty Shopping Policy', *The Tax Lawyer*, n° 4, 1990.
Kingson 1981, 'The Coherence of International Taxation', *Columbia Law Review*, vol. 81, n° 6, 1981.
Knechtle 1979, *Basic Problems in International Fiscal Law*, Kluwer, Deventer, 1979.
Kornikova 2008, 'Solving the Problem of Tax-Treaty Shopping Through the Use of Limitation on Benefits Provisions', *Richmond Journal of Global Law & Business*, vol. 8, n° 2, 2008.

Kosters 2004, 'The United Nations Model Tax Convention and Its Recent Developments', *Asian-Pacific Tax Bulletin*, n° 1/2, 2004.
Lagares 2001, 'El nuevo régimen de retenciones para las inversiones financieras en los Estados Unidos', *GF*, n° 201, 2001.
Lang 1998, *Multilateral Tax Treaties*, Kluwer, London, 1998.
Lang 2000, *The Application of the OECD Model Tax Convention to Partnerships*, Kluwer Law International, 2000.
Lang 2014, 'BEPS Action 6: Introducing an Antiabuse Rule in Tax Treaties', *TNI*, n° 7, 2014.
Langereis/Van Herksen 1997, 'International Aspects of Dutch Financing Companies', *Intertax*, n° 6/7, 1997.
Lerner/Lebovitz/Pridjian 1992, 'Treaty Shopping and U.S. Tax Policy: New Approaches', *TPIR*, n° 10, 1992.
Lesser 1996, P., 'Access to Tax Treaty Benefits: Procedural Aspects. United States', *TMIF*, n° 3, 1996.
Levine/Miller 2016, *U.S. Income Tax Treaties: The Limitation on Benefits Article*, Bloomberg DNA database, 2016.
Lodin/Gammie 1999, 'The Taxation of the European Company', *ET*, n° 8, 1999.
Lodin/Gammie 2001, *Home State Taxation*, IBFD, Amsterdam, 2001.
Loengard 1993, 'A (Modest) Proposal to Reconsider the Limitation on Benefits Provision of US Tax Treaties': *Essays on International Taxation*, Kluwer, Deventer, 1993.
Loukota 1989, 'International Tax Planning and Treaty Shopping-An Austrian View', *Intertax*, n° 8/9, 1989.
Lucas 2000, *La tributación de los dividendos internacionales*, Lex Nova, Valladolid, 2000.
Lukoff 1977, 'Dividends, Interest, Royalties: The 'Beneficial Ownership' Change in the 1974 Amendments To the OECD Draft Convention', *Taxes-The Tax Magazine*, n° 8, 1977.
Lüthi 1989, 'Countering the abuse of tax treaties-A Swiss view', *Intertax*, n° 8/9, 1989.
Lyal 2015, 'Compatibility of National Tax Measures with EU Law: The Role of the European Commission in Tax Litigation Before the European Court of Justice', *EC Tax Review*, n° 1, 2015.
Malherbe/Delattre 1996, 'Compatibility of Limitation on Benefits Provisions with EC Law', *ET*, n° 1, 1996.
Mangas/Liñán 1996, *Instituciones y Derecho de la Unión Europea*, McGraw-Hill, Madrid, 1996.
Manokhin 2013, 'Limitation on Benefits Clauses in Tax Treaties', *Limits to Tax Planning*, Linde, Viena, 2013.
Marino 1999, *La residenza nel Diritto Tributario*, CEDAM, Padova, 1999.
Martínez Laguna 2016, 'Institutional Hybrid Financial Instruments and Double Non-taxation under Domestic Rules and Tax Treaty Law: The Example of Spain', *Intertax*, n° 6/7, 2016.

Martín Jiménez 1995, 'EC Law and Clauses on Limitation of Benefits in Treaties with the US after Maastricht and the US-Netherlands Tax Treaty', *EC Tax Review*, n° 2, 1995.

Martín Jiménez 1998, 'Jurisprudencia del TJCE', *REDF*, n° 99, 1998.

Martín Jiménez 1999a, 'Jurisprudencia del TJCE', *REDF*, n° 103, 1999.

Martín Jiménez 1999b, *Towards Corporate Tax Harmonization in the European Community*, Kluwer, London, 1999.

Martín Jiménez 2001, 'El concepto de ayuda de Estado y las normas tributarias: problemas de delimitación del ámbito de aplicación del art. 87.1 TCE', *NUE*, n° 196, 2001.

Martín Jiménez 2002, 'Domestic Anti-Abuse Rules and Double Taxation Treaties: A Spanish Perspective – Part I', *BIT*, n° 11, 2002.

Martín Jiménez 2004a, 'The 2003 Revision of the OECD Commentaries on the Improper Use of Tax Treaties: A Case for the Declining Effect of the OECD Commentaries?', *BIT*, n° 1, 2004.

Martín Jiménez 2004b, 'La tributación de los cánones y regalías': *Comentarios a los convenios para evitar la doble imposición y prevenir la evasión fiscal concluidos por España*, Fundación Pedro Barrié de la Maza, La Coruña, 2004.

Martín Jiménez 2010, 'Beneficial Ownership: Current Trends', *World Tax Journal*, n° 1, 2010.

Martín Jiménez 2012, 'Towards a Homogeneous Theory of Abuse in EU (Direct) Tax Law', *BIT*, n° 4/5, 2012.

Martín Jiménez/Calderón 2000, *Imposición directa y no discriminación comunitaria*, Edersa, Madrid, 2000.

Martín Jiménez/Calderón 2002, 'Los establecimientos permanentes, los casos triangulares y el Derecho Comunitario. (Un comentario a la sentencia del TJCE Saint-Gobain)', *NUE*, n° 214, 2002.

Martín Jiménez/Calderón 2003, 'La jurisprudencia del Tribunal de Justicia de las Comunidades Europeas y el Impuesto sobre Sociedades': *Manual del Impuesto sobre Sociedades*, IEF, Madrid.

Martín Jiménez/Calderón 2017, 'La Directiva UE 2016/1164 contra las prácticas de elusión fiscal que inciden en el mercado interior', *RCT*, n° 407, 2017.

Martins 2016, 'Limitation on Benefits and EU Law': *Preventing Treaty Abuse*, Linde, Wien, 2016.

Mason 2005, 'U.S. Tax Treaty Policy and the European Court of Justice', *Tax Law Review*, n° 65, 2005.

McCarthy 1997, 'Switzerland: New Tax Treaty with the United States', *ET*, n° 4, 1997.

McDaniel/Ault 1998, *Introduction to United States International Taxation*, Kluwer Law International, The Hague, 1998.

McLure 2004, 'Corporate tax Harmonization in the European Union: the Commission's proposals', *TNI*, vol. 3, n° 1, 2004.

Menck 1993, 'Das OECD-Musterabkommen in der Revision 1992-Eine Übersicht', *IStR*, n° 6, 1993.

Miller/Stone 2008, 'The Evolution of Limitation On Benefits, Beneficial Ownership, and Similar Rules: Recent Trends and Future Possibilities', *TMIJ*, n° 12, 2008.

Morrison/Bennett 1993a, 'The New U.S.-Netherlands Treaty: Part I-Limitation on Benefits and Related Issues', *TNI*, n° 2, 1993.
Morrison/Bennett 1993b, 'The New U.S.-Netherlands Treaty: Part II', *TNI*, n° 3, 1993.
Muntendam 1996, 'Luxembourg: New Tax Treaty with the United States', *ET*, n° 12, 1996.
Navarro/Parada/Schwarz 2016, 'The Proposal for an EU Anti-avoidance Directive: Some Preliminary Thoughts', *EC Tax Review*, n° 3, 2016.
NMB Bank 1988, *Trust and Management Services in the Netherlands*, NMKB trust, Amsterdam, 1988.
Nouwen 2017, 'The European Code of Conduct Group Becomes Increasingly Important in the Fight Against Tax Avoidance: More Openness and Transparency is Necessary', *Intertax*, vol. 45, n° 2, 2017.
O'Connor 2016, 'Revised Procedures for Obtaining Assistance From U.S. Competent Authority, Including Discretionary Relief', *The Tax Adviser*, vol. 47, n° 1, 2016.
OECD 1986, *Double Taxation Conventions and the Use of Conduit Companies*, OECD, Paris, 1986.
OECD 1987, *International Tax Avoidance and Evasion. Four Related Studies*, OECD, Paris, 1987.
OECD 1990, 'Tax Treaty Override', *TNI*, n° 1, 1990.
OECD 1996, *Controlled Foreign Company Legislation*, OECD, Paris, 1996.
OECD 1997, *Model Tax Conventions on Income and on Capital*, II, OECD, Paris, 1997.
OECD 1998, *Harmful Tax Competition: An Emerging Global Issue*, OECD, Paris, 1998.
OECD 1999, *The Application of the OECD Model Tax Convention to Partnerships*, OECD, Paris, 1999.
OECD 2000, *Issues Related to Article 14 of the OECD Model Tax Convention*, OECD, Paris, 2000.
OECD 2003, *2002 Reports Related to the OECD Model Tax Convention*, OECD, Paris, 2003.
OECD 2004, *The OECD'S Project on Harmful Tax Practices: The 2004 Progress Report*, OECD, Paris, 2004.
OECD 2008, *Attribution of Income to Permanent Establishments*, OECD, Paris, 2008.
OECD 2013, *Action Plan on Base Erosion and Profit Shifting*, OECD, Paris, 2013.
OECD 2015a, *Preventing the Granting of Treaty Benefits in Inappropriate Circumstances, Action 6 – 2015 Final Report*, OECD/G20 Base Erosion and Profit Shifting Project, OECD, Paris, 2015.
OECD 2015b, *Aligning Transfer Pricing Outcomes with Value Creation, Actions 8-10 - 2015 Final Reports*, OECD/G20 Base Erosion and Profit Shifting Project, OECD, Paris, 2015.
OECD 2015c, *Countering Harmful Tax Practices More Effectively, Taking into Account Transparency and Substance, Action 5 – 2015 Final Report*, OECD/G20 Base Erosion and Profit Shifting Project, OECD, Paris, 2015.
OECD 2015d, *Limiting Base Erosion Involving Interest Deductions and Other Financial Payments, Action 4 – 2015 Final Report*, OECD/G20 Base Erosion and Profit Shifting Project, OECD, Paris, 2015.

OECD 2016, *Multilateral Convention to Implement Tax Treaty Related Measures to Prevent BEPS*, OECD, Paris, 2016.
O'Donnell/Marcovici/Michaels 2000, 'The New U.S. Withholding Tax Regime: To Be or Not To Be, a Qualified Intermediary', *TPIR*, n° 6, 2000.
Offermanns/Romano 2000, 'Treaty Benefits for Permanent Establishments: The Saint-Gobain case', *ET*, n° 5, 2000.
Ogley 1993, *Principles of International Tax*, Interfisc Publishing, London, 1993.
Oliver 1989, 'Access to tax treaties', *Intertax*, n° 8/9, 1989.
Oliver/Libin/Van Weeghel/Du Toit 2000, 'Beneficial Ownership', *BIT*, n° 7, 2000.
Oliver 2001, 'The Parent-Subsidiary Directive of 23 July 1990: a United Kingdom perspective', *EC Tax Review*, n° 4, 2001.
Osterweil 1999, 'OECD Report on Harmful Tax Competition and European Union Code of Conduct Compared', *ET*, n° 6, 1999.
Osterweil 2009, 'Are LOB Provisions in Double Tax Conventions Contrary to EC Treaty Freedoms?', *EC Tax Review*, n° 5, 2009.
Özgenç 2017, 'Limitation of Benefits Clause and Turkey's Approach: From Policy to Legal Order', *Intertax*, n° 5, 2017.
Palao 1966, 'El fraude a la ley en Derecho tributario', *RDFHP*, n° 63, 1966.
Palao 1977, 'La elusión fiscal mediante sociedades', *REDF*, n° 15/16, 1977.
Palao 1996, 'Notas a la Ley 25/1995, de 20 de julio, de modificación parcial de la Ley General Tributaria (II)', *RCT*, n° 155, 1996.
Palao 1997, 'Tipicidad e igualdad en la aplicación de las normas tributarias (La prohibición de la analogía en Derecho tributario)', *Anuario de la Facultad de Derecho de la Universidad Autónoma de Madrid*, n° 1, 1997.
Palao 2001, 'Algunos problemas que plantea la aplicación de la norma española sobre el fraude a la ley tributaria', *CT*, n° 98, 2001.
Palao 2003, 'Normas anti-elusión en el Derecho interno español y en el Derecho comunitario europeo', Asociación Argentina de Estudios Fiscales, 2003 (http://www.aaef.org.ar).
Palao 2004, 'The New General Tax Law in Spain, Including a New Anti-Avoidance Clause', *BIT*, n° 3, 2004.
Palao 2015, 'OECD Base Erosion and Profit Shifting Action 6: The General Anti-Abuse Rule', *BIT*, n° 10, 2015.
Panayi 2016, 'International Tax Law Following the OECD/G20 Base Erosion and Profit Shifting Project', *BIT*, n° 11, 2016.
Paz-Ares 1999, 'Uniones de empresas y grupos de sociedades', *Revista Jurídica de la Universidad Autónoma de Madrid*, n° 1, 1999.
Peters/Holdem/Smith 1995, 'Dividend Mixer Companies and the Bew US/DUTCH pact', *ITR*, n° 2, 1995.
Philips/Collins 1985, 'The Assessment and Collection of tax from non-residents', *CDFI*, vol. LXXa, Kluwer Law and Taxation Publishers, Deventer, 1985.
Phillips 1995, *International Tax Treaty Networks*, vol. I, ESC International, 1995.
Picciotto 1992, *International Business Taxation*, Quorum Books, New York, 1992.
Pijl/Hählen 2001, 'The New Advance Pricing Agreement and Advance Tax Ruling Practice in the Netherlands', *BIT*, n° 12, 2001.

Pistone 2002, *The Impact of Community Law on Tax Treaties*, Kluwer Law International, London, 2002.
Plansky/Schneeweiss 2007, 'Limitation on Benefits: From the US Model 2006 to the ACT Group Litigation', *Intertax*, n° 8/9, 2009.
Polesi 2016, 'LOB – Article X (3) of the OECD MC: Active Conduct of a Business': *Preventing Treaty Abuse*, Linde, Wien, 2016.
Rädler/Lausterer/Blumenberg 1997, 'Tax Abuse and EC Law', *EC Tax Review*, n° 2, 1997.
Rädler 1999, 'Limitation of Treaty Benefits in Germany': *International Studies in Taxation: Law and Economic*, Kluwer Law International, London, 1999.
Ramallo Massanet 2001, 'La directiva 90/435/CEE relativa al régimen fiscal común aplicable a las sociedades matrices y filiales. La experiencia española', *Información Fiscal*, n° 43, 2001.
Rapakko 1989, *Base Company Taxation*, Kluwer, Deventer, 1989.
Rasmussen/Bernhardt 2001, 'The Limitation on Benefits Provisions in the Tax Treaty with the United States', *ET*, n° 4, 2001.
Raventós 1994a, 'A Fiscal Cold War', *ET*, n° 10/11, 1994.
Raventós 1994b, 'Strict limitations on benefits in new Spain/U.S. pact-Part 3', *ITR*, n° 4, 1994.
Raventós 1995a, 'El *treaty shopping* en los últimos convenios de doble imposición firmados por España', *RESE*, n° 21, 1995.
Raventós 1995b, 'Tax Authorities Recant on Luxembourg SOPARFIs', *ET*, 1995.
Raventós 1998, 'Practical Issues in the Application of Double Tax Conventions', *CDFI*, vol. LXXXIIIb, Kluwer Law International, The Hague, 1998.
Reinarz 1996, 'Swiss/US Pact Sets Strict Limitation on Benefits', *ITR*, n° 12, 1996.
Reinarz 1999, 'Switzerland: Revised Swiss Anti-Treaty Shopping Rules', *BIT*, n° 3, 1999.
Report of the Committee of Independent Experts on Company Taxation (Ruding Report) 1992, Office for Official Publications of the European Communities, Bruselas, 1992.
Rivier 1987, 'The Fiscal Residence of Companies', *CDFI*, vol. LXXIIa, Kluwer, 1987.
Rivier 1998, 'Le recours à un critère subjectif pour definir l'usage abusif des conventions de double imposition conclues par les Etats-Unis: conclues par les Etats-Unis: l'exemple de l'Euro-holding', *RDADF*, n° 3/4, 1998.
Rohatgi 2002, *Basic International Taxation*, Kluwer Law International, The Hague, 2002.
Rosenbloom/Langbein 1981, 'United States Tax Treaty Policy: An Overview', *Columbia Journal of Transnational Law*, vol. 19, 1981.
Rosenbloom 1983, 'Tax Treaty Abuse: Policies and Issues', *Law and Policy in International Business*, n° 15, 1983.
Rosenbloom 1988, 'Review: OECD Report Double Taxation Conventions and the Use of Conduit Companies', *Intertax*, n° 6/7, 1988.
Rosenbloom 1991, 'Toward A New Tax Treaty Policy For a New Decade', *American Journal of Tax Policy*, vol. 9, n° 1, 1991.

Rosenbloom 1993, 'Derivative Benefits: Emerging US Treaty Policy': *Essays on International Taxation*, Kluwer, Deventer, 1993.

Rust 2015, 'Annex to Article 1: Improper Use of the Convention': *Klaus Vogel on Double Tax Conventions*, Kluwer Law International, Alphen aan den Rijn, 2015.

Sadiq 2001, 'Unitary Taxation –The Case for Global Formulary Apportionment', *ET*, n° 7, 2001.

Sancho 2001, 'La teoría de la sede y el Derecho comunitario: a propósito de la sentencia Centros', *Revista Jurídica de la Universidad Autónoma de Madrid*, n° 4, 2001.

Sanz Gadea 1996, *Transparencia fiscal internacional*, Centro de Estudios Financieros, Madrid, 1996.

Sanz Gadea 2001, 'Medidas antielusión fiscal', *Documentos del IEF*, n° 22, 2001.

Saunders 1991, 'Principles of International Tax Planning', *TPIR*, 1991.

Saunders 1995, 'How Much Longer will Treaty Shopping Be Allowed?', *TPIR*, n° 1, 1995.

Saunders 2000, *International Tax Systems and Planning Techniques*, Sweet & Maxwell, London, 2000.

Schaffner 1997, 'Highlights of the New United States-Luxembourg Double Tax Treaty', *BIT*, n° 4, 1997.

Schaffner 1998, 'Luxembourg Soparfi Regime Remains Attractive', *BIT*, n° 8/9, 1998.

Schinabeck 1996, 'The Limitation on Benefits Article of the U.S.-France Tax Treaty', *TMIJ*, n° 1, 1996.

Schuch/Toifl 1998, 'Austria: Highlights of the New Tax Treaty with the United States', *ET*, n° 1, 1998.

Schwarz 1994, 'Economía de opción (*treaty shopping*) en tratados fiscales y rentas del capital', *Zergak. Gaceta Jurídica del País Vasco*, n° 3, 1994.

Shannon 1988, 'The General Definition of Residence under United States Income Tax Treaties', *Intertax*, n° 8/9, 1988.

Shay 1993, 'Re-examining Chapter 3 Income Tax Withholding and the Role of the Withholding Agent', *Essays on International Taxation*, Kluwer, Deventer, 1993.

Sheppard 2016, 'Why the New U.S. Model Treaty', *TNI*, n° 8, 2016.

Soler Roch 1997, 'Una reflexión sobre el principio de residencia como criterio de sujeción al poder tributario', *Presente y Futuro de la Imposición Directa*, Lex Nova- Asociación Española de Asesores Fiscales, Valladolid, 1997.

Soler/Ribes 2001, 'Tax Treaty Interpretation in Spain': Lang (ed.), *Tax Treaty Interpretation*, Kluwer Law International, The Hague, 2001.

Sparagna 2015, 'Court Grants Judicial Review of Denied U.S. Tax Treaty Qualification Ruling', *TMIJ*, vol. 44, n° 10, 2015.

Spector 1993, 'Limitations on Benefits under the New US-Netherlands Income Tax Treaty', *BIT*, n° 4, 1993.

Spector/Salou 1995, 'The New U.S.-France Income Tax Treaty: Vive la Difference', *TMIJ*, n° 2, 1995.

Spitz 1991, *Planificación fiscal internacional*, Deusto, Bilbao, 1991.

Stone 2015, 'LOB Provisions in the 2015 Draft U.S. Model Tax Treaty', *TNI*, n° 7, 2015.

Bibliography

Strauch 1997, *Limitation on Benefits- Article 16 of the New Double Taxation Convention Between the United States of America and the Federal Republic of Austria*, University of Vienna, 1997.

Streng 1991, 'The U.S.-Netherlands Income Tax Convention: Historical Evolution of Tax Treaty Policy Issues Including Limitation of Benefits', *BIT*, n° 1, 1991.

Terr 1989, 'Treaty Routing vs. Treaty Shopping: Planning for Multicountry Investment Flows under Modern Limitation on Benefits Articles', *Intertax*, n° 12, 1989.

Terra/Wattel 2001, *European Tax Law*, Kluwer Law International, The Hague, 2001, 3th ed.

Terra/Wattel 2012, *European Tax Law*, Kluwer Law International, Alphen aan den Rijn, 2012, 6th ed.

Thacker 2004, 'India-Mauritius Tax Treaty: The March of the Law', *Asia-Pacific Tax Bulletin*, n° 1, 2004.

Thill/Milhac 1995, 'French Treaty Brought up to Date', *ITR*, October, 1995.

Thömmes/Kiblböck 1994, 'Anti-Treaty Shopping Provisions', *ET*, n° 4, 1994.

Thömmes/Eicker 1999, 'Limitation on Benefits: The German View Sec. 50D(1A) Individual Income Tax Act and EC Law Issues', *ET*, n° 1, 1999.

Tobin 2016, 'The U.S. Model Treaty Is Out!', *TMIJ*, vol. 45, n° 5, 2016.

Trost 2001, 'El *trust* en la planificación fiscal internacional': *Fiscalidad internacional*, Centro de Estudios Financieros, Madrid, 2001.

Troup 1993, 'Of Limited Benefit: Article of the New U.S./Netherlands Double Tax Treaty Considered', *BTR*, n° 2, 1993.

Turro 1992, 'U.S. and the Netherlands Sign Tax Treaty; Limitation-on-Benefits Article Breaks New Ground', *TNI*, n° 27, 1992.

Uckmar 1956, 'Influencia del domicilio, de la residencia y de la nacionalidad en el Derecho tributario', *RDFHP*, n° 24, 1956.

Uckmar 1983, 'Elusión fiscal y evasión fiscal', *CDFI*, vol. LXVIIIa, Kluwer, Deventer, 1983.

UN 1988, *Contributions to International Co-operation in Tax Matters (Treaty Shopping, Thin Capitalization, Co-operation Between Tax Authorities, Resolving International Tax Disputes)*, Ref. ST/ESA/203, UN, New York, 1988.

US Department of the Treasury 2007, *Report to The Congress on Earnings Stripping, Transfer Pricing and U.S. Income Tax Treaties*.

Valente 1998, 'Elusione fiscale internazionale: strumenti unilaterali di contrasto e disposizioni convenzionali in materia di *treaty shopping*', *Diritto e Practica Tributaria*, vol. 69, n° 2, 1998.

Valente/Magenta 2000, 'Analysis of Certain Anti-Abuse Clauses in the Tax Treaties Concluded by Italy', *BIT*, n° 1, 2000.

Vamvoukos 1985, *Termination of Treaties in International Law (The Doctrines of Rebus Sic Stantibus and Desuetude)*, Clarendon Press, Oxford.

Van Brunschot/Van Weeghel 1993, 'Netherlands-United States: The New Tax Convention', *ET*, n° 6/7, 1993.

Van den Ende/Smit 2001, 'Netherlands/Portugal: European Tax Law Influences the New Tax Treaty', *ET*, n° 3, 2001.

Van der Weijden/Doets 2004, 'The New Protocol to the Netherlands-United States Tax Treaty', *BIT*, n° 7, 2004.

Van Herksen 1996, 'Limitation on Benefits and the Competent Authority Determination', *BIT*, n° 1, 1996.

Vanistendael 1994, 'The Limits to the New Community Tax Order', *Common Market Law Review*, n° 2, 1994.

Vanistendael 1997a, 'Reinventing Source Taxation', *EC Tax Review*, n° 3, 1997.

Vanistendael 1997b, 'Judicial Interpretation and the Role of Anti-abuse Provisions in Tax Law': *Tax Avoidance and the Rule of Law*, IBFD, Amsterdam, 1997.

Vanistendael 1999, 'Impact of European Tax Law on Tax Treaties with Third Countries', *EC Tax Review*, n° 3, 1999.

Vanistendael 2000, 'Reflexiones sobre los convenios de doble imposición entre la Unión Europea y países terceros', *RESE*, n° 34, 2000.

Vanistendael 2001, 'Looking Back: A Decade of Parent Subsidiary Directive – The Case of Belgium', *EC Tax Review*, n° 3, 2001.

Van Raad 1986, *Non discrimination in International Tax Law*, Kluwer, Deventer, 1986.

Van Raad 1988, 'The Netherlands Model Income Tax Treaty', *Intertax*, n° 8/9, 1988.

Van Raad 1993, 'The 1992 OECD Model Treaty: Triangular Cases.', *ET*, n° 9, 1993.

Van Raad 2001, 'International Coordination of Tax Treaty Interpretation and Application', *Intertax*, n° 6/7, 2001.

Van Thiel 1989, 'Planificación fiscal y derecho de establecimiento en Europa', *Impuestos*, 1989-I.

Van Thiel 2002, *Free Movement of Persons and Income Tax Law: The European Court in Search of Principles*, IBFD, Amsterdam, 2002.

Van Unnik/Boudesteijn 1993, 'The New US-Dutch Tax Treaty and the Treaty of Rome', *EC Tax Review*, n° 2, 1993.

Van Weeghel 1996, 'Abuse of Tax Treaties', *ET*, n° 1, 1996.

Van Weeghel 1998, *The Improper Use of Tax Treaties*, Kluwer, London, 1998.

Vargas 2004, 'Beneficial Ownership Lacks Proper Meaning', *International Tax Review*, vol. 15, n° 5, 2004.

Vega 2003, *Las medidas contra el treaty shopping*, Instituto de Estudios Fiscales, Madrid, 2003.

Vega 2004, 'Ámbito de aplicación personal': *Comentarios a los convenios para evitar la doble imposición y prevenir la evasión fiscal concluidos por España*, Fundación Pedro Barrié de la Maza, A Coruña, 2004.

Vega 2006, *Limitation on Benefits Clauses in Double Taxation Conventions*, Kluwer Law International, The Hague, 2006.

Vega 2016, 'Las medidas antiabuso en los convenios bilaterales para evitar la doble imposición internacional', *Manual de fiscalidad internacional*, Instituto de Estudios Fiscales, Madrid, 2016, 4th ed.

Vega 2017, 'The Special Tax Regimes Clause in the 2016 U.S. Model Income Tax Convention', *Intertax*, vol. 45, n° 4, 2017.

Verdoner 2003, 'Mayor Economic Concepts in Tax Treaty Policy', *Intertax*, vol. 31, n° 4, 2003.

Viñuales 1977, 'Informe sobre la Legislación Fiscal y los procedimientos de imputación parcial de beneficios de las empresas con actividades en varios países', *HPE*, n° 46, 1977.
Vischer 1994, *International Encyclopaedia of Comparative Law*, vol. III, Mohr Siebeck, Tübingen, 1994.
Vitko 2013, 'The Use of Tax Treaties and Treaty Shopping: Determining the Dividing Line', *BIT*, n° 1, 2013.
Vogel 1988a, 'Worldwide vs. Source Taxation of Income: A Review and Re-evaluation of Arguments (Part I)', *Intertax*, n° 8/9, 1988.
Vogel 1998b, 'Worldwide vs. Source Taxation of Income. A Review and Re-evaluation of Arguments (Part II)', *Intertax*, n° 10, 1988.
Vogel 1994, 'Steuerumgehung bei Doppelbesteuerunsgabkommen': Haarmann (ed.), *Grenzen der Gestaltung im Internationalen Steuerrecht*, Otto Schimdt, Cologne, 1994.
Vogel 1997, *On Double Taxation Conventions*, Kluwer Law International, London, 1997.
Vogel 2001, 'Treaty News', *BIT*, n° 3, 2001.
Vogel 2002, 'Which Method Should the European Community Adopt for the Avoidance of Double Taxation?', *BIT*, n° 1, 2002.
Vogel/Shannon/Doernberg/Van Raad 1989, *United States Income Tax Treaties*, Kluwer, Boston, 1989.
Walsh 1997, 'An Irish View of the New U.S.-Ireland Tax Treaty', *TNI*, n° 5, 1997.
Ward 1985, 'The Business Purpose Test and Abuse of Rights', *BTR*, n° 2, 1985.
Ward 1990, 'The Other Income Article of Income tax Treaties', *BIT*, n° 8/9, 1990.
Ward 1995, 'Abuse of Tax Treaties', *Intertax*, n° 4, 1995.
Wardzynski 2014, 'The Limitation on Benefits Article in the OECD Model: Closing Abusive (Undesired) Conduit Gateways Adrian', *BIT*, n° 9, 2014.
Wattel 1996, 'Home Neutrality in an Internal Market', *ET*, n° 5, 1996.
Weber 2000, 'The Proposed EC Interest and Royalty Directive', *EC Tax Review*, n° 1, 2000.
Weber 2016, 'The New Common Minimum Anti-Abuse Rule in the EU Parent-Subsidiary Directive: Background, Impact, Applicability, Purpose and Effect', *Intertax*, n° 2, 2016.
Wijnen/Magenta 1997, 'The UN Model in Practice', *BIT*, n° 12, 1997.
Wijnen 1998, 'Towards a New UN Model?', *BIT*, n° 3, 1998.
Williams 1998, 'Practical Issues in the Application of Double Tax Conventions', *CDFI*, vol. LXXXIIIb, Kluwer Law International, The Hague, 1998.
Winandy 1996, 'Limitations on Benefits in the Proposed U.S.-Luxembourg Income Tax Convention', *TPIR*, n° 7, 1996.
Wurm 1992, 'Treaty Shopping in the 1992 OECD Model Convention', *Intertax*, n° 12, 1992.
Yan 1995, 'Portuguese Negotiations Finally Over', *ITR*, october, 1995.
Zagaris 2001, 'Application of OECD Tax Haven Criteria to Member States Shows Potential Danger to U.S. Sovereignty', *TNI*, n° 19, 2001.

Zornoza 1984, 'Significado y funciones de las consultas a la Administración en materia tributaria', *CT*, n° 50, 1984.

Zornoza/Báez 2010, 'The 2003 Revisions to the Commentary to the OECD Model on Tax Treaties and GAARs: A Mistaken Starting Point': *Tax Treaties: Building Bridges Between Law and Economics*, IBFD, Amsterdam, 2010.

Zuk 2013, 'The Beneficial Ownership Concept in Tax Treaties', *Limits to Tax Planning*, Linde, Wien, 2013.

Index

A

Ability to pay, 6, 37, 51, 285, 291
Abuse of law, 56–58, 62, 63, 252, 278
Active trade or business, 163–179, 182, 183, 185, 186, 197, 201–203, 268–270
Activity clause, 3, 66, 86, 94, 97, 98, 100, 106, 108, 112, 162–185, 187, 201, 202, 234, 258, 263, 267–271, 278, 279
Advance tax ruling, 30
Amortization, 160, 161
Anti-Tax Avoidance Package (ATAD), 54, 251, 253, 278
Arm's length principle, 31, 38–40, 43, 45

B

Back-to-back loan, 32
Base company, 20–23, 28–30, 45
Beneficial ownership, 25, 67, 77–86, 93, 169
Bona fide clause, 66, 97–100, 111, 112, 163, 166, 181, 203, 208, 225–238, 258, 271–273, 277, 282–284, 290, 292
Branch tax, 18, 87, 106, 111, 127, 129, 130, 153, 191, 213, 228, 230, 236, 237

C

Capital Export Neutrality (CEN), 11, 12, 101

Capital Import Neutrality (CIN), 11, 12
Common Consolidated Corporate Tax Base (CCCTB), 43
CFC rules, 21, 34, 36, 45, 46, 189, 203
Citizenship, 5, 74–76, 113–115, 152, 153
Closely held companies, 132
Code of Conduct, 54, 280, 281, 292
Coordination, financing and distribution centres, 33–34

D

Derivative benefits clause, 112, 123, 143, 144, 187–196, 223, 233, 263
Directives
　Anti-Tax Avoidance Directive (ATAD), 274
　Interest and Royalties Directive, 79, 265
　Merger Directive, 274, 275
　Parent-Subsidiary Directive, 254–255, 265, 274
　Savings Directive, 10, 79, 255
Discretionary relief, 236
Disproportionate class of shares, 110, 123, 124, 126–129, 135
Dual residence, 114

E

Equivalent beneficiary, 96, 178, 190–192, 194–196
European company, 265
EU, NAFTA and EEA residents, 140–141, 187, 190, 191

Index

Exchange of information, 50, 92
Exclusion clause, 89, 102, 111, 112, 204–225, 279, 280
Exemption method, 1, 11, 12, 14, 19, 74, 198, 200, 284
Exit tax, 20

F

Fiduciary arrangement, 23–27
Formulary apportionment, 37–46
Freedom of capital and payments, 251, 277
Freedom of establishment, 3, 232, 251, 257–261, 263, 264, 267, 268, 270, 275, 277
Freedom to provide services, 261, 262, 264, 277

G

General Anti-Avoidance Rule (GAAR), 52, 53, 55–67, 76, 82–84, 86, 94, 98, 99, 102, 103, 249, 276, 278
Gift tax, 26
Governmental entities, 115–117, 138, 151
Gross income, 16, 143, 144, 146, 155–161, 174–176, 182–184, 186, 201, 211, 223, 239, 243, 261
Guarantee fees, 211, 214–216, 220, 222, 224, 238

H

Harmful tax competition, 4, 10, 53–55, 102, 206, 209
Headquarters company clause, 112, 170, 178, 184–187, 234
Holding company, 32–33, 167, 170, 232, 233, 269, 270, 278–280
Holding period, 153–155

I

Incorporation theory, 70–72

Indirect Shareholding, 126, 141–143, 147, 149–151
International tax planning, 1, 2, 5–35, 196

J

Joint venture, 149

L

Liability for breach of EU law, 283
Limitation on benefits clauses, 35–292
Look-through approach, 86, 146

M

Madeira, 210, 281
Multilateral instrument, 65, 88, 101, 198–201, 203
Multilateral tax treaty, 8, 252, 290, 292
Multinational corporate group, 184–186
Mutual agreement procedure, 91, 117, 205, 223

N

Notional interest, 142, 235, 238

O

Ownership and base erosion clause, 3, 66, 67, 86, 94–98, 106, 112, 119, 125, 126, 137, 138, 140–165, 185, 187, 190–192, 196, 223, 259, 262, 263, 270, 271, 278

P

Partnerships, 23–27, 68–69
Patent box, 220, 221
Penalties, 243–245, 247
Pension funds, 96, 112, 117, 120–123, 145, 151, 159, 191, 221
Permanent establishment clause, 112, 196–203

Preferential tax regime, 3, 27, 28, 34, 54, 89, 118, 121, 187, 204–211, 213, 214, 221, 222, 232
Primary place of management and control, 123, 124, 126, 133–134
Principal Purpose Test (PPT rule), 53, 62, 64–67, 100, 103, 252, 278

Q

Qualifying intermediate owner, 142, 145

R

Real seat theory, 70–73
Reciprocity principle, 47, 51
Recognized stock exchanges, 123, 126, 127, 131–134, 136, 137, 139, 258, 259
Residence certificate, 241
Royalties, 1, 9, 14, 19, 29, 30, 32, 47, 48, 78, 86, 91, 111, 160, 179, 187, 188, 191, 193, 195, 200–205, 211–216, 220–222, 224, 238, 253, 263, 265, 267, 279, 284
Ruding report, 251, 287
Rule shopping, 19

S

Safe harbour, 98, 99, 174, 182–184
Saving clause, 153
Separate accounting, 37–46
Special tax regime, 54, 89, 142–144, 195, 211–225, 232, 238
State aid, 54, 210, 280, 292
Stock exchange clause, 3, 67, 94–97, 106, 108, 112, 117, 123–145, 147–151, 157, 164, 169, 187, 258, 259
Subject to tax, 1, 6, 8, 18, 27, 33, 35, 44, 69, 73, 86, 116, 202, 204

Substantiality test, 171–176, 180–184, 202

T

Tax avoidance, 2, 36, 43, 56–59, 63, 64, 86, 98, 103, 154, 274–276
Tax evasion, 2, 50, 51, 53, 55, 64, 103, 208, 212, 274, 275, 277
Tax-Exempt Organizations, 118–119, 121, 144
Tax justice, 51, 208
Tax return, 43, 221, 239, 243
Technical Explanation, 81, 110, 118, 127, 133, 137, 141, 160, 161, 168, 169, 177–180, 185, 215, 218, 224, 226, 228, 230, 234, 236
Territoriality principle, 12, 40
Tested group, 143, 144, 157, 161
Thin capitalization, 29, 31, 36
Transparency, 37, 54, 69, 146
Treaty override, 103–108, 137
Treaty shopping, 15–67
Trust, 23–27, 81, 85, 93, 115, 117, 121

V

Value Added Tax (VAT), 268, 269, 280
1969 Vienna Convention on the Law of Treaties (VCLT), 62, 103, 104, 110, 223

W

Wholly artificial arrangement, 273, 275–276, 278
Withholding agent, 240–249
Withholding tax, 3, 11, 195, 239, 240, 241, 243, 246, 247

Z

ZEC entities (Canary Islands), 210

EUCOTAX Series on European Taxation

(1) Peter HJ Essers, Guido JME de Bont & Eric CCM Kemmeren (eds), *The Compatibility of Anti-Abuse Provisions in Tax Treaties with EC Law*, 1998 (ISBN 90-411-9678-1).
(2) Gerard TK Meussen (ed.), *The Principle of Equality in European Taxation*, 1999 (ISBN 90-411-9693-5).
(3) Michael Lang (ed.), *Tax Treaty Interpretation*, 2001 (ISBN 90-411-9857-1).
(4) Pasquale Pistone, *The Impact of Community Law on Tax Treaties: Issues and Solutions*, 2002 (ISBN 90-411-9860-1).
(5) René Offermanns, *The Entrepreneurship Concept in a European Comparative Tax Law Perspective*, 2002 (ISBN 90-411-9887-3).
(6) Michael Lang & Mario Züger, *Settlement of Disputes in Tax Treaty Law*, 2002 (ISBN 90-411-9904-7).
(7) Carlo Pinto, *Tax Competition and EU Law*, 2003 (ISBN 90-411-9913-6).
(8) Michael Lang, Hans-Jörgen Aigner, Ulrich Scheuerle & Markus Stefaner, *CFC Legislation, Tax Treaties and EC Law*, 2004 (ISBN 90-411-2284-2).
(9) Mattias Dahlberg, *Direct Taxation in Relation to the Freedom of Establishment and the Free Movement of Capital*, 2005 (ISBN 90-411-2363-6).
(10) Michael Lang, Judith Herdin & Ines Hofbauer, *WTO and Direct Taxation*, 2005 (ISBN 90-411-2371-7).
(11) Dennis Weber, *Tax Avoidance and the EC Tray Freedoms: A Study of the Limitations under European Law for the Prevention of Tax Avoidance*, 2005 (ISBN 90-411-2402-0).
(12) Félix Alberto Vega Borrego, *Limitation on Benefits Clauses in Double Taxation Conventions*, Second Edition, 2017 (ISBN 978-90-411-6135-2).
(13) Michael Lang, Josef Schuch & Claus Staringer, *ECJ-Recent Developments in Direct Taxation*, 2006 (ISBN 90-411-2509-4).
(14) Reuven S. Avi-Yonah, James R. Hines Jr. & Michael Lang, *Comparative Fiscal Federalism. Comparing the European Court of Justice and the US Supreme Court's Tax Jurisprudence*, 2007 (ISBN 978-90-411-2552-1).
(15) Christiana HJI Panayi, *Double Taxation, Tax Treaties, Treaty-Shopping and the European Community*, 2007 (ISBN 978-90-411-2658-0).
(16) Dennis Weber, *The Influence of European Law on Direct Taxation: Recent and Future Developments*, 2007 (ISBN 978-90-411-2667-2).
(17) Michael Lang & Pasquale Pistone, *The EU and Third Countries: Direct Taxation*, 2007 (ISBN 978-90-411-2665-8).
(18) Oskar Henkow, *Financial Activities in European VAT: A Theoretical and Legal Research of the European VAT System and Preferred Treatment of Financial Activities*, 2007 (ISBN 978-90-411-2703-7).
(19) Michael Lang (ed.), *Tax Compliance Costs for Companies in an Enlarged European Community*, 2008 (ISBN 978-90-411-2666-5).

(20) Michael Lang (ed.), *Source versus Residence. Problems Arising from the Allocation of Taxing Rights in Tax Treaty Law and Possible Alternatives*, 2008 (ISBN 978-90-411-2763-1).
(21) Ioanna Mitroyanni, *Integration Approaches to Group Taxation in the European Internal Market*, 2008 (ISBN 978-90-411-2779-2).
(22) Rolf Eicke, *Tax Planning with Holding Companies. Repatriation of US Profits from Europe:Concepts, Strategies, Structures*, 2008 (ISBN978-90-411-2794-5).
(23) Peter Essers et al. (ed.), *The Influence of IAS/IFRS on the CCCTB, Tax Accounting, Disclosure and Corporate Law Accounting Concepts: 'A Clash of Cultures'*, 2008 (ISBN 978-90-411-2819-5).
(24) Tonny Schenk-Geers, *International Exchange of Information and the Protection of Taxpayers*, 2009 (ISBN 978-90-411-3142-3).
(25) Raymond Adema, *UCITS and Taxation: Towards Harmonization of the Taxation of UCITS*, 2009 (ISBN 978-90-411-2839-3).
(26) Michael Lang, Jianwen Liu & Gongliang Tang (eds), *Europe–China Tax Treaties*, 2010 (ISBN 978-90-411-3216-1).
(27) Michael Lang, Pasquale Pistone, Josef Schuch & Claus Staringer (eds), *Procedural Rules in Tax Law in the Context of European Union and Domestic Law*, 2010 (ISBN 978-90-411-3376-2).
(28) Sjaak J.J.M. Jansen, *Fiscal Sovereignty of the Member States in an Internal Market: Past and Future*, 2011 (ISBN 978-90-411-3403-5).
(29) Dennis Weber & Bruno da Silva, *From Marks & Spencer to X Holding: The Future of Cross-Border Group Taxation*, 2011 (ISBN 978-90-411-3399-1).
(30) Claus Bohn Jespersen, *Intermediation of Insurance and Financial Services in European VAT*, 2011 (ISBN 978-90-411-3732-6).
(31) Sabine Heidenbauer, *Charity Crossing Borders: The Fundamental Freedoms' Influence on Charity and Donor Taxation in Europe*, 2011 (ISBN 978-90-411-3813-2).
(32) Michael Lang, et al., *The Future of Indirect Taxation: Recent Trends in VAT and GST Systems around the World*, 2012 (ISBN 978-90-411-3797-5).
(33) Harm van den Broek, *Cross-Border Mergers within the EU: Proposals to Remove the Remaining Tax Obstacles*, 2012 (ISBN 978-90-411-3824-8).
(34) Michael Lang, et al. (eds), *Tax Treaty Case Law around the Globe – 2011*, 2012 (ISBN 978-90-411-3876-7).
(35) Dennis Weber (ed.), *CCCTB: Selected Issues*, 2012 (ISBN 978-90-411-3872-9).
(36) Daniël Smit, *EU Freedoms, Non-EU Countries and Company Taxation*, 2012 (ISBN 978-90-411-4041-8).
(37) Rita de la Feria, *VAT Exemptions: Consequences and Design Alternatives*, 2013 (ISBN 978-90-411-3276-5).
(38) Karin Simader, *Withholding Taxes and the Fundamental Freedoms*, 2013 (ISBN 978-90-411-4842-1).
(39) Madeleine Merkx, *Establishments in European VAT*, 2013 (ISBN 978-90-411-4554-3).
(40) Carla De Pietro, *Tax Treaty Override*, 2014 (ISBN 978-90-411-5406-4).

(41) G.K. Fibbe & A.J.A. Stevens (eds), *Hybrid Entities and the EU Direct Tax Directives*, 2015 (ISBN 978-90-411-5942-7).
(42) Gerard Staats, *Personal Pensions in the EU*, 2015 (ISBN 978-90-411-5953-3).
(43) Michael Lang & Ine Lejeune (eds), *VAT/GST in a Global Digital Economy*, 2015 (ISBN 978-90-411-5952-6).
(44) Massimo Basilavecchia, Lorenzo del Federico & Pietro Mastellone (eds), *Tax Implications of Environmental Disasters and Pollution*, 2015 (ISBN 978-90-411-5611-2).
(45) Cristina Trenta, *Rethinking EU VAT for P2P Distribution*, 2015 (ISBN 978-90-411-6137-6).
(46) Marie Lamensch, Edoardo Traversa & Servaas van Thiel (eds), *Value Added Tax and the Digital Economy: The 2015 EU Rules and Broader Issues*, 2016 (ISBN 978-90-411-6612-8).
(47) Raffaele Petruzzi, *Transfer Pricing Aspects of Intra-Group Financing*, 2016 (ISBN 978-90-411-6732-3).
(48) Mario Grandinetti (ed.), *Corporate Tax Base in the Light of the IAS/IFRS and EU Directive 2013/34: A Comparative Approach*, 2016 (ISBN 978-90-411-6745-3).
(49) Bruno da Silva, *The Impact of Tax Treaties and EU Law on Group Taxation Regimes*, 2016 (ISBN 978-90-411-6905-1).
(50) Michael Lang, Alfred Storck & Raffaele Petruzzi (eds), *Transfer Pricing in a Post-BEPS World*, 2016 (ISBN 978-90-411-6710-1).
(51) Marta Papis-Almansa, *Insurance in European VAT: Current and Preferred Treatment in the Light of the New Zealand and Australian GST Systems*, 2017 (ISBN 978-90-411-8360-6).
(52) Wolfgang Speckhahn, *Real Estate Investment Trusts In Europe: Europeanising Tax Regimes,* 2017 (ISBN 978-90-411-8360-6).
(53) Frank J.G. Nellen, *Information Asymmetries in EU VAT*, 2017 (ISBN 978-90-411-8837-3).